Judge Harley and His Boys

Judge Harley and His Boys

The Langdale Story

John Lancaster

Mercer University Press

Macon

ISBN 0-86554-823-4
MUP/H622

First Edition.

∞The paper used in this publication meets the minimum requirements of American National Standard for Information Sciences—Permanence of Paper for Printed Library Materials, ANSI Z39.48-1992.

Library of Congress Cataloging-in-Publication Data

CIP data are available from the Library of Congress

To My Wife

Kathleen Cavanah Lancaster

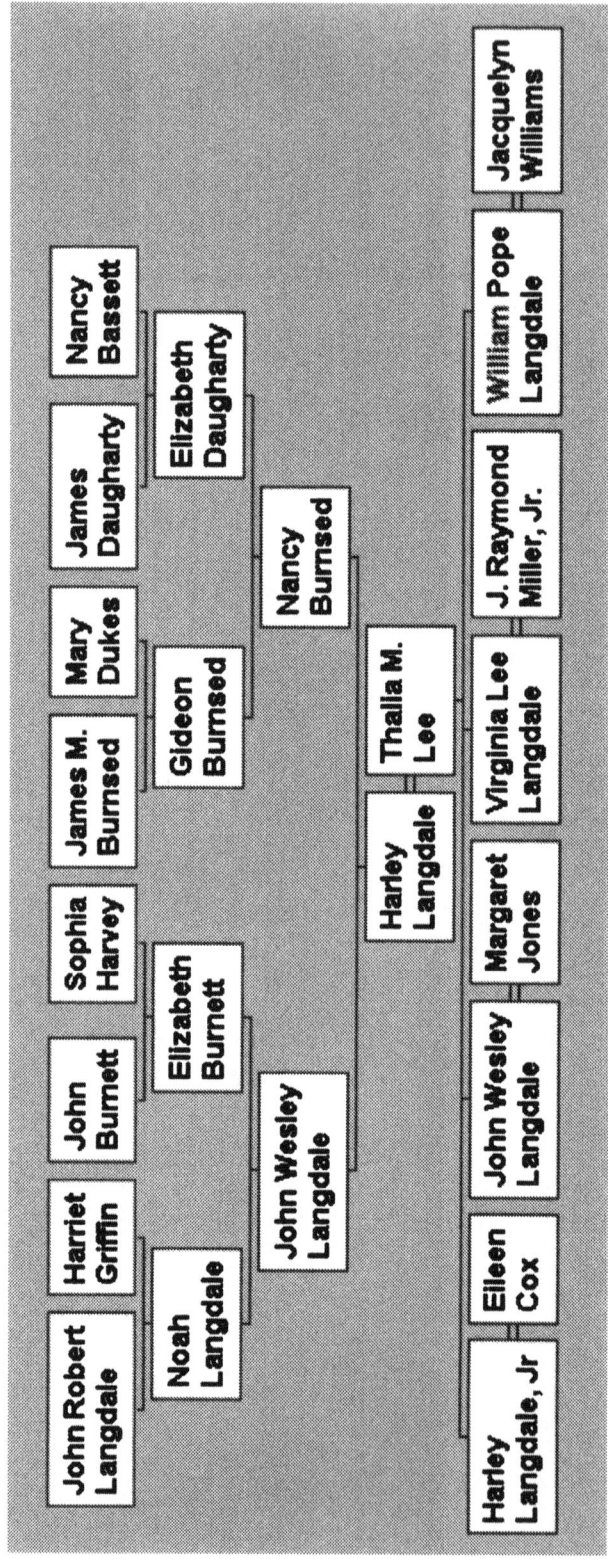

Family tree / ancestry chart:

- John Robert Langdale
  - Harriet Griffin
- Noah Langdale
- John Burnett
  - Sophia Harvey
- Elizabeth Burnett
- John Wesley Langdale
- James M. Bumsed
  - Mary Dukes
- Gideon Bumsed
- James Daugharty
  - Nancy Bassett
- Elizabeth Daugharty
- Nancy Bumsed
- Harley Langdale
  - Thalia M. Lee
- John Wesley Langdale
  - Margaret Jones
- Virginia Lee Langdale
- J. Raymond Miller, Jr.
- William Pope Langdale
  - Jacquelyn Williams
- Harley Langdale, Jr.
  - Eileen Cox

Contents

viii

Preface

Seven generations of Langdales have lived in south Georgia, concentrated in Lowndes, Berrien, Clinch, and Echols Counties. This study focuses on the men of the third, fourth, and fifth generations, starting with John Wesley Langdale of Council, Georgia, and ending with his grandsons, Harley Langdale, Jr., John W. Langdale, and William P. Langdale of Valdosta. This focus results from the plan to include in the study some account of the development of the Langdale Company, one of the major contemporary businesses of south Georgia, to which these three brothers made very significant contributions. Of course, Judge Harley Langdale, father of the three brothers, laid the foundations for the Langdale Company and dominates much of the story. Among others important to this narrative were the two John J. Langdales, father and son, who for many years ran the separate J. W. Langdale Company. This company consisted mainly of the estate of the first John Wesley Langdale. He lived, at the turn of the century, close to the western edge of the Okefenokee in the vicinity of the Suwannee River's outflow. From there, at the location of the later village of Council, he started his branch of the family on the way to unusual success in the forest products industry.

Each individual's prominence in this work is somewhat proportional to his involvement in the Langdale businesses and in public life. Obviously, this is not a history of the entire Langdale family; neither is it a detailed economic and financial analysis of the Langdale Company from a strictly business standpoint. One might say it concentrates on events and personalities at the intersection of the two worlds of the Langdale companies and the family that built them.

The Langdale family and their businesses are of interest to many people. During the hundred-year history of their forest products enterprises, the Langdales have developed one of the larger and more influential agricultural and industrial concerns in Georgia. In the 1990s, the Langdale Company owned about twenty subsidiary corporations, including automobile dealerships and a bank, to which others were added in the new century. It owned in fee simple substantially more than 200,000 acres of land, conducted one of the bigger farming operations in Georgia, and sold hundreds of millions of dollars worth of lumber, poles, oriented stranded board, and other forest products annually. Langdale manufacturing equipment and practices were among the most advanced in the country. Their extensive enterprises involved the company and individual members of the family in questions of regional and national scope, such as those affecting the environment. For decades they—especially Judge Harley Langdale and Harley, Jr.—were noted, and officially honored by government and non-government entities, as conservationists. They both took great pride in this.

Judge Harley Langdale organized the American Turpentine Farmers Association, a national cooperative, in the 1930s. As its chief official and spokesman, he traveled regularly to Washington to lobby congress and the administration on behalf of turpentine producers. This organization secured an exclusive contract with the US Department of Agriculture to funnel federal loans to farmers throughout the several states of the turpentine belt. In connection with his activities on behalf of ATFA, Judge Langdale frequently visited and corresponded with congressmen and senators from Georgia and several other states. Through his contacts with the government and officials, he endeavored to influence not only domestic policy, but also the economic foreign policy of the United States, notably in the area of tariffs. When World War II started, Judge Harley joined other leaders of industry summoned to Washington to discuss ways to increase production for the war effort.

Judge Harley's eldest son, Harley, Jr., likewise held major state, regional, and national positions in the fields of forestry, conservation, and forest products. Harley, Jr. accepted leadership posts in several professional organizations. He also served on advisory committees of the federal government and testified before the US Congress. Often he exerted influence quietly behind the scenes to shape law and policy.

Aside from the economic significance of the Langdale enterprises, members of the Langdale family have taken leading roles in social, religious, educational, and political affairs. John W. Langdale served in both houses of the state legislature, as a member and chairman of the University System of Georgia Board of Regents, and as a district governor of Rotary International. William P. (Billy) Langdale, for sixteen years chairman of the Lowndes County Commissioners, subsequently represented the Valdosta district on the Georgia Transportation Board, upon which he still sat in 2002. The Langdales supported Valdosta State University enthusiastically. In appreciation for their support, the university named one of its dormitories for John Wesley Langdale (grandfather of Harley, Jr., John W., and Billy), whom the Langdales regard as the founder of their family business. As chairman of the Board of Regents, John W. assisted Valdosta State in ways, consistent with the impartiality for which he always strove. He also served for years as a trustee of the VSU Foundation. Harley, Jr., too, gave the university firm support in financial and leadership matters. In the year 2000, in appreciation for his support, the university named its business school in his honor. This institution became known henceforth as the Harley Langdale, Jr. College of Business Administration.

For all of these reasons, the story of the Langdale family and the businesses they built are important to the history of Georgia and the southern United States. It is an interesting and wide-ranging story spanning centuries of time and the territory of several states. Although every effort is made to relate the facts accurately and fairly, this account is not entirely objective. It is favorable to the Langdales. This is primarily because so much of the information comes from Langdale papers and extensive interviews with the Langdales. The author acknowledges, too, his admiration for some members of this family.

There was a suggestion that the title given to this work might be *Suwannee River Ponderosa*. Older readers and watchers of re-runs will remember the long-running television series, *Bonanza*, which featured a family surnamed Cartwright living on and operating an enormous ranch. These included a wise father and three sons. There was a practical, business-like older son; another son who was jovial, loved a good time, and occasionally got slightly out of bounds; and a third who was more introspective and sensitive. If this parallel is not taken too seriously, one might equate Judge Harley Langdale to Ben Cartwright, Harley, Jr. to Adam, Billy to Hoss, and John W. to Joe. Instead of *Suwannee River Ponderosa*, however, we have opted for *Judge Harley and His Boys,* which perhaps more precisely reflects the content.

John E. Lancaster
Macon, Georgia
31 March 2002

Acknowledgments

The writer is grateful for the cooperation and support extended by the Langdale Company and by all Langdale family members to whom requests were made in researching this book. The company arranged for tours of its plants and use of its facilities as needed. Harley Langdale, Jr., and his siblings, plus other members of the family, gave generously of their time for interviews and consultations to achieve the utmost factual accuracy. A substantial grant from the Langdale Company for research expenses helped immensely in the early stage of work. Mr. James D. (Jim) Hickman of Langdale Forest Products Co., the writer's designated contact person with the Langdale Company, responded promptly and efficiently to all requests for appointments, for documents, and for other needed information. His able and generous assistance, which included technical advice on forestry and manufacturing processes, made this work much easier than it might otherwise have been.

For help with the genealogical aspects of this book I owe much to Dr. George Wilfred Langdale of Athens, Georgia. His paper, "The Langdales of Colleton," revised 1990, included valuable documentation and helped immensely in clarifying this portion of the story. Several other Langdales assisted by exchanging and sharing information via e-mail. Among my very helpful South Carolina/Georgia Langdale correspondents were Jennett Crosby Pearson, Dudley J. Pearce, Deborah Miller, Jim Burress, Gretta Hancock Holcom, and Mrs. Dan Garris. Descendants of Samuel Langdale of Philadelphia and Ohio who gave important assistance included Evelyn P. Sanders of Missouri, Robert Lee Langdale of Oregon, and, especially, Carla Kelley White of Tonkawa, Oklahoma. Thanks also to Gil Skidmore of the Sowle Press, Reading, England, for information she provided, in addition to the partial autobiography of Josiah Langdale that she published just in time, fortunately, for use in this work.

I wish to thank Jane Twitty Shelton, who generously shared her audio taped interviews of Judge Harley Langdale, which she and her late husband, Tom, made in the late 1960s. These provided first-person information and perspective directly from Judge and in his own voice, an important enhancement to the story. To Virginia Langdale Miller, also, I express my thanks for allowing use of the personal letters from her Aunt Nan Langdale, without which the story of John Wesley Langdale's family in Council and Jasper would have been spare indeed.

A debt of appreciation is likewise owed to the Department of History of Valdosta State University. The university provided time off from teaching, which helped considerably.

To several colleagues and friends who read the manuscript and made valuable suggestions I am also thankful. These include William M. Gabard, professor of History Emeritus of Valdosta State University; F. Lamar Pearson, professor of history, Valdosta State University; H. David Williams, head of the Department of History of Valdosta State University; Hugh C. Bailey, professor of history and president of Valdosta State University; E. L. "Boe" Williams, Jr., chairman of the board of the Huxford Genealogical Society, Homerville, Georgia, and William H. Mobley, manuscript historian, retired, at the Library of Congress. All of these gentlemen were very helpful, and of course none are to blame for the work's remaining shortcomings.

The staffs of several libraries were very helpful. The Library of Congress, the National Archives, the Huxford Genealogical Library, the Bryn Mawr, Haverford, and Swarthmore Libraries in Philadelphia, the Lowndes County Historical Society, the Colleton County, South Carolina, Memorial Library, and the Odum Library of Valdosta State University all gave valuable assistance.

To my wife, Kathleen Cavanah Lancaster, I am exceedingly grateful. She typed transcripts of all interviews and a number of other documents. She helped me with research in Washington, Philadelphia, Atlanta, and elsewhere. She encouraged me and sometimes pushed me a little to finish the job. She is due much credit for many unnamed contributions.

Abbreviations

Photo Credits

TLC   Langdale Company Photo
Photos from Langdale Company archives, photographer unknown.

TLF   Langdale Family Photo
Photos contributed by Langdale family members, photographer unknown.

JDH   By James D. Hickman, the Langdale Company

KCL   By Kathleen C. Lancaster

JEL   By the author

1

Origins

*I*n the United States and the world, the Langdale name is rare. In 1997 a commercial publisher of books dedicated to individual surnames could list only 797 Langdale households in the entire world.[1] Over half of those (436) lived in Great Britain and twenty-eight percent (227) in the United States. Within the US, the five states of Florida (with fifty), South Carolina (with forty-four), California (with thirty-three), Georgia (with eighteen), and North Carolina (with fifteen) contained seventy percent of all the Langdale households listed. For Georgia, six of its eighteen Langdale households had Valdosta addresses.[2] These are the Langdales whose family and business relations are the focus of our study.

The Langdales of south Georgia arrived from South Carolina. They trace their descent from John Robert Langdale of Colleton District, South Carolina, who moved to Georgia in the 1830s. John Robert Langdale was the son of William B. Langdale, who was a son of Josiah Langdale. Although not proven beyond doubt, available evidence suggests that Josiah Langdale came to Colleton District, South Carolina, from Philadelphia, Pennsylvania, where he had been born in 1739 into a prominent Quaker family. Josiah Langdale of Philadelphia was a grandson of Josiah Langdale of Bridlington, Yorkshire, a Quaker minister and missionary, who was the immigrant ancestor of the Philadelphia Langdales and, it is believed, those of South Carolina and Georgia.

Josiah Langdale of Yorkshire was not the first Langdale to appear in British America. Records exist of others who preceded him. For example, William Langdale arrived in Virginia in 1665; Robert Langdale arrived in Barbados in 1669;

---

[1] A more determined search would have produced more names, but Langdales obviously do not compare in number to people with such surnames as Smith, Jones, or Taylor.

[2] *The New World Book of Langdales* (Bath OH: Halbert's Family Heritage, 1997) 6.1–41.

and Duke Langdale arrived in Virginia in 1714.[3] It has been suggested that "Duke" may have been an abbreviated form of Marmaduke, a name applied to several Langdales of Yorkshire including the seventeenth-century general, Marmaduke Lord Langdale. How these earlier Langdales related to Josiah Langdale is unknown and is not part of our story. [4]

As a young man living in Yorkshire around 1690, Josiah Langdale left the Church of England to become a member of the Society of Friends, frequently referred to as Quakers. He became associated with the Quaker congregation in Bridlington, a name that Yorkshire Quakers transferred to America in the variant form of "Burlington." They gave this name to a center of Quaker life and worship in New Jersey located only a few miles from Philadelphia. During missionary journeys, which Josiah undertook usually in the company of another Quaker missionary, he visited and participated in religious meetings in Philadelphia, Burlington, Barbados, and other places in English America.

Relatively late in life Josiah married Margaret Burton, also a devout member of the Society of Friends and herself an experienced traveling missionary. They became parents of two children, Mary and John. Then in 1723, having decided to make a new home in America, the family bade their friends in Bridlington goodbye and boarded a ship bound for Philadelphia.

Josiah did not survive the trip. He died enroute, presumably of illness, and Margaret arrived in Philadelphia with her two young children. After about a year, she remarried to a man named Samuel Preston, a well-to-do Quaker businessman, prominent in religious and civic affairs. Margaret Burton Langdale Preston bore no

---

[3] Peter Wilson Coldham, *English Convicts in Colonial America*, vol. 1 (Middlesex New Orleans: Polyanthos, 1974–1976) 151.; Nell Marion Nugent, Abstractor, *Cavaliers and Pioneers: Abstracts of Virginia Land*...Reprint ed. (Baltimore: Genealogical Publishing Co., 1969) 623.; and Nell Marion Nugent, Abstractor, *Cavaliers and Pioneers: Abstracts of Virginia Land*. vol. 3 (Richmond: Virginia State Library, 1979) 148. Cited in *The New World Book of Langdales*, 1–22.

[4] In addition to the works cited above, useful information on early immigrants to America has been found on the following compact discs: Ancestry.com, *The Great Migration Begins: Immigrants to New England 1620–1633*, CD, Ancestry.com, *South Carolina Records and Reference* (1998), CD, Broderbund, *Family Archives CD #017, Birth Records: United States/Europe, 900-1880* (1995), CD, Broderbund, *Family Archives CD #170, Immigrants to the New World, 1600s-1800s* (1997), CD, Broderbund, *Family Archives CD #181, English Origins of New England Families, 1500s-1800s* (Genealogical Publishing Company, 1997), CD, Broderbund, *Family Archives CD #350, the Complete Book of Emigrants, 1607-1776 & Emigrants in Bondage, 1614-1775* (Genealogical Publishing Company, 1996), Broderbund, *Family Archives CD #516, Genealogical Records: Early Georgia Settlers, 1700s--1800s* (Genealogical Publishing Company), and Broderbund, *Family Archives CD #517, Genealogical Records: Early South Carolina Settlers, 1600s--1800s* (Genealogical Publishing Company.)

more children, and her children by Josiah Langdale perhaps enjoyed growing up in the relatively comfortable surroundings provided by their stepfather.

When they reached maturity, both of Josiah Langdale's children married well.[5] Mary, the eldest, married Samuel Coates from another well-to-do Quaker family. Many of their descendants have lived and prospered in Philadelphia down to the present, and some have achieved great distinction. Mary's younger brother, John, married Sarah Hudson, daughter of William Hudson, Jr., who operated a tanning business in Philadelphia. Sarah's grandfather, William Hudson, Sr., had once served as mayor of Philadelphia. The Hudsons were also Friends.

John Langdale, like his father-in-law a tanner by trade, seems to have lived out most of his life in the Philadelphia area as a committed member of the Society of Friends. He did move around some, however. He did not always live in the same house or even in the same city. For some years during (and perhaps preceding) the French and Indian War he resided in Isle of Wight County, Virginia, and was a member of the Friends' Western Branch Monthly Meeting established there.[6] This implies, for one thing, that the Langdales of Philadelphia knew something about life in the Southern colonies and they undoubtedly knew the roads leading to them.

John and Sarah Hudson Langdale had eleven children, three of whom died in infancy. Of the eight who lived beyond childhood, there were four of each sex. Our concern here is only with the males. John and Sarah named their eldest son Josiah, presumably in honor of his grandfather. The other males were John, Jr. (in honor of his father, one assumes), William Hudson (in honor of his mother's father), and Samuel (perhaps in honor of his Uncle Samuel Coates, husband of his Aunt Mary). Of these four boys, only Josiah, the eldest, and Samuel, the youngest, born in 1759, are known to have left surviving children. Samuel was exactly twenty years

---

[5] Marriage reference works used in this study include Ancestry.com, *Alabama Vital Records: Marriages 1808–1920*, CD, Automated Archives, *Marriage Records: Maryland, Virginia and North Carolina*, CD #004 (1994), Broderbund, *Family Archives CD #003, Marriage Index: Al, Ga, Sc, 1641-1944* (1995), CD, Broderbund, *Family Archives CD #004, Marriage Index: Md, Nc, Va, 1624-1915* (1996), CD, Broderbund, *Family Archives CD #226, Marriage Index: Georgia, 1754-1850* (1995), CD, Broderbund, *Family Archives CD #229, Marriage Index: Selected Counties of Ky, Nc, Tn, Va, Wv, 1728-1850* (1995), CD, Broderbund, *Family Archives CD #399, Marriage Index: District of Columbia, Delaware, Maryland & Virginia, 1740-1920* (1999), and Broderbund, *Family Archives CD #513, Genealogical Records: Virginia Land, Marriage and Probate Records 1639-1850* (1999), CD.

[6] Some significant Virginia-related genealogical sources on compact disc are Broderbund, *Family Archives CD #156, Family History: Mid-Atlantic Genealogies, 1340-1940*, Broderbund, *Family Archives CD #162, Family History: Virginia Genealogies #1, Pre 1600 to 1900s* (1996), Broderbund, *Family Archives CD #186, Family History: Virginia Genealogies #2 1600s-1800s* (1997), Broderbund, *Family Archives CD #187, Family History: Virginia Genealogies #3, 1600S–1800s* (Genealogical Publishing Company, 1997), and Broderbund, *Family Archives CD #205, Family History: Virginia Genealogies, 1600s–1800s* (1998).

younger than his elder brother, Josiah, and just the right age to be caught up in the conflict of the American War of Independence.

The period leading up to and including the War of Independence brought turmoil and division to the Society of Friends. For one thing, the Quakers became involved in a major movement to end slavery among themselves and others.[7] Some Quakers resisted the admonitions of their leaders on this subject and suffered punishment for it. Other Quakers, including many in the South, packed up and moved to the western territories where slavery did not exist to escape the controversy. So the western migration in which English colonists of all faiths generally participated, swelled in volume with Quakers seeking more acceptable social conditions, as well as economic opportunity.

A second unsettling issue for Quakers involved the fighting with England. As pacifists, Quakers were supposed to abstain from armed conflict. Yet some Quakers—some were called "fighting Quakers"—disobeyed their religious leaders and joined in the combat. Young Samuel Langdale evidently did this, for it is recorded that the Philadelphia Monthly Meeting of Friends expelled him for participating in warlike activity. Some time after the war, like many others of his faith, he moved to Ohio where some of his descendants still live. Others of Samuel's descendants have dispersed as far away as California, and a few appear to have returned from Ohio to live in the Philadelphia area.

In the meantime, a decade before the start of the Revolutionary War, Samuel's older brother, Josiah, had already come into conflict with Quaker authorities in Philadelphia over still another issue. This evidently had nothing to do with the anti-slavery movement or pacifism; it concerned marriage.

Quaker rules described quite explicitly the permissions that must be gained by a man and a woman who wished to be married, plus other requirements. They must both be Quakers, not too close kin (not first cousins), the proposed bride must have the approval of the women's meeting, and the proposed groom must have the approval of the men's meeting. The monthly meeting (acting for local congregations of Friends) wanted to be assured that the man had his finances in order and that he did not have an obligation to marry someone else. And of course Quaker authorities, not civil officials, must perform the ceremony.

Josiah Langdale evidently flaunted these rules by going out and marrying someone without permission or in violation of some procedure. As a result, the Philadelphia Monthly Meeting disowned (expelled) him from their group in 1764. From this we know that Josiah married at about twenty-five years of age. The sparse Quaker record also mentions that Josiah worked as a "house carpenter."

At this point, coinciding with the public controversy over unpopular British policies such as the Proclamation of 1763 and the Stamp Act, Josiah Langdale

---

[7] For the slavery issue, see Jean R. Soderlund, *Quakers & Slavery: A Divided Spirit* (Princeton NJ: Princeton University Press, 1985).

seems to have vanished from the records. By 1774, however, just before the trouble between the colonies and England flared into armed conflict, official records reveal a Josiah Langdale living in Colleton District, South Carolina. Unfortunately, those documents do not mention his place of origin, and they reveal precious little about his family connections.

Circumstantial evidence leads to the tentative conclusion that the Josiah Langdale of Colleton and the Josiah Langdale of Philadelphia were the same person.[8] It is surely noteworthy that Josiah Langdale, expelled Quaker of Philadelphia, disappeared and a decade later a Josiah Langdale showed up in Colleton District, South Carolina, from some unidentified place. Persons surnamed Langdale with first name Josiah appear only three times in eighteenth-century English American records (the first instance being Josiah the Quaker minister of Yorkshire, grandfather of Josiah Langdale of Philadelphia). For Josiah of Philadelphia we have a recorded birth date (18 December 1739), but no death date or place, and for Josiah of Colleton we have a recorded death date (30 November 1817), but no birth date. If the Philadelphia and Colleton Josiahs were the same, this man's lifespan would have been seventy-eight years, a perfectly reasonable term. From the perspective of religion, Josiah of Philadelphia was disowned by his Quaker congregation in 1764 for a marriage of which the congregation disapproved. In what might have been a reasonable religious migration from one denomination to another, Josiah Langdale of Colleton was or became an active Methodist, and by the end of the century served as a trustee of the Island Creek Methodist Church.

A clinching argument, perhaps, is that descriptions written thirty years and hundreds of miles distant from each other refer to the professions of both these Josiahs as that of "house carpenter," differentiating the carpentry on dwellings from that of a "ship carpenter," another popular vocation of the time. The Philadelphia Monthly Meeting minutes described Josiah of Philadelphia as such,

---

[8] In "Langdales of Colleton," 4. Dr. George Langdale lists six Langdales regarded as possible ancestors of Josiah Langdale of Colleton. These are William Langdale, who was in Virginia in 1665; Robert R. Langdale, a convict sent to Barbados in 1669; Duke Langdale, recorded as being in Virginia in 1714; William Langdale, who witnessed a will in Berkeley County, SC, in 1717; Henry Langdale, who witnessed a land survey in Port Royal Island, SC, in 1735/36; and John Langdale, a will recipient of Norfolk VA, and Haddonfield, NJ, in 1765. The evidence presented in this study identifies the last named individual, John Langdale of Norfolk and Haddonfield, as the father of Josiah Langdale of Colleton.

Some family members believe, however, that Josiah of Colleton descends from a William Langdale, presumably the one who was in Berkeley County in 1717. The writer has so far been unable to find documentation to support that view.

and a land deed by which Josiah of Colleton sold a parcel of land included for him the exact same description, "house carpenter."[9]

Josiah Langdale might have arrived in South Carolina by sea or by land. Colleton District was, of course, near Charleston, the colony's busiest seaport. There were also major roads connecting Philadelphia with this area of South Carolina, as shown by the map on the next page. One main road led from Philadelphia through Wilmington, Baltimore, Fredericksburg, Richmond, Petersburg, Warrenton, Raleigh, Elizabethtown, Cheraw, Camden, and, finally, Charleston. Although American history textbooks often emphasize the isolation of colonies from one another, numerous family histories demonstrate that travel from one colony to another had become commonplace by the latter part of the eighteenth century. To find a person born in Pennsylvania living in South Carolina would have been no big surprise.

It appears that Josiah Langdale of Colleton married twice, first to a Mary Curtes or Cleaton/Clayton, and second to a Mary Flowers. He had at least two sons and perhaps a daughter. The name of the first-born son, William B. Langdale, perhaps honored Josiah's grandfather, William Hudson, Jr. or his brother, William Hudson Langdale. His second son, John C. Langdale, may have been named for Josiah's father, John Langdale, or for John C.'s maternal grandfather, John Curtis (or John Cleaton/Clayton).

Both brothers served in the War of 1812, which officially ended in December 1814. [10] Probably some time during the war, William B. Langdale married young Jane Guthrie, who was perhaps half his age.[11] They had a son, John Robert Langdale, born in May 1815. The new mother was four months past her thirteenth birthday. The marriage of William and Jane lasted only a few years. Some time preceding 28 November 1821, William evidently died, because his

---

[9] Appendix C deals with this issue and others related to the genealogy of Josiah Langdale of Yorkshire and some of his descendants.

[10] Military service references on compact disc for the War of 1812 and the American War of Independence are Ancestry.com, *Military Records: Revolutionary War Muster Rolls*, CD, Ancestry.com, *Military Records: War of 1812 Muster Rolls*, CD, Broderbund, *Family Archives CD #144, Genealogical Records: Loyalists in the American Revolution* (Genealogical Publishing Company), Broderbund, *Family Archives CD #146, Military Records: US Soldiers, 1784–1811*, Broderbund, *Family Archives CD #147, Revolutionary War Soldiers and Sailors, 1775–1782*, CD.

[11] A note on William B. Langdale in Appendix D mentions that in 1802 he was issued a passport to enter the Cherokee country to work as a smith for James Vann, presumably the Cherokee chief of that name, whose home was at Spring Place, Murray County GA. William must have been at least a teenager by that time, so his birthdate would likely have been before 1790. The name Vann later appeared prominently in connection with the Georgia Gold Rush of the 1820s and 1830s. For the gold rush, see David Williams, *The Georgia Gold Rush: Twenty-Niners, Cherokees, and Gold Fever* (Columbia SC: University of South Carolina Press, 1993).

presumed widow, Jane, married her first husband's brother, John C. Langdale, on that date, about two months before the bride's twentieth birthday. The groom was thirty-four.

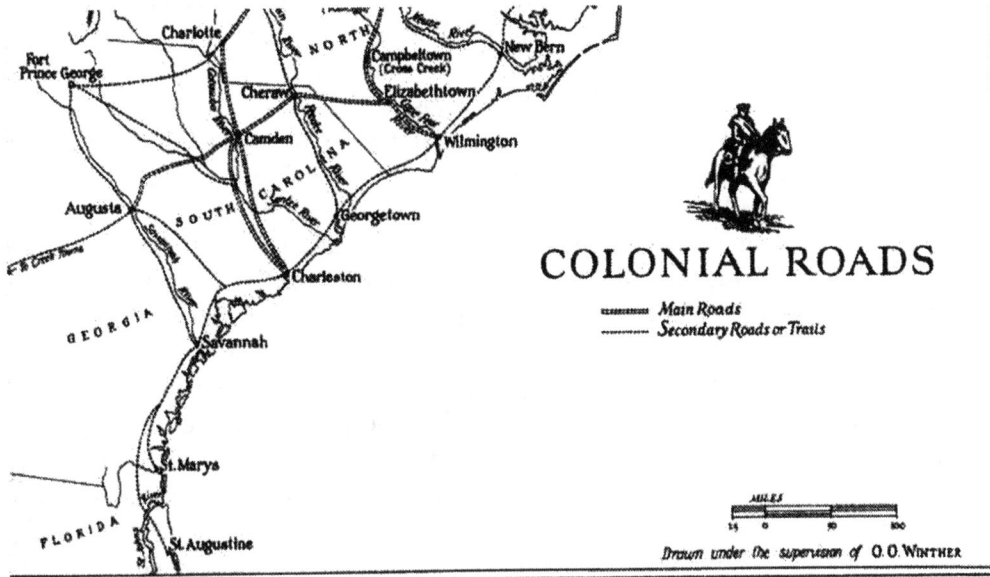

Colonial Roads.

In accord with the usual practice of the time, John C. and Jane had a large family, nine children in fact, with some of them bearing names found two generations before in Philadelphia among the children of John Langdale and Sarah Hudson. The number of these coincidences is remarkable. John C. and Jane named their eldest son, born in 1822, Josiah William Marmaduke Langdale. Undoubtedly, the name Josiah honored the child's grandfather. The name William may have honored the grandfather or the two brothers of Josiah Langdale of Philadelphia who bore that name. Marmaduke was a name given to several of the Langdales of Yorkshire, having been the name of Lord Langdale, a general for King Charles I in the English Civil War who was awarded the title of baron by Charles II for his service. According to some published genealogies and to genealogical records collected and published by the Church of Jesus Christ of Latter Day Saints, Josiah Langdale the Quaker (b. 1673) was a grandson of the first Baron Langdale, but Josiah's recently-published partial autobiography does not appear to support this connection.

Among the children of John C. and Jane Guthrie Langdale there was a John R. C. and also a John Willis, who might have been named in honor of their father, John C., or their great grandfather, John Langdale, or possibly in memory of Josiah of Philadelphia's brother, John Langdale, Jr. Their daughter, Sara Ann Caroline, may have been named in memory of her great grandmother, Sarah Hudson. Daughter Margaret O'Bryan Langdale might conceivably have been named to honor the memory of Margaret Burton, her great-great grandmother, or Margaret Langdale, a great aunt and sister of Josiah Langdale of Philadelphia. Jane and John C.'s daughter, Elizabeth, could possibly have been named for another sister of Josiah of Philadelphia who bore that name. Jane and John C. also had a daughter named Jane who may have been named in honor of her own mother, Jane Guthrie, or of Jane Langdale, yet another sister of Josiah of Philadelphia.

One of the more significant names of the children of John C. and Jane Guthrie Langdale was that of their son, Jeremiah Samuel Hudson Langdale. This name includes the name of the youngest brother of Josiah Langdale of Philadelphia, plus the maiden name of the mother of Josiah of Philadelphia. Use of all these names for the children of John C. and Jane, echoing in South Carolina the names of the Philadelphia Langdales, does not prove the Josiah of Philadelphia and the Josiah of Colleton were the same, but it *suggests* a family connection between the South Carolina and the Philadelphia Langdales. Thus, it adds a little to the argument that the two Josiahs were actualy the same one.

Among the several children in the household of John C. Langdale lived Jane's eldest child, John Robert Langdale, son of her first husband, William. He had been six years old at the time of his mother's second marriage. Perhaps as he aged John Robert felt out of place in his uncle's home, or it may have been that the peculiar wisdom inherent in teenagers convinced him that his future lay elsewhere.

As a very young man, John Robert left home in Colleton District, South Carolina, to seek his fortune. He apparently joined in a movement of families from the Colleton area who were resettling in the 1830s to southeast Georgia.[12]

Among the early Colleton immigrants to south Georgia there was John J. North (1792–1880) who settled near present-day Du Pont, just west of today's Homerville.[13] As captain, he commanded local troops in the Indian war of

---

[12] For general histories of Georgia, see Numan V. Bartley, *The Creation of Modern Georgia* (Athens GA: University of Georgia Press, 1983); Kenneth Coleman, General Editor et al., eds., *A History of Georgia* (Athens GA: University of Georgia Press, 1977); E. Merton Coulter, *Georgia: A Short History*, rev. 3rd ed. (Chapel Hill NC: The University of North Carolina Press, 1960).

[13] County and local histories useful for this study include Geraldine McLeod Clifton, chairman, and others of Book Committee, Genealogy Unlimited Society, ed., *The Heritage of Lowndes County, Georgia—2000*, vol. 1, *Lowndes County, Georgia, and Its People* (Valdosta GA: Genealogy Unlimited, Inc., 2000); Coastal Plain Area Planning and

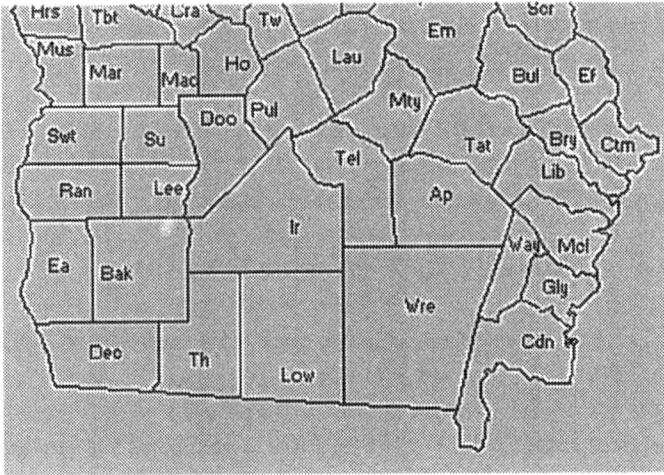

Map of South Georgia in 1838. This map shows the boundaries of South Georgia counties in 1838. This is the configuration that John Robert Langdale and other Colleton Countians found when they settled this region in the 1830s and 1840s. Irwin (Ir) and Appling (Ap) Counties, the southern boundaries of which formerly extended to the Florida line, had lost territory to Ware (Wre), Lowndes (Low), and Thomas (Th). Neither Clinch, Echols, Berrien, nor Brooks had yet been established. Map created with *Animap 2.0.*

Development Commission, *Remembered Places and Leftover Pieces* (Valdosta GA: Coastal Plain Area Planning and Development Commission, 1976); Echols County High School Composition Class, *Chinkypin*, vol. 2 (Statenville GA: Echols County High School, 1976); Hamilton County Bicentennial Committee, *A Brief History of Hamilton County, Florida*, ed. Compiler Cora Hinton (Jasper FL: The Jasper News, 1976); William F. Holmes, ed., *Struggling to Shake Off Old Shackles: 20th Century Georgia* (Savannah GA: 1995); Folks Huxford, *History of Clinch County, Georgia, Revised to Date* (Macon: J. W. Burke, 1916); Richard J. Lenz, *Longstreet Highroad Guide to the Georgia Coast & Okefenokee* (Marietta GA: Longstreet Press, 1999); Cecile Hulse Matschat, *Suwannee River: Strange Green Land* (New York NY: Literary Guild of America, Inc., 1938); Mary Lou L. and Samuel Jordan Lawson III McDonald, *The Passing of the Pines: A History of Wilcox County, Georgia* (Roswell GA: W. H. Wolfe Associates, 1984); Alexander Stephens McQueen, *History of Charlton County* (Atlanta GA: Stein, 1934); T. R. Mobley, *Old Days and Old Ways in South Georgia: A Short Story Collection* (Self-published, 1998); JaneTwitty Shelton, *Pines and Pioneers: A History of Lowndes County, Georgia, 1825–1900* (Atlanta: Cherokee Publishing Company, 1976); Inc. Valdosta-Lowndes County Centennials, Pictorial History Committee, Tom D. Shelton, Chairman, ed., *A Pictorial History of Lowndes County, 1825–1975* (Valdosta GA: Valdosta-Lowndes County Centennials, Inc., 1976).

1836–1838. He was a justice of the peace in Clinch County at the time the county seat moved from Magnolia to Homerville and was the father of twenty children by three wives.[14]

Another Colleton native, Elijah Mattox, born in 1798 the son of John Mattox, lived in Tattnall County during his youth and then moved to Waresboro around 1830. In the midst of a successful political and business career in the mid-1830s when John Robert Langdale settled in south Georgia, Elijah Mattox lived for some years at Blount's Ferry, a small settlement on the Suwannee River near the Florida line. He died at Blount's Ferry in 1856.[15] This, incidentally, is apparently the place where John Robert Langdale's son, Noah, lived at that time, so Noah and John Robert undoubtedly knew this wealthy man who came from Colleton.

Elijah's son, Dr. John Homer Mattox, who inherited much of his father's land, moved from Blount's Ferry to the location of present-day Homerville, which he is credited with establishing. He subsequently achieved its designation as the county seat in place of Magnolia. It is clear that Colleton District, South Carolina, did its part to populate south Georgia with some of its most prominent and influential citizens, and John Robert had plenty of company from South Carolina as he moved into Georgia.

One may speculate that, as a young single fellow, he simply attached himself to one of those migrating families and tagged along. It is possible, however, that he traveled separately. In either case, scanty records indicate that he spent a little time in Camden County, Georgia, then moved farther south and settled initially in the area of Lowndes County that later became part of Berrien. Although a specific account of John Robert's experience is lacking, it probably resembled that of the Burnetts, who made the move in the late 1830s, a few years after John Robert. A generation later, in the 1850s, this family provided a wife, their daughter, Elizabeth, for John Robert's eldest son, Noah. Elizabeth Burnett Langdale was the mother of the first John Wesley Langdale, whom the Langdales of Valdosta honor as the founder of the Langdale Company.

The Burnetts had reportedly come to the Colleton area from North Carolina. John Burnett and three brothers, sons of Richard Burnett, Jr., decided to join the trek to Georgia. With John went his wife, Sophia Harvey Burnett. According to a story passed down in the family, Sophia and a sister, Nancy, had come as young girls alone to America from Holland, outfitted with wooden shoes. Sophia is said to have displayed these shoes to her grandchildren decades later at the original Burnett family homestead in Echols County. John and Sophia set up this home in 1840 or 1841 about eight miles southwest of the later-established town of Fargo, GA, not far from the Suwannee River.[16]

---

[14] Huxford, *History of Clinch County*, 279.

[15] Ibid., 271–72.

[16] Harvey M. Burnette, "Burnett History" (Unpublished paper, typewritten, Burnsville NC, 1987) 1–2.

Judging by the experience of the Burnetts, the move from South Carolina typically required a couple of years. They traveled from Colleton by covered wagon with a group that included relatives and friends. When they reached Bulloch County, Georgia, they stayed a year with friends and relatives who had come there earlier from South Carolina and settled. While in Bulloch County they planted and harvested one crop. This provided them with resources for the second leg of their pilgrimage to south Georgia and enough commodities to sustain them until they could clear land and grow food for themselves and their livestock. Animals they brought with them included sheep, goats, cows, hogs, fowl, and horses.

The Burnett caravan from Colleton included John's three brothers, Benjamin, Bryant and Richard. Each of the four brothers chose to settle in a different area. Benjamin stayed in Bulloch County, John made his home in the region that became Echols, and the other two moved on to Florida, with Bryant going to Suwannee and Richard to Madison County.

Among those migrating from Carolina to south Georgia about the same time as John Robert Langdale were a family of Griffins. These Griffins trace their ancestry to a John Griffith who lived in Wales in the middle of the sixteenth century. One of John's descendants, Owen Griffith, immigrated to Isle of Wight County, Virginia. He died there in 1698. Some of his descendants, following a pattern exemplified in many families, migrated to the south and west. By the time of the Revolutionary War, Griffiths lived in Bertie and Edgecombe Counties, North Carolina, and a few were being called by the slightly different name, Griffin.

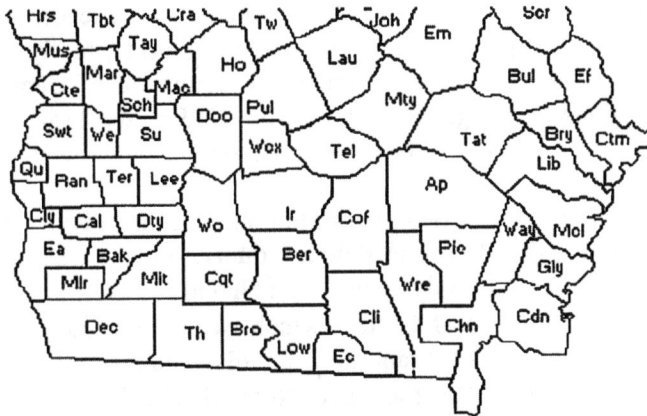

Boundaries of South Georgia Counties in 1858. This map shows the boundaries of Echols, Lowndes, and Clinch Counties after establishment of Echols County in 1858. Lowndes is abbreviated "Low," Clinch is "Cli," and Echols is "Ec." Map created with *Animap* 2.0.

From there, James Griffin, son of Francis Griffith/Griffin and Mary Byrd, led a movement of Griffins into Georgia.[17]

James Griffin and his wife, Sarah Lodge, had seven children who appear to have been enchanted by young people of the Hall and Bradford families. Six of the seven married either a Hall or a Bradford. Of the two daughters, one chose a Hall and the other a Bradford. Of the five sons, Joshua and Shadrack "Shade" married Bradfords, while Noah and Thomas married Halls. This is significant because Thomas Griffin and his wife, Nancy Hall, were direct ancestors of the Langdales of our story. Their daughter, Harriet Griffin, became the mother of all south Georgia Langdales.

Somehow in this pioneering period young John Robert Langdale became acquainted with the Griffins. In August 1835, at the age of twenty, he married their sixteen-year-old daughter, Harriet, in a ceremony conducted by Justice of the Peace Randall Folsom. Within the first year of their marriage, the young couple welcomed their first child, a son whom they named Noah. Harriet had an uncle and a brother with that name, which was later applied to a grandson and a great-grandson of the first Noah Langdale. During their lifetime, John Robert and Harriet became parents of eight other children, but those featured in this story are all descended from Noah and his wife, Elizabeth Burnett.

Information about John Robert Langdale is sparse. Military records reveal that he stood five feet, nine inches, tall. He had dark complexion. In the Indian Wars he served under Captain John Pike from April to December 1836, while newly married and father of a one-year-old child. He enrolled again as a private on 23 December 1837, under Captain W. C. Newbern. Two decades later, on 1 July 1857, records show that he enlisted at Tampa Bay, Florida, to fight Indians for at least the third time, on this occasion under the command of Captain William H. Cone. He received his discharge from service on 22 January 1858, at Tampa Bay. John Robert's twenty-two-year-old son, Noah, served with his father in Captain Cone's company.

In December 1859, about two years after his military service of 1857–1858, John Robert Langdale, then living in Echols County, bought a home site in Clinch County. Echols County was only a year old, having been created the previous December mostly from a slice of Clinch (which was only eight years old). Among the newly elected officials of brand-new Echols County, incidentally, was the eldest brother of Harriet Griffin Langdale, Noah H. Griffin. He served as one of five justices of the Inferior Court. Considering his brother-in-law's position, one might suppose John Robert would have seen some advantage to living in the new county of Echols. Yet he seems to have decided to leave Echols for Clinch. Perhaps the railroad attracted him, for the Atlantic and Gulf Railroad, laying track

---

17   John Alfred Griffin, Gedcom file 17308.ged, Ancestry World Tree, http://www.ancestry.com, 14 May 2000.

southward and westward from Savannah, reached the towns of Homerville and Du Pont in late 1859.

About the time of the railroad's arrival, on 7 December 1859, John Robert purchased a one-acre lot in the village of Magnolia, which was then the county seat of Clinch County. This appears to have been the first land owned by a Langdale in south Georgia. For this acre John R. paid $125.00 to Silas A. O'Quin of Columbia County, Florida. David O'Quin, clerk of the Clinch County Superior Court, recorded the deed in Deed Book A, Page 383, and also acted as attorney in fact for his brother, Silas, in the sale of the land. The O'Quin brothers were sons of North Carolina-born Silas O'Quin of Wayne County, Georgia.[18] Besides being a county official, David O'Quin owned one of three stores that are known to have existed in Magnolia,[19]

Incorporated in 1854, four years after creation of Clinch County from territory of Ware and Lowndes, Magnolia encompassed eighty acres of land in Lot 420 in the 12th Land District, at the approximate geographical center of the county. The town had five commissioners to govern it. A stagecoach road ran east from Magnolia to Waresboro, which was then the county seat of Ware County, and west through Du Pont to Troupville, which was the county seat of Lowndes County. A courthouse built in 1852 burned in 1856, perhaps from arson, and destroyed the county records for the first six years. Notwithstanding the fire, Magnolia had good things happening. Around 1855, for example, the town achieved the distinction of having the first Masonic Lodge in Clinch County.[20] Magnolia appeared to be on its way to success.

Unfortunately for Magnolia, its prosperity did not last. One year after John Robert purchased his home site in Magnolia, the town lost its place of honor as county seat. Dr. John Homer Mattox had moved from Blount's Ferry on the Suwannee and built an impressive estate, which he called "Homerville." The stagecoach from Waresboro stopped at Homerville on the way to Magnolia.

Then, by gift of land and other concessions, Dr. Mattox induced the Atlantic and Gulf Railroad to lay its tracks through Homerville, rather than through some other place such as Magnolia. A petition signed by about 275 citizens asked the legislature to authorize moving the county seat from Magnolia to Homerville. By December 1860, it was done; Homerville became the new county seat, and Magnolia started to wither away.[21]

The land that John Robert bought in Magnolia apparently passed out of his family's hands about four years after his death in the Civil War. There is a record

---

[18] "Deed, Silas A. O' Quin of Columbia County FL, to John Robert Langdale," photocopy of document as recorded by David O'Quin, Clerk, in Clinch County GA, Deed Book A, 383, John W. Langdale Papers, Valdosta GA.

[19] Huxford, *History of Clinch County*, 39.

[20] Ibid., 36–39.

[21] Ibid., 43–48.

showing that W. D. Griffin and Harriet Griffin Langdale as administrators sold a parcel to J. B. Giddens on 1 January 1867 for $320.00.[22] Assuming this is the same land, the relatively low price implies that John Robert never built a house on the lot in Magnolia and, therefore, may not actually have lived in that town.

In 1861, as he had in the Indian emergencies earlier, John Robert answered the call to arms. Once again he joined the army, this time that of the Confederacy.[23] He enlisted twice as a private. The first enlistment began on 1 August 1861 and ended with his discharge at Savannah, Georgia, on 18 August 1862. Less than two months later, he joined as a substitute for J. L. Sutton in Company I of the 50th Georgia.

Although it is impossible to know with any degree of assurance, this second enlistment may have been a family decision. Records show that Harriet Griffin Langdale's niece, Priscilla Griffin, married twenty-one-year-old John L. Sutton in Berrien County on 22 March 1863. If this was the same J. L. Sutton for whom he substituted in the army, perhaps John Robert enlisted as a favor to a family member. Conceivably, his wife could have even encouraged it. One might imagine it as sort of a wedding present to her niece. That would cast John R. in a sacrificial role, instead of—as some might envision this scenario—as a war-infatuated man going off to play soldier while his wife slaved at home to feed, clothe, and look after the children. Today, one can only guess about John Robert's reasons for enlisting a second time.

In any case, this second enlistment, beginning 7 October 1862, cost John Robert his life. He died of pneumonia in a Fredericksburg, Virginia, hospital on 2 March 1863, about three weeks before Harriet's niece married young Mr. Sutton, having probably no knowledge of John Robert's fate. Three comrades from south Georgia, W. E. Connell, John M. Griner, and W. W. Griner, later testified that they were in the same company, saw him die, and helped to bury him.[24] He left a middle-aged widow with several young children, the youngest of whom, Malinda, was born the year of her father's enlistment.[25]

From the twentieth-century standpoint it seems remarkable that a man over forty years of age with a large family would enlist, not once, but twice, as a private

---

[22] Folks Huxford"Langdale Folder," Huxford Genealogical Society Library.

[23] For some Civil War military service records on CD-ROM, see Ancestry.com, *Military Records: Civil War Muster Rolls*, and Broderbund, *Family Archives CD #119, Military Records: Confederate Soldiers, 1861–1865.*

[24] Harriet Griffin Langdale, and others, "Pension Applications of Harriet Griffin Langdale, Widow of John Robert Langdale, drawer 274, roll 70," Microfilm, Pension Applications of Confederate Soldiers and Widows who Applied from Georgia, Georgia State Archives, Atlanta GA. In her application for a Confederate pension on 6 June 1891, Harriet lists the date of her husband's death as 2 March 1863, and states she has lived in Georgia since 8 January 1822.

[25] Huxford, "Langdale Folder."

in a war from which so many did not return alive. Presumably, he thought his older children could help Harriet take care of the family in his absence, which he may have expected would be brief. Children of John Robert and Harriet as of 1862, with their approximate ages in that year, included Noah, twenty-seven; Mary Polly, twenty; Rebecca, sixteen; Mitchell Griffin, fourteen; Nancy, eleven; John C., nine; James D., six; Martha N., three; and Malinda, the baby.

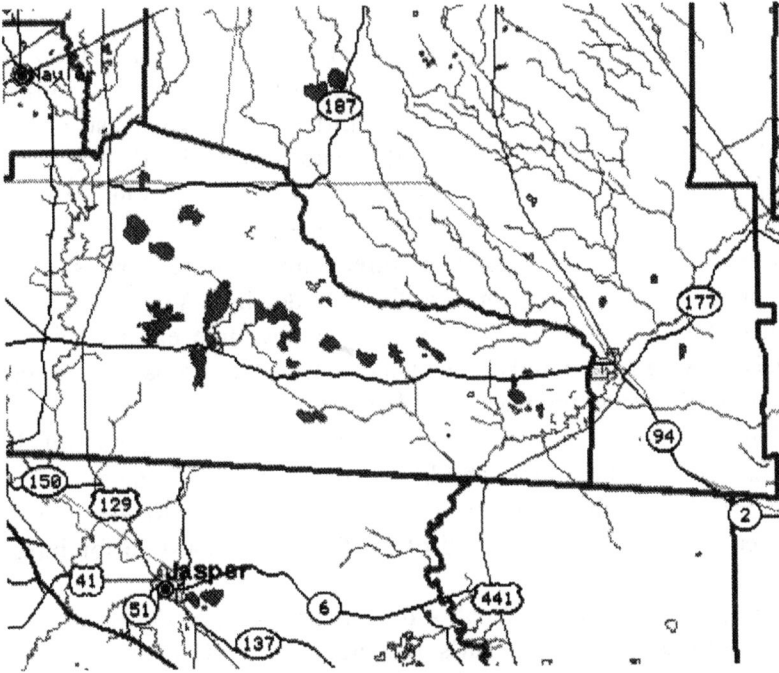

Homerville, Blount's Ferry, Jasper Area Map. This map shows the region of Clinch and Echols Counties where John Robert, Noah, and John Wesley Langdale were active in the 19th century. Homerville was just north of Magnolia. Fargo and Council were not founded until decades later, about 1900-1908. Columbia County, FL, adjoined Echols. From Tiger Mapping Service, U.S. Census Bureau.

The eldest son, Noah, may have been able to assist his mother in the absence of his father during part of John Robert's first enlistment, but could not possibly have done so during the second. In 1857, at age twenty-two, he had married Elizabeth Burnett, daughter of John and Sofia Harvey Burnett, and started his own family. Noah and Elizabeth lived at Blount's Ferry on the east bank of the Suwannee near the state line.

Perhaps his service in the Indian Wars led Noah to see promise in this place and to settle there. He may have been one of the soldiers who camped at Blount's

Ferry during the Seminole War. If a man as well educated, wealthy, well-placed, and experienced as Elijah Mattox thought Blount's Ferry had good prospects, as implied by the fact that he made his own home there, it probably did. The place appeared important enough to have a US post office operating from 1845 to 1859.[26] River transportation on the Suwannee undoubtedly attracted settlers, probably including Noah. Before his departure for the army, Noah might have shipped gum from Blount's Ferry to Pensacola or some other place for processing.[27]

By 1862, Noah and Elizabeth had three children: Mary Jane, John Wesley, and Jefferson Davis. Birth dates of the children were, respectively, 1858, 1860, and 1862. Less than two months after the birth of his youngest child, Noah enlisted at Blackshear, Georgia, in the Confederate army. The date was 4 March 1862, when he joined Company A, 50th Georgia Volunteers (Pierce County—Satilla Rangers). His father, John Robert, had five months yet to complete his first enlistment. In less than three months after Noah's enlistment, on 20 May 1862, about a year before his father's death in Virginia, Noah died in military service. Yet nobody in the family knew at the time exactly what became of him. Precisely when his family concluded that Noah probably was dead and would not be returning from the war is not known.

When Noah departed Blount's Ferry to fight in the war, he left his wife responsible for looking after three children under age five. It must have been a hard life for Elizabeth, who lived as a widow until 1878. At that time, John Wesley, 18, her eldest son, became head of the family, responsible for himself and his siblings.

Judging by the testimony of Noah's descendants in the 1980s and 1990s, it appears that, from this period, Noah's line never had close contacts with the Langdales descended from Harriet's other children or with Harriet Griffin Langdale herself. Significantly, Noah's granddaughter, Nan, who wrote several lengthy letters in the 1980s describing her family's life at Council, Georgia, and Jasper, Florida, appeared oblivious to the existence of her great-grandmother, Harriet, or to the brothers and sisters of her grandfather, Noah. Nan understood that both of their grandfathers, Gideon Burnsed and Noah Langdale, as well as Noah's father, John Robert Langdale, had died in Confederate service. She heard that their father's ancestors had lived in South Carolina and that their mother's family, the Burnseds, had lived somewhere nearby.[28] Except for Elizabeth Daugharty Burnsed,

---

[26] Hamilton County Bicentennial Committee. *A Brief History of Hamilton County, Florida.* Edited by Compiler Cora Hinton. (Jasper FL: The Jasper News, 1976) 83.

[27] John J. Langdale, Jr., Interview by author, audio tape, Valdosta GA, 17 April 1996.

[28] Nan Langdale Campbell, "Typed Copies of Handwritten Letters, 1986–1987, to Virginia L. Miller," Transcripts of original letters prepared by John Lancaster, John W. Langdale Papers, Valdosta GA. 42 pages.

who was their maternal grandmother and the widow of Gideon Burnsed, said Nan, she and her siblings never knew a grandparent.

Although Nan and her sisters might have been too young to remember their great-grandmother, Harriet Griffin Langdale, or to recall comments they heard about the family's history, the same would be less true of their brothers. In fact, it does appear that the youngest of Nan's brothers, the future Judge Harley, knew a bit more about the family's origin. Judge recalled in the late 1960s that at some time long ago, unknown to him, one branch of the Langdale family was said to have arrived in South Carolina and another branch reportedly settled in Ohio. In South Carolina, as he remembered the story, the oldest brother acquired the family property and the younger ones scattered to various places. At that time, John Robert Langdale came from Colleton District, South Carolina, to Berrien County, Georgia; later, he moved farther south. John Robert's son, Noah, born in Berrien County, married Elizabeth Burnett, who had been born in Colleton County, South Carolina, Judge recalled. Thus, the Langdales and the Burnetts had Colleton, South Carolina, connections. Noah and Elizabeth became the parents of Judge's father, John Wesley Langdale, and his siblings.[29]

From his father and perhaps from other older members of the family, Harley Langdale, Jr. formed a general impression of his Langdale origins. As he commented in 1986, "We had very humble beginnings in Clinch County. My forebears came from England and migrated down to Walterboro, South Carolina, and migrated to Clinch County. My father always said he couldn't understand why they passed over such good fertile land and settled on the western edge of the Okefenokee Swamp."

Harley, Jr.'s mental picture extended to the way the early Langdales made a living in south Georgia. "After my father's people came down," Harley, Jr. said, "they ran woods cows. The cows ranged over the Piney Woods. In the spring they would gather them. They also ran woods hogs, and then they hunted. Then the railroad came down, and they got interested in the timber business, then in the turpentine business in 1894."[30]

The first John Wesley Langdale, who never knew his father, may not have talked much about his parents, especially to his young daughters. Nan stated in 1986 that she never knew anything about her father's mother or father. Even the eldest son, John J., seems to have had little information on this subject, or else he chose not to share it. He almost never talked about it, said his son, John J., Jr.[31]

---

[29] Harley Langdale, Sr., Interview by Jane and Tom Shelton, audio tape, Valdosta GA, 4 November 1969.

[30] "Langdale Company Brings Work Ethic to Forefront," *Valdosta Daily Times*, 27 April 1986.

[31] Campbell, "Letters to VLM" ; Langdale, interview 01; and Langdale, Judge Interview01. Also, see US Census of 1880.

Judge Harley & Sister, Nan. Nan Langdale
Campbell and her brother, Judge Harley Langdale,
at Judge Harley's home in Valdosta, Georgia, in the
1930s. Nan's letters to her niece, Virginia Langdale
Miller, are the main source for information on home
life in the John Wesley Langdale family of Council.
TLF.

John J., a quiet man, not given to much talking, probably knew more than he
told his children. His younger brother, Harley, recalled hearing conversation about
the family's struggles to make ends meet following the Civil War "many times."
"Everything was just destroyed, you know…. They lost everything—didn't have
anything. And it was just a question of eking out a living and maybe going to
school very little and planting cotton, long-staple cotton, down there, which
wasn't necessarily suitable. And they had a few cows and hogs. Just kind of eked
out a living."[32]

Although John Wesley understood his father had died in the war, none of the
family knew the circumstances or place of Noah's death or burial. About a century

---

[32] Langdale, Judge Interview 01.

after the war, Noah's great-grandchildren learned his tombstone was in the Confederate Section of Magnolia Cemetery at Augusta, Georgia.[33]

Noah's death in the Civil War seems to have essentially cut the connection between his descendants and the remainder of the Langdale family in south Georgia. His widow presumably felt closer to her own family, the Burnetts, and her children evidently had no contact with the family of her husband.

This interruption of contact seems to have applied to John Wesley's grandmother, Harriet Griffin Langdale, even though she lived nearby. She was the eldest living person on John Wesley's father's side of the family living in south Georgia when John Wesley grew to manhood. Like his mother-in-law, Elizabeth "Betty" Daugharty Burnsed, and his mother, Elizabeth Burnett Langdale, John Wesley's grandmother, Harriet Griffin Langdale, had lost her husband in the service of the Confederacy. Harriet, like Betty Burnsed, lived to draw a widow's pension from the State of Georgia for a few years in the 1890s before her death. Part of the time, as she grew old, Harriet Langdale apparently stayed with her son, John Wesley's uncle, Mitchell Griffin Langdale of Homerville and Lakeland, with whom there also seems to have been no visitation from Noah's descendants. In 1997, John W. Langdale, grandson of John Wesley and son of Judge Harley, could not remember anyone in the family ever mentioning the name of Mitchell Griffin Langdale and he knew of no contact between his family and Harriet Griffin Langdale.[34]

As the widow of John Robert Langdale and the mother of his several children, Harriet could undoubtedly have told John Wesley's children much of their family history. She might have entertained them with stories of how John Robert emigrated as a teen-ager from South Carolina in the 1830s, became the ancestor of all Langdales in south Georgia, fought in the Indian wars, enlisted twice in the Confederate army, and died of pneumonia in Virginia. Harriet lived until 1898. She could certainly have been known to John Wesley's boys, the youngest of whom, Harley, was ten at her death. Yet, sadly, it appears that none of John Wesley's children ever knew their great grandmother, Harriet. Noah's descendants simply lived apart and pursued their lives in a businesslike way with little notice of the other Langdales. They were perhaps so busy making a living and so much involved with their nearby kinfolk and neighbors that they did not feel a need to seek out and maintain contact with other descendants of John Robert Langdale. Absent evidence to the contrary, one surmises the other Langdales felt much the same way.

In summary, the available evidence suggests that the Langdales of Colleton, South Carolina, and of south Georgia descend from Josiah Langdale, a Quaker

---

[33] John W. Langdale, Interview by Author, 1 May 1995, Langdale Residence, Valdosta, Georgia, Audio tape, John W. Langdale Papers, Valdosta, Georgia. Comments not included on transcript.

[34] Ibid.

minister and missionary from Yorkshire, England, whose widow and children settled in the Burlington-Philadelphia area in 1723. Josiah's son, John, and his wife, Sarah Hudson, had a large family, which included a son, named Josiah, born in 1739. This Josiah somehow ended up in Colleton District, South Carolina, before the Revolutionary War. From his two sons, William B. Langdale and John C. Langdale, all of the South Carolina and south Georgia Langdales descend. The south Georgia group look to John Robert Langdale, son of William B., as their progenitor.

Presumably by chance, John Robert and his eldest son, Noah, married women from large families. As a result, notwithstanding the premature deaths of John Robert and Noah in the Civil War, the south Georgia Langdales are related to an impressively large number of people in the area, starting with the Griffins, Halls, Burnetts, Burnseds, and Daughartys. Among their relatives, they can also list members of the Register, Crews, Carter, Mims, Leviton, and Foreacre families, plus others. It probably helped them in business and politics to have relatives distributed here and there throughout the region who could serve as contacts, sources of information, and, sometimes, business associates. This appears to have been without any calculated plan on their part, for they made no apparent effort even to maintain contact with their relatives surnamed Langdale. Yet family connections did play at least a minor role in the business success of John Wesley Langdale, which is next to be discussed.

2

Council

John Wesley Langdale, age twenty-four, and Nancy Burnsed Langdale, age twenty-one, married in 1884. They lived for the first eight or nine years of their marriage in a log house located in Clinch County, Georgia. Attracted in part by the abundance of game in the vicinity, John Wesley built his house on an Indian pathway, the Miccosukee Trail, almost within a stone's throw of the Florida border and nearer than any other homestead at that time to the western edge of the Okefenokee Swamp. This particular bit of land apparently was unowned until John Wesley moved in and built there.[1] He and Nancy lived about a mile and a half or two miles west of the future town of Council. That town came into existence in 1908, thanks in large measure to John Wesley's business initiatives.[2]

For some time prior to marrying and settling on the Miccosukee, John Wesley had scouted the territory as he hunted and fished in the Okefenokee and on its periphery.[3] Having been born near there, probably at Blount's Ferry on the

---

[1] Langdale, JJLJr Interview 01.

[2] Langdale, Judge Interview 01; Campbell, "Letters to VLM" ; Langdale, JJLJr Interview 01.

[3] For an introduction to the Okefenokee Swamp and its people, see Kay Lorraine Cothran, "Such Stuff as Dreams: A Folkloristic Sociology of Fantasy in the Okefenokee Rim, Georgia" (Ph.D. diss., University of Pennsylvania, University Microfilms, 1972); E. Merton Coulter, "The Okefenokee Swamp, Its History and Legends," *Georgia Historical Quarterly* 48 (1964); Echols County High School Composition Class, *Chinkypin, Ii;* Lenz, *Georgia Coast & Okefenokee;* Matschat, *Suwannee River;* Alexander Stephens McQueen and Hamp Mizell, *History of Okefenokee Swamp*, 1939 ed. (Clinton SC: Jacob Graphic Arts Co., 1939); Franklin Russell, *The Okefenokee Swamp*, ed. Charles Osborne, *The American Wilderness* (New York: Time-Life Books, 1973); Albert Hazen Wright, *Our Georgia-Florida Frontier: The Okefinokee Swamp, Its History and Cartography* (Ithaca NY: Cornell University Press, 1945).

Suwannee, he had come to know well the area between Blount's Ferry and the Okefenokee. Blount's Ferry is today about half a mile below the Florida line in Columbia County, but was then in Echols County, Georgia. As he hunted and scouted around, John Wesley evidently developed a vision of his future life and business in this place. He had a plan.[4]

His plan involved harvesting livestock, hogs and cows that ran wild in the woods, and various other products of the forest. These included alligator hides and bird feathers. From the forest, as time passed and opportunities arose, he produced firewood, shingles, lumber, and turpentine. Starting in 1898 when the railroad arrived, crossties became an important product.[5]

John Wesley Langdale of Council. Copy of a photograph displayed in the lobby of The Langdale Company main office. TLC.

Railroad construction required crossties, and this was a railroad-building age. Since 1830 when Peter Cooper's Tom Thumb made a thirteen-mile rail trip, Americans had built iron roads at an impressive rate. By 1840, the country had

---

[4] Langdale, JJLJr Interview01; Langdale, Judge Interview 01.

[5] For information on the forestry and naval stores industries, see James Boyd, "Fifty Years in the Southern Pine Industry," *Southern Lumberman* 144/1817 (1931); Carroll B. Butler, *Treasures of the Longleaf Pines: Naval Stores* (Shalimar FL: Tarkel Publishing, 1998); I. James, Jr. Pikl, *A History of Georgia Forestry, Research Monograph Number 2* (Athens GA: Bureau of Business and Economic Research, University of Georgia, 1966).

3,000 miles of railroad, and, in 1860, on the eve of the Civil War, the United States boasted 30,000 miles of track, predominantly in the North. As of 1869, rails linked the Atlantic and Pacific coasts. From 160,506 miles of track in 1880, the rail network grew to a peak of 254,000 in 1916.[6] For the last dozen or so years of his life, starting from the time of the Spanish-American War, John Wesley profited from the railroad boom.

Clearly, John Wesley stayed alert to the opportunities for profit, whether conventional or not, presented by the forest and the swamp. Besides that, as Judge Harley Langdale commented in his later years, "My father was a very thrifty fellow and a hard worker. We worked six days a week, you know."[7] This thriftiness, in the opinion of Judge Langdale's son, John W., goes a long way toward explaining the success of John Wesley and succeeding generations of Langdales. As John W. put it, "I think, the main thing is—and the same thing is true of my generation—it's not the making of the money, it's saving. We never have spent much—just never have had any inclination much for high living and throwing money away. I think that must have been true of him."[8]

From the start, John Wesley saw the need to acquire land, and he set an example that the next two generations of Langdales followed. On 10 November 1885, a few months after the birth of his first son, John, he paid $675.00 for 4,410 acres of land in nine lots from H. M. Hitt of Richmond County, Georgia. Each lot, all of which were in the 13th Land District of Clinch County, had 490 acres. Although this amounted to a price of only a little over fifteen cents an acre, it was a considerable lump-sum expenditure for the time.[9]

Where a young man from a poor family, just married, came up with enough money to buy 4,410 acres of land in those tight-money days, even at fifteen cents an acre, is an interesting question. Borrowing does not appear to be the answer. Turpentine producers often financed operations through borrowing, but John Wesley got into naval stores in a major way only in 1894, nearly a decade after his first land purchase. A partial explanation from his descendants is that he spent much time as a young man hunting alligators in the Okefenokee Swamp for their hides. His alligator-hunting technique was to locate their eyes by the light of a pine torch, then chop them on the head with an ax, according to his son, Harley.[10] He

---

[6] United States Department of Agriculture, Economic Research Service. *A History of American Agriculture, 1776–1990: Transportation* [cited 15 September 1998]. Available from http://www.usda.gov/history2/back.htm.

[7] Langdale, Judge Interview 01.

[8] Langdale, JWL Interview 14.

[9] "Deed, H. M. Hitt of Richmond County, Georgia, to John Wesley Langdale, 10 November 1885," photocopy of document as recorded 14 December 1889 in Clinch County Deedbook, 245., John W. Langdale Papers, Valdosta GA.

[10]Harold H. Martin, "He Converted a Wasteland," *The Saturday Evening Post*, 23 July 1955, 91–92.

also spent time collecting bird feathers for sale in the Jacksonville market. Probably, the best answer is that he rounded up unbranded swamp hogs and cattle and herded them to market at Jacksonville or St. Augustine to raise the necessary money. His income preceding 1894 seems to have depended primarily on the livestock business.[11]

According to Judge Harley, his father excelled at calling hogs. John Wesley could call swine from as far away as three to five miles. "He [John Wesley] would go out in the woods and spend the night and call hogs. He [Judge] said in the morning he'd look around and there would be three or four hundred hogs that he'd [John Wesley had] called up during the night."[12] Then, as Judge told his son, Billy, "They'd feed those hogs a little corn, and they would separate them and get the ones they wanted to keep and leave the others and tote them some twenty-five or thirty miles and trade them to a fellow that made wine."[13] They'd bring the wine back and sell it through the commissary to the workers.[14]

After the first major purchase of nine lots, John Wesley acquired three single lots, one at a time, in the period 1886 through 1888. While his wife was pregnant with two more sons, he bought three more lots of land. One came from Henry C. Williams of Wilcox County, Georgia. For this he paid $200.[15] Another lot, purchased in January 1888, from Henry Gay of Colquitt County, Georgia, cost $250.[16] Then in May, 1888, John Wesley paid C. B. Hitt of Richmond County, Georgia, $250 for a lot containing 430 acres.[17] As a result of these acquisitions, by 6 May 1888, three months past his twenty-eighth birthday, John Wesley Langdale owned at least twelve lots amounting to 5,800 acres.[18]

With each succeeding purchase, the cost per acre of land increased. It went from fifteen cents to forty-one cents, to fifty cents, and finally, to fifty-eight cents per acre. Viewing these transactions from the perspective of the late twentieth-century, all of those prices seem incredibly low. Even for the time, this

---

[11] JJLJr. Interview 01; Rose L. Johnson, interview by author, 13 June 1996.

[12] Wm. P. Langdale, Interview by H. Steen, 1991. Harley Langdale Papers.

[13] Ibid.

[14] Ibid.

[15] "Deed, Henry C. Williams of Wilcox County, Georgia, to John Wesley Langdale, 1886," photocopy of document as recorded by S. W. Register, Clerk, 22 June 1899 in Deed Book, 27, John W. Langdale Papers, Valdosta GA.

[16] "Deed, Henry Gay of Colquitt County, Georgia, to John Wesley Langdale, January 1888," photocopy of document as recorded 19 June 1900 by S. W. Register, Clerk, in Deed Book, 563, John W. Langdale Papers, Valdosta GA.

[17] "Deed, C. B. Hitt of Richmond County, Georgia, to John Wesley Langdale, May 1888," photocopy of document as recorded 19 June 1900 by S. W. Register, Clerk, in Deed Book, 564, John W. Langdale Papers, Valdosta, Georgia. .

[18] Harley Langdale, Jr., "Brief Facts on the Langdale Company," Fact sheet, Harley Langdale, Jr., Papers, Valdosta GA.

land cost very little. In neighboring Hamilton County, Florida, land reportedly sold in 1885–1886 for $1.25 to $6.00 per acre.[19]

John Wesley's brother, J. D. (Dave) Langdale, also held substantial acreage during the 1890s. He acquired five lots of land in 1892 from W. M. Jones and still owned them as late as 1899. By 1907, however, this land belonged to A. B. Swearingen. Some time after that, prior to 1920, it came into the hands of John Wesley or his heirs.[20]

While John Wesley participated in the turpentine business, becoming much more active in 1894, he also engaged in buying and selling timber for lumber and crossties. For example, on 28 November 1899, he and four other landowners sold Solomon Mobley, Jr. (1822–1907) of Clinch County a sixty-day option to buy timber suitable for lumber and crossties located on fourteen lots of land that the four owned in Echols and Clinch Counties. For the option, Mobley paid $1.00 per land lot, agreeing to pay $150.00 per lot upon which he exercised the option. Of these fourteen lots, five belonged to John Wesley, five to John Wesley's brother, Dave, three to F. R. Allen, and one to John S. Manhim. F. R. Allen signed the legal paper with his mark, so apparently he alone of the five could not write. He and Dave Langdale lived in Echols County, the others in Clinch.[21]

A seller of timber in the case of the 1899 Mobley transaction, John Wesley also, at least on one occasion, bought timber rights, perhaps for resale. On 20 June 1901, he purchased from Lucy Crews of Clinch County all timber on land lots 566 and 567 in the 13th Land District. The contract, which had actually been concluded between the parties a month previously but not written down, provided a ten-year period for exploitation of the timber. As frequently occurred in south Georgia in this period, when many people could not write their names, Lucy Crews signed with an 'x' mark The delay in putting a contract of this type in writing suggests a considerable degree of trust between Lucy Crews and John Wesley.[22] This is easier to understand when you note that Lucy Crews was John Wesley's aunt, his mother's sister.

---

[19] *Florida State Gazetteer*, as cited in Hamilton County Bicentennial Committee, *54*.

[20]The J. W. Langdale Company, "Application to Register Land, Clinch County GA, 17 May 1920. Photocopy." In John W. Langdale Papers. Valdosta, Georgia. Among the adverse deeds listed in the attachment to the petition is one from W. M. Jones to J. G. Langdale, dated 2 March 1892, recorded in Book "R," 249–50, conveying lots 561, 562, 563, 564, and 565.

[21] "Option to Purchase Timber, John Wesley Langdale and Others to Solomon Mobley, Jr., 28 November 1899," photocopy of document as recorded 14 December 1899 by S. W. Register, Clerk, Deed Book, 246–47, John W. Langdale Papers, Valdosta, Georgia.

[22] "Contract for Timber Purchase, Lucy Crews to John Wesley Langdale, 20 June 1901," photocopy of document as recorded 29 June 1907 by S. W. Register, Clerk, in Deed Book, 523–24, John W. Langdale Papers, Valdosta GA.

In 1905 John Wesley moved Nancy and the girls to Jasper, Florida, where he thought his daughters could be better educated. He, himself, continued living at the home place, though not alone. John Franklin Register, who worked for him as a stiller, moved in, as did Mrs. Register, the former Texas Johnson. Some years later, John Register died in this house, struck by lightning while standing or sitting near the water pump located on the back porch.[23]

Since 1894, more than a decade before settling his wife and daughters in Jasper, John Wesley had been concentrating heavily on the turpentine business. Evidently, he had been engaged in turpentining on a limited scale for years before that date, since Nan remembered being told that he held off building a frame house until 1893 to keep some of his larger trees in turpentine production.[24]

Historically, the American gum naval stores industry originated in Virginia, strengthened in North Carolina and, over time, moved south through Georgia and west as far as Texas. Besides the United States, chief producing countries have been France, Greece, Portugal, Spain, and Mexico.

Naval stores, so named because originally they were essential to the maintenance of wooden ships, came to be categorized as either gum naval stores or wood naval stores. Wood naval stores emerge by chemical and pressure extraction from lightwood stumps and other deadwood, the sap and bark of which have rotted away, leaving the heartwood. The heartwood is typically shredded and processed to derive pine oil, wood turpentine, and a resinous material called wood rosin.

Gum naval stores, on the other hand, come from oleoresin (commonly called gum or pitch) collected from living pine trees that have been cut or scraped on the surface to induce the flow of gum. Oleoresin consists of turpentine oil within which resins are dissolved. Steam distillation separates the turpentine, leaving residual material that hardens into solid rosin that is translucent and typically pale amber in color.

The gum naval stores industry played an important role in southern agriculture in the first half of the twentieth century, but gradually lost economic viability after World War II and almost died out by the 1970s. In the 1990s, only a very few markets remained in south Georgia for gum naval stores.

In the heyday of the gum naval stores industry in Georgia, distillers sent their rosin and turpentine to market in barrels. John W. Langdale, grandson of John Wesley Langdale of Council, recalled that the turpentine stills always employed a cooper who supervised manufacture of rosin barrels. Unlike turpentine containers, which had to be leak-proof and, therefore, factory made, rosin barrels could have small leaks without losing any of the product. Although they would not hold water, they would hold rosin. Rosin cooled quickly when poured into the barrels and

---

[23] Campbell, "Letters to VLM" ; Langdale, JWL Interview 01.
[24] Campbell, "Letters to VLM" ; Langdale, JJLJr Interview 01.

hardened before any significant quantity could leak out, automatically sealing any cracks in the container.[25]

Although they assembled rosin barrels on site, the Langdales in Judge Harley Langdale's time bought commercially-produced materials to make them. They obtained headers and staves, for example, from Tart Cooperage Company of Valdosta. These were made of rough, unplaned hardwood of low quality. Round, flat, and appropriately grooved, headers became the tops and bottoms of the barrels. Staves, which were slightly curved, about two to two-and-a-half inches wide, slightly narrower at the ends, and designed to fit into the grooves in the headers, formed the sides. It took about twenty staves and two headers to make a barrel, plus two steel wire rings to slip on the barrel from each end for holding it together. The cooper tightened the rings with a wedge and a mallet.[26]

The names of John Wesley Langdale and his descendants stand out among the leaders of the southern gum naval stores industry. In 1894, John Wesley expanded this aspect of his business dramatically. At that time, he went to South Carolina and recruited a number of turpentine workers, blacks and perhaps Indians or part Indians, as one of his grandsons recalled the story. Aside from the South Carolina recruits, there were two loyal workers, Chappy and Beatty, who had grown up with John Wesley and worked with him for years in turpentine. They liked him and stuck with him, apparently regarding him as a friend. Chappy had a son and Beatty had five sons who worked in turpentine. Some of these continued to work for the Langdales as late as the 1930s and 1940s.[27]

During their boyhood, John Wesley's three boys, John, Noah, and Harley, began to work in the turpentine business with their father. John Wesley, a qualified stiller, located his stills (distilleries) in the woods near the source of gum to minimize the transportation problem. He used mules and wagons to haul barrels of gum to the stills. Only decades later did trucks and tractors begin to supplant the mule-wagon combination, and, even then, the use of mules continued because they could go where trucks could not. Workmen known as "dippers" collected the crude gum (oleoresin) from boxes hacked in the trees and carried it to the barrels. To induce the gum to run, workers called "chippers" made wounds in the trees at strategic positions above the boxes. The products of John Wesley's stills, turpentine and rosin, apparently went to market by barge on the Suwannee until the railroad, which arrived in 1898, provided a better option.[28]

John Wesley wanted his boys to learn the turpentine business. "Back in those days," explained Judge Harley in his later years, "you had to train a fellow to do the physical work in order to operate, supervise properly, a turpentine

---

[25] Langdale, JWL Interview 01.

[26] Ibid.

[27] Langdale, JJLJr Interview 01.

[28] Langdale, Judge Interview 01.

operation."[29] "My father," he declared, "before I got to be this high, put me out to chipping. We had boxes then. That was before cups. We cut a hole in the tree, and we had to learn the trade so that then we could be in position to supervise it."[30]

As Judge's comment reveals, at the time his father started in the turpentine business, some naval stores technology had changed very little for generations. At first, in colonial Virginia, producers had extracted gum from pine trees by boring holes in them and letting the oleoresin run into holes dug in the ground at the foot of the trees. Then they advanced to the method, still in use during Judge Harley's boyhood, of cutting "boxes" in the trees themselves to collect the gum. From these boxes chopped into the trees with axes, they dipped out the oleoresin and boiled it in large iron vats over which they stretched the hides of sheep to catch evaporated turpentine. The fleece had to be wrung out by hand to put the turpenine into containers for shipment.

Although turpentine men still chopped boxes in trees during Judge Harley's boyhood, the method of separating turpentine from rosin had markedly improved with the adoption of the distillation process similar to that used in the manufacture of whiskey.[31] Another advance came in the twentieth century with the adoption of clay, glass, and metal cups, replacing boxes hacked in trees, as collection reservoirs for raw gum.

Mules & Wagon. Mule-drawn wagons employed by John Wesley Langdale and others in the turpentine business, as well as many Georgia "dirt farmers" until after World War II, resembled those presently in use at the Agrirama in Tifton, Georgia, an agricultural museum open to the public. JEL.

---

[29] Ibid.

[30] Ibid.

[31] Martin, 91.

After working as a chipper, Harley also gained experience as a dipper and as driver of the mules pulling the wagonloads of gum. He remembered that his eldest brother, John, worked as a "rough woodsman" and bookkeeper, and that Noah also handled the mule-wagon duties. "All of us boys went through with that training," Judge recalled. [32] Years later, in the 1930s, Judge put his own boys through a similar regimen.

With all this work, John Wesley's sons had little opportunity for play or school. "We didn't have much recreation," Judge recalled. We worked, and, of course, we'd go to the banks of the creek and go in swimming, and we'd fish some a little bit and that's about all. We had a little country school and we played little games around there. We didn't have but three months a year."[33]

Handling Crossties. Three workers for the Langdale Company around 1960 are shown carrying a crosstie. Moving such timbers must have been quite a challenge for John Wesley's three boys sixty years earlier. TLC.

Harley never owned a gun until he was about sixteen years of age, he declared in the 1960s. Why? "We had to work too much," he said. For that matter, he never shot a deer until after starting his law practice in Valdosta, although he did once shoot a bear that the dogs treed down at the Double Run Creek. This was not for recreation, however; he and his father and others were after the bear to keep it from their hogs. Harley was about fifteen at the time of the bear incident.

In 1898, another way of making money presented itself to John Wesley, with the coming of the railroad and its need for crossties. Especially in the wintertime when pine gum did not run, he put all three of his boys to work cutting and shaping crossties. These had to be dragged or carried out of the woods, frequently from swampy terrain. Sometimes the boys, who ranged in age from thirteen to ten in 1898, had literally to pick these timbers up and carry them out by hand, but more often they could use oxen to snake them out. A sled-like device, upon which one

---

[32] Langdale, Judge Interview 01.
[33] Ibid.

end of the log or crosstie rested, reduced the weight of the load pulled by the ox and avoided the problem of the front end of the log hanging on roots and bushes.[34]

Oxen worked better in the swamp than mules because they weighed less and had better footing. Oxen were steers trained from the time they were calves to submit to a yoke and the discipline of pulling burdens. To control oxen, drivers might put halters on them and rings in their noses. Guiding the oxen sometimes required leading them, but often they needed very little guidance because they traveled along narrow Indian or animal trails and had little opportunity to stray off course.

The Langdales also used oxen on some occasions to bring their annual or semi-annual supply of flour and other provisions from Jasper to Council. These trips, having a one-way distance of about thirty miles, took three days. The first day's travel brought them by late afternoon to the eastern outskirts of Jasper on what is today called Short Route 6, where they camped for the night. Other people also camped at this place, which seems to have been something like the nineteenth-century equivalent of a twentieth-century truck stop, with no facilities except water. They slept in tents or in (or under) their carts or wagons. The second day, entering town, they shopped for supplies, and the third day they returned home. Eldest son, John, sometimes took his mother on these oxcart trips to buy supplies in Jasper.[35] Occasionally, the Langdales went to Lake City for supplies, a distance about ten miles farther than Jasper.[36]

Sometimes oxen worked in teams of four or six. John J. Langdale, Jr. recalled hearing that his Uncle Noah had used such a team to transport gum to Blount's Ferry for loading on a barge there.[37]

Around 1906, John Wesley offered his brother, Dave, a position in his growing business as manager of his new commissary. John Wesley had erected a row of quarters for his turpentine hands and built a new commissary nearby. It replaced the former commissary located just south of it, which had become too small. The old commissary afterward contained a barber chair and served as a little barbershop.[38] At this time, John Wesley built a house for his brother's use, and Dave moved in. The house had six rooms, two on the right and four on the left. Later John Wesley added two more rooms on the right and, later still, other improvements.[39]

John Wesley's most important, or largest, business deal came in 1907. This made it possible for a large sawmill operation to start up on his adjoining land and for the town of Council to be founded. It involved a trust agreement concluded by

---

[34] Langdale, JJLJr Interview 01.

[35] Ibid.

[36] Langdale, Judge Interview 01; Langdale, JWL Interview 01.

[37] Langdale, JJLJr Interview 01.

[38] Ibid.

[39] Campbell, "Letters to VLM."

five landowners, including John Wesley and F. R. Allen. The five signatories designated these two of their group as trustees to manage, to control, and to sell their timber collectively on auction for milling. The trustees, John Wesley and F. R. Allen, agreed to pay $500.00 to each of the five members creating the trust, including themselves, which, of course, was a zero-net transaction for the two trustees. The other three members, recipients of $500 each for granting the trusteeship, were all Swearingens. They were A. B., J. D. and Walter S. Swearingen, the last named being represented by his attorney-in-fact, John L. Swearingen.

Land contributions of the five persons to the trust were as follows: John Wesley Langdale contributed nine and one-half lots of land, from which he excluded timber and crosstie rights on three lots. Walter S. Swearingen supplied eight lots. A. B. Swearingen put in nine lots, including the five that had belonged to John Wesley's brother, Dave, in 1899. J. D. Swearingen contributed two lots, plus the timber on another. F. R. Allen added one lot, excluding the timber, which had already been leased. Two of the signatories of this trust agreement, Allen and J. D. Swearingen, signed with their marks. Nancy Langdale witnessed the signatures.[40]

Some, or perhaps all, of the land placed in this trust eventually became the property of John Wesley or his descendants. In 1919, eight years after John Wesley's death, his sons incorporated his land and business as The J. W. Langdale Company. Several lots owned by the company at that time appeared, in Harley's opinion, to have titles that might conceivably be challenged. These lots all were among those included in the trust agreement of 1907. One of the lots (#547) had belonged to John Wesley at that time, six (#418, #561, #562, #564, #564 and #565) were lands of A. B. Swearingen, and one (#546) had been the property of F.R. Allen. To remedy any possible weaknesses, Harley petitioned in 1920 on behalf of The J. W. Langdale Company, of which he, Noah, and John were stockholders, to have these lots registered under the provisions of Georgia's Land Registration Act and their titles thereby perfected.[41]

The petition valued these lands at $2.00 per acre and stated that the assessed value for taxation purposes was $1.25 per acre. No lien against any of the properties existed, other than a mortgage held by Operators Naval Stores of Jacksonville, Florida, and no easements existed except for roads and railroads actually in operation.[42]

Shortly after concluding the trust agreement of 15 April 1907, John Wesley and his associates leased to the American Manufacturing Company, a corporation

---

[40] "Trust Agreement, John Wesley Langdale and Others, 1907," photocopy of document as recorded 29 April 1907 by S. W. Register, Clerk, in Deed Book, 444–45, John W. Langdale Papers, Valdosta GA.

[41] The J. W. Langdale Company, "Application to Register Land, Clinch County, Georgia, 17 May 1920. Photocopy." In John W. Langdale Papers. Valdosta GA.

[42] Ibid.

owned principally by brothers John M. and C. M. Council of Americus, Georgia, milling rights on the land placed in trust. For several years previously a large sawmill had been operating about six miles up the railroad at Fargo. Built soon after the Georgia, Southern and Florida laid its track through this area from Valdosta to Jacksonville in 1898, the Fargo operation belonged to George S. Baxter & Company.[43] Now, as a result of the deal negotiated by John Wesley, the Councils set up their mill in 1908 across the road from Dave's house and the Langdale store. According to Judge Harley, John Wesley donated 490 acres of land, one lot, to facilitate this. The Councils also built houses for their managers, engineers, and workers. They constructed a commissary and a church. To move timber to the Council mill, the company built two trams through the leased property, one toward the Okefenokee and the other running south. This settlement, known as Council, grew rapidly and soon had a population of several hundred.[44]

The tram roads built by the Council Company and other sawmill operations eventually became part of the railroads connecting Valdosta, Jacksonville, and other local towns. In the 1960s, Judge Langdale remembered some of these: "Dowling Upchurch had a mill at Moniac, or Baxter, Florida, right on this side of Moniac. They had a tram road. And part of that roadbed was used to build this railroad between here and Valdosta. Of course, Pixson and Mitchell had a mill on the Coastline and they had built a tram road all the way down to the Suwannee River. We used to dip our rosin and turpentine and get our groceries over that tram road from Valdosta. We'd buy 'em sometimes from A.S. Pendleton and Company."[45]

While building his business from 1884 to 1907, John Wesley had also been building a family. During the first four years of living in their log house, John Wesley and Nancy became the parents of three boys, John, Noah, and Harley in 1885, 1886, and 1888. None of the boys had middle names, but John and Noah later added middle initials and were known as John J. and Noah N. Langdale. Harley refrained from following his brothers' example in this respect. While serving for twelve years as judge of the Recorder's Court in Valdosta, however, people began addressing him as Judge Harley Langdale,[46] and this practice continued for the remainder of his life. So the three brothers were, in order of birth, John J., Noah N., and Judge Harley.[47]

After Harley's birth, five years passed without another child. Then, from 1893 to 1900, four girls, Sadie, Isabel, Nancy (called Nan), and Susie (nicknamed

[43]Huxford, *History of Clinch County*, 85.

[44] Campbell, "Letters to VLM" ; Langdale, Judge Interview 01.

[45] Langdale, Judge Interview 01.

[46] Archie McKay, "Langdale Lived to See Dream Come True," *Valdosta Daily Times*, 1975.

[47] Langdale, JWL Interview 14. Comments not included on transcript.

Dick by Harley) joined the Langdale family. All of the girls were born in the new frame house that John Wesley built in front and a little to the right of the log house around 1893–1894.[48]

In appearance, John Wesley Langdale was short, with dark complexion, small dark eyes, and a beard. Among his children, Noah resembled him most in height. Only the second daughter, Isabel, who died of diabetes as a teenager, inherited his dark brown eyes.

Nancy Burnsed Langdale, tall and erect, with light complexion, had the greater genetic influence on the appearance of their children. In stature, according to her daughter Nan, she resembled her daughter-in-law, Noah's wife, Jessie. All of the children inherited Nancy's light complexion. John, Harley, Sadie, and Nan all looked more like their mother than their father.

Nancy Burnsed Langdale at home Jasper, Florida, 1910. TLF.

Today, except for stone markers set up by the Langdales to identify the location, the original home site is without visible sign of either the log or the frame structure. Only memories, first and second-hand, provide information about those early days. Most of our knowledge about the Langdale houses, social life, and family life comes from a series of reminiscences in the form of letters written by

---

[48] Campbell, "Letters to VLM."

eighty-eight-year-old Nan Langdale in 1986–1987 to her niece, Judge Harley's daughter, Virginia Langdale Miller.

John Wesley apparently used his original log home for other purposes after moving into his new house. Behind the kitchen of the new residence, Nan Langdale remembered there being a small log building the family used for storage. A similar one across the road from the house served as the "store," and a third found its place at the end of a row of houses that John Wesley built for his turpentine hands. Nan guessed these were three disassembled parts of the original log house that had been the family home before her birth.

As his business grew around the turn of the century, John Wesley built two rows of houses for turpentine hands. One row extended down the road to the right side of the house toward the future location of Council, and the other stretched to the left toward Double Run Creek. It was the latter group that included the log building that resembled the store, presumably a section of the original Langdale cabin.

From the time of his marriage, several years passed before John Wesley saw his way clear to replace the log cabin with the house built of lumber. Undoubtedly, he needed to accumulate the necessary capital. Yet, he was putting a lot of money into land. Also, being in the turpentine business, he wanted to wait until he could afford to do without the resin production from the large pine trees that he wished to saw for lumber. The family said he chose the largest and tallest pines on his property and used only the heart lumber for the new house. He bought a one-man saw, Nan was told, and, with the aid of his regular crew of Negro laborers, sawed the lumber. The four men he then employed were Beatty, who could dip nine barrels of gum a week; Chappy and P. J., who were dippers, streakers, or pullers; and Bill Brinkley, called by the family, "Uncle Bill."

Uncle Bill, old and gray, worked around the house as handyman, took evening meals from the Langdale table, and sometimes entertained the family with his fiddle and accordion. In son John's room, which doubled as a parlor, the family usually gathered after supper. Except for Sundays, these brief periods in the evening afforded virtually the only respite from work for John Wesley and Nancy. Uncle Bill sat in his special chair near the fireplace to play his fiddle and accordion and sing. "It was the prettiest music we ever heard," Nan Langdale recalled. [49]

The Langdale home had three chimneys. When over the years they sometimes needed repair, John Wesley called on Uncle Alex Swearingen. In addition to being a top fiddler for square dances, Uncle Alex excelled at chimney repair. Nan remembered, as a young girl, watching Uncle Alex "mixing up clay, moss and water to slap between different lengths of slats graduating them perfectly so that the chimney wouldn't smoke."[50]

---

[49] Ibid.

[50] Ibid.

Langdale Home at Council, Georgia. This photo, showing the house in bad condition, was made shortly before it was torn down. TLF.

By the 1990s, John Wesley's frame house had outlived its usefulness and been taken down by his descendants. As his grandson, John W., explained in 1991, "We saw that it was deteriorating and wouldn't be there very long, and people were beginning to carry off some of that heart pine material, so we salvaged some of that heart pine. I went down there and got some boards. And I built some furniture out of some of that heart pine material. And it is beautiful close-grained pine."[51]

As one entered the Langdale house from the front, John's room appeared first on the right. On the left, across from it, a large bedroom with two beds provided sleeping accommodations for John Wesley and Nancy, as well as for the two younger daughters, Nan and Dick. Just behind this room, another bedroom with a hand-made pine four-poster bed belonged to Sadie and Isabel, the two older daughters. The house had an attic in which there stood an old spinning wheel belonging probably to Grandma Betty.[52]

If it is good for children to know their grandparents, thank God for Grandma Betty. Since Nancy's father, Gideon Burnsed, and both of John Wesley's parents were long since deceased, Elizabeth "Betty" Daugharty Burnsed carried the banner for her generation and all previous ones with John Wesley's offspring.

Grandma Betty had grown up near the future site of Fargo on a farm of some size. Born in 1828 the daughter of James Daugharty and Nancy Bassett, she was the granddaughter of South Carolina-born Dempsey Daugharty, and his wife Mary Pearce.

---

[51] John W. Langdale, interview by Harold Steen, 1991.
[52] Campbell, "Letters to VLM."

Betty married Gideon Burnsed on 25 April 1855. He went into the army about 15 May 1862, and died of an intestinal disorder about 25 October 1862.[53]

The name Burnsed is a variant of Burnside, which appears to be the predominant version. Gideon was the son of James M. Burnside/Burnsed and his wife, Mary Dukes, of Bryan County. Gideon's paternal and maternal grandparents had come to Georgia from North Carolina. Some of his relatives moved on into Florida.[54]

Nan Langdale heard from her brother, John J., that their grandmother probably continued to live on the family farm until their grandfather, Gideon Burnsed, went into the Confederate army. By reason of her husband's death in Confederate service, Betty drew a small pension from the State of Georgia, starting in 1891. In her brighter days, as Nan remembered, "she was 'the Queen' in that part of the country. She had her own little buggy and pony," which she drove around to visit cousins and friends. She often brought little gifts, especially—it seemed to Nan—for the boys in the family. For example, said Nan, she gave a square glass hobnail dish to John, a diamond-shaped glass dish to Noah, and a stem glass tall cake plate to Harley. Those rough, tough woods-wise boys must have thought it remarkable that their grandmother would bring them such delicate gifts.[55]

Betty Daugharty Burnsed spent much of her life taking care of others. She is credited with rearing her little sister, Martha, who was only three when their mother died in 1845. Martha, like her older sister, Betty, lost her husband in the Civil War. He was James Samuel Tumblin. Five years after the war she married James "Jim" Burnett, brother of Elizabeth Burnett Langdale, John Wesley Langdale's mother. James and Martha Daugharty Burnett's nine children were, therefore, related to John Wesley Langdale's children through their mother and through their father, both of whom were first cousins of those Burnett offspring.[56]

Grandma Betty lived with her daughter's family for several years preceding her death, so the children knew her well. Like many older women of her time and region, Betty always wore a bonnet and apron. She spent most of her waking hours walking in the garden or sitting in her rocking chair on the back porch, smoking her corncob pipe. On her upper left arm Grandma Betty developed cancer, which led first to a partial and then to a complete amputation. Years later, Nan Langdale remembered how her Uncle Jim and Aunt Martha Burnett, in what was to them an

---

[53] Elizabeth Burnsed, and others, "Pension Applications of Elizabeth Burnsed, Widow of Gideon Burnsed, drawer 272, roll 8," Microfilm, Pension Applications of Confederate Soldiers and Widows who Applied from Georgia, Georgia State Archives, Atlanta GA.

[54] Pat Glasscock, Gedcom file patg.ged [cited 20 January 2000]; available from http://www.rootsweb.com.

[55] Campbell, "Letters to VLM."

[56] Burnette, "Burnett History," 3; Griffin, "17308.Ged."

act of tenderness, took the amputated limb home with them and buried it in a bed of purple violets next to their porch.[57]

Grandma Betty's surgeon was Dr. John Franklin Hall who lived at Howell and was married to Grandma Betty's niece, Elizabeth Burnett, one of the daughters of Jim and Martha Daugharty Burnett.[58] Dr. Hall also treated other members of the family. Once he performed minor surgery on John Wesley's youngest son, Harley. This resulted from an injury to Harley's foot when a mule team ran away with him, seriously lacerating it and doing other damage.

As Harley's daughter, Virginia, heard the story, her father and one of the old black men employed by John Wesley were working together. Suddenly, the mules bolted and Harley's foot got caught in the singletree. The mules dragged him around until the old man stopped them. The family stretched Harley out on the front porch, poured turpentine on his wounded foot, and sent for Dr. Hall. At the time, Harley feared he'd never again be able to walk. The injuries included a broken bone on top of his foot that never healed properly. It left a lump that required him always to buy oversize shoes.[59]

After a long time the physician arrived and did such repairs as he could. Dr. Hall made the Langdales' front porch his operating room and stitched the wound up without anesthesia while the family looked on and the girls shed tears of sympathy for the suffering Harley.[60]

On another occasion Dr. Hall treated Nan Langdale for a broken collarbone sustained in an accident. Nan admitted she caused it. Though forbidden, adventurous Nan tried her hand at chopping wood in the woodpile. Little sister Dick, more obedient, shouted to mother about Nan's misconduct. Terror stricken for fear of punishment, Nan ran from the woodpile and jumped on a hay rake, which fell, breaking her collarbone. Nancy then rushed her daughter to the doctor. This required a hasty buggy ride to the train crossing at Eddy, Florida, at least twelve miles distant, and a trip on the train to Dr. Hall's office at Howell.

For her buggy drives, Nancy had her own special horse. She sometimes took the children in the buggy to visit neighbors and nearby relatives, such as Aunt Nancy and Uncle Sam Register, who lived just on the other side of Double-Run Creek.

Although the children had little knowledge of their grandparents' generation, they fared better with respect to family in the age group of their parents. They were well acquainted with their father's sister, Jane, and his younger brother, Dave, who lived nearby. Jane, two years older than John Wesley, and her daughter, Lou, lived at Edith, Georgia, the location of one of John Wesley's turpentine stills. Both Jane and Lou were "good workers." John Wesley paid his sister to cook for

---

[57] Campbell, "Letters to VLM."
[58] Griffin, "17308.Ged."
[59] Virginia L. Miller, interview by author, 9 June 1995.
[60] Campbell, "Letters to VLM."

his turpentine hands at Edith. Lou stayed at John Wesley's home "lots helping mama, especially in the busiest times," Nan recalled. Dave, as mentioned, also became an employee of his brother when he became manager of the commissary around 1906.

John Wesley Langdale, a tough woodsman and hard-working businessman, had a softer side visible to his wife and children. At Christmas and other holidays he ordered large crates of oranges and grapefruit for the family. Sometimes he peeled the fruit for the younger children, pleasing them. "Those were the sweetest times of our lives," remembered Nan. Christmas was also an occasion for candy and presents, which Nancy usually bought for the children in Valdosta. Once she bought China-head dolls for Nan and Dick, plus a camel-back doll trunk, *with tray.*[61]

This warm and comfortable picture of Christmas at the Langdales probably had more validity for the girls than for the boys, who were older and seem to have spent their early childhood in more Spartan circumstances. Nan's brother, Harley, known for most of his adult life as Judge Harley, remembered Christmas differently. For him, the glow one senses from Nan's description was not there. "We'd usually get a little candy in a…stocking and have an orange maybe in it and an apple and something like that. And that's about all," he recalled.[62]

John Wesley took pains to help his wife, Nancy, around the house and to see that she had other help when needed, so testifies daughter Nan. For example, in winter, he got up before daylight to start fires for the family. As Nancy cooked breakfast, he often sat before the big hearth in the kitchen gripping a little square coffee grinder between his knees and grinding beans to make the morning coffee. At suppertime, John Wesley often placed sweet potatoes in the hot ashes of the fireplace to bake and cooked cornbread or biscuits in a large iron skillet supported by three tall legs (a spider). There may have been less of this than Nan remembered. If Harley observed this domestic behavior described by his younger sister, he does not appear to have been impressed to imitate it in his own marriage.[63]

The Langdale kitchen included for Nancy's use a large iron stove, probably among the best available in that day. Across the top it had a warming compartment; on one end it had a tank for heating water. When ironing clothes in this pre-electric era, the Langdales used the stove to heat four or five irons at a time. Among household tasks, Nancy excelled at sewing. She sewed, not for the girls alone, but also for the men in the family. She usually bought sewing materials from Belle and Beny Levitons' general store near Blount's Ferry. Occasionally, Nancy let the girls stay with the Levitons and their children, Bloomer and

---

[61] Ibid.

[62] Langdale, Judge Interview 01.

[63] Campbell, "Letters to VLM."

Mineola, for a day or two. Belle treated them generously and sometimes gave them material for dresses. "We were all closer to them than any of our other relatives,"[64] remembered Nan. Belle (Isabel) was one of the children of James "Jim" Burnett and Martha Daugharty who were first cousins of both of Nan's parents and nieces of Grandma Betty.

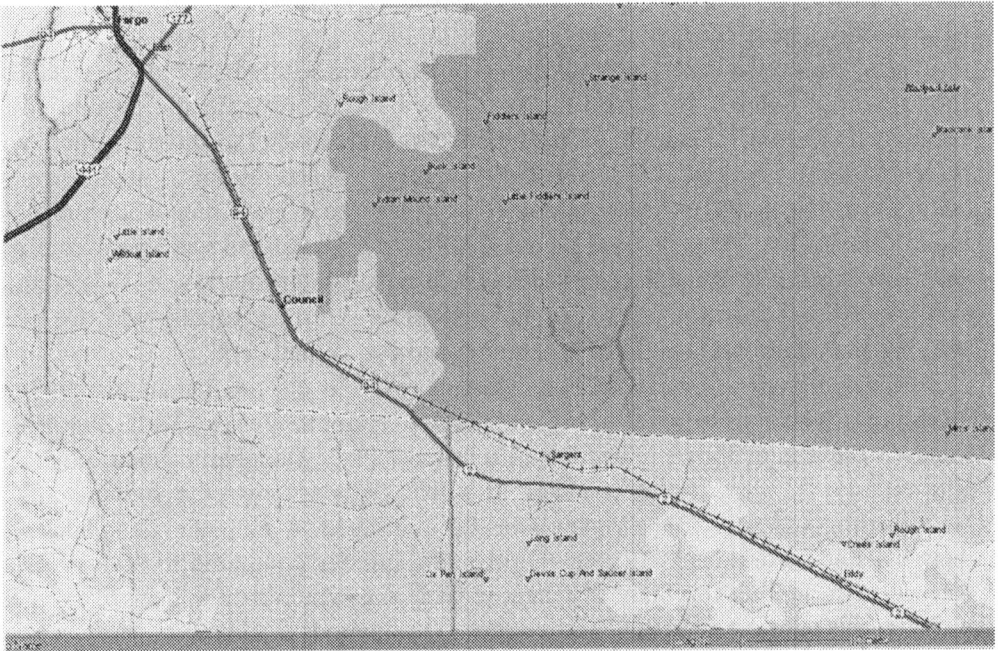

Map of Fargo to Eddy Area. This map shows the location of the Langdale home place in relation to Eddy, FL, where for a few years the Langdales boarded the train, and Fargo, GA.

Around the time the Langdale girls moved to Jasper (1905), the Levitons moved to Fargo. Other families, too, were moving out of the immediate area from about this time. The arrival of the railroad in southern Clinch County and in Echols spawned several new settlements and apparently contributed to this population movement.

---

[64] Ibid.

John Wesley Langdale loved his family and strove earnestly to provide for their needs. He could also, upon occasion, extend kindness to animals of the forest that were more typically his quarry. Daughter Nan recalled a time when her father found in the woods a fawn whose mother had been killed, and he brought it home in his arms for the girls to look after. He put the orphan deer in the log storehouse behind the kitchen. The girls cared for it and fed it warm milk from a syrup bottle. Perhaps John Wesley's behavior reflected simply a love and appreciation of nature gained from spending most of his life in the woods. Maybe he wanted to please his young daughters and develop their maternal instincts. Or perhaps, having grown up fatherless, he felt a special sympathy for the motherless fawn. We can only guess.

John Wesley kept very busy. Most of the time he worked six days a week, but once a year, in season, he took time off for a hunting trip into the swamp. With his favorite horse, a couple of old blankets, and double saddlebags filled with "keeping food," he struck out for Billy's Island. "Keeping food" included such favorites as bacon and sweet potatoes that would "keep" whether wet or dry. He entered the swamp through Edith, located north of Council and just south of Fargo on the railroad, a path made easier today by a paved highway, Route 177, running parallel to the Suwannee. In two or three days he returned, usually with his pony carrying the additional weight of a deer and turkeys he had shot.[65]

John J. Langdale, Jr. remembered talking with an old gentleman named Mett Swearingen who used to hunt with his grandfather, John Wesley. Mett Swearingen came to the Council area in 1888 and married Nancy Daugharty when they were both elderly. He went on cattle drives with John Wesley down the Indian trails to Jacksonville, and after John Wesley's death, continued to help the Langdales with their livestock work. In Mett's view, not many hunters compared to John Wesley. According to him, "everybody that hunted with him would rather hear his gun fire with the expectation of getting some meat than anybody he knew of."[66]

Sometimes John Wesley's hunting skills helped him protect his property. One night, when he and Nancy still lived in the log house, he heard a hog squeal. Hogs were then crucial to his livelihood. From the sounds, John Wesley could tell a bear had attacked a hog. He went out with his gun to kill the bear, telling Nancy on the way out, "When you hear my gun fire, turn the dogs loose." His idea was that, in case he just wounded the bear, the dogs could prevent it from getting away. As it turned out, however, the dogs had no work to do. When they arrived, John Wesley had already killed the bear.[67]

Religious life for the Langdales focused on Bethel Primitive Baptist Church. Primitive Baptist churches were conservative, independent congregations that

---

[65] Ibid.
[66] Langdale, JJLJr Interview 01.
[67] Ibid.

rejected centralized administration, Sunday schools, missionary societies and other organizations not mentioned in the New Testament. They accepted the literal infallibility of the Bible. Many of these congregations seceded from Baptist associations in the 1820s and 1830s over such issues. Primitive Baptist ministers required no special training, such as attendance at seminary, for these churches contended that God might call any individual to the ministry. They were strict Calvinists, believing firmly in predestination and the salvation of the Elect. They looked forward to the Second Coming of Christ. Primitive Baptists, such as the members of Bethel Church, regarded themselves as responsible as a congregation for the behavior of members, and did not hesitate to expel any member who misbehaved and remained unrepentant. One could be clerk of the church one day and ex-communicated the next, or even the same day. They enforced discipline strictly.[68]

Bethel Primitive Baptist church occupied a site about a mile and a half north of the Florida line on a dirt road known to people in the area as the "Woodpecker Route." This road constituted the shortest route from Fargo to Jasper. The church sat on the eastern side of the road, about a quarter of a mile from the western bank of the Suwannee River.[69]

People usually referred to Bethel as "Boney Bluff" Church. Some say the name came from the adjoining cemetery located on high ground near the river. Another explanation is that the name derived from bones seen lying around the place, the unburied residue of a battle with Indians. This cemetery was apparently the only one around there on the western side of the river at that time. Church facilities consisted of a small white meeting house with outside privies.[70]

Although church records list no member of the John Wesley Langdale family as a member of the church, the Langdales did sometimes attend. How often is unclear. Unlike John Wesley's younger brother, Dave, and his wife, Lizzie (Mary Mims Langdale), who were at times very active in the church, John Wesley's involvement with Bethel seems to have been more peripheral to his life and to have emphasized practical matters. Evidently he did not fully accept or fully meet the Primitive Baptist qualifications for membership. Even so, Nan Langdale stated in 1986 that her father supported the church more than most through clean-up and maintenance work. After her father's death, said Nan, her brother, John J., continued this practice.

---

[68] For more information on Primitive Baptists in south Georgia, see John G. Crowley, "Origins and Development of the Union Primitive Baptist Association of Georgia" (M. A. thesis, Department of History, Valdosta State University, 1981); John G. Crowley, *Primitive Baptists of the Wiregrass South, 1815 to the Present* (Gainesville FL: University Press of Florida, 1998).

[69] Campbell, "Letters to VLM" ; John W. Langdale, letter to John Lancaster, typewritten, 22 April 1997, Valdosta GA.

[70] Campbell, "Letters to VLM"; Langdale, JJLJr Interview 01.

It is clear that the family identified with this church at least in a cultural sense or as part of a family tradition. John Wesley's mother had been a member there when he was a child. In later years, after 1905, Nancy Langdale, described by her daughter as "a most devout person," demonstrated strong Primitive Baptist leanings when she took her girls regularly to Primitive Baptist services in Jasper, Florida, even after the girls had officially affiliated with the Methodist church there.[71]

To say that John Wesley did not unite with Boney Bluff Church is not to say that he was irreligious. His daughter Nan relates that he and Nancy always regarded Sunday as a sacred day. They forbade the children to go fishing on Sunday, did not allow them to ride the mules or horses on Sunday, and did no work on the Lord's day except in an emergency "to pull the ox out of the ditch."[72]

Harley, Jr., John J., Jr., and Virginia Langdale (Mrs. John J., Jr.) at Bethel Primitive Baptist Church Cemetery in April 1995. JEL.

Every autumn the Langdale family attended "Big Meeting" at Boney Bluff Church. A social and religious highlight of the year, this was an all-day affair with preaching, prayer, singing, foot washing, and dinner on the grounds.

The younger children, aside from enjoying the wagon ride to the church, cared most for the food and fellowship. Each family put together immense

---

[71] Campbell, "Letters to VLM."
[72] Ibid.

quantities of their best food, enough for themselves and some others. At mealtime they spread tablecloths on the ground—there were no tables or shelters—and put the food on the tablecloths. Some families chose to spread their food together, as did the Langdales, Daughartys, and Burnetts, setting themselves a little apart from others, many of which they scarcely knew.

Some of the people who came to Big Meeting, being poor, brought extra bowls and baskets in which to carry food home. The Langdales and others more affluent brought extra food because they knew from experience that these poorer folk would come by their spread to fill plates or bowls for "take-home."[73]

At the Langdale home at the turn of the century, food abounded. Their garden provided plenty of vegetables; fruit trees produced peaches and apples; and the Langdales enjoyed grapes from their own vine. To make curd, Nancy warmed skim milk, placed it in a small salt sack, and hung it on a limb of the apple tree to drip until it became firm enough for slicing. Nan Langdale liked curd with syrup and sometimes with cream.

Although the Langdales had one thoroughbred Jersey cow—the only one around in that area—to provide milk, most of their cows and hogs were of the scrub type that roamed freely in the woods. "Piney Woods Rooters," the hogs were called. These swamp-bred animals, both hogs and cows, fended for themselves and remained usually very lean, not to say skinny. Consequently, their meat was tough. To overcome this problem, to improve the quality of the meat, a few weeks before hog-killing time each fall, John Wesley sent his range riders to round up the animals and drive them into corrals that he had built here and there throughout the swamp. Then, for a few weeks, he sent wagonloads of corn to fatten the animals. Daughters Nan and Isabel, tomboys, loved to ride on the corn wagons when occasionally allowed to.

For meat dishes, the Langdales relied heavily upon pork and beef. Some time after building the new house, John Wesley erected a large smokehouse for preparing and keeping the family meat supply. At hog-killing time, following rural custom, John Wesley and Nancy shared fresh meat with their neighbors. In those days refrigerators and home freezers did not exist, so everyone considered it a treat to have fresh meat.

Curing and preserving meat took special effort and considerable time. Typically, John Wesley sent wagons into the forest to bring out large palmetto leaves which he placed on the floor of the smokehouse and upon which he laid pork sides, heavily salted, for curing. They used rock salt or other coarse salt intended for the purpose, not table salt. This produced salt pork, a favorite food for the Langdale family. Salt pork served as seasoning for peas, beans, greens, and soups, and the Langdales fried it to eat with sweet potatoes. Some of the pork sides and shoulders John Wesley selected to be hung with sides of beef for the smoking

---

[73] Ibid.

treatment. These items hung in rows from poles suspended from the smokehouse rafters.

Sausage making also played a prominent role at hog-killing time. John Wesley set aside some of the meat, a lot of lean meat, for this purpose. They stuffed the seasoned and ground sausage meat into hog intestines that had been cleaned and thoroughly washed. The cleaning procedure involved scraping the small intestines to remove their contents, thorough washing in running water in Double Run Creek, and washing again in a large washpot located in the woodpile (near the fuel supply). Unused sausage casings became chitterlings.

Slaughter and meat preservation went on for several days each fall. At the end of it, the smokehouse contained large quantities of hams, shoulders, sausages, and sides of pork and beef hanging from the poles and rafters. Slabs of salt pork rested on the floor of palmetto leaves. For some days after the slaughtering time, a smoldering hardwood fire filled the interior with smoke, flavoring and curing the meat.

A milkhouse, resting on stilts at the end of the back porch near the kitchen, housed dairy products. In the milkhouse one found large yellow crockery bowls filled with milk, cream, butter, and clabber. A large butter churn of the up-and-down, plop-plop, type converted the cream into butter and buttermilk. The Langdales then washed and molded the butter. The girls liked to drink the buttermilk mixed with cane syrup.

Syrup Kettle. John Wesley's syrup boiler would have resembled this one on display in 1999 at the Agrirama in Tifton, Georgia. JEL.

John Wesley always had a big patch of cane from which he made syrup for his family. The syrup-making operation took place just outside the backyard gate. A shelter covered the large, iron syrup kettle, placed conveniently near the wood-shed. Into this kettle, John Wesley and his men poured cane juice to be boiled and condensed into syrup. A wood-fired furnace supplied the necessary heat.

The juice came from a simple cane mill standing near the boiler. This mill had two large steel rotating cylinders that pressed juice from the cane as an operator fed the stalks into it. Juice flowed from the mill into a barrel covered with a cloth strainer. A dipper hung near the barrel for the use of anyone wishing to quench his thirst with sweet cane juice.

Mule-Powered Cane Mill. A cane mill of the type used by John Wesley Langdale was on display in 1999 at the Agrirama in Tifton, Georgia. JEL.

Animal power drove the cane mill. Typically, a mule, hitched to a lever about twenty feet in length (usually made from a log), walked in a circle all day long turning the mill. After a while, a shallow circular rut marked the path of the mule's endless trek, round and round. Sometimes the bored mule just closed its eyes. "He knew he wasn't going anywhere,"[74] recalled Nan Langdale.

John Wesley and Nancy Langdale loved, carefully supervised, and protected their children. "There was plenty of love," remembered Nan, "but not that touch-ing, hugging, kissing display as is generally displayed in later generations...."[75] John and Nancy's strict moral guidance included prohibition of sibling squabbling. Although the children did their share of "picking at each other" when their parents were not around, they learned to avoid doing so in their parents' presence. When punishment had to be administered, Nancy used a thin switch, which she required the transgressor to provide. John Wesley simply said, "Stop," and whatever activity he disapproved of immediately stopped. The children knew his word—even a single word—was law.

---

[74] Ibid.
[75] Ibid.

The younger children loved to get into their father's store—the commissary for John Wesley's turpentine business—located across the road from the Langdale home. Various commodities in barrels and sacks filled the place. There were great boxes of salt pork slabs, patent medicines, and—especially intriguing to daughter Nan—two brands of snuff. One brand, Railroad, found its greatest popularity with blacks; the other, Thistle, appealed more to whites. Nan knew her mother used Thistle, and she decided she must try it. She filled her cheek with a generous wad and in a few minutes became very sick. Fearing death more than a whipping, Nan called for her mother's help and rejoiced when mother mercifully spared the rod. Evidently, Nancy thought the child had suffered punishment enough.

Another time Nan got into trouble for taking property she did not own. This happened the same day she broke her collarbone and had to be taken to the doctor in Howell. Nan and her mother had returned by train from Howell to the section foreman's house at Eddy. This was their equivalent of a train station, from which they had to return home by buggy. While Nancy visited for a few minutes sociably with the section people, little Nan, with her arm in a sling because of the broken collarbone, looked around the yard curiously. She found the most beautiful round, tapered, green glass object she had ever seen, and she just had to have it. So she slipped it into the compartment under the buggy seat. On the way home, Nancy heard this thing, an electrical insulator, rolling around and making noise. She wondered what it might be, but Nan said not a word.

As soon as they got home Nancy found the insulator and declared that Nan must take it back *immediately after supper* because it belonged to somebody else. Nan "was petrified," because after supper it would be night, and she feared the scary trip in the dark. Nancy let her worry until after supper, then, compassionately, told Nan they would return it the next day.

Nan remembered that her brothers, John, Noah, and Harley, several years older than the girls in the family, had few opportunities for courting, or "sporting" as people called it then. Living in rural isolation, they probably felt, as some might say today, romantically deprived.

The boys tried to enhance their social opportunities. Once, for example, they persuaded their mother to let them hold a taffy-pulling party and dance. Nowadays essentially a lost art, taffy-pulling around 1900 could be a good excuse for a get-together. As Nan described it, "syrup was boiled down—two people take a big ball of candy opposite each other 'pull and slap, pull and slap, 'til it was creamy white."[76]

Another time, the boys planned to attend a community square dance to be held at the end of a day's harvesting. This event, the harvesting followed by the dance, was to take place at the Fouraker Place, owned by relatives of the Langdales and noted for its dense population of rattlesnakes. Although Nan and

---

[76] Ibid.

her sisters were considered too young to go to the dance, the girls thought there was a slim chance they might get to attend because they were to be at the Fourakers' home all day beforehand with their mother. Hope and anticipation fed their excitement.

On the big day, as planned, Nancy took the girls with her to the Fourakers' to help with the quilting bee. Quilting was an all-day task, at which the women busied themselves while the men and boys, including Nan's brothers, all joined together in the work of harvesting. At the end of the day, the workers rewarded themselves with the celebratory square dance. All the young men and young women looked forward eagerly to the dance. The top fiddler in that area for such occasions was Uncle Alex Swearingen. The leading dancers, Nan remembered, were her brother, Noah, and Norwood Swearingen.

For the Langdale females, Nancy and her daughters, the day produced, along with the pleasures of visiting and working with neighbors, a few frustrations. In Nancy's case, she found herself distracted from quilting as she kept busy trying to keep the girls cooped up in the yard and safe from rattlesnakes. As for the square dance, the girls did not get to attend; Nancy took them home before it started. Not only did she protect them from rattlesnakes, but from grown-up entertainment as well.

Considering the challenges of a rural environment, the Langdales, Nancy and John Wesley, supervised their children closely. For example, they rarely permitted them to spend nights away from home. Among the few exceptions to this rule, Nan recalled, was the time her parents allowed her to spend a whole week with her Uncle Dave and Aunt Lizzie.

John Wesley's brother Dave and his wife lived at that time over near the river, "about where the highway runs from Edith to Lake City." They had ten children, five boys and five girls. The boys were Jim, McElroy, Barney, Dewey, and Ewell; the girls were Lillie, Rosa, Bertha, Donella, and Nellie. From the week Nan spent with Uncle Dave's family, her most enduring memory concerned guineas. Dave and Lizzie had a large number of these birds. Guineas made noises frightening to Nan as they flew over the house, and guinea dishes appeared on the Dave Langdales' menu almost daily.

When Nan returned home from the visit, Uncle Dave and Aunt Lizzie gave her a guinea to take with her. John Wesley and Nancy had no enthusiasm for this gift, for they disliked guineas. The only fowl they raised were chickens and turkeys, although some of their neighbors had geese and ducks. Nan's guinea, unwelcome from the start, got into serious trouble when it turned out to be predatory toward her mother's baby chicks running around the yard. According to Nan, it swallowed them whole. So the little girl had to give her bird away. She did not really mind, though, because by that time she had come to despise it, too.[77]

---

[77] Ibid.

For Nan, one of the most memorable aspects of childhood was school at Big Pond. Six of the Langdale children, all three boys and three of the four girls, attended this one-room log school. The schoolhouse stood on the opposite side of the pond from the Langdale home.

Big Pond occupied a spot on the Miccosukee Trail near the point of the intersection of the present Highway 441 and the Echols County Line and about three or four miles from the Langdale homestead. More of a swamp than a deep-water pond, it differed from the majority of so-called "round ponds" typical of this area. Besides being larger and perhaps having been formed through a different geological process, it contained a mixture of hardwood and cypress trees, whereas most round ponds were essentially cypress ponds. Cypress ponds provided good material for crossties when John Wesley went into that business. After John Wesley's children incorporated the estate in 1919, Big Pond lay well within the boundaries of the incorporated land. (Every year egrets roosted at Big Pond and shed their feathers. As Nan recalled, John Wesley collected these feathers and sold them in Jacksonville for $5.00 each.)[78]

On the way to school at Big Pond, the children had to cross a small stream by footlog. On one occasion, Noah and Harley, who were still in school there, both were overcome with eagerness to help a pretty girl across. They fell to competing a little too vigorously for the attention of the young lady, and both slipped into the water. When they arrived home dripping wet, they had the misfortune immediately to encounter their father, who had little tolerance for such foolishness. "Come let's go with me," John Wesley directed, and the boys followed him down to the edge of the swamp. Knowing full well what was to happen, Nancy and the girls stood teary-eyed on the front porch while waiting for the inevitable sounds of corporal punishment.[79]

By implication, at the time of this undated event so clear in Nan's memory, the Langdale family had already entered into the initial stages of dispersal. Education was the reason. Since the eldest boy, John J., was not "still in school at Big Pond," he presumably had already enrolled in school at Abbeville, Georgia, to which he was the first of the three boys to go for higher (beyond Big Pond) education. The girls, on the other hand, needed the cultural advantages of urban life, in John Wesley's opinion. Accordingly, in 1905 he sent them under the care of their mother and second-son, Noah, to live in the nearby town of Jasper, Florida. An account of the Jasper years, 1905–1911, follows.

---

[78] Ibid.; Langdale, JJLJr Interview 01 ; Langdale, JWL to JEL Letter.
[79] Campbell, "Letters to VLM."

3

Jasper and Abbeville

John Wesley and Nancy placed education at the top of their priorities for their children, at least for the girls. To provide a better chance for their daughters, as soon as the youngest (Susie) reached the age to start school, in 1905, John Wesley moved his family—though not himself—to Jasper, Florida, where they would have the advantage of a superior school system and an urban environment.[1]

Notwithstanding the Jasper move, John Wesley seems to have had mixed feelings about formal education. He, himself, had received very little. Regarding this subject, Judge Harley once commented, "Well, my father was deprived of any education much. He could read and write, but on account of the fact that he came up in Reconstruction… but he was in favor of education. And he was perfectly willing for us to go to school."[2]

Willing, yes; enthusiastic, perhaps not, except in the case of the girls or perhaps later in life. One might argue that, for some period of time, John Wesley considered formal schooling more important for his daughters than for his sons. To provide the girls a better education, he bought a house and moved the whole family to Jasper. On the other hand, he sent the boys to school only three months out of the year. The rest of the time they worked in the woods learning skills and performing the hard physical labor their father had found important to his success. As Judge Harley remembered, "He was in the turpentine business and crosstie business and livestock business and very successful, but he trained all of us boys—he wanted us to follow naval stores or turpentine operations, because he said you could always sell it, and he had been right prosperous in the turpentine business, and that was kind of the height of his ambition that we make a success in life, and he thought the best way to do it was in the naval stores business."[3]

---

[1] Ibid.

[2] Langdale, Judge Interview 01.

[3] Ibid.

When Harley, after studying at schools in Abbeville, Douglas, and Decatur, Georgia, decided he wanted to attend law school, he found his father disapproving. Lawyering did not appear to John Wesley nearly as good a way to make a living as turpentining, and he tried to dissuade Harley from going to law school by offering to get him a turpentine place.[4]

John Wesley's differing esteem for formal education as it applied to his sons and daughters may have had something to do with his concept of different roles for the sexes. Whereas he placed heavy work demands on his sons, even when they were very young, he seems to have required hardly any labor of his daughters. In the series of letters she wrote late in life describing her childhood, Nan Langdale gave no indication that the girls in the family had anything like the work demands expected of the boys. By comparison, it appears the girls, who were, of course, several years younger, had it very easy.[5]

It is possible, however, that moving the family to Jasper in 1905 represented, not just special treatment for the girls, but an enhanced appreciation for education on the part of John Wesley for his daughters *and* his sons. The experiences of John, Noah, and Harley, as they took concentrated courses to overcome their educational deficiencies, probably gave John Wesley a better understanding of the value of formal education for boys as well as for girls. He may have wished he had sent his boys to school more and worked them a little less in the swamp. Of this, we have no way to know.

John had finished at Big Pond and gone on "before 1902," as Nan remembered, to study at the normal school in Abbeville, Georgia. Nancy and John Wesley missed their eldest son tremendously, and Nancy wrote him regularly on Sunday mornings. Little Nan sat by her mother on the porch and felt privileged to look on as Nancy penned her weekly letter to "Dear Johnny" or "Dear Son."[6]

Following in John's footsteps, Noah and Harley also went away, one after the other, to further their education at the Georgia Normal College and Business Institute in Abbeville. Two professors, W. A. Little, principal, and A. A. Kuhl, commercial department director, operated the school. Mrs. Kuhl taught shorthand and telegraphy. The school offered courses of study in teaching, business, science, music, shorthand, typing, and telegraphy. "These people came from Ohio," remembered Judge Harley in the 1960s, "and they were very good people."[7]

Professors Little and Kuhl had moved to Abbeville directly from Jasper, Florida, presumably leaving teaching positions there. Probably they had been associated with the Jasper Normal Institute, which was founded in 1890 and subsequently absorbed into the Jasper public school system.[8]

---

[4] Ibid.

[5] Campbell, "Letters to VLM."

[6] Ibid.

[7] Langdale, Judge Interview 01 ; McDonald, *Wilcox County*, 36.

[8] Hamilton County Bicentennial Committee, passim.

The two professors opened the institute in Abbeville with the support of local citizens, so Abbeville must have offered them a more attractive situation than they had in Jasper. The Jasper connection probably explains how the Langdales knew about and trusted this school at Abbeville.[9]

In his later years, Judge Harley referred to the Georgia Normal College and Business Institute as the "Little and Kuhl school" and described his program there as a cram course. A student could do in one year what normally took four years, he said. Courses took ten weeks to complete.[10]

The school probably offered the Langdale brothers exactly what they needed, given the quality of education available at Big Pond and their limited attendance there. That school had one room and no differentiated grades. Even if Big Pond had offered the best academics in Georgia, however, Harley and his brothers would have had serious educational weaknesses because they attended only a third of the time each school year. There must have been many gaps in their education to be filled in by the program at Abbeville.[11]

Citizens of Abbeville took great pride in the Georgia Normal School and Business Institute. Its establishment in 1898 has been described in a local history as the most important event of the period for Abbeville. The school occupied three buildings with a total of 40,000 square feet. Mrs. D. J. Ryals operated the dormitory, called the "Central Hotel," a large wooden building in which many students, including the Langdale boys, boarded. In 1899, perhaps two years before John, the first of the Langdales, arrived, one hundred of the school's four hundred students were boarding students. In 1906–1908, Harley paid $7.50 per month to stay at the dormitory, which did not yet have electric lights.[12]

The *Abbeville Chronicle* on 27 April 1899, credited the school with attracting twenty-five additional families to Abbeville. In 1906 the school published a thirty-five-page brochure showing its modern buildings and boasting of an aggregate enrollment of 5,000 during its eight years of operation. For several years, the school seemed to thrive, but, following its commencement of 14 June 1908, it closed its Abbeville operation and reopened the next year in Douglas, Georgia.

Upon arriving at the Abbeville campus in 1906, Harley felt ill at ease. He had only two shirts, so he alternated washing and wearing them. His hands appeared so rough and callused from the hard work in the turpentine woods, he felt embarrassed to shake hands. At age eighteen, having already reached adult height, he towered over the young high school students with whom he had classes.[13]

---

[9] McDonald, *Wilcox County, 36*.

[10] Langdale, Judge Interview 01.

[11] Ibid.; McDonald, *Wilcox County*, 36.

[12] Langdale, Judge Interview 01.

[13] Miller, VLM Interview 01.

Soon, however, Harley found he enjoyed school at Abbeville. "He loved the kinds of things he learned about—he said he loved to carry the girls' violins for them and carry their books and go back and forth, and they invited him into their homes. That just opened up worlds to him." "He said those little girls were so nice to him. They were students there in Abbeville, much younger and more refined. He talked a lot about the way he felt during that time, that he was ashamed of being so rough. He was determined he was going to shape up." Years later, when a couple who had grown up in Abbeville, the Olivers, lived nearby, he "could talk for hours…about the school and about the town," Virginia remembered.[14]

Photo of Harley's Teaching Diploma from Georgia Normal College and Business Institute at Abbeville. His diploma for the Scientific Course was dated 1910, which was after his experience at Donald Fraser Military Academy. JEL.

Harley had studied two years at Abbeville by the time the school moved to Douglas. During the summer between his first and second years, he had also worked as a public school teacher. In those days, some counties, after crops were laid by, had a special session of school. A scarcity of teachers, he recalled, gave him the chance to teach. Harley received at least three diplomas from this school, one of which was for completing a course on teaching.

---

[14] Ibid. Virginia L. Miller has a newspaper photo with this caption: "Captain Harley Langdale, Sr., 1909, commanded at the inauguration of William Henry Taft." This implies he graduated from the military academy in 1909 and probably started at Mercer in the fall of that year.

In the fall of 1908, Harley followed the faculty to Douglas to continue his studies at the Little and Kuhl school.[15] On the way to Douglas, he must have felt like a veteran traveler, compared to the time when he first left home for Abbeville two years before. That had been only his second time ever to ride a train.[16]

With two years and part of another at Little and Kuhl, Harley left the Douglas school to enroll (perhaps temporarily, under the direction of Little and Kuhl) in the Donald Fraser Military Academy in the Atlanta suburb of Decatur. There he enjoyed the military routine. He excelled and received the school's highest honor as student commander of cadets. A highlight of his career at Donald Fraser came when he led a contingent of Donald Fraser students in the inaugural parade of President William Howard Taft in 1909.[17]

Cadet Commander Harley Langdale Leading his Troops for the Inauguration of President William Howard Taft. TLF.

---

[15] Langdale, Judge Interview 01. In his interview with the Sheltons, Judge said he attended two years in Abbeville and one year in Douglas. He must have meant that he did three years' work. He could not have spent a year in Douglas after June 1908 and also commanded the Donald Fraser cadets in the inaugural parade in January 1909.

McDonald, *Wilcox County*, 36–38, 79–80.. Page 36 of this book mentions that the new Wilcox County Courthouse was built in 1903, so photos of Harley and others on the steps of the courthouse could not have been made earlier than 1903. Page 80 says that, later, W. A. Little taught until his death at the University of Florida, and the Kuhls operated a business school for the remainder of their lives in Douglas.

[16] Langdale, Judge Interview 01.

[17] John W. Langdale, "History of the Langdale Law Firms," in John W. Langdale Papers (Valdosta GA: May 1996). This paper mentions that Donald Fraser Military Academy is now known as Riverside.

After studying at Donald Fraser and receiving a final certificate from Little and Kuhl, Harley enrolled in Mercer University against the advice of his father. John Wesley urged him to go into the turpentine business, instead. "My father repeated this many times," recalled Harley, Jr. "His father came to him when he was supposed to catch a train to go to Mercer ... and said, 'if you won't go and study law, I'll try to buy you a turpentine place and then you'll be in business.'"[18]

Grandma Betty, who supported Harley in his wish to study law, may have been the decisive influence in this case. She helped him with school expenses. As Virginia put it, "He said his Daddy didn't encourage him, so his grandmother helped him." "I really think she's the key to his getting out of there."[19] With a law degree from Mercer, Harley settled in Valdosta in 1912 and opened his law practice.[20]

Harley's oldest brother, John, first of the three to attend the Georgia Normal School and Business Institute, went through the commercial program in one year. John, who had an aptitude for mathematics and excelled at bookkeeping, then taught at the Abbeville school for a year after getting his diploma.[21] Being very skilled at handwriting and lettering, John was given the responsibility of preparing diplomas for graduates. He also made business cards for people who needed them and did it so expertly that they could pass for printed cards.[22]

From Abbeville, John returned to work briefly with his father at Council. At this time, John Wesley had recently gone into the business of shingle manufacturing. The procedure called for cutting cypress trees as much as three feet in diameter into shingle-length sections and rolling these out of Double Run Swamp. The sections then had to be split by hand into shingles. After taking his ease for so long as a student and teacher in Abbeville, John found this work not so much to his liking. He soon moved on to Jacksonville to work at the Barnett Bank. According to John's sister, Nan, John Wesley, who had become an important customer of the Barnett Bank by this time, helped him secure the job.[23]

A year after John enrolled in the Georgia Normal School and Business Institute, Noah followed him from Big Pond to the school at Abbeville. Like John, he received his teaching certificate; unlike John, Noah took a teaching job. This was back home at Big Pond. As a result of Noah's career move, probably influenced by his father, when little Nan started the first grade at Big Pond in 1904, she found her brother, Noah, as her teacher. One day, to Nan's great embarrassment, Noah called on her to recite her ABCs, and she failed the test. He

---

[18] Harley Langdale, Jr., interview by Harold Steen, typed transcript, 1991.
[19] Miller, VLM Interview 01.
[20] Campbell, "Letters to VLM."; Langdale, Judge Interview 01.
[21] Langdale, Judge Interview 01.
[22] Langdale, JJLJr Interview 01.
[23] Campbell, "Letters to VLM."

took her into the cloakroom and administered the standard switching, which she did not like and never forgot. Spankings and education went together at Big Pond.

Occasionally, said Nan, if the turpentine wagons had a little free time, the girls could catch a ride to school at Big Pond. It must have been a challenge for little girls to sit in these turpentine wagons for a trip to school and avoid arriving sticky with gum on their clothes and bodies. Most mornings, the wagons were busy, and the children walked to school on the Miccosukee Trail. They started out before daylight when the ground and grass were wet with dew. Sometimes they took off their shoes (each child had only one pair), violating their mother's instructions and ignoring her warnings about the perils of ground itch. Nan missed school fairly often, she recalled, because her parents kept the children home in bad weather.

At age six, Nan liked school. She especially enjoyed going there when she had her little tin lunch bucket. This usually contained for lunch a sweet potato, bacon, an apple or peach turnover, biscuits, and a small bottle of syrup water.

In transplanting his family—all female members, plus Noah—to Jasper in 1905, John Wesley took the advice of a close business friend, Mr. Vickers, who lived about half way between the Langdale home and Jasper. A large landowner and turpentine producer like John Wesley, Vickers assured him that Jasper had one of the best schools around, with levels from first grade through normal college. It may have been through Vickers that John Wesley learned of Professors Little and Kuhl.

Concerning the move to Jasper, if the Langdale girls had been asked for their opinions, none would have voted for it. They enjoyed the open spaces, the freedom of roaming through the woods, the opportunities to observe the flight and nesting of birds, and the beauty of rain falling in sheets through the pine trees. In Jasper, they could not go out after a rain and scoop up minnows with a fruit jar for their fish bowls. They would not have access to their wagon-chain swing suspended from the rafters of the buggy shed or to their merry-go-round made from a long plank pinned at its center to a pine stump. Would there be in Jasper a little colored boy who would give the girls a ride in his apple-box wagon pulled by a nanny goat? No, but John Wesley believed the change would be good for his daughters, and that settled it.

Transporting the family and their goods to Jasper required two vehicles. John Wesley, Nancy, and Dick, took the buggy. The older girls rode with Noah, who drove the wagon laden with furniture and supplies. This included beds and a hand-made dining table, plus kitchen implements and an abundant quantity of food that Nancy prepared for the trip.

The little caravan departed very early in the morning. At noon they stopped for lunch with relatives, the Fourakers. There Nan and Isabel, though carefully groomed, with their hair neatly braided by their mother and dressed in their best outfits for traveling, wandered away from the others and discovered a barn filled with cotton recently harvested. They could not resist walking on the snowy stuff, then burying themselves in it, and generally having a great time playing. When John Wesley and Nancy got ready to leave the Fouraker place, they had first to find the girls, who now had innumerable wisps of cotton in their hair and on their clothes. The girls paid for their fun, enduring a stern parental lecture, but were relieved to escape a spanking.

About dark they arrived at their new home in Jasper. They set up the beds, lighted their oil lamps, and started the wood stove to make coffee and to warm some of the food Nancy had brought.

For the most part, the house had still to be furnished. The day after their arrival in Jasper, the adults and Sadie went shopping for furniture. They purchased a player piano, a six-piece parlor set, a wool rug, center tables, rocking chairs, a buffet, chairs to go with the dining table from the home place, two pictures for the dining room, and high-backed rocking chairs for the porch. For the dining room, they also bought a twelve-place setting of china, a punch bowl with twelve cups, and a chocolate set with twelve hand-painted cups.

John Wesley had secured an attractive and spacious dwelling for his family in Jasper, a comfortable place in which they could take pride. The house sat on a large lot, which also included a roomy and neatly-painted barn, a large vegetable garden, and a number of pecan trees. A white frame two-story house, freshly repainted, with maroon trim and with a white picket fence across the front of the lot, it had a wide central hall. Entering at the front by way of this hall, one found the parlor on the left and, behind that, a large bedroom. On the opposite side of the hallway, three bedrooms stretched, one behind the other, to the back of the house. Upstairs, the Langdales had two more large bedrooms.[24] Whether the Langdale home had a telephone is unknown. Some people in Jasper had them and could talk long-distance to Valdosta. The telephone company had completed the line connecting the two towns about 1899.[25]

Passing down the hall to the rear of the house, one arrived at the back porch, from which doors led into the kitchen and the dining room. At the end of the back porch a walkway connected to a large pantry that John Wesley kept well stocked with cured meat. He also brought "Old Pearl," their purebred Jersey cow, from the home place and installed her in the barn to provide milk. Nancy, as she had in the country, also kept chickens to supply eggs and meat.[26]

Although no record has been found of any trouble with the neighbors over wandering chickens, the country habit of keeping yard fowl had already attracted the unfavorable attention of some of the Jasper ladies. They formed the Woman's Club about 1905 and, before long, started agitating to get hogs and chickens off

---

[24] Ibid.

[25] Hamilton County Bicentennial Committee, 5.

[26] Campbell, "Letters to VLM."

the streets. They also pushed for city garbage collection. Jasper was definitely moving toward modernity.[27]

From the back porch of the Langdale residence, one also gained access to a room especially equipped for taking baths. The bathing room included large zinc tubs that the Langdales filled by drawing water in zinc buckets from a deep well accessible from the porch. The house had no indoor plumbing. An outdoor privy stood just beyond the garden. Slop jars avoided the necessity of going outside at night.[28]

Across the street stood the public school, a sprawling two-story structure. Fenced on all four sides, its grounds occupied an entire city block. On each side a stile—steps up on one side of the fence and down on the other—allowed people to enter or leave the grounds.[29] Facing NW Third Street, this building, or part of it, originally belonged to the Jasper Normal Institute before it became the public school complex. This school burned in 1924 or 1925, long after the Langdales moved to Valdosta, and the Woman's Building took its place on the site.[30]

The girls dreaded starting school. They had never been around city folk, and they knew nobody at the Jasper school. They felt insecure, intimidated, like country bumpkins. Nevertheless, it had to be done; Dick entered the first grade and Nan the second. The younger children had classes on the first floor. The older girls, Isabel and Sadie, went to their rooms on the second floor. Noah got a job as a teacher.[31]

Soon the girls felt pretty much at home. They made many friends in Jasper. They felt a little self-conscious because they did not have "boughten" dresses like the city girls, but Nancy's skill and good taste as a seamstress met their wardrobe needs very well. She saw to it that their clothes were always clean, starched, neat, and tasteful.

Nancy, herself, like other ladies of her generation, typically wore blouses, called "shirt-waists," and skirts. For dress-up occasions, she generally wore a black blouse. Neither Nancy nor the girls, as they grew older, used lipstick in those days; that was, in Nancy's view, for women of bad reputation.

For her teacher in second grade, Nan had Miss Mozell. Miss Mozell liked to give the children aphorisms such as "An idle brain is the devil's workshop" and "Lost between sunrise and sunset, two golden hours—no reward offered for they are gone forever." She wrote one of these wise sayings on the blackboard each morning. Each Friday afternoon Miss Mozell had the children engage in a spelling bee, which Nan usually won. At least, that's the way she remembered it when she was much older.

---

[27] Hamilton County Bicentennial Committee, 77.

[28] Campbell, "Letters to VLM."

[29] Ibid.

[30] Hamilton County Bicentennial Committee, 53.

[31] Campbell, "Letters to VLM."

Noah also had an interest in Miss Mozell. They dated for a while until an unfortunate incident involving Nan spoiled their budding romance. In the second grade, if a child needed to go to the bathroom one signaled it by holding up two fingers to gain permission. One afternoon, toward the end of the school day, seven-year-old Nan held up two fingers but received no acknowledgment from Miss Mozell. She kept holding up two fingers, and still Miss Mozell did not notice. Eventually, the inevitable happened—wetness and horrible embarrassment. Little Nan put her head on her desk and could not bear to look up as the other children left for the day.

Hearing of this humiliation of his little sister, Noah stormed over to have a frank talk with Miss Mozell. After this, he never asked her out again, remembered Nan with satisfaction.[32] Well, maybe. One might have a little skepticism, though, that a young man would break off a promising relationship with an attractive young woman for the sake of his little sister's wounded pride. Nan may not have known the whole story. Neither do we.

Down the middle of Jasper, a town of about one thousand persons in 1900 and seventeen hundred in 1915, ran the Atlantic Coast Line Railroad. Jasper had profited from the railroad since the waning days of the War Between the States. In 1865, construction crews of the Pensacola and Georgia Railroad Company completed the line between Live Oak, Jasper, and Du Pont, Georgia. About a mile north of Jasper at that time, which is the present location of Hately and NW Central Avenue, they built a depot to serve passengers and freight. In 1911 the Atlantic Coast Line built a new depot a block north of the original one.[33]

By 1905 when the Langdales moved there, two rail lines served Jasper. The Atlantic Coast Line offered passengers, cattle, and bales of cotton an opportunity to go south at 10:00 a.m. or north at 4:00 p.m. The Georgia, Southern and Florida, which laid its tracks to Jasper in 1889–1890, had four trains coming through each day. Two came in the morning at 6:00 and 9:00, and two came in the evening at 6:00 and 9:00. The 6:00 P.M. arrival attracted a crowd and gave the townspeople a good opportunity to socialize. The GS&F had its depot slightly farther north than that of the ACL.[34]

In the decades after 1865, businesses occupied sites near the depot, and on each side of the ACL tracks, prominent families built fine houses. In this setting, the First Methodist Church had also placed its parsonage. There the Methodist pastor, the Reverend Mr. Smith, lived with his family. This was a magnificent place, the Langdale girls thought. The parsonage took up a whole block and had a

---

[32] Ibid.

[33] Ibid., Hamilton County Bicentennial Committee, 87; Population figures from *Debow's Review* as cited in Hamilton County Bicentennial Committee, *Hamilton County*, 53. The US Census, including Negroes, placed the population in the range of ten to twelve thousand in the 1900 to 1910 period, according to the same source.

[34] Hamilton County Bicentennial Committee, 77.

beautiful wire fence around it. At a time when the streets and sidewalks of the town had yet to be paved, the minister's residence had a concrete walk running from each corner of the lot to the house.[35]

In time the girls became good friends with the daughters of the Reverend Mr. Smith. Nan regarded Esther Smith, who was in the same grade, as one of her best friends. It hurt her feelings, though, that although she frequently went over to play with Esther at her house, the Smiths never allowed Esther to play at the Langdale home. Esther's older sister, Lillian, became friendly with Sadie, and the two studied together. Years later, Lillian became famous as author of the novel, *Strange Fruit*, which she based upon people and scandalous events in Jasper.[36]

It seemed to the Langdales that most of the upper class in Jasper attended First Methodist Church. Invited by some of their friends to revival services there, the girls went every night. "We all fell under the spell of all that soulful preachin'," wrote Nan. "And the last service we all joined the church."[37] From that time on, the girls went to First Methodist worship and Sunday school every Sunday morning. This required some dedication, for the Methodist church stood a number of blocks away from the Langdale home, at the corner of E. Central Avenue and Fifth Street, and they had to travel by foot.[38]

Nancy encouraged the girls in their Methodism, but she, herself, remained staunchly Primitive Baptist, attached in her mind to Boney Bluff. In Jasper, she also took her daughters to Baptist services on Sunday evenings and to Baptist prayer meetings on Thursdays. Perhaps she thought they needed regular doses of *real* religion to go along with the society variety. In any case, it would appear that the Langdales were adequately churched in Jasper. One attraction of the Baptist services may have been that the walk to the Baptist church, located downtown, was much shorter than the trip to First Methodist.

For the most part, the girls had to make their own recreational opportunities in Jasper. Sometimes they went down to the edge of the swamp to pick wild flowers. Occasionally they played in the large sinkhole across from Judge Horne's home about a mile out of town on the Valdosta highway. Once, exploring the bottom of this crater, Nan found a fifty-cent-piece. She was thrilled.

---

[35] Campbell, "Letters to VLM." This house is apparently the one referred to in the 1976 *Brief History of Hamilton County, Florida*, 79, as the Staten-Smith-Corbett house. This chapter, Chapter Seventeen, written by Virgie Hyman, tells of a Mr. C. W. Smith who moved into Jasper from the country, the Mitchell Settlement, she thought, with a large family, including eight children. One of these was Lillian Smith, author of *Strange Fruit*. "Mr Smith was prosperous, but the depression came and he sold his holdings and went to Laurel Falls, Ga. where they had a summer hotel. Lily died two years ago in Atlanta and is buried in her loved mountain top, but her influence is strong."

[36] Ibid.

[37] Ibid.

[38] Ibid.; Hamilton County Bicentennial Committee, 43.

In their second year at Jasper, two house guests, Maybell and Norma Vickers, came to live with the Langdales in one of their upstairs bedrooms. They were daughters of Mr. Vickers, John Wesley's business friend, who had recommended the Jasper school. Having decided now to send his own girls to school in Jasper for a year, Mr. Vickers made arrangements for them to stay with the Langdales.

Maybell and Norma brought with them a Shetland pony and a little cart for it to pull. This made them all the more welcome to the Langdale girls, who hoped to enjoy lots of rides in the cart. But it did not happen. The Langdale sisters got only one invitation to a cart ride. Maybell, who was about Nan's age, preferred to keep the pony and cart to herself and her sister. For Nan, this took some of the glow off the relationship.[39]

In time, the girls found boyfriends. Nan had one named Pennywell who gave her daily rides on his bicycle handlebars after school. This ended when he held her hand and scratched her palm as they were walking to a party. It frightened her to death. She had heard what that meant. She ran straight home—forget the party—and never rode his handlebars again.

Eldest daughter Sadie started dating but ran into trouble with her father. Seventeen years old by 1910, Sadie had grown to be a lovely and popular young woman. As Nan put it, "Sadie was really a beauty. She was a typical 'Gibson type,' buxom, well-corseted, lots of black hair, big blue eyes, and peaches and cream complexion, and all the eligible young men in town were trying to date her."[40]

As Sadie matured in her teen-age years, Nancy began allowing her to have dates on weekends. Evidently, however, Nancy had neglected to clear this with her husband. In Jasper on one of his regular visits, John Wesley answered a knock at the door and found a young man standing there who said he was calling on Sadie. "Go home," John Wesley told him, and he did. Sadie, her mother, and her sisters just cried. They did not argue or complain, but they may have wished they dared. The young man happened to be Frank Smith, the First Methodist preacher's son, seen by Jasper females as a prize catch. "Guess my beloved dad had heard all about the city slickers and the country gals,"[41] observed Nan.

John Wesley visited his family in Jasper every two or three weekends, usually arriving on Saturday. Sometimes he traveled on horseback, but more often he took his fancy buggy or buckboard pulled by two matched high-stepping horses. These horses, said Nan, were "his pride and glory." "You could see it all over his face when he would drive them up to our house in Jasper."[42] Neighbors waited around and watched for his arrival. For them it was the Saturday show, and John Wesley seemed to enjoy being the main attraction.

---

[39] Ibid.
[40] Ibid.
[41] Ibid.
[42] Ibid.

Sometimes, especially at the long Christmas vacation from school, Nancy and the girls came back from Jasper to visit the home place and spend time with John Wesley. When they did, they traveled by train. For example, at Christmas the year Harley was in military school (1908), Nancy took the girls for one of these home vacations and coincidentally met Harley on the train. He was on the way home, too, dressed in his military uniform from Donald Fraser Military Academy. It was shortly after this that Harley led the Donald Fraser cadets in the inaugural parade for President Taft.

Until the Council sawmill came and created the town of Council in 1908, there was no railroad depot in the immediate vicinity. To get to the home-place, Nancy and the girls left Jasper on the Atlantic Coast Line train bound for Waycross. At Haylow they changed to the Georgia, Southern and Florida train, which took them to the crossing at the section-foreman's house at Eddy, Florida. This was about twelve miles south of the future location of Council. John Wesley met them at the Eddy crossing. The train stopped to let them off there, and, when they flagged it down, it stopped to pick them up for the return trip. Before construction of the depot at Council, the Langdales went to the Eddy crossing to board the train for Jacksonville or Valdosta.

The change from one railroad line to another at Haylow required a little extra doing. The Southern train on the way to Jacksonville normally crossed the Atlantic Coast Line tracks at Haylow a few minutes ahead of the Jasper-to-Waycross train. To facilitate the Langdales' transfer, the station agent at Jasper called ahead to Haylow and asked the Southern train to delay its departure from there. It nearly always did. Only once, when the train from Jasper ran very late, did the Southern fail to wait. That time the Langdale girls had their first experience at staying overnight at a hotel. At least, this was Haylow's equivalent of a hotel, a kind of bed-and-breakfast farm house. The girls enjoyed it, especially the country food.

The procedure for the return trip required flagging down the Georgia, Southern and Florida at the Eddy crossing and taking the train to Valdosta. There they had to wait most of the day for a train to Jasper. When they arrived in Valdosta, as Nan remembered the routine, Dr. Wilson met them at the station with his touring car and delivered them to the Valdes Hotel where they waited. In the afternoon, as time approached for the Jasper train, Dr. Wilson came in his touring car to ferry them to the station.

Nan found this trip very exciting, especially the ride in the car. It had neither top nor doors. She sat on the floorboard with her feet on the running board. Thrilling and scary it was. Nan loved it. She also liked the ice cream that Dr. Wilson bought them.[43]

---

[43] Ibid.

One year, Christmas 1908, the year Harley wore his cadet unifrom home on vacation from Donald Fraser,[44] they returned from their stay at the home place to find in Jasper, to their great surprise, a new family member. Noah had gotten married. He and his new wife had already set up housekeeping upstairs.[45]

Noah had married Jessie Catledge, a lovely, black-haired girl whom he had met at the Lyceum recently held at the Jasper school. The Lyceum ranked at the top of annual attractions in Jasper, and that particular year William Jennings Bryan spoke. He gave a lecture, as Nan recalled, on "The Little Train That Could Hardly Make It" but said "I think I can, I think I can," and, upon succeeding, said "I thought I could, I thought I could."[46]

Jessie, recently home from college, attended the lecture. Noah saw her and found her irresistible. The two hit it off from the start. "We left for Council for long vacation and in 10 days they were married," wrote Nan.[47]

The Langdales all liked Jessie; Nancy and Sadie, especially, found her to be wonderful company. About a year later, Jessie and Noah became parents of a little girl, Marguerite, who grew up to become a lawyer in Washington DC. Following John Wesley's death in 1911, they moved to Council and Noah assumed responsibilities as manager of the turpentine still at Edith. Later, Noah moved to Valdosta where Harley lived, there being insufficient work to provide a livelihood from the family estate at Council.[48]

While the Langdales lived in Jasper, Isabel, the second daughter and the only brown-eyed child in the family, became ill. Eventually, the family physician, Dr. W. M. O'Cain, whom they regarded as Jasper's finest, diagnosed the problem as diabetes. John Wesley and Nancy took Isabel to the Holmes Sanitarium in Valdosta, considered the best hospital in the area. They arranged for diabetes specialists from as far away as Atlanta to examine and treat her. None of them seemed to know anything much to do, other than put her on a strict diet. This did not seem to help. Months passed, and she appeared worse, rather than better. Isabel's weight dropped by a third and she had dark pieds over her body. The family visited her often. She begged to go home and for sweets to eat.[49]

Finally, John Wesley and Nancy gave up on medical treatment. They took their daughter home to Jasper and permitted her to eat whatever she wanted. To the casual observer she probably appeared normal and happy, though the family knew she suffered painfully at times. After several months she died. It was 3 September 1910.

---

[44] *Valdosta Daily Times*, 19 January 1909.

[45] Campbell, "Letters to VLM."

[46] Ibid.

[47] Ibid.

[48] Ibid. ; John J. Langdale, Jr., interview by Harold Steen, 1991, typed transcript, The Langdale Company Offices, Valdosta GA.

[49] Campbell, "Letters to VLM."

They carried Isabel's remains to Boney Bluff for burial. Adding to the sorrow of her loss, there was now the unexpected struggle with nature to lay her to rest in peace. Merely moving her body across the Suwannee to the cemetery turned out to be a test of endurance. Weeks of rain had swollen the river beyond its banks, and the bridge, normally a bit rickety, appeared quite unsafe. The funeral party, with Isabel's casket, had to row themselves across the river by boat.[50]

The following April 1911, John Wesley became ill. He had been on a hunting trip to the Okefenokee, had run out of water in his canteen, and had drunk several times from a lake in the swamp. He went to Jasper for medical treatment. It turned out that he had Typhoid Fever, but medical opinions differed about how to treat his illness. Every day the Langdales' family physician, Dr. O'Cain, visited him. Daily, also, Dr. Wilson, hired by the family to share duties with Dr. O'Cain and add his expertise, traveled from Valdosta to see him. In late May and early June, with summer coming on, the temperature soared, adding to John Wesley's discomfort. The family did their best to cool his body through constant fanning. Harley, who had not yet graduated from the law school at Mercer, arranged for a nurse to come from Valdosta to help. All efforts failed. John Wesley died on 7 June 1911, after an illness of six weeks and was buried at Boney Bluff Cemetery.

Perhaps John Wesley could have survived this illness if he had had one physician, instead of two, or if the two had agreed on the treatment. Some weeks later, the nurse, a pretty young woman whom Harley was dating, revealed that she had observed problems between the two physicians. Dr. O'Cain had appeared jealous and resentful that Dr. Wilson had been brought in from Valdosta. Each time Dr. Wilson prescribed medicine for John Wesley and returned to Valdosta, she said, Dr. O'Cain cancelled the order and prescribed a different medication.

Although the truth of this report is uncertain, it is clear that Nan Langdale Campbell, at least, placed greater confidence in Dr. Wilson and tended to believe the allegation. Except for this, "everyone felt like Dad would have pulled through," she wrote. It also appears that, by revealing the dispute over treatment long after anything could be done to resolve it and possibly save John Wesley's life, the nurse spoiled her relationship with Harley. Why didn't you warn us? He must have asked. Although the family had thought Harley and the nurse appeared very much attracted to each other, this apparently soured their relationship.

Commenting on his father's untimely death in 1955, Judge Harley attributed it to medical ignorance. "They treated him for malaria when he had typhoid," said Judge. "He was stout as a mule. All the Langdales have been strong men. I had a great-uncle who could walk a footlog carrying a two-hundred-pound sack of guano under each arm. I had another uncle who could hold a barrel of whisky up to his

---

[50] Ibid. Since both Jasper and the cemetery are west of the Suwannee River, it would seem unnecessary to move Isabel's body across the river, as described by Nan. Considering, however, that when John Wesley died in 1911, the family had his body shipped by train from Jasper through Valdosta to Council, it is likely that the same occurred with respect to Isabel.

lips and sip it like he was drinking from a glass."[51] Some might suspect Judge exaggerated a little the physical prowess of Langdale men, but there seems to be no reason for doubting the sturdiness of John Wesley's physique before his illness.

At the time of his death, John Wesley had become one of the more prominent and successful businessmen in Clinch County. His obituary published in the Valdosta *Times* noted that he died at age 51 "in the prime of life" and credited him with a reputation as a "good citizen," a "splendid neighbor," and generous friend to many. According to the newspaper's sources, his estate had a value on the order of $150,000, including $35,000 to $40,000 in the bank.[52]

For that period, $35,000 was a large amount of cash. To see this in the perspective of that day, consider that the Bank of Abbeville, Georgia, had been organized in 1904 with a capital of $25,000 and proudly reported deposits as high as $40,000 by 1908. The Bank of Homerville, started in 1903 with capital of $15,000, claimed $25,000 in 1916.[53] These were small banks in small towns. Still, if John Wesley actually had $35,000 to $40,000 in cash, as stated in the obituary, he had enough liquid capital at the time of his death to open his own bank.[54] That is an impressive achievement for a fellow who grew up without a father or formal education and who lived all his life in the backwoods of one of the poorest regions of a poor state.

The substantial estate that John Wesley left to his wife, three sons, and three daughters is a tribute to his resourcefulness, strength of character, and hard work. It is clear that he stayed alert to the possibilities of profit, orthodox or unorthodox, from the resources of the forest. An accomplished woodsman and hunter, he killed alligators for their hides, collected bird feathers for sale to the suppliers of hat-makers, and made large profits from the sale of hogs and cows native to the woods and swamps of that area. He purchased thousands of acres of forestland and entered into firewood, crosstie, shingle, and lumber production. In the naval stores business he operated two turpentine stills, one at Edith and another at Council. He negotiated with other landowners and brokered a deal that resulted in the establishment of the Council sawmill and the town of Council. He did all of these things with, so far as is known, little or no formal education and with no family wealth to give him a start. He provided for the education of his children and prepared them, as best he could, for financial success. The story of John Wesley Langdale is a story of admirable achievement by an American pioneer. He deserves the praise and thanks of his descendants and the admiration

---

[51] Martin, 92.

[52] "John Wesley Langdale Obituary." *Clinch County News*, 16 June 1911.

[53] Huxford, *History of Clinch County*, 52..

[54] McDonald, *Wilcox County*, 38.

of those who value courage, self-reliance, and individual initiative. John Wesley's heirs enjoyed the advantages of a substantial estate, which his sons later incorporated as the J. W. Langdale Company.

4

The J. W. Langdale Company, 1919–1965

With John Wesley's death, Nancy called upon her sons for help with the business. Eldest son, John, who had already been given management responsibility by John Wesley, assumed the primary administrative role. After completing school in Abbeville, he had worked with his father for a brief period before employment for about two years with the Barnett Bank in Jacksonville. He subsequently left the bank, his son and daughter recalled, for a job with one of the railroads in Jacksonville. Some time prior to John Wesley's death, John J. returned to Council at his father's request. This must have been no later than August 1910, for he was appointed a notary public for District 1219 in Clinch County on 8 August 1910.[1] It seems the railroad wanted to transfer John to the northeast, and John Wesley invited his son, instead, to come home and help run the business. Still single, John moved in with his Uncle Dave. He continued to live with Uncle Dave, apparently, until the latter's departure from the business and, eventually, John occupied the same house with his wife and family.[2]

Noah gave up teaching in Jasper to become manager of the still at Edith. He, Jessie, and their baby, Marguerite, moved into a small new house—five rooms and a bath—built for them next to the larger house occupied by Dave Langdale and his family, plus John J., at Council. After managing the still at Edith for a year or two, Noah moved to Valdosta where Harley had located in 1912[3]

A family conference between Nancy and her sons concluded that she and the girls should also leave Jasper. Their new home was to be Valdosta, where Harley now had a room at the Brinson House. This boarding house stood on the corner of Central Avenue and Lee Street, directly across the street from the location in 2001 of the Valdosta city hall. By that time the Brinson House had long since

---

[1] Huxford, *History of Clinch County*, 210.
[2] Langdale, JJLJr Interview 01.
[3] Campbell, "Letters to VLM."

been replaced by a parking lot. In 1912 Nancy and the girls moved into their new place a few blocks from the Brinson House at 508 East Hill Avenue.

Judge, Thalia, and Harley Jr. about 1915. TLF.

Busy starting his law practice, Harley still found time to attend his mother and sisters. In the summer, he took the girls to Blue Springs, out the Quitman highway, driving them in his new Bell automobile. There he taught Nan to swim. As Nan remembered, he carried her into the middle of the spring and let her go. She dog-paddled her way out.[4] This is an instructional technique that Harley later employed with his sons.[5]

Harley also used his new car to court a young lady he met at the Brinson House. She was Thalia Lee of Virginia, whom he married the next year. Thalia may not have said so at the time, but she thought Harley's sisters were overprotected and pampered. Years later, she made no secret of this opinion in comments to her daughter, Virginia. "Mama said those girls were awfully spoiled,"

---

[4] Ibid.
[5] Langdale, JWL Interview 14.

remembered Virginia. "She said she was hard on me because she wasn't going to let me grow up like those girls." Thalia blamed Harley for helping to spoil his sisters because "every time she'd complain to him about them, he said, 'Oh, leave them alone, Thalia, they'll grow out of it.'"[6]

Harley Langdale in 1911.
From a Mercer U. Fraternity
Picture. TLC.

Meanwhile, the Council sawmill operation, which John Wesley had played a crucial role in bringing to Clinch County in 1908, provided jobs for local workers and brought new people into the area. The new industry and the town it spawned had both an economic and a social impact on local people, including the Langdales. For example, James McCabe, an engineer with the Council company romanced and married Dave's daughter, Bertha Langdale. One of the top executives of the company had a romantic interest in John Wesley's eldest daughter, Sadie. And, recalled Nan, "even Dick and I both had our special admirers."[7]

After moving from Jasper to Valdosta, Nancy visited often in Council where John J. lived with his Uncle Dave and looked after the family business. Presumably, she had her say on how it should be run. On one of these visits to her son's home, on Sunday, 23 November 1913, Nancy suddenly took sick and died within three hours. The Valdosta newspaper attributed her death to apoplexy, which today would be called a stroke. Harley, Noah, and their three sisters received the news by telegram and rushed to Council the morning after their mother's death. Like her husband only two years before and her daughter Isabel previously,

---

[6] Miller, VLM Interview 01.
[7] Campbell, "Letters to VLM."

Nancy was laid to rest at Bethel Primitive Baptist Church Cemetery. She was only fifty-two.[8]

Nancy's girls' romantic interests in Council increased after the death of their father in 1911 and their mother in 1913. When Nancy died, the girls ranged in age from twenty to thirteen.[9] In this period they spent vacations from school with Uncle Dave and Aunt Lizzie. Being about the same ages as their cousins, Rosa, Bertha, and Donella, they had much in common and enjoyed their times together.[10]

At Council they went to church and Sunday school every Sunday. John led the singing and urged Nan to play the pump organ, which she struggled to do. The music lessons her mother had arranged for her (and sister Sadie) in Valdosta after their move from Jasper in 1912, following the death of John Wesley, did not prepare her well, Nan thought, for playing this instrument.

After Sunday dinner in Council the girls usually went for walks with their boy friends along the railroad tracks. As they strolled they sometimes picked water lilies from the railroad ditches. In Council, around the period of World War I, courting activities had narrow scope.

Aunt Lizzie liked it that way, as she made plain to Nan one Sunday. That particular weekend Nan had invited a friend, Marie, from Valdosta to visit Council with her. Nan wanted to introduce her to a good-looking young man named Malcolm. After Sunday supper, still in daylight, Nan's friend Alex came over, bringing Malcolm along. The two couples sat on the porch, talking. As it started to get dark, Aunt Lizzie appeared with a lighted lantern, which, without a word, she placed right between the couples. Taking the hint, the two fellows hurried off toward the railroad tracks while Marie and Nan, totally shaken, retired to their room. Nothing was ever said of this to Nan, but Aunt Lizzie and her lantern had made her point.[11]

By 1915, the eldest Langdale sister, Sadie, found a husband. Actually, she had been seeing this fellow for a long time. He was Preston Sandlin a banker's son and

---

[8] "Mrs. J. W. Langdale Dead: Well Known and Highly Esteemed Woman Died at Council," *Valdosta Daily Times*, 24 November 1913; "Funeral of Mrs. Langdale," *Valdosta Daily Times*, 25 November 1913.

[9] The Langdale children evidently had no information about the death of their grandmother, Nancy. As John explained, "I never did think to ask while Daddy was alive. We just never did ask him much unless he volunteered on personal things. With him, it was always business." Langdale, JWL Interview 14. With respect to Harriet Griffin Langdale, the widow of John Robert Langdale, who died in 1898, John had a similar response. "I never heard Daddy discuss whether he had ever seen her or not. I feel like if he had seen her he would have told me." Langdale, JWL Interview 14.

[10] Campbell, "Letters to VLM."

[11] Ibid.

one of the most "eligible" young men from Jasper. With far more social than business experience, Preston had a reputation as an excellent dancer.

Preston learned to dance well, it is said, around 1906 when the lovely Miss Irnie Irvine, whose sister and husband operated a hotel in Jasper, organized a dancing class. Preston and several of his friends signed up to learn the waltz and the two-step. Unfortunately, dancing had not won complete social acceptance in Jasper. Only two local girls danced, and they declined to join the class. As a result the fellows practiced, reportedly, with chairs as partners. Finally, as a kind of graduation ceremony, they hired an orchestra and held a big dance. Judge Mallory Horne and his wife chaperoned. The dance, scheduled for a Monday night, turned out very well, except that on the previous Sunday one of the local ministers had something pointed to say. The title of his sermon was "From the Ball Room to Hell."[12]

Preston and Sadie had been dating before Nancy and the girls moved to Valdosta in 1912. Afterward, Preston's interest continued. Each Sunday, he took the first morning train to visit Sadie in Valdosta and returned to Jasper by the last evening train. On these weekly trips, he usually brought Sadie a box of chocolates, one or two of which little sister Nan helped herself to on the sly.[13]

The Sunday visits continued after Nancy's death in 1913. Eventually, on a Sunday in April 1915, Preston and Sadie called in Harley and Thalia, who had themselves been married less than two years, and announced their determination to be married that very day. Although Harley and Thalia urged them to wait, as Nan understood it, the two couples went directly to the preacher's home and the marriage took place. The newlywed Sandlins lived for a time in the Langdale home at Jasper, which had been vacant since Nancy and her daughters left there in 1912.[14]

Sadie's younger sisters, Nan and Susie (Dick) remained single until November 1920. Attending college in Cleveland, Tennessee, they met two local young men of the Campbell family. Nan married Roy Simmens Campbell and Susie married Horace Elbert Campbell.

By this time, only the eldest sibling, John J., busy running the family business, remained unmarried. His time came in 1923, when, at the age of 38, he married Rosalie Talley Cornelius of Homerville. John and Rosalie met when she came to teach school at Council. She had been teaching since graduating from high school about two years previously.

Rosalie was a member of the Baptist church in Homerville; for the convenience of attending a church nearby, she joined the Methodist church in Fargo. Although, for some time following the deaths of his parents, John J.

---

[12] Virgie Hyman tells this story in Hamilton County Bicentennial Committee, 78.

[13] Campbell, "Letters to VLM."

[14] Ibid.

apparently displayed strong interest in church and regularly led the singing in services at Council, he never officially joined a church. In this particular matter, for whatever reason, he seems to have followed his father's example.[15]

In other respects, John J. proved to be community minded. While operating the J. W. Langdale Company, he served as a member of the Clinch County Consolidated School Board, and, for at least fifteen years, he was Clinch County Commissioner.[16]

On 1 April 1919, John J. and his brothers petitioned to incorporate the family business in Clinch County as "The J. W. Langdale Company" with a capital stock of $50,000 and the privilege of increasing it to $200,000. The petition requested authorization to operate any or all of a long list of business types. These included real estate, naval stores, lumber, other manufactured wood products, farming, livestock raising, and mercantile businesses, both wholesale and retail.[17]

The corporation became effective on 9 May 1919. Reflecting the wishes expressed by John Wesley before his death, five of the six children owned eighty shares each of the company's stock; John J. received a hundred shares. John Wesley had promised John a larger portion of the estate as an inducement to come home and help run the business before his fatal illness of 1911.[18]

John J. served as president and manager until his death in 1955. At that time his hundred shares of stock passed equally to his two children, Rose and John J., Jr. By then the company had acquired substantially more land, several thousand acres of it in Florida. In 1997 the total of the J. W. Langdale Company land came to 21,134 acres.[19]

Another company, set up in 1937, was Langdale Woodlands. It included about 7,500 acres purchased for $1,500. This land was in Columbia County, Florida, and much of it was swampy. Four different persons owned part of the Langdale Woodlands Company in 1937. Jay and Joe, sons of John J., Jr., owned seventeen shares of this company in 1992.[20]

For years after 1911, John J., as president and manager, struggled to make ends meet for the family business. The turpentine industry had ups and downs, and much of this period was in the down part of the cycle. Money was in short supply. In the naval stores business, an operator needed always to keep in mind that, regardless of how profitable the business might be in one period, a down-cycle

---

[15] Langdale, JJLJr Interview 01.

[16] Langdale, JJLJr Interview 1991.

[17] Harley Langdale, Sr.,"Petition to Incorporate the J. W. Langdale Company, 1 April 1919," John W. Langdale Papers, Valdosta GA.

[18] "Order of Incorporation of the J.W. Langdale Company, Clinch County GA, 9 May 1919," John W. Langdale Papers, Valdosta GA. ; Langdale, JJLJr Interview 1991 ; Langdale, JJLJr Interview 01.

[19] Langdale, JJLJr Interview 01.

[20] Langdale, JJLJr Interview 1991.

would certainly come and he would need a large cash reserve to keep his business afloat without borrowing. Lacking an adequate reserve, the operator would find himself at the mercy of the turpentine factors and their high interest rates. Consequently, a wise operator would restrain his temptation to spend his surplus on houses, cars, and a lavish life-style. He would be smart to put the money away for a rainy day.[21]

Naval stores producers in the 1920s and 1930s strove constantly to keep their businesses afloat, and many failed. The J. W. Langdale Company itself never made enough profit to afford payment of dividends to its stockholders until after World War II. The first dividends came only in the 1950s, after the growing market for pulpwood and saw-timber bolstered profits.[22]

Turpentine workers for the J. W. Langdale Company, as was true generally in the industry, had to be fed out of the company commissary. John J. negotiated from time to time with the naval stores factors in Jacksonville to get operating money. One arrangement, resembling a barter transaction, required the Langdales to ship a certain quantity of rosin and turpentine to the factors; in return they sent groceries in a boxcar to Council for off-loading into the commissary.[23]

There being no refrigeration, fresh meat could not be kept. To supply this necessity, John J. had cows slaughtered in the woods and the meat brought to the commissary. He then sold the beef or otherwise distributed it to the hands before it spoiled. Sometimes John dried meat by laying it in the sun on hardware cloth stretched between timbers and covering it with pepper, spices, and meal to keep insects away. Such meat was very hard on the outside, but edible.

Under John J.'s management, livestock continued to play an important role in the J. W. Langdale Company business. By 1992, however, this aspect of the business had been phased out.[24] From the time he was old enough John J., Jr. remembered helping with the livestock. Each spring they rounded up the cattle, separated the steers from the herd and sold them. They marked the other calves for identification and released them to run free until the next spring. "Our mark was two under bits and a split," recalled John J., Jr.

To handle the swine enterprise, they used about sixty traps especially designed to capture wild hogs. Such a trap consisted of a two-section pen with a trapdoor and another door on the side. The whole trapping and sorting operation took six days. First, corn as bait attracted the hogs, and the trapdoor dumped them into the first pen. After three days, the trappers—John J., Jr. and others—went to the trap, drove the captured hogs into the secondary pen, and reset the trap. The hogs in the secondary pen made noise, attracting other hogs that spotted the corn and took the bait. After three more days, the trappers returned, took the hogs they

---

[21] Langdale, JWL Interview 14.

[22] Ibid.

[23] Langdale, JJLJr Interview 01.

[24] Langdale, JJLJr Interview 1991.

wanted to sell, and released those they wanted to keep. Those taken to market brought only ten to fifteen cents per pound. To load the selected hogs into cages on wagons for transport out of the woods, the trappers did not use a chute. They simply grabbed these wild, toothy creatures, some of them grown hogs weighing 250 pounds, pulled them out of the pen over the fence (or through a door in the fence), and placed them into the cages. This job might have merited hazardous-duty pay, but did not generate it.[25]

In addition to turpentine and livestock, the J. W. Langdale Company continued to produce timber products, notably crossties. Occasionally, also, John J. brought a sawmill onto the estate to saw lumber, so there was some involvement in lumber production.

Notwithstanding the challenges of keeping the J. W. Langdale Company afloat in the 1910s, 1920s, and 1930s, John J. enjoyed business. He liked dealing with his labor, and he found pleasure in raising and harvesting timber. In fact, he liked all aspects of forestry, except coping with wildfires.

A Controlled Burn. Fire is typically set to back into the wind, keeping flames low and fire movement slow across the land. TLC.

Wildfires could originate in several ways. A controlled burn that got out of hand could lead to a wildfire. This hazard was inherent in the turpentine business because, to gain access to the pine trees, producers needed to burn out underbrush, weeds, and briars each year. The controlled burn also removed some undesirable trees.

More often, however, John J. found that wildfires started on somebody else's land and spread to Langdale property. People in this area had always been in the practice of burning the woods each year to stimulate the growth of new grass for their livestock. In the period before fences confined all livestock to their owners' property, it might not seem like a problem to some neighbors for their fires to

---

[25] Langdale, JJLJr Interview 01 ; Langdale, JJLJr Interview 1991.

spread and create the conditions for new grass on adjoining land owned by someone else. Their cows could eat that grass, too.

Still another possible threat of wildfire came from bootleggers. Manufacturers of non-tax-paid liquor found one market among workers in the turpentine and timber camps of south Georgia. Sometimes they even peddled small quantities of the stuff, like peanuts or fruit, on the trains that stopped at Fargo. They shipped some of their product in fast, specially-modified cars to such cities as Macon, Columbus, and Atlanta.

Whatever the market, illegal distilleries had to be hidden, and a bootlegger might choose to locate his still on someone else's land, if he considered it safe from discovery. Some of the J. W. Langdale Company land, being distant from populated areas and fairly inaccessible, must have appeared attractive to such persons. Some liquor stills, mostly small ones, did show up on Langdale land. Whether large or small, they usually did not stay in one place very long. After about two weeks, typically, their owners moved them. Paths to stills could too easily be detected by revenue agents.

The era of really large moonshine stills came in the two or three decades after World War II. According to reports, one of these might have seven tanks about six by eight by four feet deep. Each tank, capped by a worm, could have a burner beneath it. In the summer a batch might cook off every day, with each tank producing twenty-five to thirty five-gallon jugs of moonshine.

The possibility of illegal stills on the land created a dilemma for John J. and for any large landowner who might face the same situation. First, the very existence of a still, requiring fire for the distillation process, brought the possibility of an accidental wildfire. Second, a confrontation with the illegal operator or reporting him to the authorities might lead to retaliation. Retribution could come in the form of personal violence, destruction of vehicles and physical property, or, most likely, intentionally-set fires that could wipe out a forest and ruin the operator involved.

Considering the alternatives, the Langdales chose to see no evil and hear no evil. On the one hand, they cooperated with law enforcement officials when asked. On the other hand, they looked for no still, tried to avoid seeing a still, kept their distance from any suspected still, reported no still, and rejoiced when any still on their land closed down and moved to somebody else's property. The farther away, the better.

Always conscious of the fire hazards, including occasional lightning fires, John J. and other forest farmers of this era spent much of their time worrying about and working to prevent wildfires. Sometimes, in very dry years, he spent nights in the woods to keep a watch for possible fires.

John J. and Rosalie became the parents of two children, Rose, born in 1925, and John J., Jr., born in 1927. Rose Langdale married David Johnson and moved to

Tallahassee. Her brother prepared to follow in his father's footsteps in the forest products business.

John J., Jr. attended school in Fargo and Homerville, then went to Georgia Military School for his final year of high school. In February 1945, preferring not to be drafted into the army, he enlisted in the Navy and served for about eighteen months.

John J. Langdale Jr.,
1965. TLC.

John J., Jr. then resumed his education. He started at the Savannah division of the University of Georgia in 1947, transferred to the main campus at Athens the next year, and earned a forestry degree from the University of Georgia in 1951. He returned to work at Council with his father until John J. died in 1955. John J., Jr. then succeeded his father as president and manager of the J. W. Langdale Company and served in this capacity until 1965. In the meantime, John J., Jr. had married Virginia McDonald. He and Virginia had two sons, Jay and Joe.[26]

At the invitation of his cousin, Harley Langdale, Jr., John J., Jr. moved to Valdosta to become chief forester and land manager for the Langdale Company in 1965. He served in that capacity until his retirement in the late 1990s. Subsequently, he and his family sold their interest in the J. W. Langdale Company and Langdale Woodlands to the Langdale Company.

In summary, after John Wesley Langdale's death his eldest son, John J., managed the estate, which was incorporated in 1919 with John Wesley's three sons as stockholders. During his lifetime John J. Langdale played a major and positive role in political and civic affairs in and around Homerville, Georgia. John J. continued his father's livestock business, tried to stay out of trouble with moonshiners, fought against wildfires, and struggled with the ups-and-downs of the turpentine business. John J. and his wife, Rosalie Cornelius, had two children to survive them, Rose and John J., Jr.

---

[26] Ibid.

At his death in 1955 John J.'s son, John J., Jr., took his place as president of the J. W. Langdale Company. John J., Jr. later took an executive position with the Langdale Company, a separate entity from the J. W. Langdale Company, as vice president and land manager. He and his wife, Virginia McDonald, had two sons, Jay and Joe, who were in college in the late-1990s. After retirement, John J. and his family sold their J. W. Langdale Company and Langdale Woodlands shares to the Langdale Company.

Except for John J. and his family, the remainder of John Wesley Langdale's children and his widow, Nancy, moved to Valdosta within a year or so after his death. Nancy Burnsed Langdale survived her husband for only a year, dying suddenly of a stroke. The eldest daughter, Sadie, married Preston Sandlin. The younger two daughters, Nan and Susie, soon went off to college in Cleveland, Tennessee. They both married men surnamed Campbell from that area of Tennessee.

For the remainder of their lives, Noah and Harley made their homes in Valdosta. Although not examined in this account, Noah engaged in several businesses, including turpentine, wholesale groceries, and building materials. He also ran successfully for political office in Valdosta, serving on the city council. His daughter, Marguerite Langdale Pizer, succeeded as an attorney in Washington DC, and his son, Noah N. Langdale, Jr., became a football hero, a lawyer, a teacher, president of Georgia State University, and a noted orator. It is the story of Harley, the youngest son of John Wesley Langdale, to which we now turn.

5

The Harley Langdale Family in Valdosta

Great things were happening in 1912. While the country was busy narrowly electing Woodrow Wilson as the first Democratic president of the twentieth century, young Harley Langdale was starting a new phase of his life in Valdosta, Georgia. Fresh out of Mercer Law School, he had a new legal practice, a new car, and a room at Brinson's Boarding House. At Brinson's he met a young woman from Virginia whom he courted assiduously until she consented to become his wife. She was Thalia Maude Lee.

Born 14 February 1885, Thalia Lee was about three years older than Harley. She was in the millinery trade. A local store, Burruss's,[1] needing a professional milliner, or hat-maker, had brought her on temporary assignment from Virginia to Valdosta.[2]

Thalia was the daughter of Silas Watkins Lee of Gretna, Virginia, near Lynchburg. Although unrelated to the family of General Robert E. Lee, Silas served in Lee's army at the time of the general's surrender at Appomattox Courthouse. Gretna being very near Appomattox, Silas Lee simply walked home to his farm after the surrender.

Silas Watkins Lee made his living as a farmer, a shoemaker, and in later years, as a Baptist lay preacher. He sometimes wrote religious verse, and at least two of his poems have survived. In 1990 Silas's grandson, John W., attempted to set his Grandfather Lee's verses to music. One of them proved too difficult, but the other, the longer one, fell right into place. The shorter poem, as John said, "didn't have any meter, and I couldn't do anything with it. So I took the longer piece that

---

[1] John W. Langdale, "Memorandum, with Attachment, to John Lancaster," in author's files (Valdosta GA).

[2] Langdale, JWL Interview 14.

he did and within an hour the music just came to me out of that. And I wrote it down using a little keyboard I borrowed from my granddaughter and picked out the melody to that song."[3] In January 1991, by request of the choir director, he performed the song as a solo at Valdosta's First Baptist Church.

Thalia Maude Lee Langdale, 1913. TLF.

In 1900, Silas Lee died, leaving his wife, Martha Senie Coleman Lee, a widow at an early age. Crippled by arthritis and unable to work, Martha moved with her three children, Thalia, Richard Ivey, and Ernest, to Lynchburg, where the children sought employment. Thalia, who was fifteen at her father's death, eventually found work in the millinery department of a large store. There she came to the attention of a couple named Burroughs who traveled around the country training people in the millinery craft. They took her with them to New York for more training, and afterward sent her for specified periods of time to various stores that requested the service. She fashioned hats for the ladies to match their dresses and often modeled the hats she made. Thalia was a lovely young woman who accumulated friends easily wherever she went, and she kept in contact with some of these friends for many years.[4]

Assigned to Valdosta and staying at the Brinson House, she soon became acquainted with the young lawyer, Harley Langdale. Thalia also became a good friend of Mildred Brinson, daughter of the owners. At that time, Mildred was dating a lawyer named Dukes—they called him Colonel Dukes—whom she

---

[3] Ibid.
[4] Miller, VLM Interview 01.

eventually married. It worked out that Mildred and her husband-to-be double-dated sometimes with Harley and Thalia. At least they went for drives together in Harley's stylish new open car.[5]

Martha Lee with Ernest and Thalia, 1908-09. TLF.

After completing her tour of duty in Valdosta, Thalia returned to Lynchburg. Harley wrote to her, and she responded. It took Judge eleven months to persuade Thalia to marry him.[6] Finally, he went to Lynchburg, and they were married there. They honeymooned in North Carolina, their daughter, Virginia recalled.[7] Harley may not have suspected at the time, but he had strong competition for Thalia's hand. Thalia told Virginia about this toward the end of her life, after Judge's death. There was another man who proposed marriage to Thalia. He impressed her with gifts, including several pieces of jewelry. It was while Thalia was showing Virginia some of her jewelry that she confided this to her daughter.[8]

So why did Thalia choose Harley? "He was handsome," said Virginia. Besides that, "he was so aggressive that it almost overwhelmed her. She may not have ever known a male figure who was so positive and aggressive as he was. He could be very persuasive and very charming. I tell you, she loved him, and she did everything she could that would please him and help him in what he wanted to do."[9]

The assertiveness and confidence with which Harley courted Thalia Lee presumably owed much to his natural personality. As an elderly man talking with

---

[5] Ibid.

[6] "They've Promoted Pine Trees," *Valdosta Daily Times*, 26 June 1970.

[7] Miller, VLM Interview 01.

[8] Ibid.

[9] Ibid.

his daughter many years later, however, "he attributed a lot of it to the encouragement he got from his grandmother—Grandma Betty." "He said she really encouraged him. See, he was the youngest of the boys, and evidently she took him under her wing."[10] Whatever the explanation, Harley clearly saw in Thalia the woman he wanted for his wife.

He chose well. Thalia, as her daughter remembered, "had a strong sense of duty." If anyone were to ask her what she liked to do, she would have replied that she liked doing for other people. "She probably wouldn't tell you what she really loved to do." "You see, said Virginia, "Mama was a nurturing person. She was nurturing us and Granny and all these other people all the time. Daddy had not a worry as far as anything going along smoothly at home."[11]

Virginia remembered her mother as "composed." She wasn't a person who would waiver after she made up her mind." People always knew where she stood on an issue. Sometimes, after patiently enduring much for the sake of Judge Harley, "she'd let him know." It may not have altered his course, "but anyway it got it out of her system."[12]

Thalia loved people and enjoyed doing things with others. She had many friends. Once, Virginia remembered, Thalia and several other ladies took swimming lessons together from a young man Virginia was dating. Thalia and her friends also worked on little projects, such as refinishing furniture. Later, after the children had left home, she enjoyed several trips that she and Judge took with Eileen and Harley, Jr. The trips were carefree times that Thalia enjoyed immensely. After Virginia graduated from college, her mother and she, plus some of Virginia's friends, went on a trip to Williamsburg, Virginia, and other places in that area. That was the first time, as Virginia recalled, that Thalia ever went out of town without either Judge Harley or Granny Lee with her. On this occasion, she arranged for a young woman from Tifton to stay with Granny Lee.[13]

Thalia's mother, Granny Lee, as the Langdale children called her, moved to Valdosta from Lynchburg when Harley, Jr. was a baby and spent most of the remainder of her days with her daughter's family in Valdosta. She died in 1942.

Granny Lee had a hearing problem. At one time, she used an ear trumpet and evidently supplemented its effect with lip reading. This is apparent for, as Virginia recalled, she could hear best when the speaker stood directly in front and spoke straight into her face. Eventually, she replaced the ear trumpet with a hearing aid.[14]

Victorian in dress and manner, Granny Lee spent much of her time knitting or sewing. She read the Bible, often with one of the children on her lap, and

---

[10] Ibid.
[11] Ibid.
[12] Ibid.
[13] Ibid.
[14] Ibid.

sometimes read the newspaper, using a magnifying glass. She never read novels. Hobbled by arthritis, she used a cane and walked no more than necessary. The arthritis kept her from negotiating the long, steep steps to First Baptist Church, where Thalia and the children attended. She rarely left the house, although, once in a while, Thalia would get her into the car and take her for a ride. She enjoyed the attention she received on her birthdays, which Thalia and the children celebrated with cake and candles.[15]

"She was a kind, sweet person," Virginia remembered. The children, mostly Virginia and John, took turns looking after their grandmother in the afternoons when they came in from school. This gave Thalia an opportunity to attend church meetings, run errands, and get together sometimes with friends. Granny Lee had a large brass bell which she rang if she needed assistance. The rule was that the child on duty should stay close enough that Granny's bell could be heard if she rang it upstairs. Sometimes, during high school and before, Virginia brought a friend home from school, and while they studied or made candy, they kept an ear open in case Granny sounded her bell. Virginia used to write letters for her grandmother, and when Virginia was twelve, she escorted her grandmother, who was then in her eighties and walking with crutches, to visit her family in Lynchburg. They traveled by train.[16]

Judge Harley accepted his mother-in law's permanent presence in their home with a little reluctance. At a time of tight money, her living there brought extra expense and other complications. Caring for her absorbed much of the family's energies. He probably thought his wife's brother, who was a supervisor in a shoe factory in Lynchburg, VA, should share the care-giving duties and keep her part of the time. Judge never said anything about this in front of the children, but appeared sometimes to express displeasure by ignoring his mother-in-law. The boys noticed and, to some degree, assumed their father's attitude out of loyalty to him. Of the children, Virginia was closest to their grandmother. Mrs. Lee gave no sign she noticed or was bothered by Judge's attitude.[17] Whatever tensions resulted from Granny Lee's presence in their home, the children never heard their parents discuss the issue.[18]

Harley and Thalia Lee Langdale became the parents of four children, the first of whom they named Harley, Jr. Two and a half years after the birth of Harley, Jr., a second son, John, came, and another two years brought a sister, Virginia. Two years later, brother Billy's arrival completed the family.[19]

When it came time for the delivery of her first child, Thalia returned for that purpose to her family's home in Lynchburg, Virginia. She stayed there for about a

---

[15] Langdale, JWL Interview 14.

[16] Miller, VLM Interview 01.

[17] Langdale, JWL Interview 14.

[18] Ibid.

[19] Ibid.

month, where the Lee family physician, Dr. Ramsey, attended her. So Harley, Jr. was a Virginian by birth.[20]

Birthplace of Harley Langdale Jr., Lynchburg, Virginia. TLF.

The second son, John, was born in Valdosta in the home his parents rented on Patterson Street. That house, located at the southeast corner of Patterson and Force Street, was in 2002 the site of a retail store, Betty Webb's Collectibles.[21] In those days, physicians made house calls, and Dr. Wilson, a general physician who lived about two blocks down the street, attended Thalia Langdale at the birth of John. Virginia, too, was born while the Langdales lived in this house.

The Langdales moved from Patterson Street when Harley, Jr. was about five and John W. was about two years old. Their father rented a place at 316 E. Hill Avenue, which was next door to where Church's Fried Chicken was located in 2000.[22] While they lived there, around 1920 to 1926, Judge Harley bought the family's first radio, an RKO cabinet model. Judge enjoyed listening to it, picking up a station out of Cincinnati, Ohio.[23]

Although the Hill Avenue address is in a commercial area today, that was not so in the early 1920s. In those days, one found Valdosta's business center near the intersection of Patterson with Central Avenue or Hill Avenue. The northern limit of commercial stores extended perhaps a block north of Valley Street. As one traveled from downtown toward the east on Hill Avenue, Lee Street marked the division between commercial and residential areas. There, on the corner of Hill Avenue and Lee Street, stood Dan's Grocery, which had a candy counter that

---

[20] Langdale, HLJr Interview 1991.
[21] Langdale, JWL Interview 14.
[22] Ibid.
[23] Langdale, JWL Interview 14. ; Langdale, "JWL to JEL Memo."

attracted the boys' interest. They liked to go there for a jawbreaker or a sucker, when they had a penny.[24]

Harley Langdale Jr. as Infant & Young Child. TLF.

The home on Hill Avenue had a dirt yard, not a grass lawn. The soil was a white, sandy loam, as John W. remembered. Not a very large yard, either, and Judge Harley had a dog pen in the back yard in which he kept one or two dogs. "You would call it a poverty-stricken area today," said John W. "We accepted it."[25] In 1995 he recalled that, at about age four, he fell off the porch of that house and hit his head on a piece of granite lying on the ground. This was perhaps his earliest recollection of childhood. Later, when John W., whom the family called Bud, made some mistake growing up, they often joked about this accident. That's what's wrong with Bud, they would say. He fell off the porch and broke his head.

For years the family also poked gentle fun at John W. about a craving for peanuts he displayed at age four, the year Judge tried dirt farming. At peanut harvesting time, Judge brought home a huge bag of raw peanuts. They were raw, but too dry to boil. John loved those peanuts. He filled up a little cup with them and went around the house eating raw peanuts and dropping hulls on the floor. His mother scolded him for scattering hulls all around. Family members reminded him when he was older that he would select a peanut to eat, try it, and, if it was not good, throw it down, declaring "No good peanut."[26] His mother enjoyed re-telling this story. As time went by, when John W. made a mistake, they would tease him,

---

[24] Langdale, JWL Interview 14.

[25] Ibid.

[26] Ibid.; Langdale, JWL Interview 14.

saying, "That must be what's wrong with Bud. He had too many peanuts when he was young."[27]

Children of Harley and Thalia Langdale. Virginia, Billy, Harley Jr., and John W. Langdale in April 1923. Presumably, this was on the porch of the rented house on Hill Avenue, since the date was in the middle of the period when they lived there. TLF.

On Hill Avenue, a shell-shocked veteran of World War I, a Mr. Shinholster, lived next door to the Langdales on the side toward town. In addition to a German Lugar pistol that would not shoot, Mr. Shinholster had a BB gun, an air rifle that afforded him his main recreation. He often sat on his back porch shooting at targets, which included tin cans and sparrows. In those pre-conservation years, nobody had a second thought about shooting birds at any opportunity. Little John W. took an interest in this man and his air rifle, visited him, and occasionally received the privilege of shooting the BB gun.[28]

At this time, Valdosta had a street railway system. One line ran out Hill Avenue as far east as Bray's lumber mill. There the car turned around and traveled west. John W. remembered riding the streetcar and, once, overcome with curiosity, he and an accomplice placed a penny on the track to see what would happen to it as the streetcar ran over it. The result: "It mashed it pretty flat."[29]

Before starting regular school, John W. went to kindergarten. A lovely young woman named Claudia Jackson, the daughter of a prominent Valdosta lumberman, operated the kindergarten at the corner of Webster and Troop Streets. Several years later, Claudia took a Sunday school class at First Baptist that included John among its members. John W. admired Claudia for her beauty of person and spirit. "She was the one who witnessed to me when I was nine years old and told me about how to get to heaven," remembered John W. "And I give credit to Claudia and to

---

[27] Langdale, JWL Interview 14. ; Miller, VLM Interview 01.

[28] Langdale, JWL Interview 14. ; Langdale, "JWL to JEL Memo."

[29] Langdale, JWL Interview 14.

another woman named Leola Smith who took charge at BYPU [Baptist Young People's Union]." "And I accepted Christ at age nine because of those two people."[30]

John's connection with Claudia's family continued many years later. After returning from World War II and before his marriage, John W. became a Sunday school teacher at First Baptist, as Claudia had been when he was nine. She had long since married and now had children, one of whom, Billy Finley, happened to be in his class. John W. taught Billy and the other boys the basics of taxidermy, which he had learned as a boy. John recalled in 1995 how he and his Sunday school boys killed a squirrel and proceeded to skin and mount it at the Jackson-Finley home at 508 E. Moore Street, next door to the former Shoney's Restaurant on Ashley Street.

After kindergarten with Claudia Jackson, John W. attended Central Grammar School, a red brick structure located where the First Baptist Church now has its Fellowship Hall parking lot. Every day, from his home on East Hill, he walked through the downtown area to school and back. Sometimes he found exciting things to watch, as when they first started construction of the Daniel Ashley Hotel. Walking along Hill Avenue on the north side, he stopped to observe and marvel at what seemed to him a skyscraper under construction across the street.

The boys, Harley, Jr., John W., and young Billy, went barefoot most of the time, even during the winter, except for very cold days, and they wore overalls. "We didn't have to buy them pre-faded," remembered John W. with a laugh, "they got that way naturally." The boys liked wearing overalls and, on Sundays, always rejoiced to get home from Sunday school and church to shed their dress-up clothes and get back into their denim outfits.[31]

In July 1926, when Harley, Jr. was about eleven, John W. about nine Virginia about five, and Billy about three, the Langdales moved to 700 North Patterson Street, partly, as Virginia recalled, to be a little closer to the schools the children were attending. This residence, known to some as the Ashley House, belonged to Mayor J. D. Ashley at that time and was in 2001 the location of the Robert Cork law firm. Judge paid rent of $100 per month.

Virginia, who had not yet begun first grade, remembered this place vividly. "It sat up off the ground and had that gray powdery sand underneath the house," and we could go under there and play and hide, and get dirty," she recalled. There were "doodle bugs" under this house, small grayish bugs that lived in the soil and could be found at the bottom of tiny round indentations. The children sometimes amused themselves by stirring (doodling) with a small stick or straw in these soil-dimples and chanting a little rhyme, something like this: "Doodle-bug, Doodle-bug,

---

[30] Ibid.
[31] Ibid.

where've you been? Around the world and goin' agin." When the doodle-bug emerged, it was time to start over with another doodle-bug hole.

"That was the nicest house we had had,"[32] said Virginia. It had a large master bedroom on the front for Judge Harley and Thalia. On cold mornings Virginia went in her parents' room to get dressed by the fire. Although every room had a fireplace, that was the only fire they had for dressing. Harley, Jr. and John W. usually kindled the fires. This house included a solarium with a brick or tile floor where Thalia kept plants and a sunroom on the side toward North Street where the Langdales liked to sit. Harley, Jr., John W., and Billy shared a room, and Virginia slept in Granny Lee's room.

The family had a radio and, in a booth downstairs, a telephone. At night, if the telephone rang, someone had to rush downstairs to the phone booth. Nighttime calls frightened Thalia because she worried that Judge had had an automobile accident somewhere. He often came in late from a day-trip to one of the Florida turpentine camps. He drove often to his turpentine camp located between Savannah and Charleston, sometimes staying overnight. Roads were narrow and, before the legislature required farmers to fence in their livestock, one never knew when a cow or a hog would wander onto the road.

According to Virginia, "Mama was always afraid he would have a wreck, which he did. If there was a place to get stuck, he got stuck. My recollection is that he didn't ever get himself out. He usually just sat back and smoked his cigar and waited for somebody to come help him get out."[33] Well, maybe he sometimes put some palmetto branches down to get out, she conceded.

One thing that impressed Virginia about traveling with her father was that "He loved to kill snakes in the road. He never carried a gun, so far as I knew, when he was carrying us around, but he would stop and make a big thing over killing that snake with an old rotted limb."[34]

Although the Ashley house exceeded by far the spaciousness of their former home on Hill Avenue, the Langdales did not necessarily have more room for themselves. For one thing, they often had company, such as Judge Harley's sisters, other relatives and, occasionally, some of Judge's friends or clients from Clinch or Echols County. Once in a while a cousin, a client, or a turpentine business associate whom Judge brought to dinner slept over before returning home. Many years later Thalia related to her daughter how difficult it had been for her to deal with all these unexpected guests, but, at the time, she kept quiet about it.

In addition to Judge's family and business guests, the Langdales had other people in the house. They rented a room to college girls, two at a time, enrolled at Georgia State Womans College, a few blocks up Patterson Street. By the late

[32] Miller, VLM Interview 01.
[33] Ibid.
[34] Ibid.

1920s, Harley, Jr. had reached the age when he began to notice these young women. "Harley can name all the girls that stayed there," observed Virginia. [35]

In 1931, Judge Harley bought his first house to live in and moved his family there in the month of April. Located at 1006 N. Patterson, and of solid brick construction, it had belonged previously to Mr. Will Strickland. Judge still owned this house when he died in 1972. In addition to a kitchen, breakfast room, dining room, and living room, it had four bedrooms and a sleeping porch upstairs. This is where the family lived when Harley, John, Virginia, and Billy attended Valdosta High School. When John came back from the Navy, still single, in 1945, he returned to live with his parents in this house. Billy's son, William P. Langdale, Jr. an attorney, owned it in 2001. [36]

Among the Langdale children, no question ever existed about who held authority. Seniority ruled. From earliest childhood, John W. always accepted the leadership of his older brother, Harley, Jr. "I always had a lot of respect for Harley," he recalled. 'He taught me a lot, and I followed Harley on a lot of things during those early days." Sibling rivalry between the two boys rarely appeared. As John put it, Harley, Jr. "was entitled to more respect than I was. He was the senior." Harley generally led in deciding what games and activities the boys would engage in.

As young children, Harley, Jr. and John W. liked to play common childhood games, such as Hide and Seek. A little later, they played a variation on that game, which they called "Kick the Can." As John W. described it, "You would stack up five or six empty cans, and on the signal everybody would run and hide, except the one who was 'it.' The one who was 'it' had to find one of the hidden players, call out the discovery, and then get back and touch that stack of cans before the one he discovered could run back and kick 'em down. Now, if any one of those who were hidden could get back and kick the cans before the one who was 'it' could go back and touch 'em, then he who was 'it' had to remain 'it.' It was a game that kept us occupied and was inexpensive."

They also played Cowboys and Indians. Once Santa Claus brought John a cowboy suit for Christmas, and another time, an Indian suit. [37]

Harley, Jr. and John W. were very close. As John put it, "I probably got most of my general education from Harley—things that you learn that you don't get in school. I had a lot of respect for Harley. Even as a child, Harley was pretty serious. What he said I knew I could well rely on." [38]

There was one time, however, when Harley, Jr. gave his little brother a hard time. Harley had been in school a couple of years and John W. had still not learned to read. Opening up the local newspaper, the Valdosta *Times*, eight-year-old

---

[35] Ibid.

[36] Langdale, JWL Interview 14 ; Langdale, "JWL to JEL Memo."

[37] Langdale, JWL Interview 14.

[38] Ibid.

Harley assumed his most adult posture and pretended to read. Then, with great seriousness, he said, "Well, I see in the paper that Bud Langdale is dead." John ran to his mother and complained, "Mama, Harley says I'm dead. I ain't dead, mama." Seeing the effectiveness of his stunt, Harley, Jr. did it a few more times, tormenting his little brother, but this was rare behavior for him. John W. could not remember another example of such sibling abuse on Harley's part.[39]

Harley, Jr. may have been serious and mature for his age, but, like any boy, he occasionally crossed the line of acceptable conduct. His sister, Virginia, recalled once when the two older boys were preparing to travel alone to visit their aunts in Cleveland, Tennessee. Their mother sent Harley, Jr. to the barbershop to get a haircut. She wanted him well groomed for the trip. He came back with his hair almost shaved off "and made some smart remark that he got a haircut like he wanted."[40] Thalia was most upset. Harley, Jr. had the prettiest hair, she thought, and now he had ruined it.

Another time Harley, Jr., as a small child, got into a bind by putting his head where he shouldn't. Climbing around on the iron bed, he stuck his head in between two spokes in the headboard. Thalia had to call Judge home from the office to extricate him.[41]

Like most parents of their time, Judge Harley and Thalia Langdale emphasized punishment, rather than rewards, in managing their children. Wrongdoing usually resulted in a spanking or switching. Occasionally, however, the boys found themselves confined to the house, denied outside playing privileges, or some lesser punishment. At school, besides the risk of spankings, misbehaving children sometimes had to stand in the corner.[42]

In later years, all four children agreed that their mother deserved a major share of the credit for their moral upbringing. She took them to church and she was around perhaps ninety percent of the time, compared to their father's ten percent. Ten percent, though, was enough for Judge Harley to exert a strong influence. He was "so stern in being the dominant male,"[43] and the punishments he gave had a powerful deterrent effect on inclinations to misbehave.

As the eldest, Harley, Jr. took the greatest heat from their father. Judge Harley expected more of him than of the other children. Harley, Jr. got the most whippings, John W. recalled. "They didn't need to give me as many because I was observing the pain and suffering on his part and it was hurting me too. But he got several, and Daddy was stern with us. Of course, Daddy was not there very often,

---

[39] Ibid.

[40] Miller, VLM Interview 01.

[41] Ibid.

[42] Langdale, JWL Interview 14.

[43] Ibid.

but when he would get home and Mama would report to him what had occurred, he would administer the needed punishment with his belt, and it was effective."[44]

Although Harley, Sr. usually delivered the punishment to the children, occasionally Thalia did so in his absence. Instead of a belt, she preferred a small camphor switch. "It was not big, but it would sting you," recalled John.[45]

When their sister, Virginia, arrived to join the family, the relationship between the two older boys changed little. They usually did not play with their little sister because she was much younger, and, besides, boys in those days avoided playing with girls, lest they be judged "sissy." Virginia had her own playmates, other girls from the neighborhood and from school, with whom she spent time.

Virginia described her childhood as happy. The four Langdale children got along well, she said, with a minimum of fussing and bickering as they were growing up. They respected and obeyed their father, who almost never raised his voice in dealing with them. The children understood the behavior he expected of them and did not question it. "Daddies weren't buddy-buddy back then; they were in control," said Virginia. Relations between the four siblings have grown closer as they have aged, she observed, although they are less demonstrative than many families.[46]

In childhood, Virginia spent more time with Billy than with the older boys and felt closer to him. Harley, Jr. and John W. had an older set of friends. Among them were the Dukes boys, sons of Mildred Brinson Dukes, with whom Thalia had become friends when she lived for a while at the Brinson House before her marriage. The Dukes brothers joined Harley and John at hunting and fishing. There were three Dukes brothers, one each about the age of Harley, John, and Billy. Virginia knew Billy's friends better because they came around the house more.

Virginia noticed the different personalities of her brothers. "Billy was the baby," she said, "and everybody favored him." "Harley wanted to have a good time. He didn't take to the books until he got into forestry."[47] Billy followed Harley's example in finding more interesting things to do than schoolwork. John was different. "Bud was sort of quiet and always a little old man," she said. Thinner in physique compared to Harley, and especially compared to the robust Billy, John appeared more introspective and reflective. He and Virginia did their homework dutifully, but Thalia had to keep after the other two.

As for Virginia, she was quiet. She liked to read, and she had a favorite tree where she could be alone and enjoy her books. In the afternoons after school, she sometimes took an apple to munch on and headed for her special tree.

---

[44] Ibid.

[45] Ibid.

[46] Miller, VLM Interview 01.

[47] Ibid.

At the age of twelve, Virginia experienced one of the sad events of her life. When living at 700 North Patterson, the Langdales had a neighbor couple named Ed and Suzie Oliver, who had moved to Valdosta from Abbeville, Georgia. The Olivers had one child, a daughter of Virginia's age, who became her closest friend, her "bosom buddy." When Virginia wanted to get away from all the boys, she went to play with her friend at the Oliver house. Sometimes her friend preferred to play at Virginia's, for she considered it more exciting. Sadly, when they were twelve, in the sixth grade, this girl became sick and died with Scarlet Fever and Diphtheria. For Virginia, it was like losing a sister.

Virginia went to grammar school on Adair Street and then, following in the footsteps of her older brothers, went to junior high in sixth grade. Also, like her brothers, she remembered playing "Kick the Can." She and her friends also played "Hop-Scotch" and "May I."[48]

High school left Virginia with good memories. She and her friends felt safe and free to go places and do things that in more recent times would be considered unsafe. At that time they needed no driver's license. She and others could pile in a car and ride down to Twin Lakes, several miles south of town. Other times they strolled around Brookwood Park, rode bicycles, or skated down the sidewalk. She felt fortunate to have grown up in a town the size of Valdosta at a time that permitted such freedom.

From the standpoint of recreation, during high school the Langdale children had good reason to count their blessings. Their father owned memberships in the Valdosta Country Club, Ocean Pond, and other private clubs. With these memberships, and the large amount of land Judge Harley owned by this time, the boys and Virginia had no shortage of outdoor recreational opportunities.[49]

Sometimes the boys went with their father and his friends to the hunting camp the Langdales had near Big Pond. Their Aunt Rosalie had named this camp Jonohala, using the first two letters of the names John, Noah, Harley, and Langdale. As its main building, Camp Jonohala had a rough, uninsulated, one-room frame structure used for sleeping. About 24 by 30 feet, it could accommodate about sixteen cots. Unable to sleep because of the volume of snoring in this place, Judge later built himself a private sleeping house about 10 by 12 feet in size. A separate shed served as a kitchen and dining room for the camp.[50]

John W. recalled that, as a boy, he attended hunts there with his father, his Uncle Noah, and others. They used to position standing hunters around the Big Pond and send someone into the pond with dogs to drive deer out to the standers. This dog-hunting technique, though illegal in Lowndes County, met the law's requirements in Clinch County. As effective a hunting system as it was, it

---

[48] Ibid.

[49] Ibid.

[50] Langdale, JWL Interview 14.

sometimes failed. Because Big Pond was so large, a deer could in some cases elude the dogs and avoid being driven into range of the hunters.

In later years, starting right after World War II, Judge held annual deer hunts at Jonohala to start the deer season. These events usually encompassed two days, including the first Saturday of the season. Judge invited friends and business associates to these, and he paid all expenses. For subsequent hunts during the season, guests participated on a dutch-treat basis. Naturally, the first hunt of the season, for which Judge paid all costs, was the most popular.

Whereas recreation for the boys typically involved hunting or fishing, their sister, Virginia, had more parties. Thalia liked to give parties, occasionally for the boys, but more frequently for Virginia, and especially on her birthdays. Virginia recalled that Ocean Pond became the site of one of her most elaborate birthday celebrations. On this occasion Thalia invited more than fifty of Virginia's friends to celebrate her fourteenth birthday. Mrs. Langdale also hired Valdosta's premier professional photographer, Veran O. Blackburn, to photograph the party guests.[51]

Harley Jr., Teenaged Fisherman. Judge Harley encouraged his boys to hunt and fish, considering it a means of directing their energies into wholesome channels. TLF.

Not only did Virginia have more parties than the boys, John W. recalled, but she also had more overnight company. Sometimes the boys had friends to stay overnight, such as Boy Scouts with whom they also went camping, but it happened infrequently. With four children in the house, one room assigned to Virginia, and their grandmother staying with them from around 1920 until her death in 1942,

---

[51] Miller, VLM Interview 01.

the place seemed pretty crowded, even without overnight visitors. They could put pallets on the floor to accommodate guests, but seldom did.[52]

Even though she had more parties and more friends visiting overnight, Virginia remembered the Langdale home, in which she was the only girl, as "male-oriented." As she put it, "Daddy was teaching the boys about things, the woods and all that. He didn't see any reason to teach me, you know." "He never did think women needed to know about the business at all." "I think his idea was that you take care of the women and don't let them know what's going on." Like his father, John Wesley, Judge had a clear idea of the proper roles of men and women. Men made a living, and women kept the home. Virginia would probably have liked a little less protection and a little more involvement in the family business.[53]

An illustration of what Virginia meant by "male-oriented" is the way she chose to attend Shorter College, or rather, her father and brother chose for her to go there. As she recalled, a lady representing Shorter came over from Quitman. "She came and Daddy was very impressed with her. Harley was impressed. He had known a girl who went to Shorter. I never did go to see it like they do now. They just put me on the train and I just went. Stayed four years." "I never questioned it. They wanted me to go and I thought that was fine. I thought that was what you did."[54]

Although she had little choice about going to Shorter, she enjoyed the school. "I had four very happy years and it was very meaningful," she said, "but I came out not knowing how to do anything. I took a little business course after that."[55]

Among the four Langdale children, the closest bond existed between Harley, Jr. and John W. From early childhood they were a twosome. Yet even this very tight relationship had its limitations. There were things that each did not know about the other. For example, John W. never knew until 1995 the story of the young Harley's unauthorized departure from the Citadel and his return there after a stern talk by his father (related below). Nor did John W. know that, while attending the Citadel, Harley, Jr. had in mind going from there to law school but was inspired by Senator Walter F. George to enter forestry school instead. John had always been under the impression that Harley had been programmed by their father and intended from the start to go into forestry.[56]

Judge Harley's and Thalia's children got along well with their parents and held both in high esteem. There were, however, differences in how they related to them. Although all four children certainly loved their mother and seem never to have missed an opportunity to praise her, the boys felt less comfortable about discussing personal problems with her than with their father. She was a

---

[52] Langdale, JWL Interview 14.

[53] Miller, VLM Interview 01.

[54] Ibid.

[55] Ibid.

[56] Langdale, JWL Interview 14.

disciplinarian, recalled John W., and always busy. Although she displayed affection toward them, it was in a measured, restrained way. They also thought their father had a better understanding of circumstances they faced in their daily lives. Thalia had less formal education than her husband, and it seems the boys admired their mother more for her character and devotion to the family than for her worldly knowledge. When he needed to talk with a parent, as John W. remembered, he went first to his father, and Harley, Jr. did the same.

Considering Judge Harley's frequent unavailability, the children might have been expected to confide in their grandmother, who was less busy than their mother. Grandmother Lee, however, could not offer effective counsel to the children, especially the older boys. Still dressing in Victorian clothing, she appeared to them out of touch with the modern world of the 1920s and with family aspirations. Whereas Judge Harley planned for his children to have professional or business careers, she thought of them as potential craftsmen. Her husband had been a shoemaker, and others in her family had worked with their hands. Once when she saw John W. working with a small saw and hammer, she remarked excitedly to Thalia, "It looks like Bud may become a carpenter." She thought it would be wonderful if that happened, if he did something useful with his hands. That, of course, was not the type of career Judge had in mind for his boys.

In fact, John W. did learn to do things skillfully with his hands, but not as a way to make a living. In his leisure time, he became quite accomplished in woodworking, for example, and in taxidermy.

The interest in taxidermy initially involved both Harley, Jr. and John W. When they were about thirteen and eleven they decided together to send off for a correspondence course on taxidermy. Harley, Jr. soon lost interest, but John W. continued working at taxidermy for a number of years and, much later, even tried to interest his son, Johnny, in it. Johnny did not take to it at all.

John W. did a number of projects in taxidermy, starting with a squirrel. He mounted birds, including quail and ducks. He found quail easier to mount because their feathers had less tendency to fall out. He also mounted a wildcat, an owl, a deer head, fish and fish heads. He tanned the hides of various animals and snakes, including those of foxes and alligators. He made buckskin out of a deer skin and used it for years as a source of shoe strings. "I didn't ever waste anything,"[57] he said. Many years later, he worked taxidermy into his program as a Sunday school teacher, demonstrating the craft to some of his students.

John W.'s spare-time activity stands in contrast with that of his older brother ever since childhood. "I have used my leisure to advantage over the years," John observed. "I've always thought Harley's leisure was business. His recreation was business. He just devoted practically everything to business, even early on. But I

---

[57] Ibid.

could relax with some of these projects (after studies and chores were done). I couldn't enjoy doing things of that type until I had done my assigned tasks."[58]

During childhood, assigned tasks included common household chores. For these, the children took their marching orders from their mother. They had no set daily schedule of duties, however. If the yard needed sweeping, or if wood or coal needed to be brought in, Thalia gave instructions and the boys complied. Billy was too young to share the responsibilities of the older boys.

Chores at home had their equivalents at school, but the teacher assigned tasks. Having gone through Claudia Jackson's kindergarten, John W. started to Central Elementary School at the age of five. The school day ended at noon. He liked all his teachers, even Miss May, whom he remembered as very stern. She gave him the only whipping he ever got in school, which, naturally, made a vivid impression on his mind. It happened because of an incident in the fourth grade with "an overgrown boy" recently arrived from Holland. This boy, who stood several inches taller than John, sat behind him in class. Every time Miss May looked the other way, the boy tapped John on the head, tormenting him. Exasperated, John finally swung around and landed a sharp blow with his fist. Unfortunately, as John spun around, so did the teacher, and she saw nothing but the lick he delivered. It did him no good to claim self defense. Miss May called him to the front and gave him the standard "ruler treatment," which was more embarrassing than painful.

John W. demonstrated such an aptitude for spelling and reading that, when he reached second grade, his teacher persuaded his parents that he should skip a grade. As a result of doing so, he eventually graduated from high school when barely sixteen years of age. Upon reflection as an adult, John W. decided that skipping a grade had been a mistake. Remembering his school experiences, he concluded that, all along, he had been less mature than his classmates, who were older. "And as I look back on it," he laughed, "I wasn't that much smarter than anybody else."[59]

John W. enjoyed his early years in school, encountering nothing but success, but high school brought stiffer challenges. His verbal abilities did not seem to carry over to the areas of mathematics and science, for which, he said later, he had little aptitude. Although he continued to make A's in history, English, and languages, he performed weakly in math and science. "I got a very, very poor foundation in those subjects in high school," [60] he observed.

Of the three older Langdale children, John W. and Virginia performed best in high school. Harley, Jr. posted lower numbers, and continued to struggle academically when he went off to college at the Citadel. Not that he lacked ability; he just hadn't found the interest that would spark him to work on class assignments. As John W. saw it, Harley "did not really turn on his academic ability

---

[58] Ibid.
[59] Ibid.
[60] Ibid.

until he got in forestry school" at the University of Georgia. "This was something that he loved,...and he did well."[61]

About the time the Langdales moved to 700 North Patterson, John W. started junior high school. This school, which has long since been torn down, stood across the street from the Carnegie Library that has metamorphosed into the Lowndes County Historical Society Museum. The former junior high campus had become by the 1990s a parking lot for First Baptist Church. John rode his bike to and from this junior high school every school day.

After school, lacking organized recreation, the boys played games, mostly baseball or football. They seldom had enough players for complete teams, but two or three boys played against two or three others. To hold these games, they looked for a good, big yard. The Crescent, located a couple of blocks north of the Langdale home on Patterson Street, offered an ideal setting, and the owners allowed the boys to play on their large front lawn. "The problem was," as John W. reminisced, "it had a big wide sidewalk, and it seemed that, if you were running with the ball, you didn't ever get tackled until you hit that sidewalk."[62] With no pads, helmets, or any protective equipment, somebody usually got hurt, and that ended the game.

The Langdale children often had lots of time to play or study before supper, because the evening meal frequently came late. That was because Thalia held supper until her husband came home from visiting his turpentine places. The children usually did not see their dad during the day until the family sat down for the evening meal. They usually rose in the morning just in time to go to school. Their father, on the other hand, got up and hit the road long before day.

Since he left so early, breakfast at the Langdale home usually did not include Judge Harley, but the kids ate well. For a typical breakfast, they had eggs, with bacon or sausage, and grits. They chopped up the sausage and mixed it in the grits on their plates. For bread, they had biscuits or toast. Sometimes breakfast included waffles or hotcakes and Georgia cane syrup.

At lunch and supper, both of which were full meals, the family usually had vegetables. Frozen vegetables did not exist at that time, so those available were either fresh or canned. When it became necessary to resort to canned vegetables, they turned most often to English peas. These did not lose their flavor so much from the canning process as some other vegetables did.

Along with other meats common to Valdosta, the Langdales often ate beef, but not the most expensive cuts. "I just didn't know for some years there was such a thing as a fine sirloin or rib-eye," said John W., "because we never had that. We'd have country-fried steak, and Mama could do wonders with beating a cheap cut of beef into a pretty tender steak, you know, country fried, and make that

---

[61] Ibid.
[62] Ibid.

gravy that would go on rice. We had a lot of rice. Daddy would like rice at every meal, and we'd put it with the gravy. Mama made good gravy and, of course, we couldn't eat rice dry. You ate it with gravy. Or you mixed peas in with it, with your rice."[63]

As a youngster, John W. liked plain foods. Meat and potatoes, rice and peas with bell peppers, sweet potatoes with marshmallows on top, and peanut butter and jelly sandwiches appealed to his palate. He shied away from salads and couldn't stand mayonnaise. When he grew up he learned to like salads, but never acquired a taste for mayonnaise. His favorite lunch that his mother used to pack for his fishing trips as a teenage boy included a sandwich of sliced pineapple and another of peanut butter and jelly. All his life he preferred plain foods.

At mealtime, the children understood they were expected to eat everything on their plates. To do less, to waste food, would be wrong when millions around the world were known to be starving. Since they usually had good appetites, this rule caused them no problem. They had permission to talk with each other and their parents, but knew better than to become disorderly. Thalia taught them the rudiments of good table manners, but did so in a fairly relaxed way. She was no fanatic on this subject.

The Langdales frequently had guests for lunch, mostly clients whom Judge invited at the last minute. For instance, he might phone Thalia twenty minutes before lunch and say, "I've got Mr. Carter here [a client who had come in from Fargo]. "I'm bringing him to lunch." Thalia would never complain, except sometimes under her breath. She always produced a meal.

Instead of imposing on his wife on short notice, Judge might have taken his client to a downtown restaurant, of which there were one or two at that time. But, recalled John W., "Daddy thought it was a sin to eat at a restaurant. He would, if he could avoid it, never eat at a restaurant. And he thought that when his friends and clients came in that he ought to take them to a home-cooked meal. And he would do that often without giving Mama any prior notice. And she'd whip it up and make it acceptable, too."[64] If Thalia didn't have time to prepare something like beef or chicken, she'd throw together a breakfast of ham and eggs or bacon and eggs.

Thalia enjoyed a reputation as a good cook. In addition to regular meals, she excelled in preparing desserts such as angel food cake and caramel cake. Cooking almost led the list of her interests, ranking perhaps just below her WMU (Women's Missionary Union) activities at church and her "personal welfare program," as John W. called it. This referred to her longtime practice of choosing a needy family or two to help on a regular basis with food and other necessities. On Hill Avenue, where the Langdales depended on wood fireplaces for heat, Thalia

---

[63] Ibid.
[64] Ibid.

cooked with a wood stove. Later, when they moved to Patterson Street, she had a modern gas or electric range.

To help her in the kitchen, Thalia usually hired a black woman. For many years Rosa Jones worked for her. Later, for a long time, a woman named Curly helped her with the cooking duties.

Sewing also ranked high in Thalia's list of priorities. Although she left the millinery trade after marrying, she retained an interest in sewing and excelled as a seamstress. She repaired and altered the boys' clothes, and made dresses for Virginia.[65] During World War II, she and Mrs. Reese ran the Red Cross sewing room in Valdosta. Mrs. Reece was chairman, and Thalia co-chairman. Anything that came up about sewing, she could handle. In sewing and in other crafts she demonstrated artistic talent. "She loved to do things with her hands," said Virginia.[66] She (Virginia) and John W., who also displayed an artistic bent, apparently inherited or learned this from their mother.

Judge Harley, like Thalia, had a domestic helper. This young black man named Eddie Hall, perhaps sixteen or seventeen years of age at the time, came to work around the Langdale home in the 1920s and stayed for about forty-five years. Judge Harley brought Eddie from one of his turpentine camps to Valdosta as a yard worker. In time he served as Judge's driver, cook, and fishing and hunting companion. They had become almost inseparable, hunting and fishing buddies, one might say, before Judge's death in 1972. Many people around Valdosta knew Eddie as "Boy" Hall, the name he had acquired at the turpentine camp. A man of admirable character, by all accounts, he served as a deacon in his church and became a competent quail hunter through his association with Judge Harley, who gave him a shotgun for quail hunting.

Judge Harley Langdale
and Eddie "Boy" Hall
hunting birds. TLF.

---

[65] Ibid.
[66] Miller, VLM Interview 01.

For a number of years, perhaps two decades, prior to his death, Judge Harley invited friends around town to come over from time to time for breakfasts prepared by Boy Hall. They considered this a treat, and eagerly awaited an invitation. Boy Hall served Judge in many ways, and Judge felt a moral commitment to do right by him as a loyal worker and friend.

Morality, ethics, and responsibility, Thalia always believed, have their basis in religion, and parents should teach these daily to the children. Basically, Judge agreed with his wife, but with limitations. For Judge Harley, financial responsibility took the top spot in his list of ethical principles. He had no patience with a man who attempted to avoid his debts or to hide his assets from his creditors. Anyone who declared bankruptcy he classified as "sorry," except perhaps in the case of disability or serious extenuating circumstances. To emphasize and make crystal clear his views on this subject, he used to declare that even his wife's sewing machine was listed in his name.[67] At other times, however, Judge took a somewhat lighter view of bankruptcy, quipping that he never went bankrupt in his early days of business because he "didn't have the money to pay the court costs."[68]

Except for asking the blessing at meals when he was home—Thalia did this in his absence—Judge Harley had minimal involvement in formal religion for many years. Growing up in the Council area, he had gone with the family to dinner on the grounds at Boney Bluff, but had never affiliated with that or any other church. He thought it was good for his family to attend church and Sunday school because he wanted them to absorb Christian values, but he regarded church attendance for himself as a waste of his time. He had work to do. Sometimes Judge dropped the family off at church and then drove on to the office or to a turpentine place. "Daddy didn't use bad language, and he set a good example the way he lived, but he just felt like it was wasting his time to go to church,"[69] said John.

Judge Harley's aspirations for his children centered on hopes for their financial success. In this he reflected the attitude of his father, John Wesley. He cultivated conservative behavior in them. He taught them to avoid waste, to eat all the food on their plates, for example. He regarded morality, to be learned partly in church and Sunday school, as a pre-requisite for financial achievement.

He favored their involvement in church because he believed practice of Christian principles would help them become successful. As John explained his father's views,

> he felt like teaching the Bible and, particularly, the Ten Commandments, was in furtherance of that goal. He said, if you live in accordance with this code, with the Christian code, and you are a respected person

---

[67] Langdale, JWL Interview 14.

[68] McKay, "Langdale Lived to See Dream Come True."

[69] Langdale, JWL Interview 14.

and you discipline yourselves you can always do well in life. People will respect you. One expression that he gave us was, 'Let your word be your bond.' So live that your word is your bond. In other words, you don't have to give any bond to insure your performance. You are so respected that when you say you will do something, people will accept that. You've got that credibility. This was his teaching.[70]

Judge's practical view of Christianity as an aid to business success never satisfied his wife. When Thalia came to Valdosta as his bride, she quickly identified with the Baptist church and wanted Harley to do likewise, but, of course, he held back. Each time one of the children joined the church, Virginia remembered, they urged him to join with them, and he said he would later, but he always procrastinated. One factor, Virginia seemed to think, was the necessity of baptism by immersion. Probably he considered this a little too humbling for such a prominent attorney and businessman as himself.[71]

Once he joined, he became a model church member. He attended regularly and participated actively.[72] This happened about the middle of World War II. Judge underwent baptism by immersion and became a member of First Baptist Church. John W. heard about this in a letter from his mother while aboard ship in the Pacific. "Mama wrote me and told me that Daddy had joined the church, that Dr. Gibson had won him. She was elated....The pastor was T. Baron Gibson."[73]

When he joined the church, Judge was in his mid-fifties. During all their thirty years of marriage up to that time, Thalia had been the family's religious leader. She took the children to church, and she taught them a strict moral code. John illustrated his mother's ethical teaching with this account of an incident in his life in the sixth grade.

I can remember when I was in the sixth grade at junior high school, when I got home I had the pencil that I had picked up off of the floor and she didn't recognize it in my school supplies. She said, 'where did you get that pencil?' It was broken off. It was not a full new wooden pencil. It was just broke—about maybe two-thirds of a pencil. I said, 'I picked it up off the floor.' She said, 'Well, it's not yours, is it?' I said, 'No, ma'am.' She said, 'Well, when you find something like this you should turn it in to the teacher. You're not supposed to take that and bring it home.' So she put me in the car and took me back to the school and made me take that pencil to the teacher. And that impressed me, you know, concerning the commandment "Thou shalt not steal." Her concept was, that is stealing if

---

[70] Ibid.
[71] Miller, VLM Interview 01.
[72] Ibid.
[73] Langdale, JWL Interview 14.

you find something and you appropriate it to your use. The proper thing to do is to turn it in to the teacher and let her try to determine who lost that pencil.[74]

Judge saw it as his fatherly duty to manage his boys' time to keep them busy and out of trouble while they were growing up. Partly for this reason, he encouraged all three of his boys to fish and hunt. He viewed it as wholesome recreation. Far better, he thought, to encourage activities of this type, rather than allow the boys to become idle and start hanging around the pool hall or the drugstore with other unoccupied youngsters. Keeping them in the woods could keep them out of trouble, he thought, and on their way to successful lives as adults. Judge sometimes took the boys hunting and, at other times, had them ride with him to the various turpentine places when he went to check up on his managers. On these occasions, John W. usually sat in the back seat and Harley, Jr. sat in the front with his father. John, because of younger age or lack of interest, apparently learned less than Harley, Jr. about the turpentine business during these excursions. He did not see the trips as part of a training program, and he never felt like this would be his life's work.[75]

Nevertheless, when the boys reached twelve or thirteen years of age, Judge put Harley, Jr. and John W. to work in the turpentine woods in the summer time, training them for hard work as he had been trained by his father. Thalia helped prepare them for work. She took them downtown and bought them the right kind of clothes, overalls and brogan shoes, to wear in the woods. Harley, Jr. recalled that some of his friends laughed at him and John for having to go work all summer in the forest.[76]

Actually, Harley, Jr., being older, had spent some time working in the woods before this time. "When I was ten years old," Harley, Jr. recalled, "my father sent me to my uncle [John J.], who had not married at that time and lived down below Fargo. I spent several months with him down there, and I'd work in the woods and I'd be with the mules and the horses and then dipping gum."[77]

Judge next assigned Harley, Jr. to work on the place in South Carolina that Joe Wetherington managed. According to John W., "Daddy considered Mr. Wetherington to be a man of fine character and one well suited to teach his son." In South Carolina, Harley, Jr. gained experience stacking pulpwood and found that the black men who did it regularly could teach him something about it. He started out stacking the wood his own way until they showed him a superior method. The

---

[74] Ibid.

[75] Ibid.

[76] Langdale, HLJr Interview 1991.

[77] Ibid.

long trips to South Carolina also afforded Harley an opportunity to practice driving for his father, well before he reached today's legal age for driving.[78]

After his South Carolina experience, Harley, Jr. spent the next summer on the job at Tarver. Then John W.'s turn arrived. Starting when he was thirteen or fourteen, John worked as a dipper at Tarver for two summers, during part of which time Harley, Jr. was foreman of the dip squad. Years later, when Harley, Jr. graduated from forestry school, Judge put him in charge of the Tarver place as his first managerial assignment.[79]

John W. found his big brother to be a tough boss. Harley carefully avoided showing any partiality to him. For his part, John expected no favoritism and understood that it would make a bad impression on the men if he asked for it. As the owner's son, he thought of himself more as a manager in training than as a regular worker, and he did not wish to be accused of having it easier than the others in his group.[80] In addition to John W., the dip squad included five or six adult black men who were experienced dippers. Three of these, whose names John still remembered in 1995, were "Black Boy," "Cut-Eye," and "Dad." John learned to dip and chip mainly by observing them and others at work.[81]

The members of the dip squad walked parallel to each other through the woods, making a broad sweep and trying to avoid missing any cups containing gum. A good tree might exude enough gum to fill a cup in two weeks, although the average came closer to three weeks. If the dippers missed a cup, the next time through they might find the cup overflowing and gum being poured out on the ground and wasted. Operators became unhappy about that. To minimize waste, they wanted their dippers to empty the cups when most cups were about three-fourths full. Dippers preferred to find cups that were full, rather than perhaps half full, because they could dip more gum with less effort and make more money.[82] Common laborers at this time made about $40 per month.[83]

Of the dippers in his squad, "Dad" made the greatest impression on John W. Perhaps sixty years of age, he had a much younger wife whom he called his "old lady." One Friday evening, as John W. and Harley, Jr. were starting for Valdosta, Dad approached John about making a purchase for him in town. He said to John W., "I wants you to get me a dime's worth of castor oil, a dime's worth of sulfur, and a nickel's worth of Epson salts." John replied, "I'll be glad to, Dad. What you want with that?" Dad explained, "My old lady's sick, She's about to die and they tell me that will fix her up." He went on to say, "I thought if I could spend a quarter on her and save her I'd go ahead and spend it." John could never forget this

---

[78] Langdale, JWL Interview 14.
[79] Langdale, HLJr Interview 1991.
[80] Langdale, JWL Interview 14.
[81] Ibid.
[82] Langdale, JWL Interview 1991.
[83] Ibid.

remarkable commentary on the value of a human life. The old man debated whether to spend a quarter, amounting to half a day's wage, for medicine to save his wife.[84]

Evidently, the medicine worked, for Dad's old lady did not die. About three or four years later, though, John W. heard that Dad had been run over by a train and killed. According to this report, "his mind just got bad." Somehow he failed to move off the railroad track as a train passed through.[85]

Dippers like Cut-eye, Black Boy, and Dad were paid fifty cents per barrel of gum they collected from the cups mounted on trees. John received the same wage. Trees closer to the swamp produced more gum and usually had fuller cups than those on "the hill." A dipper assigned to work the hill might have to empty two or three times as many cups to get a certain volume of gum as he would if assigned to an area in or near the swamp. This required more walking. To increase his productivity and make more money, a dipper wanted to be given trees on lower ground, which was usually more fertile and better watered. Although John W. did not expect more than his fair share of the low-ground trees, it seemed to him that Harley, Jr. put him to work on the hill a little more often than necessary.[86] Perhaps Harley tried a little too hard to avoid showing favoritism to his brother.

A turpentine bucket. KCL.

John W. remembered one occasion, though, a very hot day, when Harley, Jr. sent him to work the swamp, which had water standing from a few inches to perhaps three feet deep. As John recalled, "The mosquitoes were very bad in that swamp. After I got in there, I decided that I would rest a little while, so I sat down in the water. The water came up to about my neck. Of course, that made my body mosquito free, and it relieved my suffering from the heat. And I thought I would enjoy that just for three or four minutes. And Harley caught me. He did give me a pretty good tongue lashing when he caught me in that position."[87]

---

[84] Langdale, JWL Interview 14. ; Langdale, JWL Interview 1991.
[85] Langdale, JWL Interview 14.
[86] Ibid.
[87] Ibid.

When John started dipping, he used a twelve-time bucket, the smallest they had available on this turpentine place. Using a twelve-time bucket, he needed to empty the bucket twelve times into a barrel to fill it. At Tarver they also had ten-time and eight-time buckets, but John's thin frame could not handle their greater weight.

Because it was impractical to have a separate barrel for each dipper, each bucket of gum had to be recorded as the dipper emptied it into the barrel. This duty belonged to the driver of the wagon, which moved through the woods in reasonably close proximity to the dippers. The driver, who might be older and infirm, had to be a responsible person who could be trusted to keep an accurate tally. The wagon, pulled by a mule, had a step at the back about half way between the wagon floor and the ground. Dippers used the step to boost their gum and themselves into the wagon so they could empty their buckets.

Occasionally, one of the old-timers, perhaps moved by nostalgia, would sing out a loud, forest-piercing musical call, unique to himself, to signify his dumping a bucket of gum. This had been standard practice a generation earlier to announce the completion of a bucket when the barrel had no attendant right there to observe and record the event, but by 1930 one seldom heard such calls anymore. In 1995, John still remembered one of these well enough to demonstrate it in a loud, clear, musical voice. "Put one downnnnnnn for my baby," he sang, and one felt transported to the past, sensing a little of the spirit of long ago in the turpentine woods.[88]

John W.'s father referred to such a call as a "holler." Speaking in 1955, Judge observed, "Each holler is different. One man may holler, 'Dollar Bill,' Another, 'I owe de man'; another, 'Sea-bo-o-o-a-ard,' or the name of the girl he is romancing with at the moment. There was a time I knew every holler that was hollered on my land."[89]

Judge also remembered nostalgically a similar thing called the "howl," which belonged to the era of "boxes" cut with axes, the time before cups were hung on trees to collect gum. Turpentine workers considered it a great achievement to cut a hundred boxes in a day's time. When a man neared the hundred mark for boxes cut that day, said Judge, he started "a long quavering chant," that went something like this:

"Woke up this morning aweepin' and amoanin'. Goan try to make a dollar for me...and a quarter for my ba-aybee. Said I'd cut a hundred. And looks like I'm gonna make it. So I want you boys to help me. For I'm agoin' to howl."

Other workers, hearing of the approaching triumph, joined in like deacons encouraging their preacher with "amens." "Yes, man.... Help him, Lawd.... . Oh, yes," they might say. Upon cutting his hundredth box, the day's champion climbed

---

[88] Ibid.
[89] Martin, 92.

a tree and gave a mighty shout with no discernible words, just a howl, announcing his achievement to the world of the pine woods.

"I'd give anything in the world just to hear a woods crew howl again," said Judge.[90]

Howls never happened and hollers rarely did in John W's experience as a novice turpentine worker. Heat, snakes, mosquitoes, and the hard physical labor tested his determination to be a good dipper. The hardest thing, at first, was getting his hands used to the work. His tender city-boy hands quickly blistered, the blisters broke, and gum burned his raw flesh. It took about a week, John W. recalled, for the blisters to heal and calluses to emerge.[91]

Life in the turpentine woods, though mostly hard work and drudgery, occasionally produced an adventure for the boys. Once as they crossed the swamp in water perhaps chest or shoulder deep, they encountered a poisonous snake. Harley, Jr. carried a pistol and, when they went into water that deep, he put the weapon in his hat, the only place to keep it dry. So, when the snake swam into their path, Harley whipped the pistol out of his hat and blew the serpent away. John W. was surprised that very few rattlesnakes appeared, apparently because the traffic of turpentine workers in the woods scared them away.[92]

Judge Harley did not order John W. or Harley, Jr. to work at the turpentine camp. He cultivated an attitude in the boys' minds and provided an opportunity. He had impressed upon them all their lives the value of money and the importance of earning and saving. Of course, they wanted to please their father and they surely knew what he desired, but, they also wanted to earn money. Harley had already been working, but this was John's first opportunity for significant earning. Besides the income, which for him turned out to be sixty to seventy-five cents a day, he liked the idea of doing and learning something new.[93] Within a day or two, though, John W. decided he had learned all he needed to know about dipping gum. There really was not much to discover about this particular job, and it was boring, not to mention strenuous and unpleasant because of heat and insects. In the future, he could certainly appreciate the kind of learning accomplished in a schoolroom.[94]

One of the few pleasures John W. remembered from his first summer on the place at Tarver was the warm bath available at the turpentine still. He and Harley, Jr. lived in a tent across the railroad track from the still. At the end of the day, tired, sweaty, and partially smeared with gum, John W. loved to cross the track and get a bath in the warm water produced by the still. That felt *so* good.

---

[90] Ibid.

[91] Langdale, JWL Interview 14.

[92] Ibid.

[93] Ibid.; Langdale, JWL Interview 1991.

[94] Langdale, JWL Interview 14.

A hack. KCL.

While working five days a week in turpentine, Harley, Jr. and John decided to diversify and increase their incomes through a little business activity on weekends. They usually returned to Valdosta on Friday evening and went back to Tarver late Sunday afternoon, having been to church and Sunday school earlier in the day. On the way to Tarver each week they stopped by the Foremost Dairy and bought a gallon of ice cream and a supply of cones. Back at the turpentine camp, they sold ice cream cones for a nickel a piece, making a profit of two cents each.[95]

John W. worked two summers at Tarver, dipping for fifty-cents a barrel the first summer and chipping at so much per tree the second. Although an adult might ordinarily dip two barrels a day and earn a dollar total, John thought he did well to accomplish three-fourths of that. He made a little more money the next year "chipping boxes," as it was called, but this was also very hard work and required more skill than dipping. For chipping, one used a "hack" with a five-pound iron ball built into the end of the handle to give it the weight needed for making streaks on pine trees. Wielding this heavy instrument all day long built muscles but left one very tired. In his third summer of working in the turpentine business, John W. spent his time in the office learning the bookkeeping.[96]

In the meantime, from the age of ten or eleven, fishing, encouraged by his father, played a large role in John's life. He started to develop a lifelong love of fishing when he visited his Uncle John J. Langdale a couple of times at the Langdale home at Council, at about the age of eight or ten.

For these visits, Judge Harley put young John W. on the train in Valdosta and John's Uncle John J. flagged the train down at Council. The train stopped there only if flagged. As postmaster, if the train did not need to stop for passengers, John J. hung the outgoing mailbag on a pole and a trainman on the mail car

---

[95] Ibid.
[96] Langdale, JWL Interview 1991.

snagged it with a hook as the train passed through. Incoming mailbags the crew tossed out on the ground as the train sped through Council.[97]

Uncle John J. lived about two miles from Cypress creek, which ran out of the Okefenokee and merged with the Suwannee. Young John W. got in the habit of walking the railroad track to reach the creek, where he fished for hours and returned each evening with a string of fish, mostly Jack fish.

One day, at about twelve years of age, John W. deviated from his usual route and, strolling along Cypress Creek, had a memorable adventure. "I walked up on a still," he recalled, "an illegal whiskey still. A boy about fourteen met me with a rifle.... When I came into the clearing, and I saw what he was protecting, it was quite a shock.... I told him I was fishing, he didn't need to worry about me. To show off, he took a swig of fresh moonshine whiskey out of a five-gallon demijohn. I declined his invitation to have a drink."[98]

After a while, around age fourteen, John became particularly interested in river fishing. This involved towing a boat and trailer to some point on one of the small local rivers, putting the boat in, and fishing while traveling downstream to a landing where someone would be waiting to pick up the boat and fisherman. This style of fishing required a second person to row and manage the boat. In Valdosta at that time a number of black men hired themselves out as rowers at a charge of a dollar-and-a-half or two dollars a day. Judge Harley paid this expense for John, enabling him to fish the rivers, which he liked much better than lake fishing. The river provided greater variety. "There was always something interesting around the next bend," explained John W. River fishing remained one of his favorite activities until illness forced him to give it up.[99]

John also had a lifelong interest in music, although he never pretended to be an accomplished performer. He started piano lessons at about the age of eleven with a prominent teacher in Valdosta. His sister, Virginia, took lessons at the same time. Virginia remembered that "he caught on a lot quicker than I did." Neither of them liked to practice, but John practiced a little more than Virginia. Sometimes when she tried to practice "he would come by the hall and thump me on the head. I'd holler out and Mama would tell him to quit. He said, "Oh, I'm just kidding you." Later, when Virginia had headaches, she pointed the finger at John, saying, "It's on account of your kidding me so much."[100]

John W. recalled that he had twelve lessons, enough to learn the scales, then quit. In high school, he picked up a little more musical training through an activity that was perhaps as much necessity as choice. Like most Valdosta boys, he wanted to play football; but with a top weight of 125 and brittle bones, he "didn't last long," as he remembered. A broken collarbone persuaded him to seek a less

[97] Langdale, JWL Interview 14 ; Langdale, JWL Interview 14.

[98] Langdale, JWL Interview 1991.

[99] Langdale, JWL Interview 14.

[100] Miller, VLM Interview 01.

physical extra-curricular activity. So he joined the Drum and Bugle Corps. For this, he bought a bugle and a uniform, which consisted of "a white shirt, white duck pants, and an orange and black sash around the waist." John played two years in the Drum and Bugle Corps before graduating and going off to North Georgia College.[101]

Billy Langdale, compared to his older brothers, had a much easier, less businesslike boyhood and he remembered his father very differently. From Billy's perspective, Judge Harley emerges as a warmer, more tolerant and easy-going father, more of a "buddy." Billy remembered that, from the time he was a small child, his father took him on trips to the turpentine camps.

While making such a trip, sometimes, on the spur of the moment, Judge left Billy for three or four days with friends in the country. These unplanned stays in the country happened when Billy was as young as five or six. For example, with Billy in the car, Judge might stop to talk with Jack Allen. Jack would say, "Why don't you let Billy stay with me?" Judge would reply, "If he wants to," and Billy would say, "Well, that suits me." Judge would put Billy out with no clothes but those he had on; he would come back for him in three or four days. If his clothes needed washing, the host family washed them. Billy enjoyed these experiences, and recalled with pleasure bogging down and sleeping in the goose-feather beds common at the time. Occasionally, Billy stayed like this with the Will Carter and Mann Carter families.[102]

Judge took young Billy hunting with him and had the boy accompany him on deer stands. Once when Billy was about ten or eleven, they started back from a hunting trip to the turpentine place in South Carolina and had a little more adventure than they expected or wanted. When departing, Judge stood his gun on the floorboard between them, with its barrel resting against the back of the seat. He said to his son, "Billy I'm going to load this gun because we may see a turkey going out of here. If we do, we'll shoot him." So they started out, and as they bounced along, suddenly the gun went off, blasting a hole in the seat and the back window. "Did you mash that trigger?" Judge asked. "No, Sir," [103] replied Billy. They never figured out what caused the gun to fire.

Dreading what Thalia might say when she heard about this incident, Judge cautioned Billy, "Now, don't tell your mama about this gun going off." They reached home all right, and the next morning, before daylight, Judge got up, took the car to be repaired, and borrowed a substitute vehicle. "Where's your car?" Billy remembered his mother asking. "I'm just getting something fixed on it,"[104] Judge replied.

---

[101] Langdale, JWL Interview 14.
[102] Langdale, WPL Interview 1991.
[103] Ibid.
[104] Ibid.

Judge loved quail hunting and was very good at it. For that purpose, he usually kept four or five dogs around the house. Once a week Billy had to put these animals through a dip to rid them of ticks and other insect pests. Judge kept a barrel of creosote dip in the back yard. Each summer, Judge sent the dogs to the turpentine place to get them toughened up for the forthcoming hunting season. Billy remembered that he and his father used to haul the dogs out to the woods in the car. They'd stop the car and, for three or four hours, work them, four at a time, in the forest.[105]

"I was always pulling jokes on my daddy," recalled Billy, "and my Daddy would tolerate me." Once Billy took a magneto from a Model-T Ford and built what he called a "shocking machine." A magneto normally generated high-voltage electricity when turned with a crank, igniting the fuel mixture in the cylinder of an internal combustion engine and starting it without a battery.

Judge came in from hunting, with his boots and feet wet. Following customary procedure, he said to his son, "Billy, take my boots off me." As the boy complied, Judge became engrossed in his newspaper. Billy thought this would be a great time to test his shocking machine, so he deftly attached two little wires to his father's toes. Then he turned the crank. As Billy recalled, Judge "jumped high as the ceiling."

"Billy, you know I've got a bad heart," Judge complained to his son. But there was no punishment. It's hard to imagine Billy's older brothers getting away with such a stunt.

Yet Judge did enjoy a good practical joke. For example, he loved to tell about the bear stunt pulled on Mr. George Shelton. Mr. Shelton, like Judge an old turpentine operator, was an early riser. Long before daylight each day he drove from home to a local restaurant to discuss matters of weight with a few others who got up early. Knowing well Mr. Shelton's routine, a hunting party that Judge took into the Okefenokee killed a large black bear and brought it back to Valdosta. While Mr. Shelton yet slept, they placed it in a sitting position on the passenger side, front seat, of his automobile. As usual, he rose early, slipped into his vehicle in complete darkness, and stepped on the starter (yes, starters were on the floorboard in those days). At that precise moment the bear slumped over into Mr. Shelton's lap, and he bolted like a startled deer for the safety of his house, shrieking in terror and nearly ripping off his back door in panic. Judge denied any part in this prank, but he did laugh at it.[106] So Judge appreciated a good joke, and this perhaps made it easier for him to forgive Billy for the shocking-machine episode.

His father had a good disposition, said Billy, and a good sense of humor. Billy remembered this story his dad told on himself. Judge used to ride a horse when deer

---

[105] Ibid.
[106] Martin, 92.

hunting. Once he borrowed a horse, he said, and asked the owner if he could shoot deer from the horse. "Yes, Sir," he was told. Judge rode off and, when a deer crossed his path, he fired away. The horse bolted and bucked and threw him off. When he returned the horse to its owner, he protested, "I thought you said you could shoot off this horse." "Yes, Sir, I did," came the reply, "but I didn't say you could stay on the horse after you shot."[107]

Billy saw his father putting in long working days, as much as sixteen or eighteen hours, but he noticed this involved no strenuous activity. As Judge's youngest son put it, "My daddy never was one to do much manual labor." He remembered hearing Judge tell of when, as a young fellow before going off to school in Abbeville, he had been working for his father down at Council carrying out crossties from the swamp. Sometimes he tripped over a cypress knee and the crosstie he was carrying fell on top of him. He concluded right then there must be a better way to make a living than with manual labor.

Billy recalled a story his aunt told him, illustrating his dad's aversion to physical work. She persuaded her brother, Harley, to ride with her on a trip somewhere, in case she had a flat tire. Sure enough, a tire did go flat. Judge got out of the car, and she asked, "What are you going to do, Harley?" He said, "I'm going to flag the first truck that comes by here and get him to change that."[108]

When Judge took a trip, Billy, himself, and his mother, did the physical work required in preparation. Judge Harley often made excursions to Washington on behalf of the American Turpentine Farmers Association, sometimes accompanied by Bill Ottmeier. "When he got ready to go he didn't pack a bag. He'd just telephone and say, 'I'm going to Washington...be there about three days.' And she'd lay his clothes out and have everything just right. He never touched that. I came down and put them in; he didn't carry no bag down either."[109] Billy and his mother had many opportunities to help Judge with his bags as he traipsed off to Washington and other places on behalf of the American Turpentine Farmers Association.

So ends this account of the Langdale family's domestic life, based mainly on the recollections of Judge's children. The next order of business is to explain how Judge Harley Langdale became so deeply involved in the turpentine business.

---

[107] Langdale, WPL Interview 1991.
[108] Ibid.
[109] Ibid.

6

Turpentine Places and Partnerships

he origin of the Langdale Company, as distinguished from the J. W. Langdale Company, goes back to 1922. It started with a number of turpentine partnerships established by John Wesley Langdale's youngest son, Harley, usually called Judge Harley.

As best one can determine, no money from his father's estate found its way to Judge Harley's pocketbook in the 1920s and so did not provide the means for his purchase of land or operation of his naval stores business. The J. W. Langdale Company made no distribution of funds to heirs or of dividends to stockholders during this period.[1]

Notwithstanding the lack of a direct financial connection, Judge Harley and his descendants have honored John Wesley Langdale as the founder of the Langdale Company, created mainly from Judge Harley's assets and formally incorporated in 1948. John Wesley is certainly deserving of recognition because he taught his son, Harley, a value system and cultivated in him character traits that contributed importantly to his success. John Wesley also taught Harley something about the naval stores and forest products business. The stock that Harley owned in the J. W. Langdale Company, his father's incorporated estate, probably helped him borrow money, and he undoubtedly benefited from contacts related to his father and to the company bearing his father's name. It is also true that, recently, the owners of the Langdale Company have completed the purchase of the J. W. Langdale Company stock from the other heirs. Acquisition of this stock from the original stockholders occurred from 1943 to 1996. There is certainly good reason to honor John Wesley Langdale as the sentimental founder or as family patriarch, and it is commendable that his descendants wish to honor him as founder, but the true founder of the Langdale Company, as the term is generally understood, was Judge Harley Langdale. Judge's eldest son, Harley, Jr.,

---

[1] Langdale, "JWL to JEL Memo."

essentially took over from his father and provided the vision and leadership that brought the company its remarkable success since the late 1930s.[2]

Judge Harley at his desk about 1940. TLC.

Harley, Sr. settled in Valdosta in 1912, the year after the death of his father, John Wesley. Harley's mother and sisters also moved to this south Georgia town the same year from Jasper, Florida. The presence of his family in Valdosta presumably influenced Harley's determination to locate there instead of in Griffin, Georgia, or Miami, Florida. Knowing that his late father had business contacts in Valdosta also affected his decision. "Miami was just starting," Judge once commented, "and I decided that due to the fact that I had some connections there, Valdosta would be the best place for me to locate."[3]

Harley graduated from Mercer on 7 June and arrived in Valdosta on 1 July to start his law practice. He found office space in the old Valdosta Bank & Trust Company building. A partnership with a lawyer named Clements, lasted only four months. Later, he joined Omer W. Franklin, who had just graduated from the University of Georgia, in a partnership that endured twenty-one and a half years.[4]

The partnership with Omer Franklin, which operated under the name, Franklin and Langdale, had its offices in the Strickland Building. This structure stood on the southwest corner of West Hill Avenue and South Patterson Street. Another attorney, Homer Eberhardt, joined the firm in the early 1930s and, after

---

[2] Langdale, JWL Interview 14.
[3] Langdale, Judge Interview 01.
[4] Ibid.

a while, became a partner. The name of the firm then changed to Franklin, Langdale, & Eberhardt.

Judge's outside interests as one of the world's largest turpentine producers and head of ATFA in the 1930s left him less time than his partners wished him to spend in his legal practice. Consequently, they agreed to dissolve the partnership.[5]

For a short time after splitting with his partners, Judge Harley practiced law by himself, but he soon formed another partnership. A recent graduate of the University of Georgia Law School, B. Lamar Tillman, joined Judge as an associate around 1937. Shortly afterward, J. Lundie Smith also became an associate. Within two or three years, these two younger men rose to the rank of partners, and the firm took the name, Langdale, Tillman, and Smith. At this point the three partners moved their offices across Hill Avenue to the building located immediately behind the First National Bank. This was the location of the Langdale, Tillman, and Smith offices when John W. Langdale graduated from law school and entered the firm as an associate in 1940 and worked there briefly before going off to the war.

Langdale & Langdale,
Law Partners, 1969.
TLC.

When John W. returned after the war and rejoined the firm, it had the same partners and occupied the same offices. Several years later, however, the partnership dissolved. This occurred in 1951 when Judge and John W. found they needed to spend more of their time working with the Langdale Company. These two moved their offices to the company's new corporate office building on the Madison Highway and practiced law under the name Langdale & Langdale until Judge's death in 1972. Actually, during this latter period, Judge gave his primary attention more and more to his agricultural interests and to the American Turpentine Farmers Association, while John W. handled most of the legal work.[6]

---

[5] Langdale, "Law Firms."
[6] Ibid.

After practicing law in Valdosta for a decade, Judge had no other business interest than his ownership of stock in the J. W. Langdale Company. At this juncture, as Judge recounted nearly four decades later, he received a visit from a man who had been in the turpentine business with his father. This man, whom Judge did not identify, wanted to set up his own turpentine place with Judge Harley's backing as a partner. The two agreed on terms and started a turpentine farm at Mayday, Georgia.[7] The year Judge Harley started in the naval stores business was 1922. By 1937, he had acquired 20,000 acres of land and was working for turpentine purposes nearly three million trees, operating twenty-five turpentine camps and almost as many stills.[8]

Harley, Sr.'s brief account tells us that someone offered him an opportunity to get into the turpentine business and he accepted the proposal, but it omitted the name of his visitor and other significant facts. The man who came to see Harley must have been W. W. Turner, who became his partner at Mayday, or perhaps the visitor was Judge's brother, Noah. Family members recalled that Noah had gone into the turpentine business at Mayday, and it was he from whom Judge bought the thousand acres of land, the first of many thousands of acres he acquired over the years. Harley paid his brother $2.00 an acre, with $500 down and $500 additional in each of the next three years.[9] So it appears that Judge and his partner, W. W. Turner, basically purchased and assumed Noah's turpentine operation at Mayday. Judge named this business the Langdale Turpentine and Cattle Company. Presumably, he hoped to start a cattle business there, similar to that of his father, but he never did.[10]

Judge's latter-day summary of how he got into the turpentine business also fails to explain why a young lawyer with a growing clientele would accept such a proposal, one that could be expensive and would certainly take time away from his legal practice and his family. It is possible that, if Noah wished to sell, perhaps to go into another business, Judge bought the land partly as a favor to his brother.

Judge's son, John W., thought several factors probably entered into his father's decision. Judge knew the turpentine business well, he enjoyed it, and he liked the challenge it brought. Like the forest products business of today, it was cyclical, with ups and downs. Turpentine and rosin prices did best in times of general prosperity in this country and overseas because naval stores commodities were used so much as raw materials for consumer products. Much of the turpentine and rosin went to England, the Netherlands, and other European countries.[11]

The cyclical aspect of the turpentine business challenged all operators and drove many out of business. As Harley, Jr. recalled in later years, some turpentine

---

[7] Langdale, Judge Interview 01.
[8] Langdale, "Brief Facts."
[9] Martin, 91.
[10] Langdale, JWL Interview 14.
[11] Ibid.

producers "would buy the biggest car they could buy one year, and the next year they couldn't even buy a license plate for it."[12] That happened partly because "the market was manipulated a good bit by the factors and the brokers and the exporters."[13] To succeed, a person needed to be a good planner and make preparations for the down cycle. Judge had confidence that, with his education, experience, and ability, he could do that.[14]

Judge's daughter, Virginia, agreed that her father had always retained a liking for the turpentine business, notwithstanding its inherent challenges. In addition, she said, her father had discovered he did not like some aspects of lawyering. He enjoyed the trial, but not the research and preparation of briefs. Detail work he preferred to assign to someone else.[15]

One of Judge's more famous court victories came in Echols County. In a trial there he supposedly convinced the jury his client was innocent of murder because the victim, who had been shot in the back, had been "backing down on his client in a threatening manner."[16]

Judge's youngest son, Billy, comparing his father's style as an attorney to that of his brother, John W., put it this way: "Daddy wasn't like John, my brother. You could ask him a legal question and he'd give you an answer just like that. But if you were to ask John a legal question, you'd get a long answer. He would read you what the law books say. But my daddy was not that way."

Judge liked business better than law practice, and next to that, he liked being with people. This was Virginia's impression as she grew up. He dearly loved interacting with people. Whether the people were important politicians like Senator Walter George or unknown associates in the turpentine business, Judge enjoyed and got along with them equally well. In dealing with these different types of people, Judge did not appear to alter his style or manner to accommodate their different social positions. "You never saw a person like him," declared Virginia. People accepted his leadership; they wanted to do what he wanted them to do. Virginia marveled at this ability of her father to get along with and influence others.[17]

In fact, perhaps for all of the reasons mentioned, Judge seems to have been looking for a good business opportunity, and this offer came at the right time. Already, in 1920, he had leased some land and tried row-cropping, specializing in peanuts, and been unhappy with the outcome. "Daddy always seemed to really want to get back to plain old dirt farming...like he had done down on the home place," John W. recalled. Though only four years old at the time and unaware of

---

[12] Langdale, HLJr Interview 1991.

[13] Ibid.

[14] Langdale, JWL Interview 14.

[15] Miller, VLM Interview 01.

[16] Martin, 92.

[17] Miller, VLM Interview 01.

the vicissitudes of farming, John understood later that the farming venture did not succeed financially, perhaps because of crop failure or market conditions.[18] With the disappointing dirt farming episode behind him, Judge probably thought the turpentine business offered more potential.

From the perspective of today, it is clear that, in 1920, Judge picked a bad time to try conventional farming. National statistics indicate that farmers prospered in the period from 1889 to 1919, but farm prices collapsed in 1920 ushering in an agricultural depression that lasted through 1940. In short, the Great Depression started for farmers a decade earlier than for the economy as a whole.

The low farm prices resulted from huge surpluses. Income for farmers and farm commodity prices reached their lowest point in 1932, the year of Franklin Roosevelt's election as president. By 1941, the world war absorbed the surpluses and created extraordinary additional demands. After the war, by the 1950s, the problem of surpluses returned to plague American agriculture.

Hard times on the farm help to explain why, from the standpoint of the number of people making a living from farming, agriculture has become much less important as a sector of the US economy than it used to be. Only about 2.9 percent of the country's population earned a living from agriculture in 1987, compared to 90 percent when George Washington was President.[19]

Judge Harley's Mayday partnership of 1922 established a precedent and a pattern. In years to come, other aspiring entrepreneurs, perhaps knowing of the Mayday enterprise and thinking Judge could find the capital they needed to acquire a place that was on the market, approached him about similar arrangements. To some of these propositions he agreed. As Harley, Jr. summarized the situation, "He was getting into the turpentine business by trying to pick the best partner he could pick whether he had any money or not, then borrowing money from the factors and setting up a turpentine operation."[20]

Beginning with the Mayday farm, Judge Harley soon established others at Blanton and Withers. At Mayday, where he bought his first thousand acres from his brother, and at Blanton he owned the land, but he leased the place at Withers. At this point he had three turpentine places in three different counties.[21] During the 1920s, in addition to W. W. Turner, Judge had several other partners, including the Bennetts.[22] He picked his partners carefully. He looked for honest, hard working, intelligent men who had knowledge of the turpentine business. Judge considered it critical that the proposed partner have the ability to manage the

---

[18] Langdale, JWL Interview 14.

[19] United States Department of Agriculture, Economic Research Service. *A History of American Agriculture, 1776-1990: Farm Economy* [cited 15 September 1998]. Available from http://www.usda.gov/history2/back.htm.

[20] Langdale, HLJr Interview 1991.

[21] Langdale, Judge Interview 01.

[22] Langdale, "JWL to JEL Memo."

workers. As he stated decades later in emphasizing this key point, "a lot of people never made a success in the turpentine business because they couldn't control labor."[23]

Harley, Jr. echoed his father's comment, stating in 1992, "I guess the key to his success was the ability to size up people...because if you get the right man that can handle the labor and use good judgment and work, you can make money."[24] On the other hand observed Harley, Jr. "I knew some mighty good men that would have a hard time with labor, particularly when times would get a little better and labor would be a little more difficult. They couldn't get it, and so they couldn't make any money."[25] Success in handling labor required successful recruiting and retention of workers.

The key to controlling labor, as John W. remembered it in the 1990s, was understanding the type of person who worked in the turpentine camps. In general, this was a job of last resort. "If a person could work anywhere else, he would do that," observed John W. in 1995.[26] John's comment perhaps exaggerated the situation a little, but his point was that working in the turpentine woods ranked very low in the scale of desirable occupations.

On the other hand, and more positively in Harley, Jr.'s view, these workers generally liked their lifestyle. They adopted a way of life that fit in with the piece rate method of payment. Since they were paid on the basis of how many barrels they dipped or how many faces they streaked, not for how long they labored, they had flexible working hours. Typically, a worker would go to work in the woods in the morning, taking along his little Feist dog and a bucket containing his lunch. If the dog flushed and caught a rabbit, the game might be put into a sack and taken home to become the family's supper. In the middle of the day, if the temperature rose very high, the worker could find a shady spot and take a nap if he so chose. "It was a way of life that these people enjoyed," thought Harley, Jr.[27]

Also on the positive side, workers in old age sometimes had a degree of security at a turpentine camp, not from any formal commitment, of course, but from a manager's personal kindness. Until late in the naval stores era, turpentine workers had no welfare system to take care of them in old age. There were county "poor farms," but most turpentine laborers who grew too old to work simply stayed in the camps where they had been working for years. Operators often allowed such "retired" workers to continue living in their furnished housing and gave them credit at the commissary so they could obtain food, patent medicines,

---

[23] Langdale, Judge Interview 01.
[24] Langdale, HLJr Interview 1991.
[25] Ibid.
[26] Langdale, JWL Interview 14.
[27] Langdale, HLJr Interview 1991.

and clothing. Usually, in such a case, the operator had to absorb the cost because the aged worker lacked the means to pay his bill.[28]

Even so, turpentine workers toiled year after year at piece rates on a low wage scale, and they earned little money. They lived in camps, usually located from five to fifty miles from a town of any size. In this isolated situation, they had only the recreation they found for themselves. The owner of the turpentine place provided them with shelter, consisting of small, plain houses grouped together in a sort of village referred to as "the quarters."

Typically, every worker owed money to the owner of the camp. Some of the debt came from credit purchases of food, medicine, tobacco, kerosene and other necessary items at the owner's commissary. Other debt resulted from emergencies. Because he was poor and had no savings, any crisis, such as illness or a funeral, required a worker to borrow money to pay the physician, the funeral director, or whoever provided the emergency service. People who furnished these services usually wanted to be paid in cash. After all, who would risk extending credit to a turpentine worker who obviously had no money and lived miles away in the woods somewhere? Welfare programs did not exist for these rural laborers, as they did later. In an emergency, a worker had to borrow money from his employer, if he could, because no other lender would take the risk. As a result, when the man got paid on Saturday, or once a month, he might receive no cash because his earnings went toward payment of his debt. In summary, turpentine workers tended to live beyond their means, which were slight, and to stay in debt to their employers.[29]

Small wonder that some workers, perhaps despairing of ever paying off their debts, chose to escape them by moving to another turpentine place where they might start over with less or, conceivably, no debt. A worker desiring to make such a change might get in touch by some means with another turpentine operator and offer his services. Ethical turpentine operators followed the honorable and accepted practice of paying off the debt of a worker desiring to move, although the law did not require it. In such a case, the worker did not avoid the debt, but he simply owed it to his new boss. Some operators, however, recruited workers with the promise that they would be debt-free at the new location, and they sneaked in at night to help a worker move without clearing the debt. To avoid losing their laborers and the money invested in them through credit and loans, turpentine operators kept a vigilant eye out for clandestine night-time movers. Some operators earned a reputation in the naval stores business for devious recruiting, but Judge Harley opposed such cheating, John W. recalled, and instructed his managers to operate ethically.

A successful manager of a turpentine place needed to know his workers as individuals, for he needed to be able to predict their behavior in various

---

[28] Langdale, JWL Interview 1991.

[29] Langdale, JWL Interview 14.

circumstances. In one of his roles, the manager acted like a loan officer. He had to decide, day by day, how much credit particular workers should be allowed. It suited the manager's purposes to have the worker owing money, but not to excess. Too much debt, especially if the manager put pressure on him in other ways, a worker might run away in the middle of the night, creating a need to recruit a replacement and perhaps losing the investment in credit. The cummulative amount of credit extended to all workers in the camp increased the cost of operation and reduced profitability, so the manager also needed to keep an eye on the total amount of credit granted.

Paying out too much cash on payday to some men could also create a problem. With a pocket full of money, a fellow might go down to the juke, spend his weekend drinking, and fail to report for work Monday morning. Such absenteeism reduced the camp's productivity. Obviously, the manager wanted to minimize this kind of behavior.[30]

In 1939 R. W. Wishart, a plainspoken veteran of nearly forty years in the turpentine business in Georgia and Florida, described for a Federal Writers Project interviewer typical turpentine places that he had known. Wishart had worked at a number of camps owned by different persons and located in different areas of Georgia, Florida, and the Caribbean. His perspective sheds a little more light on the turpentine farming business in the pre-war period. His descriptions and his explanation of "handling labor," have slightly sharper edges than those of the scholarly John W.

As Wishart described it, blacks did nearly all the hard physical labor in the woods and around the stills, while whites held the management jobs. "The manager, foreman, commissary men and woods riders are all white men," he explained. These officials lived in "fairly good houses" on one side of the camp, and the Negroes lived in "two or three-room cabins or board houses" in an area called "the quarters" on the opposite side of the camp. The number of workers in a camp typically varied from fifty to two hundred, depending on the number of crops (10,000 faces) being worked. Wishart recalled that he managed one group of eight camps in 1922 with a total of 120 crops and 400 Negro workmen.[31] This, coincidentally, was the year that Judge Harley went into the turpentine business at Mayday.

When possible, said Wishart, managers assigned unmarried men to dwellings in the quarters separated somewhat from those of married workers to reduce the amount of trouble over single men's attentions to married women. The separation helped, but it did not eliminate conflict. The forest at night gave cover to

---

[30] Ibid.

[31] R. W. Wishart, "Interview by Lindsay M. Bryan," in Federal Writers Project (Library of Congress, Washington DC, 2–4. Hereinafter referred to as "Turpentine Man.")

surreptitious dalliances, and managers often had to deal with fights involving knives and turpentine tools between single men and jealous husbands.[32]

Taking John W.'s observation about the nature of turpentine workers a step further, Wishart described them as "a class by themselves." They behaved differently than town dwellers or farm laborers. Most of the turpentine hands he had known were born in a turpentine camp and had never lived anywhere else. They rarely went to town, and "few of them ever saw the inside of a school house." In the typical camp, there was a "juke," which in earlier times was called a "tunk." This, said Wishart, was where "the men and women gather on Saturday nights to dance, drink moonshine, gamble and fight. Between dances or drinks, young couples stroll off into the woods and make love." The typical camp also had its "jack-leg preacher," who held church services in one of the houses on Sunday.[33]

Camp foremen preferred their workers to be married because this reduced the number of quarrels and fights. Most marriages of turpentine workers, especially in the early period of Wishart's experience, he described as "commissary marriages." These unions took place without benefit of legal licensing or ceremony, religious or civil. When the foreman and a couple agreed that a marriage should take place, the foreman simply established an account for the couple at the commissary and assigned them a house in the quarters. The couple moved in, and were considered married. Sometimes, however, a couple had a few dollars to spend for a license and wanted a legal or "cotehouse marriage." In such cases, they would go to the county seat, purchase what they called a "pair o' licenses," and tie the knot legally.[34]

In each camp, the foreman reigned supreme. Usually, except for really serious offenses such as murder, sheriffs tended to leave it up to the foreman to enforce the law in his camp. As Wishart put it, turpentine hands saw the foreman as "the law, the judge, jury and executioner." Negro workers addressed the foreman as "Cap'm." When talking to each other in his absence, they called him "the man." He had better *be a man*, too, declared Wishart, and never display weakness. "If he ever stands for any back talk or shows a streak of yellow he's through, and might as well quit." [35] The men would pretend to respect him, but would laugh at him behind his back; they would "gang up" and make his life so miserable he'd ultimately have to leave.

The men in a turpentine camp must be ruled fairly but firmly, declared Wishart. That was an important aspect of "handlin' labor," something for which Wishart believed he had a special knack derived from his lifelong association with the Negro workers and his understanding of them. Turpentine workers liked him,

---

[32] "Turpentine Man," 2.

[33] "Turpentine Man," 6.

[34] "Turpentine Man," 7–8.

[35] Ibid.

he said, and would follow him, if he asked them to, when he quit a job and moved to another place.[36]

Wishart recalled an incident in which rapport with his men proved advantageous and, to him, humorous. This happened while he managed a camp in Polk County, Florida. The incident illustrated how turpentine operators often tried to "steal," or at least entice, workers from each other.[37]

One Saturday night after payday, shortly before Christmas, about forty of his men were playing a card game they called "skin," a favorite pastime among them. It just happened that one of the out-of-state owners of that turpentine company, visited the camp and observed the illegal gambling, of which he disapproved. Without saying a word to the foreman, this owner reported the men to the sheriff and arranged for all of the card players to be arrested. The authorities fined each $35 and jailed them in Bartow, pending payment of their fines.

Wishart's boss refused to pay the fines, so the men remained in jail. Someone told the foreman of a competing turpentine camp about the situation and let him know that he could gain forty good workers just for paying their fines to get them out of jail. This man quickly did so, and sent the men on the road to his camp while remaining in town for a few days to enjoy Christmas festivities. Wishart intercepted his just-released men on the way to their new employer's place. He urged them to come back home and go to work; he'd see that nobody bothered them any more about gambling, he promised. "They all whooped for joy," Wishart recalled, "and followed me back and went to work again for me."[38]

A few days later Wishart encountered the man who had paid the workers' fines, and they struck up a conversation. This gentleman complained that "some son of a bitch stole" forty good workers from him and, he had paid $35 a head to get them. He wished he could find out who did it. "I sympathized with him plenty, and it was weeks afterward before he found out it was me got his hands." By the time the two met again, Wishart's rival had "stolen" somebody else's hands and was no longer angry. The two of them just joked about it, he said.[39]

Although they differed in certain respects, the Langdale camps and workmen clearly had much in common with those of Wishart's description. Billy Langdale's experience running the camp at Mayday testifies to that.

Released from the Marine Corps on 10 June 1945, Billy went right to work in the naval stores business with his father. He and his new bride, who was from just outside of Columbia, South Carolina, moved to Mayday, Georgia. At Mayday there had developed something of an emergency situation because the manager of that turpentine place had moved away and was in the process of trying to take much of the labor force with him. So Billy arrived at Mayday with the assignment to

---

[36] Ibid.

[37] "Turpentine Man," 9–10.

[38] Ibid.

[39] Ibid.

restore order, keep the labor together, and run that turpentine place. He managed the Mayday operation for about a year and a half.[40]

The transition from secretary to a congressman in Washington DC, to wife of a turpentine camp manager in south Georgia must have required a major intellectual adjustment for his new wife, Jackie. She had visited Valdosta before the wedding, however—came down on the bus—and perhaps had an inkling of what was in store. For the first month, until a house at Mayday could be readied, Billy and Jackie rented a place at Twin Lakes, a few miles south of Valdosta. Billy commuted daily from there to the turpentine camp. When they did move to Mayday, it was not too bad, as Billy remembered it. They had a country-style house, but with servants. They also had nosy neighbors, but enjoyed time together, for example, fishing on the Alapaha River. Jackie paddled the boat, while Billy fished. Their first child was born while they lived at Mayday.[41] This was William P. (Bill), Jr., born 1 April 1946. Their other two children were Robert Harley (Bob), born 1 May 1948, and Mary Jacquelyn (Lyn), born 5 January 1950.[42]

While operating the place at Mayday, Billy said later, he had some unbelievable experiences. "To be a manager of a turpentine place was about a fifteen hour a day job," he recalled in 1992. "You would have to run the commissary...haul the people to the woods...[and] ride the woods and check on the ones that said they completed certain work...." "Then for the ones that got sick you had to haul them to the doctor in Valdosta. If they had financial problems, you had to bail them out of that."[43]

Managing the commissary ranked high in his list of responsibilities. At this time, in 1945–1946, Billy no longer had to purchase all supplies from the factors, as had once been the case. He bought some from his Uncle Noah, who had a wholesale grocery business in Valdosta, and other items from a company called T & R. Patent medicine salesmen also called at Mayday and sold their products to him directly.

Wartime rationing remained in effect when Billy started at Mayday. This made it difficult to provide meat for his workers without resorting to the black market. Mostly the workers ate salt meat, for the commissary had no refrigeration. At least once, to satisfy the craving for fresh beef, he slaughtered some old cows, about ten or twelve years old. To fatten the cattle before slaughter, he provided them fresh green wiregrass by burning a section of woods. They fattened very well, he recalled, and yielded good meat.

At Mayday Billy applied some of the techniques of managing turpentine camps that he had learned earlier from Troy Dukes, "an old time turpentiner" who

---

[40] Langdale, WPL Interview 1991.

[41] William P. Langdale, interview by author, audio tape, Valdosta GA, 14 February 2002.

[42] Clifton, ed., *Heritage of Lowndes County*, 110.

[43] Langdale, WPL Interview 1991.

ran the place at Tarver. For example, Billy had learned from Dukes how to awaken the workers each morning. At 4:00 A.M., the camp manager started the truck and drove through the camp sounding the horn. At the other end of the row of houses, he waited to see smoke curling from the chimney or lights turned on. If lights or smoke did not soon appear, he went to those houses and banged on the doors to awaken their inhabitants.

Often on Mondays following the monthly payday, several dwellings at Mayday failed to produce either smoke or light, indicating that the worker living there felt too sick to work. At the turpentine camp, people called these "Blue Mondays." They were the result of hangovers from drinking moonshine whiskey on Friday and Saturday. Troy Dukes had taught Billy how to manage that situation, using his own special concoction made from moonshine and patent medicines from the commissary. The commissary normally stocked Syrup of Black Draught, 666 Cold Medicine, paregoric, Raymond's Little Liver Pills, and sundry other medicines. Some of these turned out to be surplus, unsaleable, because rats gnawed the boxes or they were in some other way damaged.

Jacqueline & Billy Langdale, wedding photo, June 1945. A few days later, the couple went to manage Judge's turpentine place at Mayday. LCHS.

Imitating his mentor, Troy Dukes, Billy gathered whatever surplus medicines he had available at Mayday, plus a gallon of moonshine whiskey. He then poured half the whiskey into an empty jug and put half of his medicines in each half gallon of whiskey. With this solution of uncertain formula and potency, well shaken, he could deal with "Blue Monday." If a worker found himself too sick to work on Monday morning, Billy knocked on his door and offered him a glass of medicine to cure his ailment. "The main thing in it that made it work was a strong laxative," Billy recalled. "During the day you could ride back—and most of the outhouses were right back of the house—and you could see them coming and going about all day long. The next day they would be just as slick and pretty and nice as you'd ever seen, and they'd go to work the next day."[44]

Langdale turpentine camps such as the one at Mayday usually had between twenty and fifty workers, plus their families.[45] About thirty families lived in the quarters when Billy arrived in 1945. "When I got there labor was short. You couldn't get people to work, and I got a lot of mine out of the prison system in Florida. They would be glad to throw them out if they wouldn't come back to Florida, if they'd come to Georgia."[46] "I had murderers, I had every kind. I found out murder wasn't a bad offense with that kind of labor," said Billy, because these people did not hold a grudge against a man who killed someone in a fight. They thought it was just normal for a man to get angry and attack another. If a participant in a fight ended up dead, that was simply a fact to be accepted, not a wrong to be avenged.

Once, Billy recalled, two men got into a fight at the juke in front of a room full of witnesses, using "cutters" as weapons. Cutters were sharpening tools, resembling files in appearance, but very sharp on the edges and with a point much like that of an ice pick. One man killed the other, while sustaining cuts on his arms. Ordinarily, the manager of the turpentine place took care of the administration of justice. In this situation, however, the sheriff called in the Georgia Bureau of Investigation to determine whether charges should be filed. A GBI agent, after spending several days at the camp investigating the matter, concluded that conflicting testimony from the twenty or thirty eye-witnesses made it impossible to prosecute.

Recruiting labor, criminals or not, absorbed much of Billy's time at Mayday. Turpentine managers competed fiercely for scarce workers. Without hesitation, it seems, Billy joined in this slightly comical, but very serious and sometimes dangerous game. Typically, each Saturday afternoon after working his regular six-day week, he started on a recruiting trip to Florida, equipped with a supply of moonshine whiskey. Down below Tallahassee, near a town called Crawfordville, he found good hunting grounds for potential recruits. On these recruiting trips he took with him a man who knew the territory and situation. Locating a few likely prospects, Billy and his assistant softened them up with moonshine and extolled the advantages of working at Mayday. With luck, they persuaded three or four men to go with them to Georgia. Then, on the following Monday, Billy returned

---

[44] Ibid.

[45] Langdale, JWL Interview 1991.

[46] Langdale, WPL Interview 1991.

to Florida to pay the workers' accounts and move their belongings to Mayday. Although the law did not require worker accounts to be paid when they moved, that was considered the honorable thing to do.

Sometimes Billy had to contend with efforts by rivals to recruit his workers. For example, he had a family consisting of a man and wife, several daughters and one or two young boys living at Mayday. The man, a dipper, worked hard, and sometimes his boys helped him. Billy thought well of them. A young stranger dressed in a soldier's uniform showed up one day and moved in with this family, seemingly attracted by the girls, as Billy perceived it. One day Billy came into camp and found that every one of them were on their way to the railroad depot at Mayday, carrying all they could in their hands, preparing to catch the train. "Where are you going?" Billy asked. "We're just going to town," they replied.

Billy doubted that story. They were carrying too many possessions, he thought, just to be going to Valdosta. He collared the "soldier boy" and found out the truth. A man from nearby Gainesville, Florida, Billy Belott, who was the grandson of a former partner of Judge Harley at Mayday, had been there recruiting and had given train tickets to all of them. The old man of the family had already gone to work at Gainesville. Billy forbade them to leave, contending that some of the things they wished to carry away were collateral for debts they owed him. The "soldier boy" didn't argue with Billy's position. That suited him all right, he said, because he liked it better at Mayday anyway, but they did have those tickets supplied by the Gainesville man. Billy solved this problem by collecting the tickets.

About three weeks later, Billy went to Gainesville to retrieve his worker, taking with him the man's wife, who was to serve as intermediary in persuading her husband to return to Mayday. Arriving at the Gainesville place about ten or eleven o'clock at night, Billy stopped his truck just outside the quarters and sent the wife to get her husband. He waited for an hour or so while mosquitoes nibbled on his face, neck, and arms.

When the wife did not return by midnight, Billy concluded he had suffered enough from the Florida mosquitoes; he decided to go in. He drove up to the house of the camp manager, Belott, who was standing in his front yard. Billy explained his purpose, and the other man immediately pointed a pistol at him, having already—as Billy soon learned—sent for the sheriff. As the two men faced each other, bright lights appeared behind Billy. He turned to see what it was, and Belott, Billy said, "hit me right in the jaw and got on top of me and he kind of leant away. I leaned over and gave him a sure enough good elbow."[47]

It took only a moment for Billy to discover he had bitten off more than he could chew. As he recalled many years later, "The biggest deputy sheriff I'd ever seen—must have weighed three hundred pounds—grabbed me and shook me like I

---

[47] Ibid.

was a baby, and made me promise that I would let this fellow move these laborers from my place."[48] He would agree to the move, Billy conceded, provided Belott paid their debt of about $500 in cash. Billy stipulated that he would not accept a check. Two or three days later a man drove up at Mayday to move this family, offering a check to settle the account. Billy refused it, and sent the truck back to Gainesville empty.

"The next thing I knew," recalled Billy, "the FBI man came to see me." Billy discovered he had been charged with peonage in Orange County Superior Court. A judge in Tifton helped Billy refute the charge. "If it hadn't been for him, I expect I'd be in bad shape. He took all my testimony and wrote it all down, and I wrote letters."[49]

A memorable diversion from managing the Mayday turpentine place came for Billy in 1946. At that time, as a means of raising money to build a new football stadium, the citizens of Valdosta decided to stage a football game with former Wildcat players competing against each other. They called this the "Lard Bowl." Organizers divided the players into two teams, one coached by Bobby Hooks and the other coached by Dynamite Goodloe.

Down at Mayday minding his turpentine business, Billy had no part in this until he received a visit from his old and very dear friend J. F. Holmes, for whom he had played backup tackle in high school. Holmes wanted him to play the same role again. Billy protested. He was out of shape; he had not been on a football field in years, and he was too busy to practice. That doesn't matter, said J. F. Holmes; you will just be my substitute and probably won't have to play at all. So Billy agreed.

On the day of the game he drove in from Mayday. Somebody found him a pair of shoes that were too large. They ransacked the place and found other ill-fitting equipment for him to put on. He got dressed and prepared to warm the bench for the duration of the game. Then, to Billy's chagrin, on the first play of the game J. F. Holmes got hurt and had to be carried from the field. So Billy had to play the whole game, which ended in a 0-0 tie. He laughed at the experience later, but never forgot the blue places he had all over his body for two weeks afterward.[50]

After his adventures at Mayday, Billy moved to Valdosta. Subsequently, he managed Judge Harley's turpentine places in Nashville and Lakeland, Georgia.[51]

Although not every turpentine farm that Judge and his partners operated in the 1920s and 1930s had its own still, the larger ones usually did. They resembled the one on display in 2001 at the Tifton, Georgia, Agrirama and shown in the photo essay below.

---

[48] Ibid.
[49] Ibid.
[50] Langdale, WPL Interview 05.
[51] Langdale, WPL Interview 1991.

At one time Judge had interests in about twenty-five turpentine places in Florida, Georgia, and South Carolina. In some of these enterprises he had more than one partner. His operation at Tarver, Georgia, grew to become the largest one in the country.[52]

Judge Harley kept records of the expenses and productivity of each turpentine place. From each place he required weekly reports, which he published among his various operators to allow them to compare their achievements. He did this partly to stimulate competition among them. The reports showed the number of barrels of gum produced per crop (10,000 trees). This allowed objective comparison of different size places, such as a ten-crop and a fifteen-crop operation. Still, to be fair in evaluating the effectiveness of his managers, Judge had to make mental allowances for differences in quality and concentration of trees at different sites.[53]

By publishing the reports and stimulating competition, Judge provided incentive for his managers to do a better job. The effectiveness of oversight varied, of course. Sometimes a manager, yearning for recreation not available in the woods, might leave his assistant in charge and pay a mid-week visit to town. Typically, the quality of supervision suffered in his absence. On the other hand, another manager might mount his horse and ride through the woods where a dip squad or a chipping crew had just worked to see whether any trees, perhaps one or two separated some distance from the main concentration of trees, had been missed. Finding that some had, he would call the foreman's attention emphatically to the slack performance, and the whole unit would learn that shirking responsibility wouldn't do. Judge wanted to encourage rigorous and conscientious supervision.

Judge usually chose good managers, but if he made a mistake in this respect, he soon corrected it. To give managers extra incentive, he made them partners. By sharing control, responsibility, and profit with his partners, he built a much larger business than he ever could have if he had tried to operate these places alone. The string of partnerships that he developed bore some resemblance to a franchise situation in that it allowed him to leverage his time and money.[54]

During the years when he formed these turpentine partnerships, Judge Harley continued his law practice. He worked hard and kept long hours. Typically, he got up early in the morning, well before daylight, and drove to a turpentine camp over roads that were at that time unpaved. After consulting with his partner, or whatever he needed to do at the turpentine place, he drove back to Valdosta over those rough, sometimes wet and boggy, roads, and arrived at his law office earlier, he boasted, than most other Valdosta attorneys got to theirs. After attending to

---

[52] Langdale, Judge Interview 01; Langdale, "JWL to JEL Memo."
[53] Langdale, JWL Interview 14.
[54] Ibid.

legal matters all day, he usually visited another turpentine camp in the late afternoon, often getting home at nine or ten o'clock at night.[55]

Most of these turpentine partnerships did very well. According to Judge Harley, "this thing got to expanding, I was making a success pretty good, picking good people. I picked one man that was making twenty-five dollars a month as a still hand and finally bought him out, and I paid him pretty near $500,000 for his interest. And I just kept on expanding."[56]

As he added partners and places, Harley and his partners usually leased land for gum production. Generally, they secured three-year or five-year leases, making annual payments of a certain amount per turpentine face. According to the prevailing wisdom, trees could be worked for turpentine about four or five years. Turpentine producers typically leased a place for the useful life of the trees for producing gum, then moved on. Once gum production ended, trees could provide income to the owner only if cut for fuel, poles, or lumber. Subsequently, the cut-over land had little value because it had no marketable product. Such land could be bought cheap. People did not yet realize the potential for forest regeneration, had little knowledge of forest management, and failed to see the possibilities for second-growth timber.[57]

In the late 1930s, Harley, Jr. recalled, the Langdales paid about ten cents per face per year to lease turpentine land. On the average, an acre had about twenty faces, so leases cost annually about two dollars per acre. Taxes on land at that time were only about ten cents an acre.[58]

As time passed after Judge went into turpentine, land values fell, and Judge got more and more into land acquisition. The general trend in agriculture explains this partially. Farmers were leaving the land and doing so at a faster rate.

In 1850 and in 1860, before the War Between the States, the average American farm measured about 200 acres. To a great extent because of the Civil War and its consequences, this fell to 153 acres by 1870 and 134 acres in 1880. Likewise, the percentage of the labor force making a living in agriculture dropped from 64 percent in 1850 to 49 percent in 1880. Thirty years later, in 1910, only 21 percent of the US labor force earned a living from farming, and the average size of farms was 148 acres and rising. Subsequently, the acreage of farms grew steadily as the number of farmers continuously decreased. By 1990, farmers made up only 2.6 percent of the labor force, and the average farm comprised 461 acres.[59]

---

[55] Langdale, Judge Interview 01.

[56] Ibid.

[57] Ibid.

[58] Langdale, HLJr Interview 1991.

[59] United States Department of Agriculture, Economic Research Service. *A History of American Agriculture, 1776-1990: Farmers and the Land* [cited 15 September 1998]. Available from http://www.usda.gov/history2/back.htm.

In the 1920s in south Georgia, the Boll Weevil exacerbated the general trend and the effect of the agricultural depression. Earlier in the twentieth century, many south Georgia and north Florida farmers had prospered from growing long-staple cotton. At one time Valdosta had eight cotton gins dedicated to processing this crop. That ended when the Boll Weevil arrived. Some farmers, unable to make a living from their land and unable to sell it, simply abandoned their property. They just moved off and left it, leaving it in some cases to be sold by the county for taxes. Judge bought some of this land for the price of taxes owed.[60]

Judge kept on the alert for opportunities to acquire land. According to one of his Valdosta lawyer friends, "I ran into the Judge on the street one day and told him where he could buy nine thousand acres of land for a dollar and a quarter an acre. I'll bet he didn't have ninety cents in his pocket, but he went around the corner with his shirttail popping, headed for the depot to catch the train.[61]

In these hard times for farmers, Judge Harley and his partners found it easier to acquire land, whether by lease or purchase. Sometimes, before a lease ran out, the landowner approached them about renewing it. In one instance, Judge found he could buy a place for less than he could lease it. So he did. Although he wanted land primarily for its turpentine potential, his acquisitions included a considerable amount of cultivated land. This led to diversification into production of corn, peanuts, tobacco, and other crops, as well as livestock.[62]

Judge always had an interest in livestock. Although his son, John W., had the impression row-cropping might have been Judge Harley's favorite kind of farming, John's younger brother, Billy, saw his father as more of a livestock enthusiast. And of all his agricultural interests, in Billy's opinion, Judge Harley liked the hog business best. Judge's father, John Wesley, had prospered with hogs and cows down at Council before getting into turpentine, and Judge Harley had learned the business from his father. The J. W. Langdale Company, managed by Judge's brother, John J., continued this aspect of John Wesley's business until after World War II, and of course Judge knew the practices employed there.[63]

In the days before fences, the time of the open range, farmers in the flatwoods had annual hog round-ups. On such occasions, owners marked their hogs with a certain brand. Judge Harley's mark was a swallow fork and an underbit in each ear. These Piney Woods Rooters had noses about a foot long. A common joke, Billy remembered, was that they would just about balance if you picked them up by both ears: there would be about the same amount of hog in front as behind the ears.

Judge's cattle received the same brand as the hogs, although he had some cows branded with an SA because he had bought the claim of a man who used that brand.

---

[60] Langdale, Judge Interview 01.

[61] Martin, 91.

[62] Langdale, Judge Interview 01.

[63] Langdale, WPL Interview 1991.

Later, Judge Harley used the brand HL. In the Council area, he had perhaps a thousand head of cattle, and in South Carolina around three to five hundred head of much better quality beef. Though left to run free, cattle usually didn't stray more than about seven or eight miles, as Billy recalled.

Judge had a reputation for having a keen eye and long memory for livestock. Billy remembered hearing people comment on this. Some said he could buy a claim, view the cattle once, return the next year to see the herd again, and notice a particular cow was missing. "Where is that spotted cow that was here last year?" he would ask. "I don't see her. Where is she?"[64]

Although he liked the livestock business, Judge did not allow himself to be diverted from the main profit-maker, naval stores. Land and pine trees remained the key to successful turpentine production. Before long, after some success at land acquisition, Judge Harley became excited about the possibilities of buying large amounts of land. He had a plan, he said in later life, inspired by a Valdosta sign painter who liked to do crossword puzzles. "I'd get up before day some mornings and go to a turpentine place," Judge said, "and this sign painter here would be down working a crossword puzzle. Well, I had me a crossword puzzle. I wanted to connect fee simple all these turpentine places, about fifteen miles from one to the other. That was the crossword puzzle I worked. So I finally connected it all up in fee-simple land."[65]

At other times, to his daughter, Judge described his land acquisitions as "like a quilt, piecing it together." "He would just get so excited about it," Virginia recalled, "telling me how he pieced up this and that, and how hard it was to get that little strip there, and who it was owned by. That was a challenge to him. I guess he was just in the right place at the right time when all this land came up for sale."[66]

Judge's knowledge of land and its characteristics in various areas became legendary. People said you could show him a handful of dirt and he could tell you where it came from.[67]

Some land that Judge Langdale acquired had very little immediate value, even for naval stores. This included tracts that farmers had turpentined in the 1930s, earning annually about ten cents per face. The income from turpentine during the depression helped them stay afloat for a few years. After this, they sometimes secured additional income from selling the worked out trees as saw timber, and finished by selling the cut-over land. They were then out of business, so far as their forestland was concerned.[68]

Billy Langdale remembered that his father had a reputation for being eager to buy, but very reluctant to sell land. "They said he had a cramp if you asked him to

---

[64] Ibid.
[65] Langdale, Judge Interview 01.
[66] Miller, VLM Interview 01.
[67] McKay, "Langdale Lived to See Dream Come True."
[68] Langdale, HLJr Interview 1991.

sign a deed,"[69] remembered Billy with a laugh. Judge Harley once showed Billy a tract of land that a man had given him clear title to. Judge "got a lot [one tract] of land for 25 cents an acre,"[70] recalled Billy. Some of this cheap land rose rapidly in value. The Langdales acquired land in Berrien County for nine or ten dollars an acre, Billy remembered, and just a few years later, the timber on it sold for twice as much as the land cost.[71]

Judge could buy land cheap because he had little competition for it. As of the middle 1930s paper mills had not yet arrived to create a demand for pulpwood. Sawmills preferred larger timber. Most of the land Judge bought in these early years had little use, except for turpentine. Banks even refused to accept it as collateral for a loan, classifying it as wasteland. In Valdosta, Mr. Winn, the banker, sometimes teased Judge Harley about his land. As Judge remembered thirty years later, "Mr. Winn used to kid me and ask me about if I wanted to borrow a little money how much or what collateral I had. He wanted me to tell him I had some land down there in Clinch and Echols, so he'd laugh at me. Ha. Ha. Ha."[72] On another occasion, concerning his relationship with bankers during the early days, Judge quipped, "They thought I was crazy;...bankers would see me coming and run like startled rabbits."[73] Yet Judge "had an idea that some day or another that was going to change."[74] So he went about the business of completing his crossword puzzle with fee-simple land.

Looking back in 1955, Judge marveled at the failure of other south Georgians in the 1920s and 1930s to see the profit potential of the pine tree. "Why they couldn't see that, is a mystery to me," he told an interviewer. "This coastal country is the pine tree's natural home. Land that is too pore to grow peas will grow a slash-pine tree. You don't have to do a thing with it but keep the wild-fire out of it and let it grow. The Lord knew what He was doing when He made a pine tree. He knew that men were going to butcher and burn and destroy the forests. So He put a little propeller on the pine tree's seed, so wherever an old tree was spared, its seed could float on the wind to start the forest growing again."[75]

The situation did change with respect to land and timber values, of course, much to Judge's advantage during the period encompassing World War II and the Korean War. It happened for a number of reasons, including, but not simply because of international conflicts. Reflecting those changed circumstances since the late 1930s, the Langdale Company's daily net as of August 1954 came to around $2,000. About this time one estimate put Judge's net worth at

---

[69] Langdale, WPL Interview 1991.

[70] Ibid.

[71] Ibid.

[72] Langdale, Judge Interview 01.

[73] McKay, "Langdale Lived to See Dream Come True."

[74] Langdale, Judge Interview 01.

[75] Martin, 91.

$10,000,000. He acknowledged annual income of perhaps $88,000. In 1955 the Langdales owned 130,000 acres of pineland and had long-term leases on 150,000 more. By this time the Langdale Company sold 100,000 cords of pulpwood annually at $13 a cord to the Clyattville paper mill, something Judge would not have dreamed of doing before 1937.[76] That was the year Harley, Jr. graduated from forestry school and returned to help run the family business. The period from the late 1930s to the mid-1950s saw remarkable improvement in Judge's fortunes.

In retrospect, Judge may have expressed in later years a slightly exaggerated view of his own prescience. His son, John W., doubted his father foresaw the great increase in land and timber values that actually occurred or the prosperity his company would eventually enjoy. Judge's investments turned out to be far better than he expected. As John W. saw it, Judge basically made good short and medium-term business decisions for a more profitable turpentine business.[77] Fortunately, those land purchases proved to be sound long-term investments that laid the foundation for the highly successful Langdale Company, which included some twenty corporations of various sizes and types by the 1990s.[78]

In the early days, though, back in the 1920s especially, Judge struggled. Land was cheap, and he bought much of it, but emphasizing the low price obscures the fact that he paid substantially more for it than the sales price. Since banks could not lend money on waste land and he did not have enough money of his own, he had to convince the turpentine factors to provide the capital. Soon he found himself deeply in debt to the factors and paying much higher interest rates than he would have paid on a regular bank loan.

Long afterward, Judge described his relationship with the turpentine factors, which had both positive and negative aspects.

If it hadn't been for the turpentine factors," he declared, "I couldn't have done a thing. They had to have turpentine to stay in business, and I knew how to make turpentine. The factors had complete control over me. They'd let me have money to lease land or buy land, and pay wages. They sold me the groceries I had to carry in my commissaries. They charged me eight per cent on the money I borrowed and another two and one half per cent commission when they sold my turpentine and rosin. Since I had to sell through them, they knew they'd get their money back. Some years they did. Some years they didn't. They went along with me pretty good, but sometimes, when I got in too deep, they'd cut me off. I

---

[76] Ibid.

[77] Langdale, JWL Interview 14.

[78] Ibid.

remember once, when I owed them nearly four hundred thousand dollars, I sent in a little old draft for thirty-five dollars. They turned it down.[79]

Judge Harley put his own money into land purchases, too, money that another person might have spent on his family. Rather than buy a house for his family to live in, for example, he continued to rent until around 1930, eight years after he went into the naval stores business.

In a *Saturday Evening Post* article in 1955, Harold H. Martin retold a story he heard in Valdosta about Judge Langdale and his strained finances in the pre-war period. The tale went something like this. A local fellow took a visitor down Patterson Street, pointing out with pride the impressive residences of lumber and cotton tycoons and commenting on their wealth. "There's Dr. So-and-So's house," said the guide. "He's worth a million dollars. And there's Mr. Such-and-Such's place. He's also worth a million dollars." Then, coming to the Langdale residence, the guide observed, "There's where Judge Harley Langdale lives; he owes a million dollars."[80]

Actually, Judge doubted that he had ever owed more than half a million dollars at any time, but he admitted that some years he had trouble paying his rent and worried that his creditors might attach his personal property. Possibly he owed more than he thought, Judge conceded, for he kept some of his records in his head. As Judge put it, "I've seen the time that if I had wanted to take bankruptcy I couldn't have done it. I didn't have the money to pay the court costs. If my creditors had wanted to push me, they could have put me on the street. Me and my wife and my kids would have had to walk out of the house and down the road with nothing we owned to our name but the clothes on our backs."[81]

In later, more prosperous years, Judge and others often quoted his comment that "the Lord knew what he was doing when he made a pine tree."[82] Well, Judge knew what he was doing, too, when he put everything he had in land; he was taking a big calculated risk, undoubtedly with high hopes, but with little expectation it would turn out as well as it did.

There is an interpretation of Judge Harley as a romantic visionary who saw it as his mission to restore the pine forests as they were at the time of Columbus. For example, Harold Martin said in his 1955 article, "the spectacular upswing in the judge's fortunes is due to one firm conviction to which he has clung, stubbornly, all his life. It is the judge's unswerving belief that the Lord is determined that a great forest of pine trees again shall roll in a blue-green sea along the coastal plain from the Potomac south to Florida and west to the Mississippi, as the forests stood

---

[79] Martin, 91.

[80] Ibid., 20.

[81] Ibid.

[82] McKay, "Langdale Lived to See Dream Come True."

there when the country was young. The judge, who is sixty-six now, has spent a half century assisting Divine Providence in this massive restoration project... ."[83]

Well, not exactly. Certainly Judge was not without sentiment and he saw further and clearer than most of his contemporaries, but he was more interested in making a living than in re-creating the world. The rise in his financial position resulted more from practical business decisions in the light of economic and political circumstances than from a grand design to help Divine Providence restore the primeval forest. The dramatic improvement in Judge's finances, coinciding with World War II, the Korean War, and the Cold War, certainly owed something to those events and opportunities they created. In addition, the importance of having an able, energetic, and forestry-educated son to take over and run the day-to-day operations of the company from 1937 on can hardly be over-emphasized.

Judge's decision to move aside in 1937 and permit Harley, Jr. to take charge qualifies as probably the best management move he ever made and a crucial factor in the success of the Langdale Company. Not only did this improve the management of the family forest products business at a critical period, but it permitted Judge to devote his own energies to the American Turpentine Farmers Association, which he established in the 1930s and led for many years. As leader of this organization Judge brought profit to himself and other turpentine producers throughout the turpentine belt. The story of ATFA is next to be addressed, following a photo essay on old-fashioned turpentine stills.

---

[83] Martin, 91.

Photo Essay

A Typical Turpentine Still

The stills on the Langdale turpentine places resembled the one shown in the following scenes.[1] All work on a turpentine place focused on the distillation plant, or "still." Prior to World War II the typical still, located in or near the forests that produced the gum they processed, looked much like this one maintained as a museum exhibit at the Agrirama in Tifton, Georgia, and photographed in 1999. Approaching the still from the output side, the visitor sees two small buildings, one of which is the still itself and the other the cooper's shop.

Turpentine still on display at Agrirama, Tifton, Georgia. JEL.

In the previous photo and more clearly in the next, below, a ramp made of logs is visible at the left of the still, which was the input side. Gum collected from the forest entered the still here. The next photograph, shows the ramp viewed

---

[1] The distillation process is described in Kenneth L.Thomas, Jr., *McCranie's Turpentine Still*. (Athens: University of Georgia, Institute of Community and Area Development, 1976).

from the input side of the still, with a 55-gallon barrel of gum in place to be rolled up the ramp into the still.

Input (L) & output sides of turpentine still. JEL.

Ramp upon which a barrel of gum entered the still. JEL.

The following picture provides a clearer view of the platform or "upper deck" that was the barrel's destination. Once the gum was poured into the copper kettle,

Upper deck of turpentine still. JEL.

which was called "charging the still," it received heat from the wood-fired furnace visible below the platform. The copper kettle was mounted in the brick structure above the fire chamber. Heating the gum caused turpentine mixed with steam to rise through the "cap" or "condenser" into the "worm" and through its tail pipe into the "spirit room" or shed. The kettle, condenser, and worm were made of copper and typically purchased from the manufacturer as a unit. The photo below shows the mouth of the furnace into which wood was inserted for fuel.

Furnace. JEL.

Looking at the still from a point near the cooper's shop, one can see the wooden still tub, which housed the "worm" and was filled with water for cooling and condensing the hot mixture of steam and turpentine on its way to the spirit shed. As this process heated the water in the still tub, hot water ran out the top of the tub and was replaced by cool water added through a pipe at the bottom. Turpentine was separated from the accompanying water ("low wine"), which was

Still tub & separator barrels. JEL.

heavier than turpentine, by passing the mixture through two barrels and into a third. As, in turn, each barrel filled, turpentine flowed out an opening at the top, while water settled to the bottom and passed out through a drain. The third barrel, called the "spirit barrel," served as the shipping container for the turpentine.

Tailgate, strainer, & rosin barrels. JEL

A residue of rosin and trash remained after removing the turpentine by distillation. When this had cooled to an acceptable temperature, the mixture was drawn off through a port (the "tail gate") located on the lower level behind the furnace.

Then the rosin passed through three strainers to remove all the trash and flowed into the vat.

The next photo shows the three strainers through which rosin was filtered. Each successive strainer was finer than the previous one, with the third making use of cotton batten to remove remaining impurities.

Rosin, having been cleaned and strained, went into barrels like those in the foreground of the preceeding photograph for storage or for shipment to the turpentine factor. The whole distillation process for a charge of about 500 gallons of crude gum took about three or four hours.

This is the kind of still that Harley, Jr. put out of business on Langdale property when he set up the centralized still in Valdosta during the Second World War.

Strainers & tailgate of turpentine still. JEL.

The new still, built with stainless steel components, ran for thirty years without major repairs. It required less labor, delivered better products, achieved more output per barrel of gum, and could process much greater volume of oleoresin than all the fire stills combined.

7

American Turpentine

Farmers Association

*I*n the 1930s the naval stores industry encountered a crisis with low and unstable prices. To ameliorate the situation, various individuals and groups tried to organize producers, factors, and dealers, the three basic kinds of business in the industry. Through collective influence, they hoped to improve naval stores prosperity.

Out of this period of discussion and contention, an organization emerged that worked effectively for the industry and undoubtedly saved many people from business failure. Judge Harley Langdale took the lead in forming and running this organization, known as the American Turpentine Farmers Association. "It was formed in 1936 because all the turpentine operators were pretty well broke," remembered Harley, Jr. "The thing that really broke them was the fluctuation of the price, manipulated by the factors and the brokers and the exporters."[1]

When Judge proposed the American Turpentine Farmers Association as a farmers cooperative, he put forward an idea that had already proved itself as an organizing principle. Cooperatives had by this time taken their place in the mainstream of American agricultural movements.

From the beginning of the history of the United States, farmers had established organizations to promote the interests of agriculture. As early as 1785, Pennsylvanians formed the Philadelphia Society to promote agriculture. In the 1850s, farmers set up some of the first cooperative organizations to assist in marketing such commodities as cheese, wool, and tobacco. The national Grange gave its backing to cooperatives in the 1870s.

---

[1] Langdale, HLJr Interview 1991.

Farmers turned to politics, too. By the 1890s, the Populists, a major political party advocating agricultural interests, ran candidates for the presidency of the United States.

Although they did not win the presidency, farmers gained through political influence. In the first decade of the twentieth-century, the first county agricultural agents started work. The Farm Bureau began in 1911, and, by the 1920s, farm organizations had strong lobbying efforts in Washington. Early in that decade, Congress passed the Capper-Volstead Act (1922), giving cooperatives legal standing. Thousands of cooperatives came into being, and in 1929 farmers and their representatives organized the National Council of Farmers Cooperatives. In 1930, 11,950 cooperatives boasted three million members. Within the next twenty years encompassing most of the Great Depression, World War II, and the start of the Cold War, the number of cooperatives decreased slightly, but membership more than doubled to seven million and remained at about that level in the 1960s.[2]

In 1936, with the gum naval stores industry in crisis, producers, dealers, and factors received an invitation to a great meeting in Savannah to discuss creation of an organization to serve the interests of all three groups in the naval stores industry. People came from as far away as North Carolina and Louisiana. At this meeting, Judge Harley Langdale stood up and made a speech arguing that no organization could successfully represent these three divergent interests. In particular, he thought, dealers and producers had incompatible interests because dealers, to make their profit, always strove to buy low and sell high. Producers naturally always wanted to sell high. What producers needed, declared Judge Harley, was their own separate organization.[3]

Some attendees agreed; others did not. The group decided the issue needed study. They established a committee of six with equal numbers of dealers, factors, and producers to examine the issue and make recommendations. Judge Harley and Mr. Rhodes of South Carolina represented producers on this committee.

The committee met in Brunswick. When the members arrived, they found one member, a prominent attorney and president of the Downing Company, had a plan already drawn up, which he proceeded to show the group. Before the first page had been fully reviewed, Judge Harley realized this plan called for an organization representing all three interests—factors, dealers, and producers—the very thing he had spoken against at the Savannah meeting.

Judge brought the committee meeting in Brunswick to an abrupt end. As he recalled, "I told them there may be a time when the lions and lambs lie down

---

[2] United States Department of Agriculture, Economic Research Service. *A History of American Agriculture, 1776-1990: Farm Organizations and Movements* [cited 15 September 1998]. Available from http://www.usda.gov/history2/back.htm.
[3] Langdale, Judge Interview 01.

together, but I didn't think it was time. We broke that meeting up, and two of the factors joined me. We broke that meeting up right there."[4]

Judge Harley must have taken great comfort in the support for his position he received from the factors on this committee at Brunswick. Considering that he owed a large sum to turpentine factors at that time, he entered into this organizational issue with some vulnerability and needed to proceed carefully, lest he drive the factors into opposition. In fact, Judge Harley owed so much to the factors at times, it was hard to make ends meet. As John W. recalled, "he reached a point when he and Harley practically jumped up and shouted "'Hallelujah' when they finally got in financial position to say, 'Free at last; thank God I'm free at last.'"[5]

The factors really preferred to be in the middle of everything to enhance their control over producers. Factors made high-interest loans to producers, earned commissions on sale of turpentine and rosin received from them, and made profits on sale of equipment and consumables that producers bought for their commissaries. At this particular time, some factors had enormous investments in loans to producers whose businesses were in serious trouble, considering the weak, unstable market prices. Evidently, the factors, with enormous sums of "money in the woods," as Judge put it, saw Judge's approach as a promising way of securing their own investments and, for this reason, did not oppose him. As John W., commented in 1997, "they were concerned about keeping these turpentine operators alive so they could repay their debt."[6]

Factors, such as Consolidated Naval Stores, had been a dominant force in the turpentine business since the middle of the nineteenth century, generally controlling the export market and forcing small producers to sell through them. They had some capital of their own, but they borrowed additional money from banks, which they reinvested in loans to producers. Banks could lend a turpentine farmer money with collateral of equipment, animals, supplies, or farm land, but they could not accept timberland for that purpose; it was considered waste land until the Federal Land Bank eventually changed this definition.[7] Typically, every year factors extended credit to producers to get them through the winter, and expected repayment, starting in April. In the winter, gum did not flow, so turpentine farmers had no income. Yet they had heavy expenses for equipment, their own living expenses, and costs associated with labor. Factors, in summary, financed producers in the winter and expected to collect the return on their investment in the spring and summer. They charged an interest rate of eight percent when Harley, Jr. started dealing with them in the late 1930s, a high rate for the time, and deducted two percent of the sales price as a commission for

---

[4] Ibid.

[5] Langdale, JWL Interview 14.

[6] Ibid.

[7] Langdale, HLJr Interview 1991.

turpentine and rosin sold for the producer. "It was easy credit, hard to pay back," remembered Harley, Jr. "The secret was that if you could handle the labor—most all turpentine labor was black people—if you could handle those and knew how to get the work out of them, well then you could get along with the factors pretty good because you could operate."[8]

Driving home from the Brunswick meeting in 1936, Judge Harley reflected on the deplorable situation that existed in the industry and in efforts to organize. The most pressing problem to address, he thought, was that the government had acquired a supply of rosin through a loan program and was now selling that rosin in direct competition with current production, driving prices down. In his opinion, the situation obviously called for an association of producers to influence the government. And, given the organizational fiasco at Brunswick earlier in the day, he decided to take the initiative in creating such an association.[9]

This should not be too difficult, he thought. An organization of this type had actually been formed a few years previously and had elected a president. Its charter and bylaws appeared adequate. For some reason, however, that association had died or perhaps had never really got started.

To move this project along more easily and quickly, Judge concluded, it would be smart to base his new association on the plan of the previous one. He assigned the task of drafting the new charter to Lundie Smith and Lamar Tillman, both of whom had joined him in legal practice the year before. He provided them a copy of the defunct organization's charter for guidance.

Next, with the charter nicely printed in booklet form at his own expense, Judge Harley rented an auditorium in Jacksonville and sent invitations to producers and factors throughout the turpentine belt, from North Carolina to Texas, to convene an organizational meeting. Jacksonville, he thought, would be a convenient place for everyone to come by train.

At the meeting, which was well attended, Judge Harley had copies of the proposed charter distributed among the people and arranged to have himself suitably introduced. He spoke about his plan to establish the American Turpentine Farmers Association, with a board of directors representing every state in the turpentine belt. The crowd responded enthusiastically and adopted the plan. In elections for directors, Georgia producers chose Judge Harley as one of their four directors.[10] It must have pleased Judge immensely that Harley, Jr., who was then a senior in forestry school at UGA, attended this meeting and witnessed his father's success.[11]

Afterward, a meeting of the directors elected officers. These included Robert Newton of Wiggins, Mississippi, vice president, and Colin Kelly of Madison,

---

[8] Ibid.
[9] Langdale, Judge Interview 01.
[10] Ibid.
[11] Langdale, JWL Interview 14.

Florida, secretary and treasurer. The directors picked Judge Harley Langdale as president and instructed him to go to Washington the following week to start lobbying for the interests of turpentine producers. As its first objective, ATFA wanted to persuade the government to hold on to the rosin that it owned and not sell it in competition with current production.[12]

Judge Harley and others first approached the Department of Agriculture. At that time, the department had no separate division for naval stores. One of their first contacts in the department, Milton S. Briggs, later headed the naval stores division of the department.

In his visits with the Department of Agriculture, Judge met Agriculture Secretary Henry Wallace on a number of occasions. He found Wallace's views on naval stores ambiguous. "You couldn't hardly tell what he was. He was a flighty fellow that had a lot of ideas, you know. We got along pretty well with him," Judge Harley remembered years later.[13]

Some officials questioned whether turpentine met the official definition of an agricultural product, subject to the Agriculture Department's jurisdiction. Judge Harley and ATFA argued that turpentine production was analogous to growing peanuts or corn. It was farming. In months to come, they bolstered their argument by getting several state legislatures to declare turpentine an agricultural commodity.[14]

Classification as "farmers" not only helped qualify naval stores producers for government price support, but also led to exemption from some requirements of the wage and hour laws.[15] The American Turpentine Farmers Association and other forestry associations lobbied the federal government against applying this legislation to naval stores. The Wage-Hour Act established minimum wage and overtime requirements that would have forced turpentine producers either to abandon the piece-rate method of payment outright or to retain it and add a mechanism for keeping up with the number of hours worked. This additional accounting would be necessary in order to pay a worker a supplementary amount if his wage based on the piece-rate method did not meet the hourly minimum wage standard. Besides the higher labor costs likely under the minimum-wage law, this would have amounted to an expensive additional layer of supervision. As time passed, the government amended the wage-hour laws to include turpentine workers, but exempted companies with ten or fewer workers. Later still, the law included everyone, without exception. As John W. concluded, "It was a costly thing for forestry and turpentine to comply with that act."[16]

---

[12] Langdale, Judge Interview 01.
[13] Ibid.
[14] Ibid.
[15] Langdale, HLJr Interview 1991.
[16] Langdale, JWL Interview 1991.

Required compliance with the wage-hour laws contributed, along with competition from cheap by-products of the paper mills, to the eventual demise of the gum naval stores industry. As John W. observed in 1991, "the turpentine business itself gradually died out.... And what caused that was your labor problem, mainly. It depended on that low-cost labor."[17]

ATFA became very active in state and national politics throughout the turpentine region, which included states from North Carolina to Texas. Turpentine producers raised money for their preferred candidates and helped in whatever ways they could to elect officials sympathetic to the needs of naval stores producers. In Georgia, that included Senators Walter George and Richard Russell. In Florida, they worked for Senator Spessard Holland, and, in Mississippi, Representative Bill Carmer of the Hattiesburg district, had ATFA support. Carmer "was one of our key men up there," commented Judge Harley.[18]

Political involvement proved necessary because the people they had to deal with in the Agriculture Department appeared, initially, to have little knowledge or understanding of the needs of turpentine farmers. That was Judge's opinion.

Later, ATFA sought government price support under the Agriculture Department's loan programs. It was unfair, Judge and his friends argued, for other agricultural commodities to get loan support, in effect raising the prices turpentine producers must pay for supplies, while naval stores lacked equivalent support.[19] The Commodity Credit Corporation established a program under which it loaned ATFA money to advance to producers at times of low demand and low prices. "It was a great blessing it was formed when it was," said Harley, Jr., "because we had some of that rosin when the war started and that's what carried our country over."[20]

ATFA Leaders in 1949. Shown in graphic from unidentified magazine. Clipping from Langdale Papers. TLC.

---

[17] Ibid.

[18] Langdale, Judge Interview 01.

[19] Ibid.

[20] Langdale, HLJr Interview 1991.

The Commodity Credit Corporation never lost money on this program, in Harley, Jr.'s opinion, because it sold these stored containers of rosin and turpentine at a profit during the war and afterward. In a sense, the government took the place of factors in the marketing of naval stores.[21]

Conservation soon entered into the picture. ATFA and the Department of Agriculture jointly pushed for producers to take trees less than nine inches DBH (Diameter Breast High) out of production. Studies had shown that cupping such small trees damaged them and did not pay off financially. Government payments encouraged this improved practice.[22]

Trees smaller than nine inches DBH were, of course, younger trees. Producers typically put the first cups on trees after they were eighteen or twenty years old. Sometimes, though, for example in the 1920s when gum sometimes brought a high price, some farmers put cups on younger trees, some as small as seven inches DBH. This damaged those trees, reduced production in the long run, and ruined some of these producers.[23]

The government's conservation program and the naval stores loan program won approbation from naval stores producers. "Those two things helped us considerably," said Harley, Jr. In fact, he said, "that was one program I just couldn't criticize."[24] ATFA encouraged turpentine farmers to take advantage of new knowledge gained from US Government research and new techniques to improve production and profitability. By the 1950s, farmers were practicing more conservative cupping, taking less wood off the tree with each streak, using sulphuric acid to reduce by half the number of streaks required per season, and transplanting genetically-improved seedlings to replace older, worked-out trees.

ATFA, which grew in membership from 900 to 4,000 by 1955, also dealt with the problem of turpentine distribution to consumers.[25] In 1936, if a person wanted to buy a bottle of turpentine, he had to take his own bottle to the store, recalled Judge. Many people bought turpentine as medicine. The Langdales agreed with those who appreciated turpentine's medicinal uses. John W. kept a small bottle near his desk as a first aid for minor cuts. Judge Harley, when coming down with a cold or sore throat, added a few drops to a teaspoon of sugar, which he believed to be a good remedy for such maladies.[26]

Judge touted the medicinal benefits of turpentine to a national magazine reporter in 1955. Workers at turpentine stills rarely caught colds, he contended, and seemed highly resistant to tuberculosis, perhaps from breathing vapors

---

[21] Ibid.
[22] Langdale, Judge Interview 01.
[23] Langdale, HLJr Interview 1991.
[24] Ibid.
[25] Martin, 92.
[26] Langdale, HLJr Interview 1991.

emanating from the stills. Turpentine laborers also appeared to recover quickly from knife cuts and gunshot wounds, Judge observed.

Since before the time of Christ, Judge reminded his listener, the medicinal qualities of turpentine had been known. "The ancient Greeks," he declared tongue-in-cheek, "recognized the healthful properties of the pine-tree gum. The peasant wine of Greece, called *retsina,* was made with a rosin base, and I have heard it said that when an old Greek died after drinking *retsina* all his life, it was necessary to take his stomach out and beat it to death with a stick. Rosin is an excellent preservative."[27]

Spraying acid on turpentine faces. TLC.

Harley, Jr. showing proper use of a hack. TLC.

---

[27] Martin, 91.

Although ATFA did not distribute *retsina*, the association did work on the design of containers for distributing turpentine, publicized the industry with an annual beauty pageant to select "Miss Gum Spirits of Turpentine," and conducted nationwide advertising. Judge Harley worked hard to have a successful beauty contest, one of his pet projects. He was proud of the new containers and related advertising, which, for a while, raised the price of turpentine distributed in these containers by seventy-five percent. The association won a national award for the excellent design of its containers. Unfortunately, the good sales results diminished as competition from sulphate turpentine produced by paper mills increasingly undercut the price of gum turpentine.[28]

When the paper mills first began producing byproducts in competition with gum naval stores, Judge and other producers did not expect this competition eventually to put them out of business. Chemists and others told them, and they believed, that gum naval stores were superior to the sulfate turpentine and tall oil produced by the paper mills. In time, however, Harley, Jr. and others who were better acquainted with the paper mills saw the handwriting on the wall. As he put it, "they had the money, they had the chemists, they had the people, and that was going to come about. So it really has."[29]

Harley Langdale, Jr. explaining use of a Rosin Standard Gauge, a souvenir from the turpentine era, in 2001. JEL

In their competition with the naval stores byproducts of paper mills, gum naval stores producers tried hard and went to great expense to turn out superior grades of rosin. The highest quality, grade X, had the lightest color. Other grades, from top to bottom, were called Waterwhite, Windowglass, Nancy, Mary, Kate, Isaac, Harry, George, Frank, Edward, and Dolly. According to a traditional story, the names of these grades came from the names of Negro laborers whose complexions varied from light to dark. Each barrel of rosin had to be inspected.

---

[28] Langdale, Judge Interview 01.
[29] Langdale, HLJr Interview 1991.

An inspector drew a sample from each barrel and compared it to a standard that he carried around with him. At first, the paper mills could not produce rosin of the higher grades, but later they could.[30]

Notwithstanding the efforts of ATFA, by 1939, future prospects for gum turpentine producers appeared dim. Some were writing the industry's obituary. A second-generation turpentine man, R. W. Wishart of Florida, for example, took this view. Wishart, son of the manager of a twenty-crop turpentine place near Eastman, Georgia, had been born there in the turpentine camp in 1899 and spent the greater part of forty years in the business, mostly in Florida. About the same age as Judge Harley, he had been a water boy at the age of eight, a talley man at ten, and was making boxes and streaks at age 12. He became a woods rider and foreman of a dipping squad at thirteen and a guard of convict workers on a turpentine place near Punta Gorda, Florida, at fifteen. He managed turpentine places for two or three years before joining the army and fighting in France in 1917.[31]

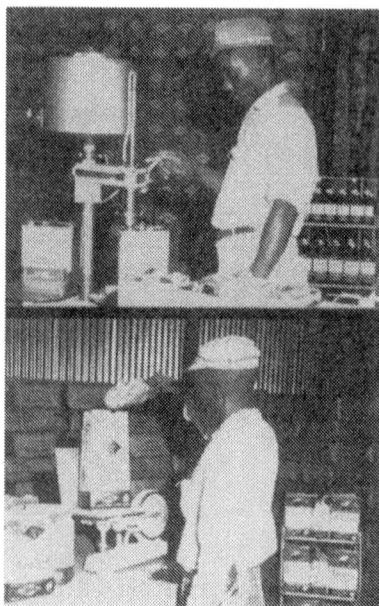

Langdale workers packaging turpentine & rosin for sale to consumers, following ATFA guidelines. TLC.

After the war, Wishart managed turpentine operations with as many as 120 crops in Florida (10,000 faces per crop). In 1934, when "the price of naval stores again hit bottom," he found work supervising a logging camp. Three years later (1937), the year Harley, Jr. finished forestry school, he returned to the turpentine business, but not in the United States. He took a job with the government of Haiti

---

[30] Ibid.
[31] "Turpentine Man," 1–10, passim.

to survey that country's naval stores and lumber resources. He set up a still for the Haitians before returning to Florida.

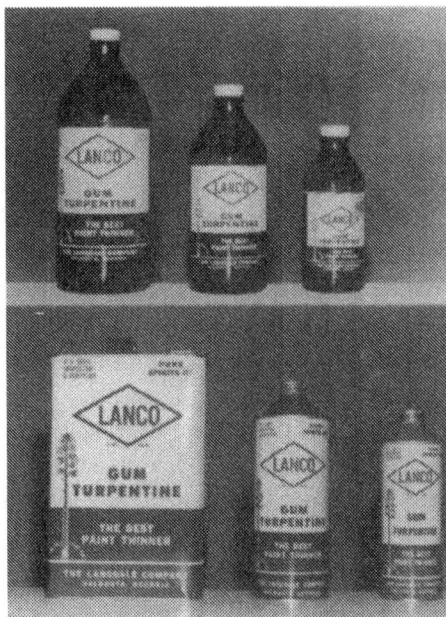

ATFA designed turpentine containers. TLC.

Interviewed on 22 August 1939, Wishart felt optimistic about Haiti's future in naval stores, partly because of their vast supply of virgin timber and partly because of their cheap labor, which came to only twenty cents a day. With labor at twenty cents a day, Haiti could compete even with the cheap synthetics, he declared. As for the United States, he said, "The turpentine business is done for in this country, and I don't think it will ever come back." For years preceding the 1934 crisis, remembered Wishart, naval stores prices had been trending down. Competition from substitutes and from wood naval stores, he said, "made it almost impossible to operate a regular turpentine business at a profit."[32] The bleak business environment Wishart described was the one Judge Harley and fellow producers faced when they organized the ATFA, and it was the situation Harley, Jr. stepped into when he graduated from forestry school and entered the family business full time.

In making his comments about the end of the gum naval stores business, Wishart did not foresee the effect of a world war, which began with the German invasion of Poland less than two weeks after his pessimistic prediction. World War II brought a windfall of prosperity to the gum turpentine industry, rescuing

---

[32] "Turpentine Man," 5–6, 10.

producers from the problem of oversupply and weak prices of the late 1930s. It perfectly fit the prescription for profitability given by Bradley Kennelly of Jacksonville, Florida, on 12 September 1939.[33]

Kennelly, who had been for nine years general manager of the naval stores yard at Jacksonville, essentially a warehouse, at municipal terminal, agreed in substance with Wishart's pessimistic assessment. He stated in an interview that he had never seen the naval stores business so slow during his nine-year tenure, and he thought records would show that the naval stores business had never been so bad. The main problem, he thought, was competition from substitutes for gum naval stores in making paints and varnishes. There existed at that time a great surplus of naval stores. For example, he said, "We have now on hand about 320,000 barrels" [of rosin]. A vast quantity of turpentine also stood unsold on the yard. "The only thing that will cause things to loosen up is another world war or some of the foreign countries and the United States to form trade relations enough to absorb this surplus we have on our hands,"[34] opined Kennelly.

As it turned out, the large surplus existing in 1939 fell far short of wartime needs. When the United States entered World War II, ATFA helped mobilize the country's resources. Early in the war, as Judge Harley remembered, the government called the heads of agricultural organizations to Washington to talk about increasing production. Of course, Judge represented ATFA. In this instance the situation of France, defeated by Germany in 1940 and partially occupied, entered into calculations. France had been a major international supplier of naval stores, but now France's part of world production was lost to the Allies. ATFA cooperated with the government in trying to increase the supply. There were problems, notably the shortage of labor, Judge recalled, but the country's needs were met.[35]

It is widely accepted that World War II, not the New Deal programs of President Franklin Roosevelt, really ended the Great Depression. Roosevelt's programs helped ameliorate conditions, but did not provide the dramatic cure that the people of the United States would have liked.

A similar point can be made with respect to the American Turpentine Farmers Association and the gum naval stores industry. ATFA and all the lobbying by Judge and others with congress and the administration on behalf of turpentine farmers certainly helped, but the war had the more dramatic effect in rescuing farmers from the problem of the surplus and increasing competition that threatened to put them out of business. Maybe World War II and the Cold War extended the viability of the gum turpentine industry in the United States for a

---

[33] Bradley Kennelly, Interview by Lillian Stedman, 12 September 1939, Jacksonville FL, Federal Writers' Project, Library of Congress, Washington DC.

[34] Ibid.

[35] Langdale, Judge Interview 01.

generation. The war certainly provided a major boost to the fortunes of Judge Harley's turpentine business in Valdosta, Georgia.

Yet the war affected the Langdales in other less desirable ways. Most obviously, two of the three brothers, like millions of other young men, soon found themselves at war. For them, concern for college grades or career advancement paled in comparison to the concerns of soldiers in combat. An account of college and the World War II period for the Langdales follows a brief photo essay about growing and harvesting trees.

Photo Essay

Trees—Planting to Harvest

The life of a pine tree begins with a tiny seed. In 1955 Judge Harley Langdale described in memorable words the natural process of reproduction. As he phrased it, God "put a little propeller on the pine tree's seed, so wherever an old tree was spared, its seed could float on the wind to start the forest growing again."[1] Pine forests depended almost entirely on natural reproduction until the twentieth century, and this is still the rule on some types of land. In the second half of the century, however, tree farmers, including the Langdales, turned increasingly to transplanting genetically-improved pine seedlings grown in nurseries to regenerate their forests.

Pine Seedlings: Containerized (L) and Bare Root. JDH.

---

[1] Martin, passim.

They also participated in experiments to improve the survival rate of transplanted seedlings. For example, in March 2001 two companies, in cooperation with the Flatwoods Chapter of the Society of American Foresters, planted a tract on Langdale land near Homerville, Georgia, with experimental variations of fertilizer and herbicides to spur initial growth rates. As depicted above, one version had been grown at the nursery in a tube to concentrate the root system and retain more soil around the root. The other was an industry-standard bare root seedling.

Hal Rowe at Homerville site. JDH.

The two companies involved were the Helena Chemical and the International Forest Seed Companies. Langdale foresters working directly with this experiment were Jim Barrett, vice president and technical forester of Langdale Company Woodlands, and Hal Rowe, forest supervisor. This being a small tract and it being late in the planting season, those in charge decided to employ an old technology, the dibble, for transplanting these young trees, rather than bring in tractors and mechanical transplanters, which have been in standard use since at least the 1950s. The dibble, of course, predates motorized transplanting equipment. The composite photo (top of next page) shows a worker transplanting a pine seedling at the experimental site near Homerville.

Jim Barrett. JDH.

Transplanting equipment similar to that shown below (bottom of page), which dates probably from the 1950s, more nearly typified the method used in large tracts at the start of the twenty-first century.

Transplanting with a dibble. JDH.

For many years the Langdales have taken great pride in the number of trees they planted from year to year. Anyone who ever talked with Harley Langdale, Jr. for very long about forestry probably heard him cite statistics about the number of trees planted on Langdale land. Harley, Jr. made it clear to all that, although the Langdale Company had moved into manufacturing on a large scale, he always regarded himself as primarily a tree farmer. He had taken to manufacturing essentially to secure markets for his trees. It pleased him immensely to be able to state that the Langdale Company had planted more trees than it had harvested since the 1930s. An important landmark in his career as a professional forester and tree farmer came on 26 March 1991, when he celebrated the company's having planted its fifty millionth pine tree. A televised ceremony with state legislators and other dignitaries in attendance memorialized the event.

Tractor-drawn transplanting machine. TLC.

Proper site preparation is obviously a prerequisite for successful transplanting of pine seedlings. The amount and difficulty of the work involved varies considerably, of course. In areas where trees have been harvested by clear-cutting, Langdale workers use bulldozers with regular blades and rootrake attachments to clean up the sites. They finish the preparation by creating beds of soil in long rows spaced properly for seedlings to be planted on them. The procedure resembles that used in tobacco farming where the farmer prepares deep beds of soil in rows as a hospitable home for young plants. In the forest, of course, the site or field is much rougher; there is more debris. Also, some bushes and the stumps of harvested trees cut off at ground level, remain in the earth. One advantage of the deep soil beds is that they cover the stumps and make it easier to transplant seedlings over the top of them.

Ceremony to Commemorate Planting 50 Millionth Tree. Those shown (L-R) are Robert Simpson III, member of the board, Georgia Forestry Commission; John Mixon, Georgia Forestry Commission director; Harley Langdale Jr.; Robert Harley Langdale Jr.; Senator Loyce Turner; Representative Tim Golden; Representative Robert Patten; and Representative Henry Reaves. Georgia Forestry Commission Photo. TLC.

Site prepared for transplanting pine seedlings. JDH.

To the inexperienced observer looking across a tract of newly-planted pines, the seedlings may be almost invisible. Young pines must compete with grass, weeds, and bushes normally found in a forest. It takes several years for pines to grow to a dominant position with respect to competing plants and to start to tower over them.

Young planted pines at Kinderlou, Georgia, Fall 2000. JDH.

One of the great dangers to young pines has always been wildfire. The threat of fire to trees, plants, and creatures of the forest appears vividly from the following photograph taken by a fire behavior analyst in the Bitteroot National Forest on 6 August 2000. Fleeing the intense fire, animals can be seen taking refuge in a stream.

Animals escaping fire. Photo, "Elkbath," by John McColgan of Fairbanks, Alaska.

The Langdale Company has always placed major emphasis on fire control. The company has cooperated with government and led in private efforts to prevent wildfires and to contain them when they occur, whether on Langdale land or not. The photo below shows a wildfire that Langdale firefighters helped to put out in 2000. This fire and the endangered small pines in the foreground were not on Langdale land. A Langdale bulldozer is just barely visible in the lower middle of the photo, working close to the flames.

Although wildfires are usually harmful and often dangerous, fire is also an important tool for managing forestland. Properly conducted prescribed burns clear away brush and other fuels that accumulate over time and increase the hazards of unplanned fire.

Langdale bulldozer
fighting a wildfire in
2000. TLC.

Prescribed burns are just one of the tools foresters use to care for trees during the long period, commonly twenty-five years or more, from transplanting to harvesting saw timber. A few others are fire breaks, forest roads, thinning, and herbicides. The last decade of the twentieth century saw increasing use of chemical fertilizers, sometimes applied by aircraft, to increase the growth rate of trees.

Prescribed burn on
Langdale land, March
2001. JDH.

A tree farmer who planted high quality seedlings, took good care of them for perhaps twenty-five years, and had the good fortune to escape fire and weather damage, might hope to see trees resembling those shown below.

Langdale pines at Kinderlou, Georgia, fall 2000. JDH.

For a tree farmer, as for a peanut farmer, the primary reason for planting trees is ultimately to harvest them. Harvesting technology has changed dramatically in the last half century. Chain saws, for example, rightly regarded as a great advance over axes and crosscut saws, have become obsolete as an instrument for felling a tree or trimming the limbs off a harvested tree. At the beginning of

Feller-buncher of directional shear type. JDH.

the twenty-first century, the tool of choice for cutting down trees is the feller-buncher. This is a heavy tractor fitted with hydraulic machines that can cut down a tree in the time it takes to snap one's fingers. Some of these behemoths can take down several trees and carry them for a while before pausing to lay them down in a convenient place.

Feller-bunchers come in various configurations. The directional-shear type feller-buncher, as depicted in the photo above, has a large hydraulic piston that pushes a blade through a tree from one side to cut it off and cause it to fall in the direction away from the piston. The type of feller-buncher used on Langdale land is the saw-type, which Langdale managers prefer because it causes less damage than the shear-type to fibres in the lower part of the tree and, therefore, allows them to get more lumber from a tree.

Feller-Buncher at work near Homervlle, Georgia, in March 2001. This is a saw-type feller-buncher. JDH.

A Saw-type Feller-Buncher at rest. JDH.

Saw & Lifting plate on saw-type Feller-Buncher. The saw, located nearest the ground, has replaceable teeth and weighs 750 lbs. The steel plate above the saw lifts the tree as the saw cuts it off. JDH.

These feller-bunchers are quick. The saw-type feller-buncher does not roll up to a tree, stop, and then saw it down. It completes the whole operation in one motion, without stopping or even hesitating. As fast as the tractor is traveling is how fast the tree comes down. The machine approaches a tree, its four robot arms immediately encircle it and hold it against the top forks, the saw cuts it off at ground level, and the hydraulic lift picks it up and either carries it or lays it down, as the operator chooses. It is an amazing machine.

Feller-Buncher grasping a tree that is being cut down. JDH.

One feller-buncher keeps two skidders busy moving logs to the loading area. And these are modern grapple skidders, not the old-fashioned kind that used cables. With the cable-type skidder, either the driver or another worker had to attach a cable to each log to be dragged out of the woods. The driver of today's grapple-type skidder simply operates levers to have the machine clutch logs in a giant hydraulic claw to carry them away.

Delimbing machine & skidder. JDH.

The loading area is where harvested trees have their limbs removed. This, too, is a quick operation. A log-loading machine fitted with a grapple picks up a tree and drags it through a delimbing machine. Taking all the limbs off a tree requires perhaps thirty seconds. This is a far cry from trimming with a chain saw.

Log loader, delimber, & skidder. JDH.

Before loading the logs on trucks, they have to be sorted. The Langdale procedure is to put logs into three categories, which are transported on separate trucks to their respective destinations. The logs of greatest value are those meeting the specifications to become utility poles. Poles are identified and marked as such while still standing in the forest. The feller-buncher and skidder operators keep poles separate from the other two categories of wood, which are sawlogs and pulpwood. Logs that are too small for the sawmill become pulpwood. Anything big enough for the sawmill to use and not suitable for a pole is sent to the mill as a sawlog. There the Fulgum crane unloads the logs and places them in position to begin their transformation into lumber.

Truckload of logs delivered to Langdale Sawmill. JDH.

Fulgum crane unloading a log truck. JDH.

In conclusion, the Langdale timber harvesting operation is thoroughly modern, mechanized, and highly efficient. The backbreaking and dangerous labor of decades past is no more. Powerful machines run by skilled operators seated in air- conditioned cabs make the harvesting of timber look as easy as the equivalent activity in traditional south Georgia farm crops like peanuts or cotton. Indeed, the Langdales think of themselves as tree farmers, primarily, so the comparison is appropriate.

8

College and War

*H*arley, Jr. enjoyed high school in Valdosta. He passed all of his classes without studying. His biggest challenge was to survive football practice, which he endured for four years. His father wanted him to play, but his size put him at a disadvantage. If he got to play in a game, it was always toward the end. When he graduated at age sixteen, Harley, Jr. was still among the smaller Valdosta Wildcat football players.

1929 Valdosta Wildcats.
Among these eight, Harley Jr.
(arrow) appears to be the
smallest. Cropped from a
wrinkled postcard. TLF.

At that time Emory Junior College had recently opened in Valdosta. Harley, Jr. attended Emory at Valdosta for a year, but did not excel. The faculty at Emory expected a person to study, and Harley, Jr. had not yet learned to do that. Besides, the forest interested him more than books.

The next year Harley, Jr. chose to enroll at the Citadel, partly because his father encouraged him to go there. Judge Harley, who had attended a military school in Atlanta, Donald Fraser, liked military training. Both Harleys, father and son, knew something about the Citadel, which was located in South Carolina, partly because they spent a good deal of time at Judge's turpentine place at Palmetto Bluff and had some contact with South Carolina people. Moreover, since their ancestor, John Robert Langdale, had come originally from Walterboro, South Carolina, they felt they had an ancestral South Carolina connection.[1]

None of that helped Harley, Jr. adjust when he arrived to start classes at the school. He knew nobody on campus or in the vicinity, and he felt lost. Still, "That's one of the finest things that could have ever happened to me coming from my background," he declared in 1995. "I didn't know a single soul in that whole area of Charleston. I went up there and I learned a lot of things that I don't think I would have learned anywhere else—to be orderly, be organized, and to be neat, and other things. And I am grateful for what the Citadel did for me. I liked the military life. I was able to march and hold myself erect and things like that, and I liked it, and I met some outstanding people."[2]

Harley Jr. as Citadel cadet.
TLF.

After completing his freshman year, Harley, Jr. returned to the Citadel as a sophomore with high hopes. He felt good when he found that he had been chosen as the number two corporal for his class. Then, shortly afterward, word came that he was ineligible to accept the corporal's post because his grades were too low. Devastating news, and too much for him to bear. "I was disappointed, more so than anytime in my life," he recalled. He quickly packed a suitcase and, without telling anyone, slipped out of the barracks and caught the train for Valdosta. He could do that because his father, as attorney for the railroad, could ride free, and this privilege extended to the family.

He reached the Valdosta depot about eleven or twelve o'clock at night and walked with his suitcase the several blocks home to 1006 N. Patterson Street. He rang the bell, and his mother let him in. Then his dad came down and talked with him for a long time in a way that he "had never been talked to before." Judge said "that I would never amount to anything if I didn't get an education—he said it

---

[1] Langdale, HLJr Interview 1991.

[2] Harley Langdale, Jr., interview by author, audio tape, Harley Langdale, Jr., Papers, Valdosta GA, 22 March 1995.

wouldn't make any difference about all this other stuff. But he talked to me about two hours and I got my suitcase and walked back to the depot. There was a train that came in something like four or five in the morning. It was dark, I remember that. I got that train back to the Citadel, and I don't think there were hardly two or three people there that had known I had gone. It wasn't easy to get out of the Citadel. They had iron bars in the dormitories."[3]

This event had an important effect upon Harley, Jr. Henceforth, he approached life with a greater degree of maturity. He remained at the Citadel and completed his second year there before transferring to the University of Georgia to study forestry.

The fact that Harley, Jr. studied forestry and his brother, John W., went into law did not result from any grand design by their father. As Harley, Jr. asserted in the 1990s, Judge basically wanted them to succeed at whatever they chose to do. Actually, at the time Harley, Jr. went off to the Citadel, he leaned toward the legal field and had secured a few law school catalogs to examine. Not that he intended necessarily to concentrate on the practice of law, but he had in mind following the example of his father and operating a forestry business, using legal training as an aid to success.[4] This aspect of his thinking, Harley, Jr.'s consideration of attending law school, he did not share with his brother, John W., who was surprised when he first heard of it in the 1990s.

Harley, Jr.'s decision in favor of a career in forestry occurred at Palmetto Bluff, where Mr. George Varn owned forestland and a hunting camp. Mr. Varn invited friends and business associates to come there and go deer hunting. Guests invited to the Palmetto Bluff camp included numerous politicians, including Senator Cotton Ed Smith of South Carolina, Senators Walter George and Richard B. Russell of Georgia, and numerous congressmen. Judge Harley, Harley, Jr., and other members of the Langdale family often participated in these hunts. Harley, Jr. recalled that he killed his first deer at Palmetto Bluff at the age of twelve. The hunting camp at Palmetto Bluff sat amidst a large tract of timber that George Varn owned (later acquired by Union Camp Corporation) and that Judge Harley turpentined under contract. Judge Harley and Varn, who also owned land in south Georgia, were good friends as well as business associates.

While attending the Citadel, Harley, Jr. went on one of these hunts that also included Senator George. It turned out that the senator and Harley, Jr. had a common interest in forestry. Harley listened attentively as the senator talked about the policies of President Roosevelt related to conservation and the CCC. Senator George foresaw good career possibilities in forestry, and he mentioned that his son was then at the University of Georgia learning forestry.

---

[3] Ibid.
[4] Langdale, HLJr Interview 1991.

Both Senator George and Judge Harley urged Harley, Jr. to follow the example of the senator's son and enter the forestry program at the University of Georgia. So, taking their advice he transferred from the Citadel to the University of Georgia. As best Harley, Jr. could determine, he was the first person from south Georgia to study forestry in a formal academic program. Reflecting on this nearly six decades later, he concluded that his career in forestry had been, as he phrased it, "one of the great blessings of my life."[5]

Harley Jr. & friends at UGA. Left to right, Eugene Brogdon, Francis Clark, Harley Jr., Jim Gillis. Jr. TLF.

When Harley, Jr. arrived at the University of Georgia he found the forestry school in some ways disappointing. The curriculum appeared generally irrelevant to forestry problems in south Georgia. The school had outdated books, mostly translated from German, and a shabby, decaying classroom building. In short, recalled Harley, Jr., the school was in a primitive stage of development.

The dean of the school, Gordon Marckworth, quickly saw in Harley, Jr. a possibility for correcting the facilities problem. He enlisted the young Valdostan's aid in a political power play. Georgia's governor at that time, E. D. Rivers, lived in Lakeland, just twenty miles from Valdosta, and Harley, Jr. knew the governor as a family friend. At the dean's instigation, Harley organized a committee of students. They went to visit the governor and the chairman of the Board of Regents, seeking a new building for the forestry school. This initiative did finally result in a new classroom building for the forestry school.

Harley, Jr. recalled in later years that four major issues absorbed the attention of students at the UGA forestry school when he attended there: efforts by the US Forest Service to establish forest regulations; inadequate fire protection; insufficient markets for forest products; and lack of money to practice the best

---

[5] Ibid.

forestry methods. When he graduated in 1937 and returned to work in his father's business, he found the last three of those issues to be major practical concerns. His efforts to deal with those issues, discussed elsewhere, continued for many years, right on through the period of World War II.

Harley Jr. (with clipboard) & UGA forestry students on a field assignment to transplant seedlings. TLF.

Unlike his brothers, John W. and Billy, Harley, Jr. did not serve in the military during the war. Not that he lacked preparation or inclination. He had military training for two years at the Citadel, of course, and he also served in the ROTC cavalry unit after transferring to the University of Georgia. When war came, he simply could not pass the physical exam. The draft board classified him Four-F for medical reasons, the result of an appendectomy at the University of Georgia that healed improperly. Leakage occurred and a tumor grew, requiring another serious operation. Surgeons had to cut out a section of his intestine and reattach it.[6]

Physically disqualified for military service and with both of his brothers serving in the Pacific war, Harley, Jr. concentrated on running the business. This had been chiefly his responsibility since long before the fighting started in Poland. The naval stores business prospered as exploding demand wiped out the massive surpluses of 1937 and called for increased production. By 1943 Harley, Jr. believed conditions were right for construction of a centralized turpentine still. This project, which is described elsewhere, coincided with a major change in Harley, Jr.'s personal life. In 1943 he met and married Miss Eileen Cox.

Eileen was the younger daughter of Decar Covington Cox (11 February 1894–13 April 1967), a naval stores producer, and his wife, Minnie Gibson (7 November 1895–10 June 1974). Her paternal grandparents were Anne and James Monroe Cox. Born in Santa Rosa County, Florida, on 24 February 1919, Eileen had lived as a young girl in South Carolina, near Smoaks and Ravanel, and had

---

[6] Ibid.

moved with her family to Valdosta at about the age of twelve. [7] Eileen and her older sister, Annie Jeannette, whose music-loving mother saw to it that they take piano lessons together in elementary and high school, also attended classes together at Georgia State Woman's College in Valdosta for three years. When Jeanette, who was a year older than Eileen, married J. F. Holmes, a Valdosta Wildcat football standout from a prominent family, Eileen decided to go away to complete her senior year at Brenau College in Gainesville, Georgia. After finishing her education degree at Brenau, she taught elementary school four years in Lowndes County, with two years each at Naylor and Pine Grove.

Eileen's sister introduced her to Harley, Jr. The Langdales had a little house down at Mayday that they used as a clubhouse. Harley, Jr. asked Jeanette and her husband to bring him a date for a Sunday outing on the Alapaha River and a supper they were having afterward. Jeanette insisted that Eileen attend, so she did. And from then on "he and I were attracted to one another and we kept seeing one another," explained Eileen. [8]

Eileen had a job that summer at the Georgia Southern Railroad station selling tickets at night, from 11 P.M. to 7 A.M. So Harley would pick her up at home for a date, and he'd put her out at the train station in time to start her job at 11 P.M. They were married 21 August 1943, about four months after they started dating, at the home of the Reverend E. L. Todd.

Shortly after their marriage Harley, Jr. completed his plans for the centralized turpentine still. "He ordered all the parts the first few months we were married," Eileen recalled. "He spent a lot of time calculating and figuring what to buy, with drawings spread out here and there."[9]

At this time they lived at Ledgedale farm out beside the Bemiss Highway, and a Moody Field family lived right next door to them. Responding to the government's call for families to plant "victory gardens" as part of the war effort, Eileen and Harley, Jr. had a little vegetable garden. They canned tomatoes, made chili sauce and catsup, and did other things to have something to eat that they had grown.[10]

In the meantime, Harley's younger brother, John W., had completed undergraduate and law degrees, had become a naval officer, and was aboard a fighting ship in the Pacific.

Having graduated from Valdosta High School at age sixteen, John W. enrolled in North Georgia College, a military school located at Dahlonega, Georgia. His dad gave him a choice: either go to Emory Junior College in Valdosta or to the military school. John chose North Georgia. The military aspect appealed to him

---

[7] Clifton, ed., *Heritage of Lowndes County, 63.*

[8] Eileen Cox Langdale, interview by author, audio tape, Harley Langdale, Jr., Papers, Valdosta GA, 14 February 1995.

[9] Ibid.

[10] Ibid.

somewhat, and he wanted to get away from Valdosta. John probably figured he had a head start on learning to march, since he had been in the Drum and Bugle Corps for two years at Valdosta High. Little did he suspect that he was about to become a paid musician at the college.[11]

It happened this way: In John's words, "I was in line at the Registrar's Office, and the military officer in the school came out in the hall and said, 'Any of you fellows blow a bugle?' I raised my hand; went in his office and he said, 'Here, blow this.' I blew reveille. He said, 'You are the school bugler.' I got the job and I didn't know it paid, but that was quite a pleasant shock to me when I found it paid $6.00 a month. And then they raised it to $8.00 a month."[12]

As school bugler, John had to blow reveille each morning before daylight. In his second year, someone played a trick on him that he never forgot. During the night, while he slept, one of the boys came into his room and set his clock ahead. When the alarm went off in complete darkness, he jumped up and blew reveille as usual. Unfortunately for him, and for the whole battalion, it was only 2:00 A.M. So the entire battalion found themselves doing exercises at 2 o'clock in the morning, and John got the blame. When the class had their fiftieth-year reunion some years ago, John offered to forgive the culprit, if only he would confess. But nobody did. "I reckon the Lord has already had his vengeance on that perpetrator," said John W.[13]

At North Georgia College John W. played cornet in the college band. He had never played anything but a bugle, and had never learned the bass clef. Playing the cornet with the basic military music they performed, however, he got along just fine with the treble clef alone. John enjoyed the music and the marching at Dahlonega, though not the hazing.

His career at North Georgia College ended abruptly when an opportunity arose for an appointment to the Naval Academy. Senator George offered this to Judge, who thought it was a great idea. John could attend the Naval Academy, get a free education, and be paid $75 per month. So off he went to Annapolis.

When he accepted the appointment to Annapolis John W. had no idea that all naval cadets earned engineering degrees. They did not train naval officers as historians or sociologists. Being weak in math, John found this to be an insurmountable problem. He struggled through two years at the Naval Academy, learned better study habits, suffered through the abominable hazing, and then dropped out and enrolled in the University of Georgia just about the time that his brother, Harley, graduated from forestry school in 1937.

At the University of Georgia, benefiting from the improved study techniques he had picked up at Annapolis, John W. cruised. He earned a bachelor's degree in

---

[11] Langdale, JWL Interview 14.

[12] Ibid.

[13] Ibid.

economics in August 1939 and a law degree in June 1940. He then returned to Valdosta and began the practice of law with his father's firm at a salary of $75 per month, the same stipend he had received as a student at Annapolis.[14]

Within a year it became apparent to John that war might come at almost any time. From the draft board he drew a low number and faced the probability of being drafted and placed in the infantry as a private. He decided to volunteer for assignment in the navy as a legal officer, but was told the navy had all the legal officers it needed. The navy offered to train him as a line officer, however, at a school affiliated with Northwestern University in Chicago.

In September 1941, two years after the onset of war in Europe, John started Naval Midshipman School, and in December he completed the course. Commissioned an ensign in the US Naval Reserve on 22 December 1941, he accepted a post as instructor in the school and served in that capacity until May 1942.

Dissatisfied with shore responsibilities, John W. applied for combat duty. The navy assigned him to a new destroyer, the *Lardner*, which made its shakedown cruise in July 1942. He served on this ship for about eleven months. The *Lardner* passed through the Panama Canal and arrived in the Pacific war zone about the time of the first landings at Guadalcanal in early August 1942. The *Lardner's* main duty for several months was to escort troop ships, supply ships, and tankers from Noumea and Esperito Santo to Guadalcanal and return. Combat actions most commonly resulted from Japanese submarine or air attacks. The *Lardner* took part in the Battle of Tassafaronga, 30 November 1942, the last of four major Japanese-US night surface actions between early August and the first of December.[15]

For his second assignment John went to another new destroyer, the *Hickox*, which followed the same pattern of shakedown cruise and transfer to Pacific as the *Lardner*. He served about three months in the war zone aboard the *Hickox* and was then appointed to the staff of Captain (addressed as Commodore) Womble, squadron commander. He served aboard the destroyer *Owen* as operations officer for Commodore Womble for about five or six months. Commodore Womble's command, DESRON 52, included nine destroyers.

About the time of the start of Okinawa operations Captain Womble received a promotion to Commodore and transferred to the cruiser *Oakland*, his flagship for command of Destroyer Flotilla II, which included two squadrons. John also transferred to the *Oakland* and continued as Womble's operations officer. He served as the "voice of the commodore" in radio communications with ships in the flotilla.

---

[14] Ibid.

[15] For a recent study of this battle, see Russell S. Crenshaw, Jr. Captain, USN (Ret), *The Battle of Tassafaronga* (Baltimore MD: Nautical and Aviation Publishing Company of America, 1995). This work includes a photograph of the *Lardner* on 46.

After the Japanese surrender, John W. landed with Commodore Womble and the rest of his staff, plus a small contingent of marines, at Yokosuka Naval Base, Tokyo Bay, to take over the base. Womble was assigned as commander of Naval Shore Activities, Yokosuka Naval Base.

A day or two after General MacArthur accepted official Japanese surrender aboard the battleship *Missouri*, John departed Japan for the United States. He had spent fifty months on active duty in the Navy, most of it in the Pacific. His decorations included the Bronze Star and the Pacific Theatre Ribbon with eleven engagement stars.[16] Released from active duty shortly afterward, he returned to Valdosta and resumed his practice of law.

In later years John commented that he regarded the four years he spent in the Navy during World War II as part of his education. The most important thing he had learned in the preceding seven years, during which he received his law degree, was discipline. His four years of wartime service broadened his cultural experience, he said.[17]

Shortly after returning to Valdosta from the war, John W. found romance. It seems to have been a case of love at first sight when he met a young woman named Margaret Jones. She was younger than he by ten years. This happened in August 1946 when Omer Franklin gave a swimming party on South Beach at Twin Lakes in honor of returning veterans. John and Margaret both attended; she went as the date of Billy Bird, and John W. took Georgia Smith to the party. The attendees swam in the afternoon and went to a restaurant for steaks in the evening. Then, as John had a car and Billy did not, the two couples rode back to town together. Later, John telephoned Margaret and asked her out. Four months later, in December 1946, they were married.

Margaret came from one of the old Valdosta families. Her parents were James Cooper Jones (23 September 1895–23 October 1968), a salesman by profession, and Elsie Stone (12 October 1900–August 1992) of Wytheville, Virginia, a school teacher. Following the Jones side of her family backward, her grandparents were Joseph Cooper Jones (b. 1847) and Cornelia Carringer (1861–1939) of Morristown, Tennessee. In deference to the staunch Methodism of her Tennessee-born grandmother, Margaret's parents reared her and her brother, James, Jr., as Methodists. The Joneses worshipped at Valdosta's First Methodist Church.[18]

Continuing backward with the Jones line, Margaret's great-grandparents were Berry Jones (1799–8 August 1854) and his second wife (m. 1846), Rebecca Perrill Cooper of South Carolina. Berry Jones had a large-scale cotton-growing enterprise on his plantation that extended from the general area of present-day western Valdosta to the Withlacoochee River. In 1851 he also acquired eleven lots of land

---

[16] Clifton, ed., *Heritage of Lowndes County,* 109–10.

[17] Brian Daughdrill, "Langdale Received Varied Education," *Valdosta Daily Times,* 24 October 1988.

[18] Clifton, ed., *Heritage of Lowndes County,* 105–107.

at Ocean Pond in southern Lowndes County. His elder brother, Francis farmed the land around Francis Lake, and it is for him that the lake is named.

The Joneses trace their descent from Francis Jones (1714–1774), who arrived in Isle of Wight County, Virginia, from Wales about 1730–1735, became a planter in Cumberland County, North Carolina, for some years, and received a large grant of land in Burke County, North Carolina, from King George III in 1765. Margaret is a descendant through Francis Jones's second marriage, to Elizabeth Huckabee (1737–1798). One of their sons, James Jones (b. 1764), received a bounty land grant as a revolutionary soldier from the State of Georgia. He died at his home in Bulloch County, Georgia, in 1822. After the death of James Jones, his widow, Elizabeth (Betsy) Mills Jones (b. 1774), accompanied their children who settled in Lowndes and Thomas Counties, Georgia. These included Francis and Berry Jones.

Margaret's family home, when growing up, was the old "home place" for the Berry Jones plantation situated between present-day Valdosta and the Withlacoochee River. This house, standing during her girlhood three miles from town, has been swallowed by the city. The site of the old Jones "home place" was occupied in 2002 by the LDS church at the corner of Jerry Jones and Gornto Roads.

At the time of their marriage John W. was already a deacon in First Baptist Church, probably one of the youngest ever. Margaret, on the other hand, although she had prominent Baptist ancestors, was a Methodist. After a while Margaret decided to change her church affiliation, and she joined her husband in being very active in the work of Valdosta's First Baptist Church for the next half century and more. For over three decades, for example, she directed the College Department of the Sunday school.

John and Margaret had three children, a son and two daughters. They named them John W., Jr. (Johnny), Lee Stone, and Margaret Elizabeth. "We had a wonderful marriage, we really did. The Lord blessed us very richly," declared Margaret in 2002.[19]

John's marriage took place a year and a half after that of his younger brother, Billy, who had also been in the Pacific theatre for most of the war. Billy had been released from active duty in June 1945, a few months earlier than John, and had immediately married. For a time during the war, John W. and Billy had served in the same neighborhood, so to speak, that of Guadalcanal. They were, however, in different branches of the military service, and neither knew of the other's presence nearby.

Unlike his older brothers, Billy had not completed a college degree when the war started. Billy's higher education career included taking courses at Valdosta State College, Mercer University, and the University of Georgia at various times.

---

[19] Margaret Jones Langdale, interview by author, audio tape, 14 February 2002, Langdale Company, Valdosta GA John W. Langdale Papers, Valdosta GA.

As Billy put it, "I wasn't an outstanding student; I never did take to college much."[20]

Billy graduated from high school in 1937 and went to the University of Georgia in 1938. Harley, Jr. had just finished at Georgia with his degree in forestry, and John W. was at Athens working on his economics and law degrees. Unlike his brother, John, however, Billy had more interest in football than in academics. In high school he had played tackle for two years for the Valdosta Wildcats. He was "a mediocre player," as he described himself modestly in 2002, backing up his friend J. F. Holmes. In football prowess, Billy said he could not match J. F. Holmes or his cousin, Noah Langdale.[21] Billy enjoyed playing, however, and even though he had no football scholarship at Georgia, he played extensively as a freshman tackle. At less than 175 pounds, he considered himself rather light for that position, especially compared to the 300 pounders who often play that position today.[22]

Billy returned to the University of Georgia for his second year but played less football because he "didn't want to pay the price," as he recalled.[23] He also did poorly in his course work and soon dropped out. He then enrolled in Mercer University at Macon but also had a short career there. He returned home, and went to work for his father at the Tarver turpentine place, which was then the largest turpentine place in the world. At Tarver, Judge Harley had a large double still supplied by several turpentine camps located around Tarver. When payday came, once a month, more than a thousand workers came to Tarver to settle up.[24]

At Tarver, Billy learned how to chip and dip. Unlike his older brothers, Harley and John, Billy had not learned the turpentine business in early adolescence. While they had gone to the woods to work, Billy, being much younger, had stayed around home and spent more time with his mother. Of course the operation at Tarver, although it was the largest, was only one of a number of turpentine places that Judge Harley operated in the late 1930s. Billy recalled that Judge had twelve or fifteen of these places on Superior Pine Products land alone.[25]

Superior Pine, which owned some 220,000 acres adjoining Langdale property in 1992 had become a major landowner in south Georgia in 1926.[26] From then until 1929, the company attempted to run a naval stores operation on their land, but lost money. The company then contracted with Judge Harley to handle their

---

[20] Langdale, WPL Interview 1991.
[21] Langdale, WPL Interview 05.
[22] Langdale, WPL Interview 1991.
[23] Langdale, WPL Interview 05.
[24] Langdale, WPL Interview 1991.
[25] Ibid.
[26] Langdale, JJLJr Interview 1991.

turpentine trees on a percentage basis. This was the first time, so far as Harley, Jr. knew, that anyone worked turpentine trees with a percentage arrangement.[27]

Judge had stills at Barnes, Pineland, Fargo, and Council. When the manager at Fargo left, Judge put Billy in charge of that turpentine place for a while.[28]

Having seen something of the real world, particularly the turpentine business, Billy happily returned to college at the University of Georgia. Once again, however, he found his interests unsuited to college life, and after a short stay at the university he left school and enlisted in the Marine Corps. This occurred shortly after the Japanese bombed Pearl Harbor, and it coincided with Billy's twenty-first birthday. Billy was born 10 February 1921.

Aside from his failing academic career and the wave of patriotic feeling sweeping the country after the Japanese attack in Hawaii, Billy had another reason for picking this particular time to enlist in military service. He had served in the Georgia National Guard, G Company, 121st Infantry, for three years during high school in Valdosta, but had resigned from the guard when he went off to college. The Valdosta guard unit had, by this time, been called into national service and transferred to Columbia, South Carolina. The troop commander sent word to Billy that he could have the rank of sergeant if he would sign up again with his old unit, and Billy decided that was an opportunity he should not pass up.

He persuaded a friend at the University of Georgia to go along with him, and the two of them packed up everything they had and went to Columbia, intending to join the National Guard unit from Valdosta. To their dismay, when they arrived they found the Valdosta guard had already shipped out, so there was no unit to join.

Billy and his friend had more or less burned their bridges with the University of Georgia and were committed to join the military, but they now had to decide which outfit to join. Billy's friend wanted to enlist in the Marine Corps because he had a cousin in the corps, and he thought this cousin might be helpful to them. Billy, on the other hand, pointed out that he had a brother in the Navy, John W., so he preferred to join the Navy to be in the same branch of service as his brother.

The two young men agreed to flip a coin to decide whether they would join the Marine Corps or the Navy. The Marine Corps won. They went to the Marine recruiter to see about enlisting, and this recruiter said to them, as Billy recalled, "Man, you're the luckiest two people I've ever seen in my life. You've come just at the right time. The Marine Corps now is giving away booze to everybody going and giving away watches, brand new watches." So, naively believing they had struck gold, the two young men signed the enlistment papers. They figured they had definitely made the right decision to join the Marine Corps. So, precisely at age twenty-one, Billy became a United States Marine. His enlistment in the

---

[27] Langdale, HLJr Interview 1991.
[28] Langdale, WPL Interview 1991.

Marine Corps extended for three years and four months, from February 1942 to June 1945.

Presently, the two friends found themselves on a bus to Savannah. They stayed in the YMCA about two days in Savannah. Then some of the group, including Billy, went from there to Parris Island where they endured about six months of basic training. After boot camp at Parris Island, the Marine Corps sent Billy to Camp Lejeune, North Carolina, and from there they sent him to American Samoa. In American Samoa, Billy found himself first assigned to the rangers, but the ranger outfit there disbanded, and the marines then assigned him to a machine gun school.

While attending this machine gun school, Billy rose practically over night, literally, from private to lieutenant. As the rationale for this remarkable opportunity for advancement filtered down to Billy, General Carwell, who was in charge there, decided to create thirty-two new second lieutenants in the field. The general, Billy was told, chose to do this to avoid having his unit filled with "ninety-day wonders." Ninety-day wonders were young college graduates who had been given ninety days of military training and then awarded officer commissions. General Carwell evidently wanted more seasoned military people to serve as officers in his command.

As a result of the general's decision, Billy received a promotion from private to corporal one day and from corporal to second lieutenant the next day. Then he went back to the same squad, the same platoon, the same company that he had been in for six months as a private. He had no insignia or any change in uniform. Only a piece of adhesive tape stuck on his collar showed him to be an officer. At the time it seemed to him that the chief benefit of being an officer was that he could now go to the head of the line and buy a whole case of beer. As a private he had been standing in line to get a limit of just two cans of 3.2 beer.[29]

From American Samoa, Billy's unit went to Guadalcanal. The battle was essentially over when they arrived, so they engaged mainly in mopping up operations. Then Billy was selected to go on a patrol to Bougainville to scout the terrain and gather information. Lieutenant Langdale had fifteen volunteers with him on this mission. They traveled from Guadalcanal to Bougainville by submarine. Billy's commanding officer at this time, Lewis Wilson, later rose to be a general and became commandant of the Marine Corps.

Accompanying Billy and his fifteen volunteers on this mission, there were three or four Bougainville natives and one Dutchman who had lived on the island previously. Billy's commanding officer, Lewis Wilson, and a Navy officer also went. From the submarine that brought them to Bougainville from Guadalcanal, the patrol traveled by rubber boat to shore. They landed about a mile from a contingent of some two thousand Japanese and buried their rubber rafts on the

---

[29] Ibid.

shore. They stayed on the island two or three days gathering information and then returned to the submarine. They flashed a blinker light from the shore to signal to the submarine their readiness to depart. Subsequently, they came back with the main invasion force and landed in approximately the same place. This time they stayed for two months engaged in battle with the Japanese. "We stayed in there 60 days, slept wet every night, dug a foxhole every night," declared Billy in 2002. "We came out on a road twice as wide as an interstate highway that the Seabees had built while we were there." As a result of this action, Billy saw a number of his comrades killed, one of whom was awarded the Congressional Medal of Honor.[30] Billy, himself, received the Bronze Star and promotion to first lieutenant.

Reflecting upon these events nearly six decades later, Billy could scarcely believe that he was the young man whose combat experiences were etched so indelibly on his mind. The portrayal of a "band of brothers" recounted in a recent book and motion picture differed from his recollection of war in the Pacific. The marines with whom he served were all young fellows, aged seventeen to eighteen for the most part, who did not stay together as a group long enough to develop the kind of personal devotion implied by the expression "band of brothers." Changes in the makeup of units resulted not only from casualties, but also from the high incidence of disease. The camaraderie among his men, in Billy's opinion, came more from their identification with each other as marines than from being well acquainted through long service together.

Perhaps the most vivid impression for Billy as he remembered events of Guadalcanal and Bougainville in March 2002 was how selfless and unafraid these young men were. Any time Lieutenant Langdale asked for volunteers, there were more than enough, regardless of the danger of the mission. Among these men he was an older fellow, being twenty-two, but in one respect he was just like them. "I can remember I had no fear in those days," he declared. "I didn't even think that I could get killed."[31]

At eighty-one years of age in 2002, Billy had not for some time been able to locate any of the men with whom he had served in the Pacific. So far as he knew there remained no other survivors of the Battle of Piva Forks. He could think of only one who might still be living, Sid McMath, his commanding officer at school in Samoa. McMath, Billy remembered, had risen to the rank of general and had later been elected governor of Arkansas. "He was an outstanding fellow," said Billy.[32]

After the Bougainville operation, Billy returned to Guadalcanal and there underwent additional training. This was in preparation for the invasion of Guam. He did not go to Guam, however. Instead, he received orders to Quantico, Virginia,

---

[30] Langdale, WPL Interview 05.
[31] Ibid.
[32] Ibid.

as an instructor. There he had to go through basic training again to be qualified to lead a class through this course. When he completed training this time, the Marine Corps officials asked him to choose where he would like to be assigned. He asked to be sent back to the Pacific. Billy liked the conditions in the Pacific better than the spit and polish atmosphere of Quantico. The Marine Corps refused to send him to the Pacific, however, because he had been sick with malaria during his previous tour there.[33]

At Quantico, the Marine Corps assigned Billy to train naval officers, recent graduates of the naval academy at Annapolis who had opted to join the Marine Corps. Billy had responsibility for about ten of these young officers, so he set up a schedule to train them for overseas duty. This work did not suit him.

Yet Billy, who always had a predilection for fun, found ways to amuse himself. As he remembered, "One day at Quantico I shot a squirrel, skinned him right there, put a stick through him and built a fire and cooked him while they were watching him cook." "They looked at me...." "You got to survive," he told the Annapolis boys.[34]

One day, interrupting his training schedule, a jeep sporting a general's star came rolling up to his group. "Where's Lt. Langdale?" the driver asked. "I'm Lt. Langdale," said Billy, wondering what kind of trouble he was in. You must come right now to Washington, declared the driver. The chairman of the House Committee on Insular Affairs from Missouri wants to talk with you about something having to do with the islands. "Get your clothes changed, and we're going to get you right on to Washington." So Billy changed to his dress uniform, went with the driver to Washington, and reported as instructed to a certain room in a House office building. Having no idea what was going on, he walked in "and there was this Country Johnston and his secretary and they had two bottles of liquor up there and they were drinking liquor and Country says, 'Billy come on in here. We been wantin' to see you.'"[35]

To find and bring Billy to Washington, they had gone through the office of Representative Carl Vinson of Georgia, chairman of the Armed Services Committee. "His secretary was in on it, and they used Carl's name...." Billy stayed and partied for two or three days. Then he went back to Quantico as if nothing had happened. "How Country could pull off something like that, I just don't know." "He was the durndest character that ever lived," said Billy. "I really enjoyed him."[36]

Henry Deering "Country" Johnston was one of Billy's best friends from Valdosta. They were at one time roommates in college. His family had moved from Fulton County, Georgia to Dasher, on US Highway 41 south of Valdosta in

---

[33] Langdale, WPL Interview 1991.
[34] Langdale, WPL Interview 05.
[35] Ibid.
[36] Ibid.

the 1920s. Henry walked to high school in Valdosta and suffered teasing as "Country Boy," a name eventually shortened to "Country." He went on to study at south Georgia College in Douglas, Georgia, Georgetown University in Washington, DC, and the University of Georgia Law School. At Georgia, he gained recognition as an outstanding orator and a leader. He was elected president of his class and of the debate team. Admitted to the bar in 1941, he was at that time the youngest ever to achieve that distinction. Having received a medical discharge from the Army Air Corps, he served as administrative assistant to Representative John Gibson of Georgia at the time of Billy's summons to Washington.[37] Later, Country won election as the youngest-ever representative to the Georgia legislature and jumped into the famous three-governors controversy. That was when newly-elected governor, Eugene Talmadge, died before assuming office and a quarrel erupted between E. D. Rivers, M. E. Thompson, and Herman Talmadge over the right to be governor. Country was a Talmadge man.

Country Johnston ran unsuccessfully for congress three times, but he came close twice. Billy laughed at a predicament his friend created for himself. "In his first race," said Billy, "he made a speech in Folkston, with his battle cry 'I don't want one nigger vote.' That was before Negroes could vote. "When he ran the second time, he tried to woo 'em and one old black came up to him and said, 'Mr. Johnston, I remember what you said last time.'" Country served as Lowndes County commissioner for four years, immediately preceding Billy's election to that post.[38]

Seeing that his bout with malaria would keep him from returning to duty in the Pacific and considering his Quantico assignment boring and insignificant, Billy decided to ask for a discharge from the Marine Corps. He justified the request for release from military service on the need to work in the naval stores industry, which was considered a critical industry for the war effort. His friends warned him he had little chance of succeeding in this. Perhaps his friends did not know he would be able to secure influential help from Representative Carl Vinson, the congressman's secretary in Washington, and Senator Richard Russell. According to Billy, they wrote letters to the Marine Corps supporting his application for discharge.[39] Although Billy did not credit his buddy, Country Johnston, with involvement in this matter, one might be justified in wondering.

At this time, Billy's commanding officer was "Chesty" Puller, reputed to be the most decorated man in the Marine Corps. Billy heard through the grapevine that Chesty Puller was very tough on anybody who wanted to get out of service. If Billy hoped to get released, according to his friends, he would have to do something to win the support of Chesty Puller.

---

[37] Clifton, ed., *Heritage of Lowndes County,* 104–105.
[38] Langdale, WPL Interview 05.
[39] Langdale, WPL Interview 1991.

So Billy concocted a scheme to flatter his commanding officer and, he hoped, soften him up. He arranged for a letter to be written bearing the signature of Representative Carl Vinson and addressed to Captain Billy Langdale. It is very likely, Billy observed, that Carl Vinson never saw this letter but that it was simply written by his secretary who signed the congressman's name. As Billy recalled, the letter said something like this: "Dear Captain Langdale. If you want to go back to serving in a critical industry where you are so much needed and you can't go back overseas in the Pacific on account of your malaria attack, you need to talk to Chesty Puller, the greatest of all the Marines."

With this flattering letter in hand, Billy asked for an appointment with Chesty Puller. The letter made a good impression on him. Whereas, ordinarily, a request such as Billy's would have been immediately scuttled, Chesty Puller forwarded his request for release from the Marine Corps without recommendation, that is, without approval or disapproval. The request moved up the chain of command and was approved. Billy left active duty in the Marine Corps on 10 June 1945, and was married on the same date.[40] Within a few days, he and his bride were living near the tiny village of Mayday, Georgia, where Billy ran a turpentine camp for his father.

Billy met his future wife, Mary Jacquelyn Williams, through Country Johnston. She had worked for the War Department in New York and had come to Washington as secretary for a congressman from California. She shared an apartment with three other secretaries, one of whom worked in the office of Congressman John Gibson with Country Johnston. Country introduced Billy to Jackie.

Jackie was the daughter of Herbert Williams and Elmer Trotter Williams of Lykesland, South Carolina. She had gone to high school in Richland, South Carolina, and to college at the University of South Carolina.[41]

Jackie and Billy started their life together in circumstances that most couples in the twenty-first century would not envy. The wedding took place at Jackie's home in Lykesland, near Columbia. Having come home to Valdosta for a visit before his marriage, Billy drove up to Lykesland with his mother and Frank Bird, his best friend and best man for the wedding. They picked up Judge Harley at Columbia, where he arrived by train from one of his Washington trips on behalf of ATFA. After the wedding, Billy, Jackie, Frank Bird, Judge, and Thalia rode in the same car down to Nahunta, Georgia, where Judge had left his vehicle when he caught the train to Washington a few days previously. At Nahunta, Billy and Jackie separated from the group and struck out on their honeymoon to Jacksonville, Florida, driving Judge's automobile. Before reaching Jacksonville, however, the car ran out of gas and Billy had to walk to find fuel. True enough, the

[40] Ibid.
[41] Clifton, ed., *Heritage of Lowndes County*, 110.

circumstances of their wedding and honeymoon were a little uncomfortable, but, after all, there was still a war going on, and love can put up with a little discomfort.[42]

Although the foregoing description of Billy Langdale's World War II experience in the Marine Corps might resemble, in the opinion of some, a synopsis of a Bill Murray movie, he declares it to be true; and probably it is, with a little coloring around the edges. Billy was always a fun-loving man. His keen sense of humor tended to make some appearance in his description of almost every event and situation. It is clear from the ranks he held and the medals he received that he performed admirably as a combat marine. A more detailed description of Billy's experience would certainly make for interesting reading, or listening.

The account given above of John W.'s naval experience from 1941 to 1945 is likewise highly compressed. Much interesting detail has been left out. John's precise recollections and thoughtful commentary could well form the basis of a lengthier study at some time in the future. Now, however, it is time to focus on the Langdale Company, which was officially incorporated after the war but operated much as it had for a decade previously. That subject will be addressed following a short photo essay on the Langdale sawmill, which has been for many years an important aspect of the company's manufacturing activity.

---

[42] Langdale, WPL Interview 05.

Photo Essay

The Langdale Sawmill

Sawlogs arrive at the Langdale Forest Products Co. sawmill by truck. A twenty-ton-capacity Fulgum crane unloads them half a truckload at the time and stacks them on the ground beneath the crane. This machine travels on a circular track installed on a concrete foundation, with its base anchored in the center of the circle. The crane operator sees to it that logs stored earliest enter the sawmill first. Logs start the process of becoming lumber when the crane places them on the log deck, visible behind the truck below. This is the beginning of what is called the "log processing" operation, which precedes actual sawmill work.[1]

Fulgum crane unloading a truckload of logs. JEL.

After the crane puts logs on the log deck, they go to one of two debarkers, which are both run by the same individual. The twin debarkers are at the start of two identical log-processing lines.

The previous Langdale sawmill had one debarker and one operator. The ability of a single operator now to control two debarkers exemplifies the greater

---

[1] Photos for this essay provided by James D. Hickman of Langdale Forest Products Co.

efficiency achieved with the new machinery. This sawmill requires only twenty-one workers per shift, seventeen fewer than the one it replaced in 1998.

Johnny Langdale & Sons Wesley (L) & Jim Harley (R). Johnny is president of the company. Wesley manages the Langdale land, and Jim Harley manages Langdale Forest Products Co., which includes sawmilling and manufacturing of other solid wood products. In the background, the Fulgum crane adds half a truckload of logs to the sawmill supply stack. JDH.

Debarkers, log deck, and fulgum crane. JEL.

Upon being debarked, logs pass through scanners and then go to cut-off saws. The scanners determine the optimal length for maximum recovery from each log. Thus, computers make the decisions about where to cut off the logs. The photo of the log processing line (second below) shows both debarkers in the distance, one of the cut-off saws at left, and the two butt saws at right. A butt saw squares off the butt (bottom) of a log.

No part of the log is wasted. Recovery of product starts at the debarking stage. Bark taken off the logs travels by conveyer to a bin and, from there, to one of three destinations. Some bark is used on site as fuel, and some is sold to a local potting soil plant. Another portion goes to the MDF plant at Willacoochee, along with chips created in the log processing stage. These so-called "crane chips" come mainly from butt cuts and tops sawed off and chipped before the logs enter the sawmill.

Jim Hickman, Langdale Technical Director, points to the steel rollers that feed logs through the debarker. The actual debarker is at right in the picture. JEL

Passing from the cut-up line, logs go to the infeed system where they are divided into two categories according to diameter and take different paths in the mill. Logs nine inches and above go to the large-saw line; those below nine inches go to the small-saw line. This nine-inch criterion is adjustable, however.

Log processing line looking toward the debarkers. JDH.

Logs in the large-saw line travel through the log turner, then to two closely-related machines called the canter-quads. The log turner, a computer-controlled machine, rotates logs to position them for sawing a cant that will yield the most lumber. The computer uses data from a scanner that scans each log as it arrives. Having been optimally rotated by the turner, logs enter the canter, which squares two sides by chipping away excess material, thus creating from each log a "cant." The cant then goes to the quad-saws, four band saws, each forty feet in length. These cut side-boards off the cant if it needs to be reduced in size.

Log deck and stepfeeder taking logs into the mill. JDH.

Log Turner. Two computer-directed steel-toothed rollers move vertically and oppositely to rotate a log positioned between them. JEL.

Quad saw assemblies viewed from the top. JEL.

Traditionally, the wood taken off the log to create a cant has been sawed off as slabs. In the previous Langdale mill, slabs went by conveyor some distance to a chipping machine. (Fifty years ago bark and slabs would have been burned along with yard bark and sawdust as waste.) This mill makes no slabs, but only chips.

That simplifies the not-used-for-lumber material's delivery to its next destination. Chips are easier to move and less likely than slabs to jam or clutter machinery.

Cant on SharpChain. JDH.

In this large-log saw line, cants with two square sides and two round sides travel through a scanner and then to a computer-controlled saw assembly, the curve-saw, that cuts the cants into lumber.

Cants on scanner deck going to scanner & curve-saw. JDH.

The saw line for large logs has much heavier equipment than that for small logs. It differs also in having a new type of saw assembly that "slews and skews," giving it the ability to saw curved cants. It makes lumber from wood that formerly could only be recovered as lower-valued products. The "curve-saw" ability depends upon the scanner located at top in the photo above. This scanner is longer than any of the cants and can determine the exact curvature of each cant through its entire length and guide the curve-saw to "slew and skew" appropriately.

Cants enter the curve-saw with their flat sides at top and bottom. The remaining two round sides are at this point squared by chipping heads mounted on the curve-saw assembly. Curve-saw blades are surprisingly small, only about nineteen inches in diameter. They can saw a cant of around twelve inches in thickness, however, because saws are mounted in opposition to each other in pairs. Each blade only needs to saw halfway through the cant to complete the cut.

Curve-saw assembly with saw blades removed. The matching shiny objects on opposite sides are chipping heads that square the two round sides of the incoming cant. JEL.

In the saw line for smaller logs the cant is squared from the outset on all four sides. The cant then goes through a vertical saw arbor (VSA) assembly, with saws oriented parallel to the ground, rather than vertically, and is processed usually into 2 x 4 or 2 x 6 lumber. The output from the small-saw line merges with that of the large-saw line on the lumber deck, which feeds lumber to the unscrambler.

Outfeed of curve-saw. This shows a cant that has been sawed into six two-inch boards. JDH.

Outputs merging at lumber deck & unscrambler. JDH.

In the photo above of the lumber deck, the output from the small-saw line is in the foreground, while that of the large-saw line is toward the back, near the unscrambler. The unscrambler picks up the lumber one piece at a time and moves it to the deck above, where it proceeds to the trimmer line and to the lumber sorter.

Sorting Station. The workman stationed here sees to it that only one piece of lumber is between any two cylindrical projections on the chain conveyors. JDH.

Before merging with the output from the small-saw line, lumber from the large-saw line is evaluated by a worker, the only human in the mill who makes routine process decisions. Pieces that meet specifications move on to join the lumber from the small-saw line on the lumber deck. Those needing to be re-edged are re-routed to the edger before being sent to the lumber deck and, via the unscrambler, to the trimmer line and lumber sorter on the deck above.

A system of chain-type conveyors carries the lumber to the trim saws. Along the way, at a position called the sorting station, a worker checks to see that only one piece of lumber is on the conveyor space where only one piece is expected to be as it approaches the electronic scanner at the infeed for the trim saws. If there were two pieces instead of one, the scanner would be confused and lumber might be improperly trimmed, that is, cut to the wrong lengths.

Trim saw infeed scanner. JEL.

Trim saws. JEL.

Output from the sorting station goes through the trim saws and to the lumber sorter, which puts each piece in its proper bin, according to length, width, and thickness. A scanner checks the dimensions of each piece to determine the bin to which the sorter should deliver it. When enough lumber has accumulated in a bin, the sorting machine automatically sends it to the stacking machine.

Sorting bins. JEL.

Lumber moving to the stacking machine. JEL.

Stacking machine. JEL.

Output from stacking machine: rough green units. JDH.

Rough green units, stacked with uniform spacing between layers to facilitate airflow, ride on trams to the kilns for drying. The kilns use a high-temperature process, with drying temperatures higher than the boiling point of water. Heat for the kilns comes from steam generated by burning pole peelings and bark from the mills.

Green lumber on trams entering dry kiln. JDH.

After drying in the kiln, rough lumber is processed through the planer mill. The planer mill turns it into dressed (smooth) lumber by shaving off the rough fibers. After planing, the boards pass through the graders cab on conveyors. There human graders—not computers—look at each piece. Graders decide whether any piece should be reprocessed to have ends trimmed, and they determine the grade each one should receive. The graders on duty put a mark on every board, indicating that someone has looked at it and evaluated its quality.

Graders cab where each board receives a grade. JDH.

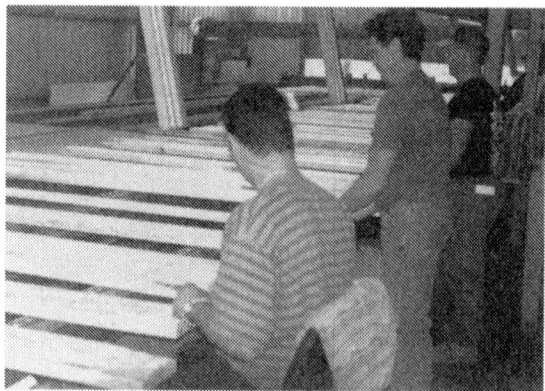

Having been graded, lumber moves on to the lumber sorter. There the sorting operator controls the sorter and its many bins through several electrical consoles, each linked to a number of bins. Every size of lumber has its own bin. One control box and the tops of several bins appear in the photo below.

Planer mill lumber sorting machine & controls. JEL.

When enough lumber accumulates in a sorting bin, it is delivered to the stacker. This machine places each board in a neat stack and sends it to the packaging machine, which binds it into lumber packages for sale.

Planer mill stacker infeed from sorting machine. JEL.

Planer mill packaging machine. JEL.

Planer mill outfeed from
packaging machine. JDH.

Langdale Forest Products Co. delivers lumber by truck, by rail, and sometimes
by ship from Valdosta, Georgia, and from Sweetwater, Tennessee. The company
has twenty-two over-the-road drivers going out each day and contracts with
independent trucking companies for some deliveries

Railroad car loaded with
Langdale lumber. JEL.

Typically, Langdale trucks carry more round-wood products, especially utility
poles, than lumber. This is because customers usually have unloading capabilities
for lumber, but not for poles, and a substantial number of customers send their own
trucks to pick up lumber at the Langdale plant.

Loading customer's
truck with lumber at
Valdosta mill. JDH.

Langdale managers in 2001 seemed well pleased with their new sawmill. Not only did it have far greater capacity for production and improved quality compared to the mill it replaced, but it also operated with a much smaller crew and recovered a higher percentage of lumber, rather than products of lower value, from the logs processed.

9

The Langdale Company

After World War II, Judge Harley and his sons decided to incorporate their land and other holdings as "The Langdale Company." This remains, more than half a century later, the official name of the parent corporation, although there are a number of subsidiaries. In the structure of this corporation Judge held the top position as chairman, but Harley, Jr. generally ran the business with Judge looking beneficently over his shoulder and nearly always acquiescing in his son's decisions.

Harley, Sr. in 1951. TLC.

In this respect, the situation remained much as it had been for a decade, since shortly after Harley, Jr.'s graduation from college. At that time (1937), as Harley, Jr. recalled, "he was mighty proud of the fact that I had gone to forestry school." Appreciative of his father's confidence, Harley, Jr. remembered that "he'd give me as much leeway as any father could give a son to go ahead and make mistakes, and he agreed most of the time with me. So he took a lesser role.... He was about fifty-one or two years old when he turned it over to me."[1]

Those familiar with the Langdale family and business, family members and others, agree that the remarkable success of the Langdale Company owes most to the personalities, values, and management skills of Judge Harley and his eldest son, Harley, Jr. The second and third sons, John W. and Billy, had important but lesser functions in the operation of the business. Their sister, Virginia, following tradition, did not work in the business.

John W., who practiced law as his father's partner after returning from the war, involved himself at the Langdale Company in this period almost entirely with legal matters. At that time, John and Harley, Jr. did not see each other every day, even though they had offices in the same building on West Hill Avenue. They talked mainly when Harley had an occasional legal issue to handle. Harley, Jr. had his office on the ground floor. They called it the Timber Office.[2]

Harley, Jr. in 1939. TLC.

John's work with the family business and his contacts with Harley, Jr. increased when they made the decision to incorporate and form "The Langdale Company." This required a large amount of research to assure he had adequate descriptions of every parcel of land and to prepare deeds from the owners in 1948 to the new corporation. The biggest problem involved, from a lawyer's perspective, was that some tracts had poor legal descriptions. None of the titles were so weak, however, as to require resorting to the registration procedure Judge Harley had used in 1920 when establishing clear titles for lands of The J. W. Langdale Company. From this time, John W. devoted more and more of his legal

---

[1] Langdale, HLJr Interview 1991.
[2] Langdale, JWL Interview 14.

practice to representing the Langdale Company and less to other clients. John also gave much of his time to civic, religious, educational, and political activities[3]

John W. in 1952. TLC.

Billy's work for the Langdale Company "was more in the woods." as Harley, Jr. summarized it in 1991. Billy excelled at handling people and making friends with almost anybody he had dealings with. He was very energetic, and when the turpentine business was important to the company, Billy could help with almost any phase of that. After the company changed its emphasis more to manufacturing, Billy concentrated on trading with people for pulpwood, saw logs, and poles.[4]

From his youth, Billy had a reputation for being less sedate and circumspect than his older brothers. Some described him as a bit rambunctious. Judge Harley seemed to support this view of his youngest son when interviewed for an article in the *Saturday Evening Post* in 1955. Extolling the usefulness of outdoor sports for developing good character in young men, Judge opined, "Hunting and fishing keeps boys out of poolrooms. I doubt that a one of my boys has ever been in a poolroom in his life. Except maybe Billy. Old Bill's a rouster."[5]

In later years, Billy dissented a little concerning the picture Judge's remarks in the *Post* implied. With respect to the poolroom comment, he said, "I think that's not quite true." "I think some of the rest of them went in there; I went in the front door and everybody else was coming in the back door." So, perhaps Billy's older brothers had learned to value discretion a little more than he did.[6]

Judge is supposed to have said he had one son who knew how to make money, another who knew how to keep it, and one who knew how to spend it. None of

---

[3] Ibid.
[4] Langdale, HLJr Interview 1991.
[5] Martin, 92.
[6] Langdale, WPL Interview 1991.

their friends would doubt that the three descriptions put his sons in order of seniority, and Billy would be the one who knew how to spend.

Billy Langdale & wife, Jackie, in 1952. TLC.

Billy acknowledged important differences between the brothers in personality. Compared to John, who had been "closer to the church group," Billy thought of himself as having more in common with ordinary people who were a little less church-oriented. He saw himself as more like his father in joining numerous organizations made up of everyday people. Billy said of himself that he had joined almost everything one could join, including the American Legion, AmVets, DAV's, and the Elks. Harley, Billy observed, kept more to himself and to organizations more strictly related to business.

Virginia Langdale Miller, 1974. TLF.

One thing Billy and Harley, Jr. had in common was a habit of early rising, which they regarded as partly a holdover from their years in the turpentine business. In the year 2001 some might speculate that a genetic predisposition could also have been involved, inasmuch as news reports said that scientists had discovered a genetic basis for early rising and retiring. Whatever the reason, every morning, including weekends and holidays, Billy said in 1991, he awakened at four o'clock. Normally by 4:30 he arrived at the Gold Plate Restaurant. He went there, he declared, because he liked to see and talk with people who got up early and who had their own opinions, rather than opinions they had picked up during the day from the radio or the TV. In contrast, Harley, Jr.'s schedule took him first thing in the morning, not to a restaurant, but to his office at the Langdale Company.

As the leader and main decision-maker in company operations, Harley, Jr. benefited from his long association with his father, with whom he had much in common as a manager. In his work heading the ATFA and in managing his turpentine partnerships, Judge often demonstrated great skill as an organizer and leader. Harley, Jr. and his brothers did not fail to notice and to adopt in some degree his techniques. As mentioned earlier, their sister, Virginia, also admired their father's ability to deal effectively with people of any background.

Billy, who often traveled or hung around with his father while the older boys were at work or in school, had numerous opportunities to observe his father in action. He admired his father's effective, easy-going manner in dealing with people.

Judge did some of his organizing during hunting trips, Billy remembered. He'd put on a deer hunt, for example, a two or three-day affair such as those he held at Camp Jonohala. At some point, Judge would get the most influential men together and persuade one to take charge of one thing and one to head up another task, and a third to do something else. Then he'd back off and let them handle their designated responsibilities. "He did that all the way through his business life," recalled Billy. "He had partners in the turpentine business, the naval stores business, and things like that. He never did tell them how to get the job done. And all his partners were so different. One would do it by getting out and working with labor, one would have a completely different way of doing it. But he had a keen ability to recognize what people had to do and recognize the importance of people and at the same time not try to dictate how they did it."[7] Once a person accepted a delegated task, Judge left it to that individual to complete the job in his own way. Harley, Jr. also observed his father's leadership techniques, including the use of hunting trips, and incorporated these into his own management system as chief executive of the Langdale Company.

As executives, both Judge Harley and Harley, Jr. typically focused on large decisions and left the details to others. John W., who worked closely with his father and brother for many years and knew both men as well as anyone could, saw this demonstrated over and over. As John perceived it, primarily because of their temperaments, neither his father nor his older brother ever had much interest in detail work.

---

[7] Ibid.

To illustrate the distaste for detail in the case of his brother, John W. told of trying to persuade Harley, Jr., who, as of 1995, had made a number of trips to England, to take time for research on the origin of their family. "He's been over there, oh I don't know, at least six times, and I tried to get him to follow up and see what we've never been able to connect up, see what ship we came on; whether we came with those indentured people or prisoners or how we came…. But Harley is just not the type to do that. Daddy was the same way." Lundie Smith, who practiced law with Judge, used to say, "Judge is a wonderful executive; if Judge ever got invited to a piano-moving party, he would always be carrying the stool."[8]

John W. Langdale, Jr. TLC.

For years, if Judge had to give a speech, Lundie Smith wrote it. Judge would simply say, "Write me a speech." When John W. first came back from World War II, speech-writing for his father became one of his responsibilities. If Judge dictated a letter, since he always had good legal secretaries, he depended upon them to get the details right. Typically, "he would say, 'Write old John…and tell him something along these lines.' And she'd have to phrase it; he wouldn't take the time to do that, to punctuate or anything."

"My son, Johnny, who's president of the company now is the same way," observed John W. "He's got good people working for him, you know." It is typical of a good executive, John thought, to concentrate on the most important points and leave the details to others. Lawyers and other people trained in specialized professions, it seemed to John W., were less likely to succeed as top executives. "They can't see the forest for the trees," he concluded.[9]

Reflecting on personality types and management styles in 1995, John W. saw himself as different from his father, his brother, and his son in that, unlike them, he had an affinity for details. For that reason, compared to them, he considered himself less suited for a top executive position. "I was not a good executive when I

---

[8] Langdale, JWL Interview 14.
[9] Ibid.

was president of the Langdale Company," declared John. "As a matter of fact, I carried the title but during that time Harley and I had a tacit understanding that he was going to keep on doing the operating part. I looked after administrative problems mostly: personnel, accounting, legal, credits, things of that nature. But he kept on doing the executive part that involved operations."[10]

Another characteristic that the two Harleys and Johnny had in common, and another difference with himself, noted John, was their willingness to work very long hours every day. The long days that Judge put in with his business interests and his legal practice kept him away from his family too much, John thought. "That was the life we had, and as I look back on it, it's not right; it's not the best life for a family, the way he was working. My son's doing the same thing now. He gets to the office between 4:30 and 5:00 every morning. He seldom gets home before 5:30 or 6:00. Harley did that for years. The business is his life. I didn't do it. I'd get down there, back when I was active, maybe by 7 o'clock."[11] So John's typical workday ran from around 7:00 A.M. to 4:30 P.M., about nine and a half hours, compared to the thirteen hours typical of Harley, Jr. or Johnny.

As one might expect, Harley, Jr. approved of Johnny's long hours and devotion to the business a little more than John W. did. "He's innovative, very dedicated and very hardworking, and nearly everyone that works at the plant or that he deals with seems to get along with him very well," said Harley, Jr. in 1991. He described John W. Langdale, Jr. at that time as knowledgeable about forestry and agriculture and eager to learn the finer points of managing the company as its president.[12]

Among his father's greatest talents, John W. listed the ability to negotiate. When negotiating in business, explained John, "you do a lot of listening, you do a lot of feinting, walking off to the side, turning your back, saying no when you mean maybe. He was a master at that. As much land as he purchased over his life time.... And the same thing could be said of Harley. That's one of his strengths. He's a patient trader."[13] In other words, a key to successful negotiation, at least sometimes, is maintaining a degree of ambiguity about one's intentions and the acceptable limits of the deal. Or to put it another way, it's usually a good idea not to show all your cards. "It's not always well to let the other person know exactly what you're thinking and be plain spoken," concluded John W. [14]

John W. observed this negotiation technique reflected in his elder brother's management approach. "Harley is not plain spoken," said John. "You have to listen very carefully. Some of his managers and other employees will tell you that about Harley—that he very rarely tells you yes or no. He gives the other party

---

[10] Ibid.

[11] Ibid.

[12] Langdale, HLJr Interview 1991.

[13] Langdale, JWL Interview 14.

[14] Ibid.

some leeway. He's never been a manager who would tell you exactly what to do. He gets his philosophy generally across to you, but he has roundabout methods, and it's very difficult sometimes. His managers sometimes want him to take full responsibility and tell them exactly what to do. He doesn't operate that way."[15] "He delegates authority and he makes his managers and his employees use their own heads and come up with their own ideas, and he has never been one to suppress individual initiative," observed John. Like his father, Harley, Jr. had the shrewdness to choose competent people to work with him and the confidence to delegate responsibility.

Following the teaching and the examples of their father and grandfather, Harley, Jr. and his brothers have practiced the traditional virtue of frugality. This applied in business and in their personal lives. Detractors have occasionally interpreted their thriftiness as stinginess, but the Langdales saw it as prudent financial conservatism. This is without question one of the most prominent values passed down from generation to generation in the Langdale family from the time of the first John Wesley down at Council. They simply took very seriously the old axiom, "A penny saved is a penny earned." With respect to his grandfather and namesake, John W. had the impression that Grandfather John Wesley made a little money out of hogs, cattle, and turpentine, but, more important, he eschewed high living and saved a large portion of his income. That observation applied also to his own generation, said John. "We haven't made the money that people would think," confided John W. in 1995, "given the fact that we have a large number of employees and a lot of land, and you look at the things that are visible. We just never have.... Well, we saved about ninety percent of what we made, except what Uncle Sam got, I guess."[16]

This habit of being close with a penny even applied in relations within the family. For instance, while John W. attended the Naval Academy an article came out in *Time Magazine* about a man, Judge Harley, down in south Georgia making a lot of money in turpentine. John received a letter from home telling him about the article, but without a clipping enclosed. His parents left it up to him to decide whether to buy the magazine from the meager funds then available to him as a student or go to the library to read the article. Most parents would perhaps have bought an extra copy of the magazine to send to their son.[17]

From time to time Judge Harley loosened his purse strings and spent money for entertainment, especially if quail or deer hunting entered into it. This occurred in connection with his promotional activities on behalf of ATFA, for example, but always in moderation.

---

[15] Ibid.

[16] Ibid.

[17] Ibid.

Billy Langdale remembered how some of Judge's political friends, knowing well his penchant for frugality, once played a joke on him. This happened at the Democratic National Convention in 1960.[18] Understanding how careful about expenditures—that is, thrifty—Judge Harley was, a few of his comrades urged him to hold a dinner for some delegates, with the hope of influencing their votes. Frank Twitty offered to take care of everything. Having in mind a group of fifteen or twenty, and an expenditure of perhaps two or three hundred dollars, Judge agreed. Frank rented a fancy place, had elaborate floral decorations, and ordered plenty of expensive hors d'oeuvres and drinks. The bill came to around two thousand dollars. "And my daddy," said Billy, "he liked to never got over it. He'd kind of color it to tell it, and he'd laugh about it later, but they really put a good one to him."[19]

Another anecdote relating to the legendary Langdale frugality is attributed to an airplane pilot who used to work for the company. According to this pilot, Judge Harley and Harley, Jr. had invited a number of friends to accompany them on a hunting trip to Latin America. Harley, Jr. showed his father a budget that he had set up apportioning a share of the expense to each guest. Judge objected, saying to his son, "Harley, we can't charge our friends for going with us on this trip. We invited them; they're our guests." Then, as reported, Judge looked over toward the pilot and muttered, "Over-trained him, didn't I?" Whether or not this story is true, Judge Harley's children certainly had effective training in the practice of frugality. In 2002, reflecting on Harley, Jr.'s attitude toward spending, little brother, Billy, commented, "Used to—he's changed a lot—whenever a dollar went out of his hands he wanted to see some wings on it to see it was coming back."[20]

Judge Harley and his first airplane. TLC.

---

[18] Langdale, WPL Interview 1991.
[19] Ibid.
[20] Langdale, WPL Interview 05.

Within the family there is unanimous agreement that Harley, Jr. provided the vision and leadership in transforming Judge Harley's turpentine business into the diversified forest products corporation it became after 1937. As his brother, John W., affirmed in 1995, "Harley deserves the credit for everything we have developed at the Langdale Company. He started working his visions when he graduated from forestry school in 1937. For example, building the central steam turpentine distillery in Valdosta did away with all of our "fire stills" as we called them.... Going into the wood preserving business was Harley's vision, and going into the lumber business...was over Judge's protest."[21]

Harley, Jr., for his part, gave other family members much of the credit for the success of the Langdale Company. "I have had the whole-hearted cooperation of the entire family for my entire career," he declared in 1991. He went on to affirm that "we could not have accomplished what we have without the family doing their part." He singled out for special praise his brother, John W., who, "being a lawyer, certainly put the company in good position to trade on property and to keep up with some of the laws and rules and regulations." In Harley's opinion, "John was and is still an excellent land attorney, and some of the most complicated deals he was able to work out—which has really been a benefit to the company." "Now, of course," observed Harley, Jr., we have to have several groups of lawyers that are working on problems of labor relations, environmental problems, and Internal Revenue Service problems."[22] Clearly, Judge's sons remained close and mutually appreciative in the 1990s, after some fifty years of working together in the Langdale Company and more than two decades after their father's death. John's admiration of his brother echoed the trust that Judge Harley had placed in him. Judge demonstrated this confidence when he virtually turned over the business to his son within a brief period after his graduation from forestry school.

Harley Jr., shirtless, with three shirtless friends in 1937. Jim Gillis Jr. is at left, then Harley Jr., Francis Clark, & Eugene Brogdon. TLF.

---

[21] Langdale, JWL Interview 14.

[22] Langdale, HLJr Interview 1991.

John W., who was then in law school, discovered the new situation when he came home for a visit. "I was surprised how much authority Daddy had given Harley and how quickly he had taken the responsibility," said John. "I really did not expect Daddy to turn over these matters as quickly as he did." So, what was the reason for this rapid transition? "For one thing, I think Daddy recognized that Harley had been studying in the field of forestry, and there were new things developing that he didn't know about, that his field of view had been limited; and I think Daddy recognized that Harley was a responsible young man and he could turn things over to him and we could be a part of these changes to our advantage.... I know he was tempted, as anybody would be, to hold on to his old ways. But he gave in to the possibility of change, I think."[23] Perhaps one should view this as another example of Judge's finding a good partner, a good manager, and letting him perform, as he had been doing for years with his turpentine partnerships.

When Harley, Jr. returned from college to help run the company as general manager, he found, as he remembered in 1991, three major problems: inadequate fire protection, shortage of operating capital, and lack of markets.[24] All of these had a negative impact on profit. Harley, Jr. saw it as his central objective to increase profit from the land. Land and everything that lived on it was Judge Harley's main economic resource, and one that he possessed in some abundance by this time. In Harley's view, whatever the land produced must be used to the fullest. Waste must be reduced. To the extent possible, markets must be found for anything that grew from the ground or foraged in the forest.

Managing the land meant controlling it, of course, but Harley, Jr. found in the late 1930s that the Langdales did not have exclusive control of the land they owned. Farmers in Echols, Lowndes, and Clinch Counties had for years hunted on land in their neighborhoods and allowed their cattle to graze on it, with little concern for who actually owned the property. At that time, Georgia's fence laws did not require farmers to fence in their livestock, but allowed the animals to roam freely. If a farmer wished to protect his property from his neighbors' free-ranging livestock, he had to fence his fields. Drivers on the state's highways likewise had to be on the lookout for cattle and hogs crossing the roads or grazing on the right of way. The biggest problem, from Harley, Jr.'s standpoint, was that these people regularly set fire to the land to burn off the wire grass and stimulate new growth. They wanted green grass for their cattle. Such fires, unauthorized by the Langdales, sometimes got out of control and damaged or destroyed their trees.[25]

This practice of burning the woods to produce green grass for livestock persisted from pioneer days. When the early settlers moved to southern Georgia they were attracted in part by the universal existence of wire grass that provided

---

[23] Langdale, JWL Interview 14.
[24] "Langdale Is Vast Forest Industry," *Valdosta Daily Times*, 18 November 1959.
[25] Langdale, HLJr Interview 1991.

sustenance for the wild cattle that roamed the forest. Acquisition of a patch of ground with wild cattle and wire grass converted one immediately from a drifter to a rancher. Although mature wire grass looked dry and lifeless, by simply putting a match to it a farmer could simultaneously thin the insect population and evoke new growth of lush green grass. He might also secure a little food by shooting animals fleeing from the blaze. By the end of the twentieth century, however, wiregrass had been substantially displaced by new crops and farming methods from its former dominance. Yet wiregrass still proved useful, for example, as soil cover to prevent erosion on ditch embankments along state roads and highways. To commemorate the traditional importance of wiregrass, some historical societies included the name of the grass in their names. At least two major highways in south Georgia had the term "wiregrass" applied to them, one being the Valdosta to Waycross highway.[26] Curtailing the practice of freely burning the woods required cultural change in the rural population and took considerable time.

Another class of people who helped themselves to the use of Langdale land and deprived them of total control of it were moonshiners. The Langdales did not dare turn them in to the authorities or try to run them off. "We really never did have any bad trouble with them, and we never did report them. We knew that if we reported them and they found out about it they would burn us from one end to the other."[27] Mostly the moonshiners had small, temporary stills. They would operate in one place for a while, then set up a still somewhere else and abandon the previous location. "We had pretty good revenue officers down here that worked to destroy them," said Harley, Jr., "but we had a policy to leave them alone."[28]

The 20,000 acres of land Judge owned in 1937 soon grew to more than a hundred thousand acres. Father and son agreed they needed more. Consequently, they had to have money to buy it. Lacking the necessary cash, they borrowed from turpentine factors, who charged a high rate of interest, and from local banks, which were reluctant to lend. In the late 1930s, Judge and Harley, Jr. found their loans difficult to repay. For a time the cash flow situation became so tight that Harley, Jr. arranged to pay off a loan in small weekly payments to a Valdosta bank. Each Saturday morning, Harley remembered vividly in 1995, he went to the bank with a hundred dollars in hand to make his scheduled payment.

Struggling to make loan payments and master his father's naval stores business while expanding and diversifying it, Harley, Jr. worked assiduously in the late 1930s to achieve his vision for the company. Continued acquisition of land, much as Judge had been doing for years, fit into this plan, as father and son easily agreed.

---

[26] Donald Davis of Valdosta, Georgia, led a group of citizens in a campaign of several years duration to achieve designation of this road as the "Wiregrass Parkway."

[27] Langdale, HLJr Interview 1991.

[28] Ibid.

During this period, the Langdales bought land for $2 to $5 per acre that by 1992 appraised for $1000 or more per acre. From the 1930s to the 1990s, Harley, Jr. always believed the company needed more land to assure sustained yield. This conviction, plus his "love of the land," have, for him, been major motivations for land acquisition. As the price of pulpwood rose in the pre-war period and afterward, Harley, Jr. took advantage of the increased revenue to buy additional forest land when he thought it had good potential for income or appreciation. Sometimes, however, he passed up the opportunity to buy land at a low price because he thought it could not be protected from fire at reasonable cost. The price of land varied greatly over the years. In view of the much higher land prices of recent times, Harley, Jr. admitted that he sometimes had regretted passing up some of those long-ago opportunities to buy land for less. The Langdale Company still had an interest in purchasing land in the 1990s, but took a less aggressive and more selective attitude than previously. In times past, the Langdales probably averaged buying eight or ten thousand acres a year, said Harley, Jr., but in the 1990s fifteen hundred to two thousand was more typical. Mostly the company bought land contiguous to theirs.

By the 1990s, the Langdale Company and individual family members owned more than 200,000 acres of land, nearly all of it forestland of some type. As of 1992, the Langdale Company possessed about 80,000 acres of planted forests and about 127,000 acres of naturally-reproduced forests. At that time, Harley, Jr. preferred natural regeneration when it would work. Hardwood occupied twenty to twenty-five percent of Langdale forestland. About thirty percent of this land, around 60,000 acres, their foresters classified as wetlands.

As for uses of the land, in 1991 the company farmed approximately 4,000 acres, down from 5,000 acres five years previously. This included tobacco, peanuts and other crops. At one time, about forty percent of the land, uplands, had been devoted to production of gum naval stores. The turpentine business ended, however, in the 1970s, and the emphasis shifted toward production of wood for manufacturing. The Langdale Company also leased land to 146 different groups, such as hunting clubs, for recreation. By this means the company derived additional revenue, earned good will, and gained some help in controlling wild fires.

Harley, Jr. always saw the land as the basis of the family business. Manufacturing was for him a means of making full use of the resources of the land, a way to secure markets for the produce of the land. Hence, he thought of himself as primarily a tree farmer and only secondarily as a manufacturer. It was the forest, he believed, that made possible the prosperity of his family, and for that matter, of a large portion of south Georgia. For example, he estimated in 1991, fifty percent of income from the Lowndes County area came from forestland or things manufactured from forest products.

For more than fifty years, the Langdales tapped the productivity of the south Georgia forests through the naval stores enterprise. When this became increasingly less profitable and they decided to get out of that business in the 1970s, the company moved more aggressively into manufacturing.

Ending the turpentine operation actually increased the productivity of the Langdale forests from the standpoint of timber growth and the output of wood for such things as poles, lumber, and pulpwood. The growth rate of trees increased significantly, declared Harley, Jr., after the company quit the naval stores business. Tapping trees for turpentine retarded their growth probably about twenty-five percent, he thought. Large turpentine trees also slowed the growth of smaller trees by shading them from sunlight. By the 1990s, Harley, Jr. observed, some Langdale land grew more than a cord per acre per year, and some, probably former farmland, even exceeded two cords per acre, although the average was lower. Jim Hickman, a Langdale executive and registered forester, mentioned in 2000 that some of the best, intensively managed, areas were then approaching four cords per acre per year.

Year-in and year-out in the 1980s and 1990s, Langdale land supplied about a third of the wood that the company processed. This varied with weather and markets. For example, in 1991, a wet year, at least fifty percent of the company's wood came from its own land. In the dry years 1988–1990, however, less than ten percent of the wood supply came from land the Langdales owned. The fact that neither the US Forest Service nor the State of Georgia owned large tracts in south Georgia made it easier for the Langdale Company to secure its wood supply mostly from other owners. It was also advantageous, noted Harley, Jr., that the Langdale land fell mostly within fifty miles of their plant in Valdosta, keeping transportation costs down.

There were, of course, concerns in the 1990s and afterward about the future of the Langdale forestland, notably the effects of fire and taxes. Harley, Jr. worried that, because less prescribed, controlled burning was being practiced, fuel was building up in the woods that could contribute to a catastrophic fire on the scale of the one in 1955 that burned 90,000 acres of Superior Pine Products land. During the half century plus of his leadership of the Langdale Company, taxes on land had increased, Harley, Jr. lamented, from about ten cents an acre to three or four dollars an acre, or more.

Still, Harley, Jr. felt optimistic about the future. "In my opinion," he said, "the area around Valdosta is going to be in a position to be a tree-growing and forest products center in the future. I see no reasons that we will not be practicing forestry and making useful products from wood that will be just as outstanding as what I have seen in Germany, Sweden or any other place that I have had the opportunity to visit."[29] John J. Langdale, speaking in the early 1990s, said he expected the Langdales and others in south Georgia to place greater emphasis on

---

[29] Ibid.

the "chip'n saw" approach in coming years. This meant using the butt of the tree for 2 x 4s or 2 x 6s and chipping the remainder for pulp mills.[30]

Although, after Harley, Jr.'s return from forestry school in 1937, Judge quickly gave him authority over operations, he had serious doubts about some of his son's new ideas. This included Harley, Jr.'s desire to go into the pulpwood business.

By the late 1930s, pulp mills had begun to move into the South. For example, the Union Bag and Paper Corporation put its new Savannah plant into operation in the fall of 1936, about the time Harley, Jr. started his senior year of forestry school and Harley, Sr. created the ATFA. The plant then had six hundred employees and produced one hundred and thirty tons of kraft paper each day. By 1953, with nine times as many workers, the plant produced thirteen times as much paper per day, and consumed about a million cords of pulpwood annually. Its annual payroll rose during these seventeen years from $1 million to $18 million. The experience of this one plant suggests the tremendous importance of this new market for wood from southern forests.[31]

In 1937 pulpwood was a new, long-term, expanding market. By 1953, pulpwood production for all of Georgia reached two million cords a year, up about fifty percent in five years and more than five times as high as Georgia's production in 1943. By October 1953, seven pulp mills operated in Georgia: three in Savannah, two in Macon, and one each in Brunswick and St. Mary's. Three others raced to go on line later in the year in Rome, Jesup, and Clyattville, near Valdosta.[32]

Back in 1937, Harley, Jr. believed the pulpwood market offered the Langdales an opportunity to improve cash flow by selling pulpwood from their land. Pulpwood money could help repay loans needed to buy more land and could also pay for improved forest practices that would create greater revenue in the long run. Although Judge had his doubts at first, as will be discussed momentarily, pulpwood sales substantially improved profitability for the family enterprise.[33] It turned out, in fact, that properly thinning timber for pulpwood actually increased the amount and value of wood produced by allowing faster timber growth. This was Harley, Jr.'s first major innovation in Langdale business operations.[34] It did not come easily, of course, for it required overcoming some of his father's long held assumptions.

---

[30] Langdale, JJLJr Interview 1991.

[31] Union Bag & Paper Corporation, "Advertisement," *Atlanta Journal and Constitution Magazine*, 25 October 1953, 4.

[32] "Dollars Grow on Trees," *Atlanta Journal and Constitution Magazine*, 25 October 1953, 49.

[33] Langdale, HLJr Interview 1991.

[34] "Dollars Grow on Trees," 49.

Judge's reservations on the subject of cutting trees came from his experience as a turpentine producer. He shared the fears of other turpentine farmers of that era that the paper mills and their appetite for pulpwood would put naval stores operators out of business. They worried that the trees would all be cut and there would be none to produce turpentine.[35]

Judge knew very well that gum turpentine production accounted for most of the income from southern pine forests of that day. He had never been able to derive comparable profit from saw logs or crossties, for example. So, for him, it appeared essential to maintain a good supply of trees for future production of turpentine, and he preferred to cut no tree that held potential for gum production.[36] In fact, Judge's personal motto, according to some, was "I like in all things to inspire youth and conserve timber."[37]

Judge Harley & the Board of Directors of ATFA. A cooperative effort between ATFA and the US Government encouraged turpentine farmers to practice conservation. TLC.

Reflecting this concern about future availability of turpentine trees, Judge had long pursued what Harley, Jr. referred to as a "conservative policy" with respect to cupping trees. To extend the life of the tree and derive more gum in the long run, Judge typically put fewer cups on a tree than some operators would have installed. For example, instead of placing two cups on a tree initially, he might put one cup and then at a later time add a second cup, allowing the tree to grow in the meantime and providing, he hoped, space for a third cup at a later date. As a result of this tree-conserving mindset, Judge had serious doubts when Harley, Jr. started into the pulpwood business. Judge used to quote an aphorism that he attributed to Benjamin Franklin: "Be not the first to try the new, nor the last to throw the old

---

[35] Langdale, HLJr Interview 1991.

[36] Ibid.

[37] McKay, "Langdale Lived to See Dream Come True."

aside."[38] Judge feared his son was moving too aggressively into cutting their trees for pulpwood.

Of course, Judge's fears concerning a shortage of turpentine trees did not materialize. Although in time paper mills became formidable competitors as producers of naval stores as byproducts of paper making, the gum naval stores business prospered far more in the 1940s and 1950s than in the previous two decades. As of 1953, the value of turpentine production in Georgia amounted to approximately $29,000,000 annually. Georgia produced seventy-two percent of the US output of naval stores, which amounted to more than half the world supply. As probably the world's largest individual producer and in his eighteenth year as president of the ATFA, Judge Harley could point with pride to the 136,000 drums of rosin and 400,000 gallons of turpentine in storage for Georgia producers at the Langdale Company.[39]

The success of Georgia's gum naval stores producers, including the Langdales, resulted in considerable measure from technological developments that permitted greater efficiency in the use of labor. Encouraged by the government's Naval Stores Conservation Program and the ATFA, almost half of Georgia's turpentine farmers applied two new technologies, bark chipping and acid stimulation, to about three-fourths of the estimated 44,000,000 turpentine faces in production as of 1953. Output per worker reportedly increased from twenty-four to seventy-six percent as a result of these new methods. A worker who previously took care of 5,000 faces could now look after 8,000 faces.[40]

Both of these technologies went into commercial use to a limited extent as early as 1942, stimulated by wartime conditions, and gradually increased in degree of application. Bark chipping, which reduced damage to the tree, lengthened its productive life and resulted in a more valuable piece of timber at the end of its service as a turpentine tree. Acid stimulation increased the flow of gum and reduced the number of necessary streaks per season. Without acid stimulation, the Langdales normally applied about thirty streaks per season. Of course, each streak required a visit to the tree and cost money for labor.[41]

In 1937, when turpentiners were hanging on by their fingernails, neither Judge nor Harley, Jr. could foresee the large profits that would be made from gum turpentine in the next twenty years, which included World War II and the first decade of the Cold War. The 1920s and 1930s had brought ups and downs in prices and profits for naval stores producers. Many had gone under, and Judge had struggled, even as he enlarged his business, to stay afloat. Now Judge's son considered it prudent, in fact necessary, to diversify and make fuller use of the products of the land. And that meant, for one thing, pulpwood. Notwithstanding

---

[38] Langdale, HLJr Interview 1991.

[39] "Dollars Grow on Trees," 48, 49.

[40] Ibid., 49-50.

[41] Langdale, HLJr Interview 1991 ; "Dollars Grow on Trees," 49-50.

his father's qualms, Harley, Jr. went around with a paint gun marking trees with two cups on them to be cut for pulpwood, even though there remained space for adding a third cup. Judge's experience led him to think it would be better to add that third cup and get gum production for a longer period. This may have been one of those times when Judge uttered another of his favorite sayings, "It is disturbing to me....".[42]

Talking with his partners in Harley, Jr.'s absence, Judge sometimes questioned his son's tree-cutting policy. "You'd better ask Harley how I got the money to send him to forestry school," he grumbled. Of course, the money obviously had come from turpentine, not pulpwood. Nevertheless, Judge tolerated Harley, Jr.'s new ideas and allowed him to lead the Langdale Company into the pulpwood business in 1938. As Harley, Jr. described the situation in 1991 in an understatement typical of his manner of speaking, "We had discussions, but he was very tolerant of me and he was very encouraging, and he carried me in every situation that I could be exposed to."[43]

Actually, Judge's initial opposition to his son's tree-cutting softened into grudging approval as he witnessed the results. "After he saw the mortality had changed and the trees were growing better consistently, he fell in line with that, and he didn't mind harvesting a stand," recalled Harley, Jr.[44] Yet, Judge remained a turpentine man at heart. A writer for a national magazine commented in 1955 that "he still has an old turpentine man's aversion to cutting a tree."[45]

From 1938 to the 1990s, the Langdale Company never missed a week producing pulpwood.[46] Harley, Jr. sold his first pulpwood for $3.50 per unit (1 1/4 cords), loaded in boxcars. The price by 1992 approached $60 per cord.

In that first year of pulpwood production, Harley, Jr. found his best market a hundred and twenty miles southeast of Valdosta, in Jacksonville. There, a Russian Jewish immigrant named Sam Kipnis established a paper mill in 1938, operating as National Container Corporation and manufacturing cardboard boxes. Kipnis set up his paper mill near the river in what had previously been a fertilizer plant. At first, Harley, Jr. found it hard to do business with Kipnis. They didn't get along well at all. Eventually, the two men became more friendly, as Harley, Jr. recalled, at least to the point that "he and I could do business without calling in all the lawyers, and we understood each other." Sam Kipnis, said Harley, Jr., "got to be a good businessman after he made a little money down there."[47]

A period of much better relations between Harley, Jr. and Kipnis started with the latter's employment of Guy H. Wesley to take charge of wood procurement

---

[42] McKay, "Langdale Lived to See Dream Come True."
[43] Langdale, HLJr Interview 1991.
[44] Ibid.
[45] Martin, 91.
[46] Langdale, HLJr Interview 1991.
[47] Ibid.

for the papermill. As Harley, Jr. evaluated the situation, "Guy Wesley was probably the best thing that could have happened to National Container Corporation at that time." A native Floridian from Point Washington in West Florida, Wesley had worked in the woods, and knew all aspects of forestry. He had been employed with the Florida Forestry Service prior to taking the job with Kipnis. A practical woodsman, Guy Wesley "didn't know but one way to do business," remembered Harley, Jr., "and that was the fair way."[48] With Guy Wesley and his wife, Anne, Harley, Jr. and his wife, Eileen, became close friends.

The confidence that Harley, Jr. and Guy Wesley had in each other played an important role in a significant expansion of both National Container and the Langdale Company in the early 1950s. At that time, Sam Kipnis wished to build on the success of his papermill at Jacksonville by erecting another mill. Harley, Jr. assured Kipnis he would work with National Container in supplying the necessary pulpwood. Kipnis sent experts to look for a site and found a suitable place near Clyattville. This location alone in Lowndes County had sufficient drop in the river level to allow adequate ponding for aeration of the wastewater coming out of the plant.

Finding an acceptable construction site solved one major problem, but Kipnis still had to assure his potential investors of an adequate source of pulpwood for his projected mill. These financial backers insisted he have a guaranteed wood supply. Lacking forestland of his own, Kipnis turned to the Langdale Company for a formal commitment. In talks with Guy Wesley, Harley, Jr. reached an agreement that the Langdale Company would guarantee a certain number of cords of pulpwood every year for fifteen years. In return, the Langdale Company would have the exclusive right in south Georgia to supply pulpwood to the mill. Other Valdosta-area producers who wished to sell pulpwood to the Clyattville mill must sell through the Langdale Company. The down side of this agreement, from the viewpoint of Harley, Jr., was that, if the Langdale Company failed to supply the stipulated number of cords of pulpwood, National Container had the right to go onto Langdale land and harvest the required amount. Harley, Jr. feared this might become a problem in wet weather, but it never did. "In the end, it all worked out where it was mutually advantageous," he said. [49]

The Langdale wood procurement agreement with National Container paved the way for Kipnis to secure financing. He invited potential backers from New York to visit Valdosta and Clyattville. They arrived by airplane early one morning. Harley, Jr. took them around the Langdale lands, traveling dusty, unpaved roads, served them lunch in the woods, and showed them more trees than any of them had ever seen before. They were impressed. Sam Kipnis borrowed the $25 million he needed to build the Clyattville plant, plus $6 million he needed to

---

[48] Ibid.
[49] Ibid.

pay off debt remaining on the National Container mill at Jacksonville.[50] The mill went into operation in 1954 with pulpwood supplied through the Langdale Company.

As a result of the new container plant and other industrial growth in the area, executives of the Southern Railway System and of the Georgia Southern & Florida Railroads anticipated a significant increase in rail traffic through Valdosta. The railway executives decided to expand their capacity for handling rail cars in Valdosta and to name the place Langdale Yards in honor of Judge Langdale. From the standpoint of who was really responsible for the greater profits accruing to the railroads, it would perhaps have been more fitting to name the yard in honor of Harley, Jr., but the son stayed in the background and the father took the bows. The new paper mill at Clyattville connected through a spur to the GS&F at a newly constructed junction named Eskay. Sam Kipnis chose the name for this place by spelling out the sound of his two initials "S" and "K."[51]

To celebrate the expected growth in business and to cultivate the good will of Kipnis and the Langdales, top officials of the two railroads came to Valdosta on 5 February 1953. Arrangements had been made for appropriate ceremonies and inspection tours.

First pulpwood
for the
Clyattville mill.
TLC.

The day's activities began for the dignitaries at 9 A.M. with a meeting of the GS&F board of directors in the boardroom of the First National Bank. Three Valdostans, Dr. C. C. Giddens, Harley Langdale, Jr., and A. J. Strickland, Jr. were members of the board. Afterward, the group took a trip by train to the National Container plant at Clyattville, stopping off at Eskay, where the new spur line from the Clyattville plant hooked onto the GS&F main line. Ceremonies there,

---

[50] Ibid.

[51] "Southern Railroad Officials Dedicate Big Yards," *Valdosta Daily Times*, 5 February 1953.

including remarks by Southern Railway President Harry A. DeButts honored Sam Kipnis. Upon return from Clyattville by train, a ceremony at the new Langdale Yards paid tribute to Judge Langdale. DeButts introduced the main speaker, Charles Bloch of Macon, GS&F division counsel. A barbecue luncheon for guests followed, and a reception for shippers and dignitaries took place at the Valdosta Country Club in late afternoon.[52]

After the ceremony. Chatting with Thalia and Judge Langdale are Harry A. DeButts, president of Southern Railway, and Charles Bloch, division counsel for GS&F Railway, principal speakers at ceremonies honoring Sam Kipnis and Harley Langdale Sr. TLC.

The Clyattville papermill prospered from the start. In time, Sam Kipnis sold the mill to Owens-Illinois Corporation. Over the years, the facility changed owners several more times. Owens-Illinois sold it to K.K.R. (famous for junk bonds), who sold it to Great Northern Nekoosa. Georgia-Pacific took over Great Northern-Nekoosa and dealt the Clyattville mill to Tenneco, parent company of Packaging Corporation of America. Through all these changes, said Harley, Jr. in 1991, "we haven't missed a week of selling them pulpwood and pulp chips."[53]

Although the Langdales earned substantial income from pulpwood, the turpentine business remained the core of their operations in the 1940s. At that time they continued to follow a silviculture practice adopted before the war, which Harley, Jr. called a "turpentine rotation." When a tree reached nine or ten inches, the Langdales placed a cup on it. When the tree became large enough, they added a second cup. When those two faces were worked out, Harley, Jr. marked the tree for cutting. With the larger trees removed, younger trees grew and after a few years reached the size for cupping. The whole process then repeated.

There existed in the late 1930s almost no market for the worked-out turpentine trees removed as part of this turpentine rotation. Logs and lumber were

---

[52] Ibid.
[53] Langdale, HLJr Interview 1991.

both in scant demand. Making the best of a bad situation, the Langdales sawed their own worked-out trees into lumber. For this they used small mills, sometimes called "peckerwood," "coffee-pot," or "push-hard" mills, located and moved about from place to place in the turpentine woods.

Similarly, in those days no market existed for thinnings. As Harley, Jr. recalled, "the only way we could thin was dead expense."[54] Superior Pine Company, which had saplings coming up naturally at the rate of 2,000 per acre on some of their land leased by the Langdales for turpentine, paid them to send their turpentine workers to thin these trees by simply chopping them down and leaving them to decay in the woods. Such waste bothered Harley, Jr. immensely and spurred his efforts to secure better markets for forest products.

The search for better markets and greater efficiency of production contributed to the second major innovation attributable to Harley, Jr., which happened to be in the field of naval stores. This change occurred during World War II, in 1943, when the younger Harley led in setting up a centralized processing plant at Valdosta. As a result, they closed all their fire stills on the various turpentine places and trucked the crude gum directly to the Valdosta facility for processing.

Getting the gum out of the woods, however, still depended on draft animals. For example, down at Fargo, they used a four-mule team pulling a "Hoover wagon" to bring as much as six barrels per load out of the forest, a distance of about ten miles. A "Hoover wagon" was a rubber-tired wagon made from an automobile chassis. With well-lubricated wheel bearings, it rolled easily, making it possible for the mules to pull heavier loads. Each barrel of gum weighed about 500 pounds, so a load amounted to as much as 3,000 pounds.

For some time preceding 1943, perhaps starting around 1941, Harley, Jr. had been preparing the way for a centralized distillery by purchasing the rights of Judge's partners in the various turpentine places. This started to happen "after the turpentine business got a little better."[55]

World War II helped make the buy-outs possible. Profits from naval stores rose sharply as a result of the war. "Rosin and turpentine were very much in demand during the war," recalled Harley, Jr. "In fact, I would say that about 1941 and '42 were the first years that we had seen that were really profitable in the naval stores business since the twenties."[56]

The decision to buy out the partners resulted in part from the reluctance of some of them to adopt the modern methods that Harley, Jr. advocated. "They were taking off more wood, and you had to take off less wood," he recalled in 1991. "We wanted to chip down to the cambium layer, not go into the wood."

---

[54] Ibid.
[55] Ibid.
[56] Ibid.

Harley, Jr. saw the old methods as wasteful, to which he had a strong aversion. "And so that was a very difficult situation," he acknowledged.[57] Harley, Jr. took the responsibility of negotiating with the partners and purchasing full ownership of the turpentine places. Having bought them out, he could move ahead with centralization in 1943 without opposition from them.

A Small "Hoover Wagon" used for collecting gum on Langdale land in the 1950s. Scanned and cropped from a published photo by Kenneth Rogers, *Atlanta Journal and Constitution Magazine,* October 11, 1952. TLC.

To obtain equipment for the new plant in the middle of World War II, the Langdales had to get government clearance. This turned out to be easy, in view of the huge wartime demand for naval stores, even though it required scarce stainless steel, brass, and aluminum components. Within six months after receiving official approval, Harley, Jr. had the plant completed and began distilling gum.

The new centralized plant could take in crude gum at the rate of one barrel every three minutes, using a procedure developed by the US Agricultural Research Station at Olustee, Florida. The Olustee process resulted in a higher quality and more uniform product, which improved its marketability. In this new facility, the Langdales also reduced their processing costs compared to the costs of fire stills and obtained fifteen pounds more of salable turpentine and rosin from each barrel of crude gum.[58]

Before adopting the Olustee method (while using the old fire stills), stillers and helpers poured crude gum into a copper still and cooked it, separating the rosin, which settled to the bottom, from the turpentine. The rosin then had to be strained through cotton batting to remove trash. The new method developed at Olustee required cleaning the crude gum before cooking it.

This Olustee-developed method of turpentine distillation had been previously adopted by George Varn, a long-time family friend and business associate of Judge Harley. Varn had built a plant on the Olustee model at Hoboken, a small town east

---

[57] Ibid.
[58] Langdale, "Brief Facts" ; Langdale, HLJr Interview 1991.

of Waycross, Georgia. When Harley, Jr. decided to move forward with the centralized operation, Varn allowed him to use his technical drawings and specifications for construction of the Langdale plant. The Varn and Langdale distilleries at Hoboken and Valdosta, respectively, were the first and second commercial applications of the new technology developed at Olustee.[59] For George Varn's generosity, Harley, Jr. was most grateful.

Construction of the Langdale plant almost did not happen, however. Harley, Jr. had everything worked out and was preparing to order the equipment when he received a telephone call from his father, who was on one of his frequent lobbying trips to Washington, urging him to hold up. Important persons with whom Judge had talked about this venture warned him against it, arguing that certain large competitors could easily put the Langdales out of business. "Too late," Harley, Jr. told his dad. Orders for the equipment had already been placed. So the plant was built, and fortunately Judge's fears were unrealized. The centralized still was a great success.

The new Langdale distillery became a very large production and storage facility and remained so for many years. As an indication of just how large, consider that in October 1958, the Langdale Company had 130,000 drums of rosin in storage for the Commodity Credit Corporation on their yard, each with a net weight of 517 pounds. The Langdales understood this was more than could be found in any one location anywhere else in the world. The 130,000 containers in storage had a market value of $5.5 million.[60]

The centralized Langdale still, viewed from the south. Empty trucks exited down the ramp that is visible from this side. The entry ramp, located on the opposite side, is not seen here. In the foreground are stored barrels of rosin. TLC.

"That was a big operation," Harley, Jr. recalled, "and it worked out fine because we could keep our records on a weekly basis, how much gum we could produce and what our expenses were, and that helped us."[61]

---

[59] Clifton, ed., *Heritage of Lowndes County,* 158.

[60] Langdale, "Brief Facts."

[61] Langdale, HLJr Interview 1991.

Judge Harley liked the new plant and the centralized distillation process his son had installed. He approved of the new system, but he left its operation entirely to the younger man. Judge chose to be uninvolved in the details of accounting, tax questions, labor relations, or plant management. Instead, during this period, said Harley, Jr., "His forte, you might say, was talking to people of the soil, farmers or people out in the woods. He liked to do that."[62]

Interior view of the Langdale Centralized Turpentine Still. TLC.

Although this state-of-the-art distillation plant prospered for a number of years, the time eventually came in the mid 1970s that the Langdale gum turpentine business could no longer compete successfully with the byproducts of the pulp mills. The Langdale Company shut down the plant and sold it to a company connected to the government of Guatemala, which wished to use it to create jobs there. The Guatemalans disassembled it, numbering each part, and hauled it away. "That, remembered Harley, Jr., "was a sad day."[63] Remarkably, the demise of the gum turpentine industry in Georgia came despite rising prices for turpentine. As Harley, Jr. observed in 1991, turpentine was then selling for eight or ten dollars a gallon, compared to twenty-five cents a gallon in the 1930s.

From the standpoint of innovations, after (1) getting into the pulpwood business and (2) centralizing turpentine processing, the wood preservative treatment plant came next, chronologically. Harley, Jr. employed a prominent engineer from Pittsburgh, Grant Shipley, as consultant to oversee construction of this facility, the most modern then available. With this plant, in 1947 they began pressure treating poles and pilings, then went into treating lumber and fence posts, as well as other materials for which there was demand.

---

[62] Ibid.

[63] Ibid.

The Langdale pole business concentrated on smaller sizes, classes five, six, and seven, as they are designated in the business, ranging from thirty to forty feet in length. They sold these mainly to utility companies, such as REA cooperatives. Occasionally, they furnished poles of loblolly pine as long as eighty-five or ninety feet, logs for which they obtained from the vicinity of Pine Grove, Alabama, and treated at the Valdosta plant. A few times they secured even larger cedar poles from the West Coast for customers.[64]

Pole peeling machine used by Langdale Forest Products Company in 2000. Rather than merely removing bark from poles, this machine shapes and smooths the pole for improved appearance. JDH.

As of 1958, the wood preserving equipment consisted of two cylinders, eight feet in diameter. One cylinder had a length of seventy-eight feet, and the other one hundred and twenty feet. Employing what was called the Rueping process, the facility treated various items, including poles, pilings, cross-arms, construction poles, crossties, fence posts and lumber with creosote and creosote coal tar solutions. Annual production in 1958 approximated thirty million board feet.[65]

Utility poles on tram exiting a treating cylinder. TLC.

---

[64] Ibid.
[65] Langdale, "Brief Facts."

Among the most advanced in the country at that time, the Langdale Company's crosstie handling equipment processed some 80,000 board feet in eight hours. That included unloading the crossties, cutting them to exact length, adzing, boring, dating, incising, and stacking them with proper spacing for drying. Split crossties were doweled with steel pins.

Crossties stacked on the Langdale yard in Valdosta. TLC.

Machinery for handling and moving cross-ties and other materials included five debarkers, which also smoothed knots on poles and posts, three cranes, and six Gerlinger lift trucks with 18,000 pound capacity. Two of the cranes were diesel electric type, and the other was diesel.[66]

Harley, Jr.'s fourth important innovation brought significant changes to the Langdale lumber business. Since the 1930s, as mentioned previously, the Langdale Company had operated several small sawmills for cutting diseased or non-productive turpentine trees. People called these little mills, which lacked the precision to cut lumber of consistent size, peckerwood mills, push-hard mills, or coffeepot mills. They remained in use on Langdale land until the 1950s. According to usual practice, lumber went from the small mills located in the woods to Valdosta, where workmen ran it through a lumber separator and then a planer mill.[67]

During the era of the peckerwood mills, not only the technology employed, but the nature of the raw material limited lumber production and contributed to waste. Compared to trees that had not been turpentined, worked-out turpentine trees had much less value as saw timber. Although these trees produced high-quality, close-grained lumber, it was always small. Only about half of a tree that had been turpentined could actually qualify as a saw log. The lower part of the tree, containing the catface, was waste; so was the top. Only the middle section went to

---

[66] Ibid.

[67] Langdale, HLJr Interview 1991.

the sawmill to be turned into lumber. About half of this log ended up as lumber, the remainder as slabs, strips, and sawdust—waste. To get rid of this waste and make room to work around the sawmill, fires burned seven days a week, creating pollution that would be highly objectionable today.[68]

A Coffee-pot or peckerwood sawmill. TLC.

By the 1950s, new debarking machines, practical models of which had been developed by the Swedes in the 1940s,[69] appeared on the market. The Langdales became convinced such a machine could dramatically improve their lumber business if combined with a modern centralized sawmill in preference to the small "coffee-pot" mills they were then using. Led by Harley, Jr., who took notice of debarkers as early as 1952, the Langdale Company installed its first debarker in 1957 and began operating it in 1958. This new technology, among other advantages, enabled the Langdales to generate income through sale of wood chips to the paper mill located at Clyattville, just eight miles distant. The wood chips, formerly wasted as part of slabs (with bark) sliced off logs that were being cut into lumber, amounted in 1991 to more than a thousand cords of chips a week—all the Langdale sawmill produced—being sold to the PCA mill at Clyattville.[70]

As of 1991, about thirty percent of revenues from the Langdale lumber operation were from sale of byproducts they once considered waste and paid people to burn or remove. In addition to the pulpwood chips going to PCA, the company sold each week approximately 2,000 tons of sawdust, bark, planer mill shavings, and end trimmings. Sale of these byproducts helped the Langdale Company's Lumber Division remain profitable during periods of low lumber prices that occurred occasionally during the several decades after 1958 and enabled the Lumber Division to remain competitive with other companies in lumber sales.[71]

---

[68] Ibid.

[69] "Langdale Company Brings Work Ethic to Forefront."

[70] Langdale, HLJr Interview 1991 ; Langdale, "Brief Facts."

[71] Langdale, HLJr Interview 1991.

Byproducts have also been used effectively as fuel and in other ways. As of 1991, the Langdale Company had bought no fuel for its plant in at least twenty-five years. The company's environmentally-approved boiler burned sawdust and bark, some of which the company also supplied as fuel to other nearby manufacturers. In another use of byproducts from the sawmill, a German-owned plant located in Valdosta converted sawdust and bark into mulch.[72]

Harley Jr. in 1958 observing debarked logs entering the new mill. TLC.

The Langdale Company's new centralized sawmill and debarker in 1958 constituted a tremendous advance over the old peckerwood technology. This new mill had the capacity to produce 50,000 board feet of lumber during an eight-hour shift. Sawlogs being used at that time remained generally small, however, because they came from worked-out turpentine trees or from selective thinnings. Fiscal Year 1958 production of white lumber totaled 12 million board feet, a volume that increased annually until, in FY 1996, the company produced more than 88 million board feet.[73] This rose to 110 million the next year and to 130 million in 2000. At that time, the company expected eventually to reach 150 million board feet per year.[74]

The procedure for turning logs into lumber in 1958, after installation of the new debarker, started with the weighing and unloading of logs brought in by truck. Fairbanks-Morse scales with a sixty-foot long platform and a double-faced dial and printometer weighed the logs and printed a scale ticket showing the weight of the load. From the weight of the logs, company officials calculated the number of

---

[72] Ibid.

[73] Langdale, "Brief Facts" ; Harley Langdale, Jr., "Lumber Prices 1951 to Present," 2 April 1997, Harley Langdale, Jr., Papers, Valdosta GA, The Langdale Company.

[74] James D. Hickman, interview by author, 19 October 2000, audio tape, The Langdale Company, Valdosta GA, Harley Langdale, Jr., Papers, Valdosta GA.

board feet in the load. (The Langdale Company was the first to buy logs by weight. By weighing the logs and converting the weight mathematically to board feet, they found they could eliminate disputes between loggers and their scalers.)[75] A Cary Lift-Loader, moved the logs from the truck to the receiving deck. The receiving deck included a kick-and-hold log-stop and loader assembly, which the debarker operator controlled.[76]

Langdale's first
debarker, installed 1957.
TLC.

The Cambio Debarker, manufactured by Soderhamm Machine Manufacturing Co., could handle logs as large as twenty-six inches in diameter. Logs exiting the debarker entered a two-way log-flipper machine installed between thirty-inch roll conveyors. This air-powered machine flipped logs to the left or the right, depending on whether they were going to the pressure-treatment plant or to the sawmill. Logs destined to become poles, etc., went to the right and soon found themselves in the pressure treatment area; sawlogs traveled to the left and went next to the cut-off saw, which was also powered by air. From the cut-off saw, logs either moved directly into the sawmill or were shunted aside into storage.

Logs entering the mill went to one of two sash gang saws equipped with Linck automatic width adjustment controls for the blades. The blades could be adjusted for openings varying from two to fifteen inches. These width adjustments and the operation of the kickers could be controlled remotely by the operator who ran that particular gang saw and was mounted on the hydraulically operated in-feed carriage. Both gang saws were of the Gebrueder Linck brand; one was Model E 28/28, and the other was a Model E 22/28. The different models had slightly different sawing capabilities.[77]

---

[75] Langdale, HLJr Interview 1991.
[76] Langdale, "Brief Facts."
[77] Ibid.

By 1991, lumber production at the Valdosta plant totaled around 80 million board feet per year. Although the company had two operable sawmills, this lumber all came from a single mill. They no longer ran their older sawmill, the one installed in 1958. It was thought to be less efficient than the more advanced model recently put into operation.[78]

This opinion changed, however, in 1992. The new mill turned out to be too labor intensive, so the company decided to resume using the 1958 mill, which had been refurbished in 1987, and to get rid of the new one. The company took the 1958 mill out of service again in 1998 upon installation of yet another new sawmill. This proved to be a permanent retirement. In 2000, the sophisticated new mill having proven itself, the 1958 mill was torn down. This newest mill could "slew and skew" to saw curved logs, could be operated with a crew of only twenty-one, and could produce in only four days of operation each week all the lumber the existing dry kilns could process. Jim Langdale, who was in charge of this operation in 2000, liked the new equipment.[79]

Lumber prices in 1991, Harley, Jr. liked to point out, had resisted inflationary pressures, making lumber products a good value and offering a hopeful sign for the future of the lumber business. Although many people believed inflation had driven the cost of everything up, he observed, that was not true for lumber. To prove his point, he cited his personally-kept records of prices, which he retained for ready reference in his desk drawer. In October 1979, his figures showed, the Langdale Company's average wholesale price received for lumber, FOB Valdosta, reached an all-time high of $301.41 per thousand board feet of white, that is, untreated lumber. For the Fiscal Year 1979 (April 1978–March 1979), the average was $272.85 per thousand, and in Fiscal Year 1991 (October 1990–September 1991) the average price came to $230.69. So the average wholesale price of untreated lumber in FY 1991, according to Harley, Jr.'s figures, had dropped about $42.00 per thousand board feet from the high of 1979.[80]

At the end of 1991, thanks in part to the strong competitive position of lumber prices with other building materials, Harley, Jr. felt optimistic about the future of the lumber business and of the Langdale Company's prospects for continued success. Income from byproducts, amounting to more efficient use of the resources of the land, and continuing improvements in technology contributed to his optimism. Location of the Langdale facilities in Valdosta and in Sweetwater, Tennessee, also seemed to him a positive factor. Thanks to good roads in the Valdosta area, Langdale trucks could bring saw logs from sources as much as 75 to 100 miles away from the plant. Most of the Langdale forestland, amounting to more than 200,000 acres, could be reached from Valdosta with less than a fifty-

---

[78] Langdale, HLJr Interview 1991.

[79] James Harley Langdale, interview by author, audio tape, 17 October 2000, The Langdale Company, Valdosta GA, John W. Langdale Papers, Valdosta GA.

[80] Langdale, HLJr Interview 1991 ; Langdale, "Lumber Prices."

mile drive. This land held substantial reserves of timber, for the company normally purchased two-thirds of their saw logs from other landowners, conserving their own resources.[81] In addition, most Langdale customers were within 500 miles of the plant in Valdosta or the plant in Sweetwater. The Tennessee plant shipped primarily to Ohio, Indiana, Illinois, and West Virginia. From Valdosta, the Langdale Company could deliver products to any part of Florida, its most important market, in one day. Furthermore, with a strong management team in place and younger members of the Langdale family moving effectively into managerial positions, he professed strong optimism about company leadership. Taken altogether, Harley, Jr. saw a bright future for the Langdale lumber business and for the company as a whole.

In the 1980s, Harley, Jr. led the company in yet another new departure. Always seeking markets for everything produced on the land, Harley had struggled for years with the issue of hardwood utilization. With twenty or twenty-five percent of the Langdale land in hardwood, he needed to find a market for this material. He attempted unsuccessfully to sell hardwood to the paper mills. The mill at Brunswick, Georgia, considered it uneconomical to ship hardwoods from the Valdosta area; the nearest Union Camp mill was also too far away. National Container Corporation mills at Jacksonville and Clyattville did not use hardwood, and Harley, Jr. could not persuade them to change their practice. The large supply of unused hardwoods on Langdale land eventually led the company in the direction of oriented stranded board (OSB). If they could not sell their hardwood to others, they could build their own plant to consume it, thus creating their own market for the produce of their land.

Utility poles arrive at Sweetwater plant. JEL.

About the time the Langdale Company entered the OSB manufacturing business, the papermill managers who had for years resisted the idea of using hardwoods to make paper changed their policy. They spent millions to install separate digesters for hardwood processing. Consequently, for the first time in the

---

[81] Langdale, HLJr Interview 1991.

early nineties, the Langdales found a ready market for their hardwoods, such as oak and hickory, with the paper mills, and they put their soft hardwoods to use in their own OSB plant. Obviously, this was a tremendous advance in the percentage of utilization of raw materials produced on the Langdale land and, as Harley, Jr. might say, "a great blessing" to him and to the company.

Harley, Jr. took special pleasure in the fact that the OSB plant enabled them to use most of their hardwoods, including some wood of low quality. A key to successful forest management, he always believed, was good utilization. Although the Langdale OSB mill did not yet take the harder hardwoods, such as oak, hickory, and beech, it could process any of the softer hardwoods. These included sweet gum, red gum, black gum, tupelo gum, water gum, and yellow poplar. In the future, Harley thought they might modify the mill so it could also handle the harder hardwoods like hickory and oak, as some other OSB mills in the country already could. In the meantime, the harder hardwoods could be sold to the paper mills, which at last had found them desirable for making paper.[82]

OSB plant aerial view. JDH.

By the early 1990s, Harley, Jr. foresaw a brighter future for the hardwood market. In-house studies showed that some of their land produced greater returns when planted in hardwoods instead of pines, and some land appeared more productive with a mixed population of hardwoods and pines. As a result, the Langdales had begun planting hardwoods such as yellow poplar and sweet gum for use as pulpwood. Some other hardwoods, notably sawtooth oak, they planted for deer management.

The notion of actually planting hardwoods represented a major shift in thinking from the prevailing view of the 1950s. Hardwoods of the type most often

---

[82] Ibid.

found in south Georgia had little market value, and foresters perceived them as an impediment to growth of the much more profitable pines. The US Forest Service at that time recommended thinning or elimination of such hardwoods by methods including the application of chemicals to allow pines more space for growth.[83]

Some evidence that pines meant profit, came from the US Forest Service's Southeastern Forest Experiment Station at Cordele, Georgia. A stand of pines planted there in 1935, according to a report, grew in value at an annual rate of approximately $16 per acre through 1952. This amounted to a return on the original investment in labor and trees of 100 percent per year. Twelve years after planting, this timber had an appraised value of $65 per acre. Five years later, in 1952, the value of pulpwood and saw timber on this tract had increased to $190 per acre, which amounted to around $25 per acre per year during the five-year period. Clearly, the money was in pines, not hardwoods, and more in saw timber than in pulpwood.[84] By the 1990s, however, technology had made feasible the use of hardwoods that might earlier have been regarded as trash. The manufacture of oriented stranded board offers a prime example.

The Langdale Company built its OSB mill in Brooks County, near Quitman, Georgia, about twenty miles from Valdosta. This highly-automated, state-of-the-art facility cost about $35 million to construct and represented an investment of around $40 million by 1992. To pay for this plant the Langdales broke with their long-standing practice and borrowed money. Previously, since getting out of their financial straits of the 1930s, they had relied on their own accumulated resources to finance business expansion. Randall Adams, president of the local branch of the C & S National Bank, was especially helpful in arranging the loan.

Reflecting on the OSB undertaking in the latter part of 1991, nearly four years after the start of production on 9 March 1988, Harley, Jr. thought they had made the right decision. They were producing OSB of high quality, and even though weakness in housing starts during the previous few years had limited the demand and depressed prices for this material, he foresaw a bright future for it. "We're proud of the plant," he said. In the future, Harley expected to see more elaborate OSB products, some with sanded finish suitable for painting, some with tongue-and-groove cuts, and some coated with vinyl, paper, or wood veneer.[85]

The success of the oriented stranded board mill and prospects for improved future OSB products helped convince Harley, Jr. that he had made a wise choice many years before in deciding against entering the plywood manufacturing business. When it first became feasible technologically to use pine for plywood, around 1960, the Langdales seriously considered going into this. They wanted to get in, Harley, Jr. said, but they eventually decided plywood manufacture would be

---

[83] "Dollars Grow on Trees," 50.

[84] Ibid.

[85] Langdale, HLJr Interview 1991.

a poor fit with other company operations. For one thing, Langdale timber tended to be somewhat small for plywood use, a problem made worse by the turpentine business in which they were then heavily engaged. Turpentine production marred the lower part of a tree, leaving only the upper, smaller part for lumber or other use. Also, many of the logs they might devote to plywood already had a market in their preservative-treated pole business. Harley, Jr. turned down an opportunity to buy a plywood factory in Waycross, Georgia, partly because he considered it a bad location from the standpoint of readily available timber. Even though slash and longleaf pine abounded in the vicinity of Waycross, much of it had been turpentined and thus rendered less suitable for plywood.

By the latter part of 1991, plywood faced stiff competition from OSB for such uses as roof and floor sheeting in housing construction. OSB cost less, and many contractors preferred it over plywood for such purposes. Harley, Jr., who kept track of prices daily, noted a steady decline of plywood prices to the point that OSB and plywood were within about eighty dollars per thousand square feet of each other. OSB sold at that time for $137 per thousand and plywood for $220 per thousand. The price differential would have been less, Harley thought, except that west coast plywood mills were shutting down, reducing supply, and there were not many plywood mills on the east coast.

Making sound decisions is crucial to any successful business. Someone once asked Harley, Jr. how he went about making important business decisions such as building an OSB plant. The first step in deciding whether to expand a business activity or to enter a new one, he replied, has always been to evaluate present and future resources from the land. As he put it, "First, we took a look at what we had and what we were going to grow."[86] The second step, said Harley, Jr., was to read widely and talk at length with knowledgeable people, such as those he met in trade associations and people with experience in the same or a related business. In other words, he did some basic research, became well informed, and learned from others what he could. In some situations, he found it useful to employ consultants, experts in the particular field, such as Grant Shipley in the matter of the preservative treatment facility, to study the situation and to prepare a prospectus. Finally, with the best advice possible from everyone concerned, he and the decision-making group, whose make-up varied with each particular situation, reached a decision that seemed appropriate.

Harley, Jr. thought of himself as primarily a tree farmer. For him, manufacturing ranked second in importance. Trees were the resources, the raw materials, produced by the land. Manufacturing was a way to secure markets for the products of the land by converting them into things for which there was more demand. Harley's goal was to achieve maximum production from the land (to grow

---

[86] Ibid.

more wood) and to secure the best markets for these raw materials (to maximize profits).

When he graduated from the University of Georgia School of Forestry, so far as is known the first person from the Valdosta area to receive such training, and returned to help run his father's business, Harley, Jr. often encountered skepticism about forestry practices he introduced. Thinning stands of trees that were too thick, transplanting pine seedlings, and steps to control fires often raised eyebrows and sometimes evoked resistance. Now, Harley observed in 1991, with the passage of time and dissemination of information, public attitudes had changed and people in south Georgia commonly applied modern forestry methods on their land.

For most of the Langdale land, and much other land in south Georgia, Harley, Jr. argued in 1992, the best and highest use is in tree farming. People in south Georgia could compete in tree farming with people in almost any area of the country, he observed, whereas they could not compete on equal terms in growing wheat, oats, rye, corn, soybeans, and other such row crops. Even peanuts and tobacco, the main cash-producing crops on Langdale farmland in the early 1990s had serious problems, he noted. As for cattle and hog production, a mainstay for his grandfather, John Wesley Langdale of Council, and important in Judge Harley's day, changing circumstances in recent decades, including changes in law with respect to liability, had reduced its profitability. Consequently, he said, the Langdales had scaled down their livestock operations.[87]

Summarizing briefly, the Langdales incorporated their business as the Langdale Company in 1948. Management continued as before, with Harley, Jr. in charge of operations. John W. and Billy had lesser roles in the business. Of the three brothers, only John W. was given to delving into technical details. Neither was Judge Harley a "detail man." Harley, Jr. studied and followed his father's management style, which emphasized delegation of responsibility. In general the Langdales have been consistent practitioners of frugality, which they refer to as "being conservative."

Upon taking charge of the business in 1937, Harley, Jr. struggled with the issues of inadequate fire protection, shortage of operating capital, and lack of markets for the produce of their land. Like his father before him, he dealt with the problem of high interest charged by factors.

In his continuing effort to achieve greater profitability, Harley, Jr. adopted new technologies for turpentine production and centralized the distillation process. He and Judge moved vigorously to acquire more land. Harley, Jr. ventured into pulpwood production, preservative treatment of round wood and lumber, debarkers in connection with a centralized sawmill, and an OSB plant.

---

[87] Ibid. Addendum of 26 May 1992.

Other major developments came in the 1990s and will be examined later. First, however, comes a photo essay on the Langdale OSB plant, followed by discussion of the Langdales' involvement in politics and public service.

Photo Essay

The Langboard OSB Plant

T he Langboard OSB facility at Quitman, Georgia, employed 117 people, as of October 2000. The entire plant could be operated with a crew of nine, although usually, counting support people, thirteen worked on a shift. The plant operated four 8-hour shifts every day of the year. Each week it shut down for four or five hours for scheduled cleaning and maintenance. The plant was typically on-line about 99 percent of the time.

Below is an aerial view taken shortly after the plant opened, before installation of the crane. The input area, where the crane would appear in a photo made today, is at the top left; the shipping area is in the right foreground.

Aerial view of
Langboard OSB plant,
Quitman, GA. TLC.

The Langboard OSB plant uses soft hardwoods as its basic resource. Hardwood logs arrive by truck. A large portable crane removes an entire truckload of logs at once and stacks them with others under the crane. This machine is so large it took twenty-two semi-trailer trucks to transport it from the manufacturer in Canada to Quitman. It has space beneath it to store 1,400 truckloads (12,000 cords). This is enough to supply the mill for two or three months, assuming usage of 370 cords per day. The crane can lift 45,000 to 50,000 pounds at a time.

Crane grasping a load of logs for the Langdale OSB plant. TLC.

Operation of this mammoth machine obviously requires skill. The crane operator, who views the truck and its load through a camera mounted near the ground, must possess the ability to estimate by eyesight the mid-point of the weight in each load of logs before seizing the load for removal. The fingers of the grappler, driven by hydraulic pressure, completely surround the load of logs.

Crane lifts load of hardwood logs from a truck. TLC.

The company decided to install this massive crane, with planning and direction from Bob Langdale, partly to deal with a problem of supply that can sometimes result from seasonal weather variations. There have been occasions when excess rain made it difficult to get into the woods for logging during an extended period. The ability to store such large quantities of wood makes sure the plant will not be idled for lack of raw material and practically eliminates concern about weather.

Besides unloading logs, the crane starts them on the way to becoming oriented stranded board when it places them on the log deck. An automated cut-off saw cuts the logs to a proper length, if necessary.

Logs being placed onto the log deck. TLC.

Cut-off saw. JDH.

Controlled by the debarker operator, a chain-link conveyor, below, takes individual logs into the debarker. The debarker machine (second photo below) is a 35-inch model manufactured by Nicholson-Rheem. Bark and other pieces of wood that cannot be used as part of the OSB product, such as tiny particles called "fines," go to burners as fuel to heat the dryers and for the press. Debarked logs go to the flaker deck (third photo below), from which they are fed into a flaker machine (fourth photo below) that shaves off "strands" resembling large potato chips. Strands are ideally 4" long, from 1/2" to 1" wide, and 25/1000" thick.

Chain-link conveyor moving logs to the debarker. TLC.

Nicholson-Rheem debarker. TLC.

Flaker deck. TLC.

Flaker machine. TLC.

Strands go to two large storage bins, wet bins, below, where they remain until needed, and then proceed by conveyor to the rotary dryers (lower photo). Wood typically has 60 percent moisture content; it must be dried until it has only 4 percent moisture.

Wet bins. TLC.

Rotary dryers. TLC.

The temperature required for drying is in the range of 800 to 1,000 degrees Fahrenheit. Heat for drying comes in part from burning bark and fines in the burners. The following photo shows the rotary screener, which filters out pieces of wood unsuitable for use as a component of OSB, notably the "fines."

Burners provide heat for drying wood. TLC.

Rotary screener filters wood. TLC.

After being dried and screened, the strands travel to two large dry bins (below), so called because they contain dried, not wet, strands.

Dry bins. TLC.

From the dry bins, as needed, the strands are sent down the square pipes shown below for weighing in the Thayer scale. It is necessary to determine the weight so the correct amount of resin can be added in the next stage.

Conveyor to Thayer scale. TLC.

Rotary blenders. TLC.

Strands having been weighed, they get mixed with resin in two rotary blenders and sent from there to three forming heads. One of these forming heads puts down a layer of strands oriented, say, north and south, to serve as the bottom surface layer of the board-to-be. The second forming head places a layer on top of the first, but with orientation perpendicular to it. The third forming head makes a layer identical to the first layer. Thus, there are three layers, with the outside (or surface) layers being oriented in a certain direction and the middle (or core) layer turned cross-ways to them on the forming line.

Forming line photo #1. JDH.

The photo immediately below, shows the appearance of the layered strands on the forming line. The forming line, upon which the forming heads lay down the three layers of resin-covered strands, is eight feet wide and eighty feet long. Near the end of the forming line, as the three layers of strands travel slowly along, a track-mounted rotary saw runs across the material on the forming line and cuts it. This sawing occurs every sixteen feet, creating 8-foot by 16-foot mats (second photo below), which load automatically into the press (third photo below).

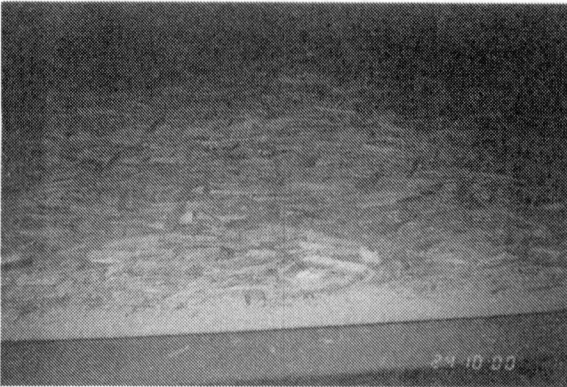

Forming line photo #2. JDH.

Forming line photo #3. JDH.

Press infeed & piston closing the press. JDH.

The press has openings for ten 8' by 16' mats. When loaded, the press heats the mats to 400 degrees Fahrenheit under pressure for four to five minutes. It then automatically unloads these mats and immediately fills up with another load.

Press outfeed showing mats being ejected. JDH.

While the new load is in the press, the just-ejected mats travel to another rotary saw. This saw cuts each 8' by 16' mat into four sheets of 4' by 8' oriented stranded board. Cut away material is burned to provide heat for the dryers.

The remaining task is to prepare the material for shipping. This involves strapping, stenciling the company name, and stacking or loading it for transport.

Stacks of OSB ready for shipment. JDH.

Summing up, the Langdales built the OSB Plant to create a market for soft hardwoods growing on their land. At the time they started construction, suitable markets did not exist, although this situation has changed since the facility went into operation. Hardwood of varying quality can be used as raw material to produce OSB. The basic process of manufacturing OSB, as shown in this brief photo essay, involves cutting the wood into flakes, glueing the flakes together in layers with alternate orientations for greater strength, and forming the product into panels with the desired smoothness, and dimensions. The Langboard OSB plant is highly automated and is operated with a small work force.

Politics and Public Service

An interviewer once pointed out to Harley, Jr. the political and public service activities of his brothers, John and Billy, and asked him what he did in the nature of public service. To this, Harley retorted, "I am working about as hard as I know how to work to make enough money that they would get enough salary to live on while they are doing public work."[1]

Harley, Jr. did much more than that, of course. Locally, he and his wife, Eileen, have supported many organizations by their attendance and participation. For example, Harley, Jr., in addition to contributing financially, has personally served as a guide for tours of historical points of interest on Langdale property for the Lowndes County Historical Society. Both Harley, Jr. and Eileen have been active in church. Eileen, a devoted volunteer with the hospital auxiliary, has made a name for herself growing roses, specializing in the Queen Elizabeth and Double Delight varieties, and generously sharing them with others. Through the Langdale Company, of course, Harley, Jr. has done much for his community over the years. An example of this is the Wildlife Expo that the company sponsored for several years.

Eileen & Harley Langdale, Jr.
TLF.

---

[1] Langdale, HLJR Interview 1991.

Wildlife Expo. Sponsored by the Langdale Company in cooperation with several other organizations, this several-day event encouraged conservation and safety in forest and wildlife activities. Photos by J. Kevin Lancaster.

Even though Harley, Jr. did not serve in elective office, he held important positions on government and quasi-government committees and boards, including some at the federal level. He also participated actively and devoted much of his time to various professional associations. These related primarily to forestry and forest industries, of course, and served his business interests.

The greatest benefit of membership and participation in any of these professional associations, said Harley, was getting to know people involved in the industry. He found it very useful to talk with people over the telephone and at meetings and social situations about issues in the industry and problems they encountered in their own business. The personal connections created through membership and service in these organizations have been helpful to the Langdale business, and "a great blessing" to him, personally, Harley acknowledged in 1991.[2]

Groups to which Harley, Jr. contributed and served in leadership positions included the Forest Farmers Association, the Herty Foundation, the Georgia Forestry Commission, and the Southern Pine Association. Each of these will be discussed briefly. He also supported the Forest Products Research Society, the Society of American Foresters and several other associations related to specific products such as crossties or to processes such as wood preservation.

In the early 1940s, while the country was at war, Harley, Jr. served as president of the Forest Farmers Association, an organization founded under the leadership of Bill Ottmeier, a close friend and business associate of Judge Harley. Bill had the idea for starting this organization while accompanying Judge to Washington for negotiations on behalf of ATFA with the Commodity Credit Corporation and the US Forest Service. Judge needed Bill's assistance in these

---

[2] Langdale, HLJr Interview 1991.

negotiations because, as a former member of the forest service, Bill Ottmeier knew how "to talk their language." Bill willingly helped Judge with the ATFA lobbying because he believed strengthening the position of naval stores producers would benefit his own company, Superior Pine Products.

During these talks with Judge Harley and government agencies, Bill Ottmeier came to see that tree farmers had nobody specifically representing their interests. He thought someone should take the initiative to form an association to represent them and he took this on himself. He met with Judge in his friend's law office, and they put together a proposed charter. Then they went down to Jacksonville and had the first meeting, much as Judge Harley had done earlier in starting ATFA. "Fifty years ago this past April," as Harley, Jr. recalled in 1991, "that's when the Forest Farmers Association was formed." Bill Ottmeier became the first president, and when he went off to the war, C. P. Kelly, from Madison, Florida, succeeded him. Vivien Whitfield became the next president, and Harley, Jr. followed him.[3]

Bill Ottmeier, founder & first president of the Forest Farmers Association, in World War II Uniform. TLC.

For some time after its formation, the organization struggled, for it had very little support. By the 1990s, however, progressive tree farmers and paper mills supported it well, and the Forest Farmers Association could act far more effectively.

Over the years, the Forest Farmers Association made its presence felt in dealing with several public issues. The association gave important support to the move to have the law changed so that, for tax purposes, tree farmers could usually count income from harvested trees as capital gains. The tax laws at one time provided that if an owner of trees had his trees cut and sawed for lumber by somebody else's sawmill, he could count income from those harvested trees as capital gains for tax purposes; but if he owned his own sawmill and cut his own trees, he had to treat the proceeds as ordinary income. The law was changed, to

---

[3] Ibid.

the great advantage of tree farmers. Aside from the tax issue, the Forest Farmers Association supported the states in efforts to prevent forest fires, to improve the quality of pine seedlings, and to increase forest growth.

Harley, Jr. as president of the Forest Farmers Association. TLC.

An Early Forest Farmers Association Board. Harley Jr. is shown standing, 3rd from left. TLC.

More than most of his public service jobs, Harley, Jr. enjoyed being a trustee of the Herty Foundation, a position to which the governor appointed him. He served longer as a trustee of this foundation than anyone else, as he understood it. He enjoyed going to the annual meetings of the Herty Foundation in Savannah.

Dr. Charles Herty, head of the Department of Chemistry at the University of Georgia, had been a leader in forest products research in North Carolina and in Georgia. In Georgia, people knew him best for the Herty cup, which he invented for use in the naval stores industry; he gained recognition also for innovations in production of newsprint. Harley, Jr. met Dr. Herty when the latter once visited Valdosta, and remembered being with Herty on two later occasions.[4]

When Dr. Herty spoke at the Valdosta meeting, about fifteen or twenty local people gathered in the courtroom of the Lowndes County courthouse to hear the

---

[4] Ibid.

talk. His topic concerned growing more and better trees for uses such as pulpwood. Herty shocked his listeners, mostly naval stores producers, by declaring that, except for wildfires, the greatest obstacles to growing trees in south Georgia were the turpentine operators who, every year, deliberately burned their woods.[5] With this accusation, he got their attention.

Herty cup. JEL.

The turpentine producers were, in fact, guilty as charged. Before setting fire to the forest each year, they "weeded" around each turpentine tree, clearing a space about two feet out from each one, in an effort to prevent the highly-inflammable catface from catching fire and destroying the tree. They reasoned that this "controlled burn" would prevent the much greater damage that would result from a wildfire that might occur at an unplanned, inconvenient time. Naval stores producers hoped in this way to protect their investment in cups, gutters, and gum accumulated in the cups. Annual burning could also help remove briars to make the turpentine trees more accessible for workers, eliminate small undesirable trees and bushes that came up in some places, and stimulate new growth of wiregrass for cattle feeding in the woods.

Herty's talk in the Valdosta courtroom occurred years after he had invented the famous clay cup that bore his name. The Langdales used and liked these cups, which had a capacity of one quart. The cups enabled them to improve the grade of rosin produced and, therefore, boost profits. Later, they installed similar cups made of glass, which were said to be superior to the clay cups. The era of glass cups ended quickly for the Langdales, however, because many of them, exposed in rapid daily sequence to a freeze, a thaw, and a hard freeze, broke and spilled their contents. They removed the glass cups and received a refund from the vendor.

The clay cups named for Herty also sometimes froze and broke, wasting their contents. To avoid this, the Langdales placed a small nail under each one in wintertime, causing it to tilt and providing space for water to expand if it froze. In later years, cups of aluminum, galvanized steel, and plastic came into use.

Galvanized cups cost less. The Langdales installed them on a "virgin" face, as they called trees that had never been cupped, very near the ground. Year by year,

---

[5] Ibid.

as the face received more streaks at the rate of thirty per year, the cup moved up the tree. A single twenty-penny nail supported the cup, which was jammed snugly up against the apron to help hold it in place, and gutters also helped stabilize the cup and guide the gum into the container.

For his forestry research, Dr. Herty had a small laboratory in Savannah. After his death, the State of Georgia subsidized this laboratory with annual appropriations. The foundation carried out Dr. Herty's ideas about ways to use wood and paper. It had a small experimental paper mill that industry researchers used with different types of wood and different kinds of chips, and sometimes with sawdust or planer mill shavings, as they tried to discover the best combination of techniques. Union Camp and other paper mills gave money to support the work of the foundation. Sometimes paper mills sent researchers to try experiments with different techniques and different woods. It saved them time and money to use the small mill at the Herty Foundation rather than try to do these experimental things with their large production paper mills.[6]

The foundation accepted contributions from industry and had contracts with different companies, as well as with government agencies, to try experimental procedures. For instance, they worked on various kinds of paper and fiber containers. In one project, Harley, Jr. recalled, Herty Foundation scientists experimented with an explosive. The foundation did some experiments for the State of Georgia and for the Georgia Forestry Commission. One of these, Harley remembered, had to do with the possible use of sycamore trees. The study envisioned clear-cutting the sycamores every five years and allowing them to sprout out from the roots.

Research by the Herty Foundation and at other facilities had a tremendous impact on the forest products business. "I never will forget," said Harley, "when it was announced that we could make paper out of southern pine." It was also a wonderful thing to hear, he said, that plywood could be made from southern pine.

The Herty Foundation did not make grants to others. Rather, it sought money to be used in its experiments. Sometimes the foundation managed to get special appropriations from the state. To do so, they arranged meetings typically with the governor. It helped that governors back in that period mostly had rural backgrounds, so they tended to sympathize with the foundation's efforts. Special appropriations could be arranged sometimes for a hundred thousand dollars or two hundred fifty thousand dollars, or something on that order. Once, Harley remembered, the foundation had to move its entire laboratory. The trustees succeeded in getting a special appropriation from the state to pay most of the expense of doing that.

---

[6] Ibid.

Winners of Georgia Forestry
Association Awards in 1962.
TLC.

Harley Jr. addressing
Georgia Forestry
Association in 1962. TLC.

Harley, Jr. also contributed much energy and time to the Georgia Forestry
Association, not to mention substantial sums of money paid by the Langdale
Company as dues. He served one term as president of the association and several
years as vice-president. The Langdale Company paid dues to the Georgia Forestry
Association in proportion to the amount of pulpwood produced and other factors.
A major goal for the association during Harley, Jr.'s presidency was reduction of ad
valorem taxes. Relief came when the state adopted a sales tax in the Herman
Talmadge administration. In Harley's opinion, the sales tax definitely helped
Lowndes County.

The Southern Pine Association also absorbed much of Harley, Jr.'s attention.
The SPA is a very good organization and has done many good things, said Harley,
Jr. in 1991, but for some of the smaller operators, it seemed to him the SPA dues
were rather high. Dues were based upon manufacturing and sales per thousand board
feet (with pulpwood not a factor). Instead of joining the SPA, some owners of

smaller mills had chosen to join the Southeastern Lumber Manufacturers Association, with headquarters in Atlanta. Dues for this organization, the SLMA, were much lower.

Southern Pine Association meeting in New Orleans, 1964. Harley Jr. is visible near center, 8th from right. TLC.

At one time Harley, Jr. tried to work out a deal to consolidate these two organizations, but could not secure agreement. He and some others thought that, by combining the resources of the two groups, they could do more advertising and have greater influence. As of the early nineties, Harley, Jr. was pleased to notice that the two organizations had begun to cooperate in some activities, but he still detected no movement to combine the two. Most of the members of the Southern Pine Association represented the bigger mills, he observed.[7]

Before Harley, Jr. became president of the Southern Pine Association, an issue had arisen over lumber standards, that is, the dimensions for two-by-fours, and so forth. This remained the hottest issue during his term. Harley remembered that when he first began with the Southern Pine Association, southeastern lumber producers were quarreling with western lumber producers over standards. Actually, as time went by, Harley came to the conclusion that the bigger problem was not the disagreement over standards, but the need to promote the use of wood in general. And there were other significant issues. These included union activities, which appeared to be increasing at that time, the greater effect of wage and hour laws on operations, and some problems with freight rates.

Still, the lumber standards issue took center stage. Much of the resistance to proposed changes came from builders, contractors, and architects. Changing the dimensions of lumber could create problems for them in some cases if they had to make changes to existing structures that had lumber of a different size. Some lumber producers preferred not to make changes just because they were used to the standards that were in effect.

---

[7] Ibid.

Agreement on changing the standards did not come easily. Hearings were necessary, and economic conditions had to be favorable. The new standards received agreement in 1979, but that never would have happened, in Harley, Jr.'s opinion, if the lumber industry had not been unusually profitable that year. His own records at the Langdale Company reflected that prosperity. According to those figures, in FY 1979 the Langdale Company averaged the highest price of any year up through FY 1991 on wholesale lumber prices. The average for 1979 was $272.85, having reached a peak of $301.41 for the month of October. Such prosperity was crucial in establishing the conditions under which the agreement on standards could be reached. It will be remembered that 1979 was in the latter part of the Jimmy Carter presidency when inflation and interest rates reached unusual heights.

Some organizations, though important and interesting to him, have not consumed as much of Harley, Jr.'s time and effort. For example, the Forest Products Research Society is an organization that Langdale Company representatives have been involved in for a long time because they thought it had an important relationship to their business. At one time Harley, Jr. served as chairman of the society's southeastern section, which included Georgia, Florida and Alabama. Subsequently, his level of personal activity diminished. The same applied, said Harley, to the Society of American Foresters, which used to have a southeastern section that he chaired for a while. A member of the Society of American Foresters for fifty years, by the 1990s Harley, Jr. no longer had to pay dues because of his seniority. Nevertheless, he continued to make small annual donations.

Harley, Jr. also resisted pressure to take a principal position in the National Forest Products Association. He went to some of the meetings, but left leadership to others. There were just so many associations, it was impossible to be very active in all of them. In addition to those mentioned above, for instance, he held memberships in the American Wood Preservers Association, the American Wood Preservers Institute, and the Crosstie Association.

The Eisenhower Administration Committee. Harley, Jr. appears 4th from left in the front row. TLC.

Government committees also required Harley, Jr.'s attention. On several occasions, he has been appointed to committees or boards sponsored wholly or in part by state and federal governments. During the Eisenhower administration he served on a committee dealing with forest research. For a number of years this committee traveled around the United States to various research facilities, studied what was being done, and then turned in a report to the federal government. Harley also served on a committee set up by the Eisenhower administration on using farm commodities for industrial use, and he found this work very rewarding.

In addition, Harley, Jr. worked on the Forest Industries Committee on Timber Value and Taxation, a congressional subcommittee. In connection with this, he appeared before the House Ways and Means Committee twice to testify regarding the treatment of income as capital gains. In this capacity he represented primarily the interests of larger landowners.

Harley, Jr. once turned down an opportunity to become a high state official in Georgia. This came after an old friend from his days at the University of Georgia, Herman Talmadge, won election as governor in 1948. Talmadge offered to appoint him state forester. Reminiscing with Herman about old times in 1991, Harley, Jr. joked that, if he had taken that job as state forester, he would already have been able to retire and would not have all the worries that he then had in business.

Harley, Jr. gave Herman Talmadge much of the credit for the state government's strong support of the forest industry in Georgia. Under Governor M. E. Thompson, Talmadge's predecessor, the state gave $125,000 a year to the Georgia Forestry Commission, recalled Harley, Jr. When Talmadge became governor, he started increasing that amount every year, and these increases made it possible for Georgia to be a regional leader in promoting the forest industry.[8]

Gov. Talmadge about 1953. From a publicity photo. TLC.

---

[8] Ibid.

During the Herman Talmadge administration, in 1953, forests and related manufactured products had an estimated annual value of $600,000,000. In pulpwood and naval stores production Georgia led the country. Although Georgia did less well in lumber manufacturing, this sector also showed rapid growth. Total lumber output in 1951 amounted to 2,193,000,000 board feet, a 35 percent increase over the 1945 figure.[9]

From the Talmadge era to the early 1990s, Harley, Jr. remarked in 1991, the forest business in Georgia had grown impressively and was then worth about twelve billion dollars a year, compared to the $600,000,000 value of 1953.[10]

During all this time, the Georgia Forestry Commission had done a good job for the forestry industry in Georgia, thought Harley, Jr. It played a leading role, for example, in achieving a good system of fire protection earlier than occurred in some other states, and the commission helped in the improvement of the quality of seedlings and in other such things.[11]

Evidence of the state's success in tree planting for reforestation appeared in the 1950s. In the winter of 1952–1953, Georgia produced more than twice as many tree seedlings for transplanting as any other state. As of October 1953, officials expected another increase in the coming winter to a total of more than 100,000,000 seedlings.[12]

Governor Marvin
Griffin talks with
Harley, Jr. TLC.

As for fire protection, in 1953 Georgia led all states in the number of acres of private woodland under fire protection. This amounted to 20,600,000 acres in 132 counties, compared to one million acres in thirty counties five years previously. The lookout towers, jeeps, other equipment, and personnel involved in such fire protection cost an estimated ten cents per acre. This appeared to be an excellent investment for the state in that the growth of pulpwood alone in Georgia during a

---

[9] "Dollars Grow on Trees," 49.

[10] Langdale, HLJr Interview 1991.

[11] Ibid.

[12] "Dollars Grow on Trees," 48–49.

year had an estimated value of $3 per acre, thirty times the cost of fire protection.[13]

Governor Griffin photographed with a group of business leaders. TLC.

Although Harley, Jr. held no public office, he did not suffer for lack of access to high government officials, including governors of Georgia and those aspiring to that position. The family friendships with Governors E. D. Rivers and Herman Talmadge have been mentioned. After Governor Talmadge, came Governor Marvin Griffin in 1954, who used to joke with Judge about their being kin, on the basis of John Robert Langdale's having married Harriet Griffin in the 1830s. Judge had no idea whether they were related, but he did not deny it.

Cousins Noah & Harley, Jr. March 10, 1962. Photo by W. Kirk Sutlive. TLC.

With Governor Ernest Vandiver, elected in 1958, the Langdales also had close ties. Harley, Jr. and Cousin Noah, president of Georgia State University, joined a group of businessmen on a trade mission to Europe led by the governor. This trip occurred between 10–31 March 1962, and was chronicled in a Savannah paper by W. Kirk Sutlive of Union Bag-Camp Paper Corporation, whose articles and photos subsequently appeared in a magazine-style brochure with the governor's picture on

---

[13] Ibid., 49–49.

the cover. While in Dusseldorf, Germany, the governor and Harley, Jr. met with and had their photo made with a former Valdostan, Miss Catherine Redles, who was then secretary to the consul general assigned to that city. Coincidentally, Harley, Jr. and Miss Redles were well acquainted, for she had once been a secretary at the Langdale Company.

Ernest Vandiver & the Langdales. Left to right, Guy Wesley, Harley, Jr., Mr. Vandiver, Judge, Billy, & John W. TLC.

Vandiver had been on familiar terms with the Langdales for a long time, as the preceding informal snapshop suggests. This photo is thought to have been made on the occasion of the dedication of the paper mill at Clyattville, which was before Mr. Vandiver ran for and was elected governor. Vandiver and his predecessor, Marvin Griffin, belonged to the so-called Talmadge faction of the Georgia Democratic Party.

This did not mean that the Langdales were all die-hard Democrats in all circumstances. They were financial conservatives, and in national politics Harley, Jr. and John W., at least, had considerable sympathy for Republican candidates and the policies they advocated. In the presidential election of 1952, when the Republican vice presidential candidate, Richard Nixon, got into trouble and gave his famous "Checkers" speech to extricate himself, Harley, Jr. communicated his support. Mr. Nixon replied with a card of thanks bearing a photo of himself and his family on one side.

Richard Nixon Family Photo Postcard, 1952. TLC.

The Langdales appear to have cared much more about issues than about names of political parties. Of course they were always polite and friendly to office-seekers of any party. Harley, Jr. seems to have striven to contribute enough money to candidates to show friendly intent and secure access, but not so much as to strain personal or company resources. One gains the impression that his financial contributions were carefully measured. To influence opininon, he really preferred to follow Judge's model and invite officials or business associates for a well-planned, relaxing, and successful hunting or fishing trip.

Turning from politics, it should be noted that Harley, Jr. held leadership positions in at least two major local organizations not related directly to forestry matters. For one thing, he served as chairman of the Lowndes County Industrial Authority for five years. During his tenure, the authority bought the first industrial park for Lowndes County and Valdosta, located between the Langdale Company offices and the municipal airport. This park turned out well, in Harley's opinion. In the 1960s, he recalled, the industrial authority tried to operate economically and recruit businesses that would pay their own way. In other words, they tried to avoid subsidizing businesses to attract them, which is consistent with the Langdale penchant for getting full value for one's investment.

On the Valdosta and Lowndes County Hospital Authority, as well, Harley, Jr. filled a crucial leadership role. He replaced his father as a member of the authority in 1972, after Judge's death, and held the post for twenty-three years. Harley, Jr. found this to be rewarding and challenging work. It seemed to him that the hospital authority had even more problems trying to pay its bills and managing its operations than he encountered at the Langdale Company. The hospital authority had more than a thousand employees, a medical staff of about one-hundred-and-forty physicians, and a large physical plant. Regarding his work with the hospital authority, Harley stated in 1991, "I am proud of the time that I have served and feel sure that we have an outstanding medical center and that, best of all, we have been able to pay our bills under very, very trying conditions." His term expired in February, 1995, and his nephew, John W. (Johnny) Langdale, Jr. replaced him as a member.[14]

Harley, Jr.'s participation and familiarity with the work of the hospital authority presumably influenced him and his family to make a major charitable contribution. Several years before retiring from the hospital authority, he participated in its decision to build and operate a senior living facility. To help bring this project into reality, the Langdales contributed both moral and financial support, some of it through the Langdale Foundation. Press reports said the Langdale Foundation gave or pledged a quarter of a million dollars toward building this senior living center, but this was an error.

---

[14] Langdale, HLJr Interview 1991.

In its early years the foundation had functioned mainly to make low-cost educational loans to college students. It had been set up partly at the initiative of Judge Harley, who was well known for supporting the 4-H Clubs and other youth programs, for that purpose. Perhaps remembering his own struggle for an education, Judge sympathized with young people in similar circumstances. As of 1970 the foundation had given several hundred low-interest-rate loans to students.[15]

As for the quarter-million-dollar gift for the senior living center, the news reports exaggerated the contribution of the foundation, which could not afford a gift of that size. The money actually came from several of the Langdale companies and families. The foundation by 1991 had less ability to give than the Langdales had intended when they set it up. Originally, said Harley, Jr., they planned to use the foundation more and more for charitable giving, and he intended to bequeath his stock to the foundation, since he had no children. But the law changed, under the Nixon administration as best he remembered, and it became difficult to do through the foundation what they had planned. As a result, the foundation had become less active by 1991 than they had intended it to be.[16]

In the year 2000, Harley, Jr. made another major philanthropic gift. This went to the business school of Valdosta State University. In appreciation for his contribution, the university named the business school the Harley Langdale, Jr. College of Business Administration.

Harley Langdale, Jr. College of Business Administration. Located in Pound Hall on the North Campus of VSU. TLC.

To sum up with respect to Harley, Jr.'s public service and government-related activities, it is clear that he gave much of his time to such things. He worked hard and provided guidance and leadership to several professional organizations and government committees. Yet most of his work in this area received relatively little press attention. Consequently, the impression emerged with many people that he concentrated strictly on running the Langdale Company and left public

---

[15] "They've Promoted Pine Trees."
[16] Langdale, HLJr Interview 1991.

service entirely to his brothers, Billy and John W. It is true, of course, that Harley, Jr. declined to run for political office, whereas his younger brothers participated vigorously in public politics.

Harley, Jr.'s youngest brother, Billy, started his political career in 1960 and was still holding public office as a member of the Georgia State Transportation Board in 2002. Regarded by many as the most personable, certainly the most jovial, of the three Langdale brothers, Billy turned his attention to politics in the year of John Kennedy's victorious presidential campaign.

As Kennedy gained the presidency, Billy won a post on the Lowndes County Board of Commissioners. He took office in January 1961 as the top vote getter of eight candidates. Billy's political style can be gauged in part from a speech he made in a political symposium at the Valdosta JayCee shack at the start of his campaign. In his speech, Billy observed: "You know my name is W. P. Langdale. Y'all know what that stands for?" They did not, so he explained. "That stands for 'Will Pave.' If you want all your children and grandchildren to see sand, you'd better go to the ocean, 'cause I'm gonna have all these roads paved pretty soon." Some people still tease him about this, calling him "Will Pave."[17]

As the commissioner with the highest vote total, he assumed the position of chairman and held that job for sixteen years. "I am very proud of the fact that he did a good job and had absolutely no criticism about mishandling the county from the money or budget standpoint," Harley, Jr. commented.[18] Billy took pride in asserting that every commission vote during his tenure was unanimous and that the county put up several new buildings without tax increases or bond issues during that period.

Billy dedicated much of his time each working day to his responsibilities as county commission chairman, probably more than any previous chairman, in Harley's opinion. Of course, since Billy worked for the Langdale Company, time spent on public duties cut into the time he could devote to company responsibilities. Billy's service as chairman cost the county very little in out-of-pocket expenses for travel and such things, said Harley, Jr.

The promise to pave roads helped Billy win the election, and he made a serious effort to keep it. Soon after taking office Billy led his fellow commissioners on a trip to see Georgia Highway Commissioner Jim Gillis, from whom they hoped to get support in paving Rocky Ford Road. When they approached Mr. Gillis about it, he said, "Billy, if you'll grade it and do everything else to get it ready, I'll put the blacktop on." Billy and his colleagues drove back home, thinking they had really accomplished something. It turned out the paving part was about a fifth of the total expense. The state's part cost about $35,000; Lowndes County's share was about $175,000. The county nearly went broke

---

[17] Langdale, WPL Interview 05.
[18] Langdale, HLJr Interview 1991.

trying to get the road prepared with its decrepit old equipment. Next time Billy went to see Mr. Gillis, the highway commissioner started the same routine, but Billy said, "Mr. Gillis, I'll tell you what. I'll do the black top if you'll do the preparation." Gillis agreed. "Go back and tell Mr. Kennedy what you want, Billy." Kennedy was the man who drew up the contracts. The relationship between Billy and Mr. Gillis was good.

Although there were actually three commissioners, one each for the northern, central, and southern areas of the state, Billy dealt only with Jim Gillis, who represented the southern area and with whom he made lots of "horseback trades." For instance, in Marvin Griffin's time they set up something called the Rural Road Authority. They had 150 million dollars from bonds. To get a road paved the main requirement was to get a right-of-way; then the state would pay for it. The road was put up for security for whoever bought the bonds. Money was scarce, though, and funding hard to get. On one occasion, Billy saw an opportunity in the Highway Department's need for an area office in Valdosta. Billy went to Mr. Gillis and offered to construct a building for use as an area office at no expense to the state if the state would pave Old Clyattville Road. You didn't have to get environmental approval by the Corps of Engineers as required today. Mr. Gillis saw it as a good deal for the state. It cost the county $20,000 for the building, and in less than two years the road was paved, Billy remembered.[19]

Billy and his fellow commissioners devoted much of their efforts to securing rights of way for road paving. During his sixteen years in office, as he recalled, the county got 150 miles of road paved, with most of the costs borne by the state and very little local expense. Their approach relied mostly on donations, not purchases, of the required right-of-way property.

The first step was to prepare surveys of property needed for road construction and draw up the requisite deeds for rights of way. Mr. Gillis would have these done whenever Billy asked for them. Billy always kept on hand a number of surveys and deeds ready to be approved for a paving contract. Then, as he explained, a typical scenario went like this: Somebody would ask him on the street, "When are you gonna pave my road? Billy would reply, "When y'all sign right-of-way deeds at no expense to the county." They'd ask, "How do we stand now? Billy would say, "Well, you've got about fifteen left." "Of course, they'd work on their neighbors, and that's the way we got the rights-of-way; we didn't spend any money." Billy and the other commissioners also approached property owners about donating property for rights-of-way. They generally had a stack of surveys piled on a table. From this stack each commissioner chose the deeds he thought he could possibly get donated and called on the relevant owner. People basically donated rights-of-way in exchange for the advantage of having a paved road. That was a simpler time, much less bureaucratic than today. After Billy left

---

[19] Langdale, WPL Interview 05.

as county commissioner, he observed, the county started offering money based on tax appraisals for rights-of-way.

For three years Billy served as a director of the Flue-cured Tobacco Stabilization Board. This board, like the American Turpentine Farmers Association, many years earlier, tried to stabilize prices of a particular commodity, in this case tobacco. The board set a minimum price for tobacco, and when the tobacco sold, the farmers who were members could put their tobacco into a stabilization program, which meant it would go into storage.[20]

The job of director was an elective position, and Billy actually had little interest in running for it. He did run, however, because Georgia Agriculture Commissioner Phil Campbell talked him into it. Campbell wanted to replace the member of the board who represented Georgia, so expecting that the Langdale name would win votes, he persuaded Billy to run for that office. And Billy won. But, said Billy, he never knew very much about tobacco, never cared much about tobacco, and after serving for three years, he retired from the board. While serving, however, he went to Raleigh, North Carolina for monthly conferences and enjoyed meeting other people involved in it.[21]

In 1987, eleven years after the end of his service as Chairman of the Lowndes County Commissioners, Billy became a candidate for election to the board of the Department of Transportation in the Second Congressional District.

The board had ten members in 1987, one from each congressional district. It set policy for the DOT and chose the DOT commissioner. Elected by state legislators from their congressional districts, members served five-year terms. Having started with eight members, as a result of Georgia's gaining representation in congress, the board increased to thirteen members by 2002.[22]

The state Transportation Board is known as a "constitutional board." As such the board is empowered to hire the DOT commissioner. The highway commissioner is allowed, in turn, to hire his deputy, a state engineer, and a treasurer with the approval of the board. The commissioner then takes care of the day-to-day operation of the highway department. If the board dislikes the policies or the management of the commissioner then the board's ultimate recourse is to fire that commissioner and hire another one.[23]

This system originated in the administration of Governor Carl Sanders. It came about as an effort to reduce political squabbling over roads and to introduce more democracy to decision-making in this area. Under the former system, Highway Commissioner Jim Gillis was thought by many to have too much power and to exercise it arbitrarily. Some alleged that Mr. Gillis ran the department as if it were a medieval fiefdom over which he was the lord. As Billy Langdale recalled,

---

[20] Langdale, WPL Interview 1991.

[21] Ibid.

[22] Langdale, WPL Interview 05.

[23] Langdale, WPL Interview 1991.

"Politicians running for office used to say, 'When I get elected, the first bus that leaves Atlanta is going to have Jim Gillis on the front seat.'"[24]

To be elected to the DOT board in 1987 Billy had to defeat the incumbent, Hugh Broome of Donalsonville, who had been on the board since its inception in the 1960s.[25] During his tenure, Mr. Broome had become well entrenched. A pilot, he used a state-owned airplane based at Donalsonville to travel around his district, and he had at his disposal a state-owned, radio-equipped car. Some people thought he encroached a little on operational matters, instead of keeping strictly to policy-making.[26]

Addressing the Albany Sertoma Club on 15 October 1987, Billy joked that his family had never lost an election, and he was doing his best to maintain the winning tradition. He acknowledged that an uncle once lost a race for tax collector, but explained tongue-in-cheek that the uncle was not regarded as "immediate family."[27]

Months of political maneuvering preceded the vote. Powerful House Speaker Tom Murphy supported Billy, while Lieutenant Governor Zell Miller and DOT Commissioner Rives backed the incumbent, Hugh Broome.

Some political observers saw this election as a milestone, showing the speaker had grown in political strength. Murphy had tried previously without success, it was said, to elect a new member to the board in place of an incumbent, but had always been frustrated by the forces of the lieutenant governor and the DOT Commissioner. Rives had assumed his DOT post only a few months previously, after the resignation of Tom Moreland.

Billy soon discovered that he had taken on a formidable task. This was far more challenging than an election for county commissioner. For one thing, he could not figure out how many votes he could count on. In his previous campaigns in Lowndes County, Billy had sometimes used what might be called a confrontational system to determine whether a man could be trusted to vote for him. He'd suddenly grab a fellow by the lapels, look him straight in the eye, ask for his vote, and then could know, in his opinion, whether this startled man was actually intending to vote for him. As he recalled in 2002, "I found out durn quick that politicking a politician ain't ordinary politicking. Them people'll lie to you and they've got the finest straight face you've ever seen." "Man, I'd travel with 'em, and I'd give 'em a jar of honey. But the other crowd would come and promise 'em asphalt. So I said asphalt is a little stronger than honey and goes a little

---

[24] Langdale, WPL Interview 05.

[25] "Billy Langdale Elected D.O.T. Board," *Valdosta Daily Times*, 15 January 1988.

[26] Langdale, WPL Interview 05.

[27] "Hiatus Over: Langdale Aims at Broome's D.O.T. Seat," *Albany* (GA) *Herald*, 16 October 1987.

further [laughter]. They always asked for a secret ballot; wouldn't stand up and be counted."[28]

On Thursday 14 January 1988, Billy won the election, but very narrowly. The twenty-seven state senate and house members from the Second Congressional District were reportedly as evenly split as they could be. According to one legislator, fourteen voted for Langdale and thirteen for Broome.[29] "They nicknamed me 'Landslide,'" said Billy.[30]

In this election Valdosta area legislators had been torn by difficult considerations. There was, of course, a natural inclination to vote for the local candidate, Billy Langdale, but there was also the rivalry between political forces at the state level. Some thought the DOT commissioner might punish Valdosta by withholding support for road projects if they voted against Broome and for Langdale. There was also concern about offending Speaker Murphy by not supporting his candidate, Langdale. After it was all over, Valdosta legislators seemed to agree that it had turned out well.

Asked for his opinion, Governor Joe Frank Harris refused to get involved. This was just normal politics, he said.[31]

Harley, Jr. appeared to give his blessing to his brother's latest political venture, perhaps to the election, more certainly to the work afterward. In his view, Billy really enjoyed this job. "I am sure they have never had a member of this board that has spent as much time as he has and attended as many meetings and at any less expense," said the elder brother, "because this is just the way he does things."[32]

As a member of the transportation board, Billy represented the Second Congressional District, which included thirty-one counties. These counties were located in the southwestern quarter of the state, from Columbus over to I-75 and down to the Florida and Alabama lines. Within this area, there were two district highway offices, one at Tifton and the other at Thomasville. If these offices encountered a problem, they usually got in touch with Billy about that. Once a month the board met in Atlanta to approve contracts for roads to be constructed in the following month. The board had at its disposal about a billion dollars a year, and these funds were allocated so much for each district.[33]

As of February 2002 Billy was unsure whether he would continue as a member of the DOT board. Redistricting in the wake of the last census placed him in the same district with a good friend whom he did not wish to run against. Lowndes was being shifted into the First Congressional District. At age eighty-one, though, Billy

[28] Langdale, WPL Interview 05.
[29] "Billy Langdale Elected D.O.T. Board."
[30] Langdale, WPL Interview 05.
[31] "Billy Langdale Elected D.O.T. Board."
[32] Langdale, HLJr Interview 1991.
[33] Langdale, WPL Interview 1991.

considered himself too young to retire from politics. Maybe he would run for state representative, he ventured. That would be fun. An argument in his favor, said Billy, was that he would not have to be trained. He already knew where the bathrooms were in Atlanta.[34]

Fun was always important to Billy, who said in 2002 that he felt sorry for people who did not enjoy life. "Of course, I feel like Harley enjoys life; I don't know whether John enjoyed life that much or not. John was very religious and serious-minded. 'Course, he had a lot of things that he did enjoy. My daddy enjoyed life, and you know one thing about my daddy, he didn't associate with old people much when he'd go out at night. When he was 75 he went with people who were 45. He'd go to fish fries and he'd go to little poker games or something like that, but his remark was that most old people want to talk about aches and pains."[35]

Mention of old people and pains reminded Billy of a story, this one involving his brother, John W. "John was visiting a nursing home one time. They had an old fella in there named Redden Parramore. John was shaking hands and saying, 'How do you feel?' People would mumble something in reply. Redden, who was on up the line, heard him and called out: 'John! Don't be asking people how they feel; they all feel like hell!'"[36]

Margaret Jones and John W. Langdale, Christmas 1952. TLC.

"Life today is more fun for me than when I was young. And I don't have any pain. And I can do damn near a man's work in a day." This from an eighty-one-year-old who had been in a hospital two days before having his arteries explored for blockages. "Everything turned out good," said Billy. The physician told him blood flow to his head was as good as if he were twenty-five; but the flow in his legs was poor. Did he not have pain when he walked? the doctor asked. "It hurts at

---

[34] Langdale, WPL Interview 05.
[35] Ibid.
[36] Ibid.

first," Billy replied, "but after walking two or three miles, it's all right." Keep walking, he was advised. When possible, Billy said he liked to take his dogs to the river swamp for a daily stroll. Walking on a track or treadmill did not appeal to him at all.[37]

A publicity photo showing Harley Jr. and John W. as chairman and president, respectively, of the Langdale Company about 1990. Always close, the two brothers had complementary interests, abilities, and personalities. Harley, Jr.'s passion was tree farming and business; yet he gave substantial time to public service. John W. was attracted more to public service, which included church and political offices, but he loyally supported his father and brother in business, especially in legal matters. John W., whose scholarly proclivities equipped him more for "detail work," as he called it, always deferred to his elder brother as the senior family member, ranking next in authority after their father.

Harley, Jr. and Billy Langdale had many notable achievements in public service, with Billy's successes coming mainly in the political arena. In a sense Billy followed in the footsteps of the middle brother, John W., who earlier succeeded in this field.

John W.'s political career began just three years after World War II, the year of President Harry S. Truman's stunning defeat of Governor Thomas Dewey for the presidency, 1948. This was also the year of incorporation of the Langdale Company, a very busy time for John W. Judge Harley, who always liked politics but never ran for office, encouraged him to run. Although John suspected that Harley, Jr. did not like the idea, apparently regarding politics as a distraction from the more important field of business, Harley did not attempt to discourage his running.[38] John ran and won his race for a seat in the Georgia House of Representatives.

---

[37] Ibid.
[38] Langdale, JWL Interview 14.

In 1949–1952, part of which time he was president of the Valdosta Rotary Club, John W. represented his constituents in the Georgia General Assembly. Subsequently, he won election and served as a state senator. From 1964 through 1971, he was a member and, for a term, chairman of the Board of Regents of the University System of Georgia.

During the late 1940s and early 1950s John's political responsibilities kept him away from home much of the time. As he and Margaret had three young children spaced about a year apart, this placed a heavy burden on Margaret for childcare. She was thankful for help from her parents who were able to assist her with the children. "It was very hard," acknowledged Margaret. Concern about neglecting his family contributed to John's decision to curtail his political ambitions after a few years. Later, when John W. served on the Board of Regents, the children were older and responsibilities for their care less onerous.[39]

Noah Langdale, Jr. speaking to the Florida Forestry Association. A distinguished scholar and popular orator, Noah several times took speaking assignments for his Valdosta cousins. TLC.

While a regular member of the Board of Regents and later as chairman, John W. had occasion to deal with his cousin, Noah Langdale, Jr., son of Judge Harley's brother and president of Georgia State University. The younger brother of Marguerite Langdale Pizer, Noah, Jr., or "Little Noah" as he was called in Valdosta, had starred in football at Valdosta High School and at the University of Alabama, where he played tackle. In 1941 he was named star student at Alabama. He went on to Harvard for a bachelor's degree in law and a master's degree in business. The University of Alabama awarded him a Doctor of Law degree. He practiced law for a while in Valdosta and taught business courses at Valdosta State College. A Rotarian, he edited the Valdosta Rotary bulletin.

From Valdosta he moved in 1957 to take the presidency of Georgia State College. This was a small evening school in Atlanta, which had started as a division of the University of Georgia and grew to become Georgia State University. By the time John W. served on the Board of Regents, Georgia State was a leading

---

[39] Langdale, MJL Interview 01.

institution within the University System of Georgia, which the Board of Regents governed. Noah was noted as an outstanding speaker and educator.[40] He retired as president of GSU in 1988. He and his wife, Alice Elizabeth Cabaniss, were parents of one son, Michael.

In the 1990s during interviews about his life, John W. spoke highly of his cousin, Noah. He was especially pleased to assert that at no time did President Noah of Georgia State ever ask his cousin, chairman of the Board of Regents John W., for any special favors for Georgia State based on their kinship.

In addition to service on the state level in a major policy-making role in higher education, John W. maintained a lively interest in education at the local level. For many years, as a trustee of the Valdosta State College foundation and in other ways, he worked closely with area public officials and leaders of the college, now Valdosta State University, to strengthen the institution through addition of facilities and programs.

John W. in May 1996. Photo taken at his home the day after he received an honorary doctorate from VSU. JEL.

John W. became the second Valdosta Rotarian to be elected governor of Rotary International District 692. He governed the district in 1967–1968, during which time he also chaired the Board of Regents of the University System of Georgia. He had previously been president of the Valdosta Rotary Club in 1949–1950. A Paul Harris Fellow, he maintained a strong interest in Rotary over the years, for example, serving as chairman of the district Finance Committee during the term of a subsequent district governor, his friend Dr. S. Walter Martin.

---

[40] Julian Miller, "To Toast Langdale," *Valdosta Daily Times*, 13 November 1977.

Brothers Harley, Jr. & John W. about 1997. TLF.

While engaged in these acts of public service, John W. carried on his legal practice. For twenty-seven years, he served as county attorney for Echols County. In business, he succeeded his brother, Harley, as president of the Langdale Company when Harley became chairman of the board after the death of Judge Harley. John was also chairman of the board of the Valdosta Federal Savings and Loan Association, director of the Citizen's and Southern National Bank of Valdosta, director of the Southern Company, former vice-president and director of the Georgia State Chamber of Commerce and past-president of the Valdosta and Lowndes County Chamber of Commerce.

Like his mother, John took a deep and abiding interest in his church. Early in World War II, aboard a destroyer patrolling the Atlantic coast, he had a religious experience that led to a lifetime commitment to God. He made a promise to serve. Subsequently, for decades he carried out the duties of a deacon in the First Baptist Church of Valdosta, and was a favorite teacher in the Sunday school. He sang in the church choir, he tithed, and he became a member of the Foreign Mission Board of the Southern Baptist Convention. He provided wise counsel. He went on church-sponsored mission trips.

John made several of these mission trips, including one to Japan. A trip to Wyoming was sponsored by Baptist laymen in Georgia. He enjoyed it and loved the people he met so much that the next year he wanted to take the whole family. The girls, however, preferred to go to camp. Johnny was in summer school at the time. Margaret's mother put him on the plane, so he flew out to meet his parents, who drove. It was about a ten-day trip, yielding about a week actually in Wyoming working at a Southern Baptist mission church. It was "a wonderful experience," said Margaret. On the way back they stopped at Cody. Johnny climbed up on a rock and found an arrowhead, with which he was thrilled.[41]

John's passion to serve continued even after he was stricken with a deadly illness, ALS, commonly called Lou Gehrig's Disease. He lived for several years as his body gradually deteriorated. An experimental drug treatment failed. He sat patiently for many hours of interviews about his life experiences. Even after being confined to a wheel chair he went regularly, almost daily, to the office and continued attending Rotary meetings and church services.

Exemplifying his belief in Christian missions even during his protracted illness, John and Margaret directed an active missionary outreach program for Spanish-speaking migrant workers in the local area. John W. took the initiative in acquiring property, raising money, and seeing to the construction of a church building for these people. From his wheel chair, he enlisted the support of many.

John and Margaret started in this migrant ministry when approached by a young Baptist woman who was then working with a Catholic group to assist migrants. These were field laborers from Mexico. John, who was active in the Baptist Men's organization, and Margaret, who was similarly involved with Baptist Women, secured the participation of those groups. Charles Harris, then president of Baptist Men, and Monteze Starling of the women's organization were two people who were particularly helpful. "When we first began the ministry it was more for reaching out for migrant workers," Margaret recalled. "We'd take food & clothing to the different camps. Then we realized the problem they had with the inability to speak English. We began meeting on Sunday afternoons at First Baptist Church to teach English. Members responded well as teachers." The church provided buses and volunteer drivers to transport the migrants. "Then, of course, they had many legal problems, so John would get involved. They had many interesting experiences." "It was a wonderful time, and we really enjoyed that." The Langdales found the migrants to be "warm and loving and interested in the Lord. It was just a wonderful experience." "We worked for about eight years," said Margaret, "and Elsie Nicholas and Ann Gunter, former Spanish teachers, took over. And they were absolutely amazed that none of us spoke a word of Spanish, and yet we were able to minister to these people for over eight years."[42]

As a result of this ministry, which was about sixteen years old in 2002, a Spanish-speaking church existed on the Quitman highway with regular attendance of about one hundred and a Spanish-speaking pastor. The pastor was a native of Paraguay; his wife came originally from Savannah. By this time migrants made up a small minority of the congregation, as most members held regular jobs in the area. It is fair to say that this church owes its existence to the leadership and personal commitment of John W. and Margaret.

---

[41] Langdale, MJL Interview 01.
[42] Ibid.

In summary, John W. provided in his final illness, which extended over a long period of time, an extraordinary example of Christian humility, courage, and intelligent use of his resources. In life he demonstrated how to live with integrity, charity, and honor. As the end approached, he accepted suffering with grace and death with dignity. He was an admirable man.

Of the four men most intimately involved in running the Langdale Company, John W. was the second to go. His father, Judge Harley, died in 1972 after years of declining health.

Four decades before his death Judge learned he had a health problem. He found out when, in his early forties (early 1930s), he applied for a twenty-year life insurance policy in the amount of $100,000. He had a large indebtedness at the time and wished to provide some protection to his family. Dr. Conrad Williams of Valdosta certified to the insurance corporation that Judge had good health. The company issued the policy, but, a month or so later, it insisted upon an exam by another physician. When the second physician found a heart murmur, the company cancelled the policy. In his early eighties, Judge laughed at what he regarded as the corporation's bad business decision. Forty years after cancellation of that twenty-year policy, he was still living. The company, as he saw it, had lost twenty years of premiums.

Nevertheless, in addition to the possible heart murmur, Judge had other serious ailments. For one thing, he had gall bladder trouble, and he suffered from the effects of an automobile accident when he was seventy-two. Billy's son, Bill, and other children witnessed this in 1960.

Early one afternoon, Judge had come by Billy's house and invited one of the boys to ride with him to the woods and drive for him. Bill, who was about fifteen at the time, jumped at the chance to drive and accompanied his grandfather on the afternoon trip. When they returned, Bill got out of the car and Judge slid under the steering wheel to drive away. At that moment, a child squealed and Judge tried to slam on the brakes, but apparently missed the brake and hit the accelerator. The car ran hard into a large oak tree, causing him serious internal injuries.[43]

Judge Harley died twelve years later at the age of eighty-four. His death occurred in the evening after a fishing trip in the afternoon. The date was 10 April 1972. He caught two big tasty fish, cleaned them, and shared a fish dinner with his sister who was visiting from Wichita, Kansas.

Recalling this sad occasion, Billy remembered that he had gone out that evening. Soon after returning home about 10 o'clock, he received a call from his mother. "Come quick. It's Daddy," she said. Judge had been practicing turkey calls, using a "yelper," preparing for a turkey hunt planned for the next morning at 3:30. "My daddy loved turkey hunting," said Billy. Judge sat in a high-backed rocking chair, working with the turkey caller. An unusually loud call attracted the

---

[43] Langdale, WPL Interview 1991.

attention of a maid, who was making a bed. She looked up and saw Judge slumped over in his chair. Thalia called a doctor, who arrived at the same time as Billy. There was nothing they could do. Judge Harley had died, apparently of a heart attack.[44]

Judge, Thalia, and the boys in 1968.

Judge had led a remarkable life. Born near the western border of the great Okefenokee Swamp and educationally disadvantaged, he had managed to overcome his deficiencies and get a law degree. For twelve years he served as municipal court judge in Valdosta and henceforth bore the honorary title or nickname, "Judge." He went into the naval stores business and gradually acquired a large amount of land, but also a large debt. He founded the American Turpentine Farmers Association and became well known in Washington as its chief representative and lobbyist. He cultivated politicians and gained political influence that served the interests of the ATFA.

Judge and Thalia about 1970. TLF.

---

[44] Ibid.

Judge about 1972. TLC.

He possessed the wisdom to recognize the abilities of his son, Harley, Jr., when the latter graduated from forestry school and to turn over management responsibilities to him. After this, Judge had the luxury of enjoying Harley, Jr.'s successful development of the Langdale Company while he, himself, devoted his attention to the ATFA, to his dirt farming interests, and to hunting, fishing, and conservation.

Judge busied himself researching and developing the best methods for curing country ham and producing the ideal hogs for the purpose. He gave his attention to raising sugar cane, using what he regarded as the right soil and fertilizer, and making from it the highest quality old-fashioned syrup. For this he used the traditional iron kettle to boil the cane juice and skim it properly until it condensed into syrup. He sent ham, bacon, and syrup as presents to friends around the country at Christmas and other times.[45]

He also created a 20,000 acre game preserve on land he held out for his private use when he and the boys set up the Langdale Company. This was primarily a refuge, or perhaps paradise is the right word, for wild turkeys and quail. Some said they could find a different covey of quail every hundred yards or so on this land. Regardless of the bountiful supply, Judge always left at least four birds in each covey that was hunted. Believing that quail needed to be well fed to reproduce well, he saw to it that they had all they wanted to eat. He planted seed-bearing plants such as millet, sesame, and buckwheat. He also had automatic mechanical feeders set up dispensing 900 pounds of grain per week. Judge made war on the enemies of his beloved birds. Enemies included flyers like Coopers hawks and crows, as well as ground dwellers such as skunks, foxes, and wildcats.

Judge loved hunting and fishing. As a leading conservationist, he helped reestablish the deer population in south Georgia after its long absence, for

---

[45]Martin, 93.

example, by having some transplanted to Langdale land. He built a number of ponds in low places, stocked them with fish, and fertilized them well. Whenever he could arrange it, he put an alligator or two in each pond. They wallowed out deep holes, he said, providing a refuge for fish in time of drought, and they kept the turtle population under control, increasing the fish survival rate. Alligators should not be killed, Judge said, until they became a danger to livestock.[46]

One of the Langdale ponds at Kinderlou. JDH.

A few years after his death some of Judge's friends nominated him for a high honor at the University of Georgia, the College of Agriculture Alumni Association Hall of Fame. Only one person each year received this honor.[47] Lamar T. Wansley of Georgia Power Company took the lead in promoting Judge for the Hall of Fame. In his letter of nomination, among other comments, Wansley stated:

> He was looked on by his peers as an outstanding farmer and conservationist. I have been associated with agricultural people throughout the state for more than thirty years, and more recently with leaders of agriculture in south Georgia and without any doubt in my mind, Judge Langdale's contributions over the years to Georgia's agriculture development exceeds anything that I know about. His influence on agricultural legislation, and his farming practices and conservation measures practiced on his own lands at his own expense have left their mark across the state.
>
> The examples he set will long continue to influence and inspire all who work in the field of agriculture. I know of no one more deserving of

---

[46] Ibid.

[47] "Judge Langdale to Be Honored Posthumously," *Valdosta Daily Times*, 7 October 1979.

this honor than Judge Harley Langdale, including those already so honored and those who have been considered.[48]

A number of influential persons endorsed Judge's nomination. These included Lowndes County Extension Agent George Kessler, who had provided Judge with expert advice and demonstrations over the years for improving agricultural practices; Craig Barnes, executive director of south Georgia Medical Center, who praised Judge's service as chairman from 1959 until his death in 1972 of the Valdosta-Lowndes County Hospital Authority; Thomas T. Irvin, Georgia's commissioner of agriculture, who wrote of "the outstanding record of service and leadership displayed by Judge Harley Langdale during his lifetime; and M.E. (Red) Coleman, who had traveled and worked with Judge in the ATFA. Coleman asserted that "the selection of Judge Langdale to receive this honor would add to the scope and dignity of all those already so honored."[49]

The list of endorsers goes on. Fellow Valdosta attorney and hospital board member Ed Barham wrote a strong, eloquent recommendation. L.W. Eberhardt, Jr., executive secretary of Georgia's Agricultural Commodity Commission for Cotton, did likewise. The Reverend Mr. James E. Pitts, Judge's pastor, wrote: "I do not know a person whom I feel more richly deserves this honor. Judge Langdale was a model of a good steward of God's good earth. He expressed his stewardship through his words and his actions. He was always cognizant that the Creator had kissed this good earth and had made us stewards to tend and preserve it. Evidences of Judge Langdale's many contributions to agriculture can still be seen around here."[50]

Testimonials on Judge's behalf came from Georgia Power engineer Clabe Chapman, Chamber of Commerce Executive Vice President Johnny B. Lastinger, County Commission Chairman Fred Deloach, Jr., and former Governor M. E. Thompson of Valdosta. Other endorsers included M. J. Lane, administrative assistant to Agriculture Commissioner Tommy Irvin, Cecil W. Chapman, C. C. Murray, and Gerald R. Varnado of Athens, J. Lamar Branch of Tifton, T. G. Walters of Lavonia, C&S National Bank Vice President Fred W. Greer, Jr. of Atlanta, Congressman Dawson Mathis, and Senator Herman Talmadge. In one paragraph of his letter Senator Talmadge emphasized Judge's support of programs for Georgia's youth. According to the senator,

---

[48] Lamar T. Wansley, " Letter to Byron Kirkland," in Harley Langdale, Jr., Papers (Valdosta GA).

[49] M. E. (Red) Coleman, "Letter to Byron Kirkland," in Harley Langdale, Jr., Papers (Valdosta GA).

[50] James E. Pitts, Rev., "Letter to Byron Kirkland."

...Judge Langdale's contribution to youth organizations was truly outstanding. He realized as well as anyone that it was as important to nurture the minds of the young as it was the soil they would one day plant. His support of 4-H, Future Farmers of America, and Future Homemakers of America enabled thousands of youngsters to benefit from expanded opportunities. He served on the 4-H Advisory Committee from the time it was organized until his death, funded a cottage at Rock Eagle 4-H Camp, and provided financial assistance for many young men and women to attend college.[51]

One of the testimonials emphasizing Judge's ability to mingle with persons of all stations came from Fritz Scarborough of Valdosta, who said he had been closely associated with Judge since 1951. Scarborough wrote:

I knew him as a farmer, conservationist, environmentalist, sportsman, innovator, businessman, churchman, philanthropist and just plain common man.

I think he would be the personification of the man in Rudyard Kiplings' poem "If when he said "if you can walk with millionairs and kings nor loose the common touch." Judge Langdale did possess those characteristics to me.

He was counsel to Presidents, Governors, Senators, Congressmen, Judges, business Magnates and many others, yet he always seemed happiest in the country crossroad store sitting on a nail keg or broken leg chair swapping stories with his many friends who frequented those surroundings.

With such an array of endorsements, the committee making the choice had to be impressed. Even though Judge had not attended the University of Georgia, the group voted to give him the honor. He was duly inducted into the Hall of Fame on 2 November 1979 at the annual meeting of the Agricultural Alumni Association, with the Reverend Mr. James Pitts as the main speaker. Unfortunately, Thalia did not live to see her husband honored on this occasion, for she had died in 1975 at the age of ninety.

In summary, it is very clear that the Langdales have been very much engaged in public service through their entire careers, though not all in the same way. Judge's interests tended toward forest products, general agriculture, wildlife conservation, health facilities, youth programs, and social or civic organizations. He was a Mason for more than fifty years and served on the Building Committee

---

[51] Herman E. Talmadge, "Letter to Byron Kirkland," in Harley Langdale, Jr., Papers (Valdosta GA).

of the St. John the Baptist Lodge #184 in Valdosta. A longtime Rotarian, he likewise took an interest in politics, though not in elective office. Harley, Jr. assumed his father's interest in health programs and his position on the board of the Valdosta-Lowndes County Hospital Authority. Otherwise, he concentrated more on professional organizations related to his business, except that, like his father, he also directed much of his attention to wildlife and other kinds of conservation. While John W. and Billy participated in several civic organizations, they differed from their father and older brother in that they turned in the direction of elective political office, and John W. devoted many of his efforts to church-related organizations. As busy as the Langdales were while building the Langdale Company, they found time for many public service activities.

Photo Essay

The Langboard MDF Plant

Harley Langdale, Jr. addressing guests at dedication of the Langboard MDF plant in Willacoochee, Georgia. JEL.

*L*angboard began production at its medium-density fiberboard (MDF) factory in Willacoochee, Georgia, on 1 September 1998. The Langdales had acquired the plant from a company in Las Vegas, New Mexico, and moved it to Georgia. The complete factory amounted to three hundred and two truckloads of material.

The Willacoochee plant differed substantially from its previous configuration in New Mexico. Langboard sent major pieces of machinery to original manufacturers for refurbishment and upgrading; factory staff overhauled other equipment on site. As one consequence of the overhaul, the plant's capacity increased 67 percent from 72 to 120 million square feet with assumed thickness of 3/4 inch. Managers attributed this result chiefly to their upgrading the refiner motors to

5000 horsepower and adding more pumps to enable faster operation of the press. In addition, a new hydraulic simultaneous closing system improved control over thickness of the MDF mats, enhancing product quality.

Aerial view of Langboard MDF plant. JDH.

The MDF manufacturing process begins with acquisition of raw materials. These include Southern yellow pine wood chips (like those used in paper manufacture), shavings from the Langdale planer mill, and sawdust from the Langdale sawmill. Chips arrive from Valdosta by truck and rail; a radial stacker unloads them onto an outdoor concrete storage area that holds 3,500 tons. A large pile of chips can be seen in the aerial photo above near the building at the upper right of the picture.

Shavings and sawdust come by truck and are dumped into a raw-material storage building with a capacity of 1,250 tons. The photo below illustrates the unloading of shavings and shows how a semi-trailer truck can be made to function as a dump truck.

A load of planer shavings being added to storage. TLC.

Early in the manufacturing process a mixture of chips and shavings goes into "refiners." These are machines that grind the raw materials into wood fiber that is subsequently blended with resin and other liquids to create medium-density fiberboard. Before entering the refiners, however, chips and shavings travel different paths for cleaning and preparation. Chips pass through a washing procedure that gets rid of sand and other contaminates; then a "de-watering screw" removes water and sends the clean chips via a "mixing screw" to bins called "refiner metering bins." Shavings, on the other hand, first enter an air-blower called the "air-density separator." This equipment separates shavings from heavy material such as rocks, metal fragments, or weighty pieces of wood. Air-blown shavings travel temporarily into the "baghouse" and later blend with chips in the "mixing screw," which feeds the mixture of chips and shavings to the refiner metering bins.

Shavings Infeed
System. TLC.

From the refiner metering bins material enters the three 44-inch steam-pressurized refiners, designated as the "face," "core," and "swing" refiners. The first feeds the "face system," and the second feeds the "core system." The "swing" refiner supplies either the face or the core system, according to need. Wood fiber going into the face system, which ends up on the surface of boards, is of higher quality than that going into the core system.

Blowline input to
flash-tube dryers. TLC

The three refiners output wood fibers to the "blowline," a pneumatic conveyor, which moves them to three seventy-two-inch "flash-tube dryers," one each for the face, core, and swing systems.

Dryer cyclones used to remove fumes. TLC.

Combustor and boiler, supplier of steam & hot dry air. TLC.

An important equipment assisting this operation is the "fluid-bed combustor" and boiler shown above. The combustor burns dust from the sander, sawdust and trim material from the saws, and purchased bark to generate steam for operation of the refiners and the press. At the same time, it provides hot, dry air to the flash-tube dryers.

Another supporting equipment, a two-field "wet electrostatic precipitator," removes dust and volatile organic compounds (VOC) from the humid air exiting the flash-tube dryers, the hot dry air from the combustor having absorbed moisture from the fibers being dried.

Wet electrostatic precipitator.
TLC.

Thayer scales weigh the wood fiber material, upon its exiting the flash-tube dryers, to determine the quantity of resin, scavenger, and wax to be supplied from storage tanks for the MDF mixture. After passing through the Thayer scales, the fiber goes into a "dry metering bin" for either the face or the core system.

Blown by conditioned air from the dry metering bins, the mixture of fiber and additives moves to the four-head vacuum forming line. The four heads lay down the material forming the "mat" that is soon to be converted into panels. Two heads each for face and core assure, in MDF terms, a good cross-panel profile (a wood density about equal to that of a fast-growing southern pine).

Forming heads. TLC

As the continuous mat flows by conveyor from the forming heads down the forming line, trim saws cut off excess material to achieve the correct width. At the proper instant another saw, called a "flying saw," moves across the line, cutting the mat to prescribed length. The newly-cutoff mat then enters a "speed-up" section of the conveyor, which moves the piece rapidly forward for injection into the press loader (photos below).

Forming Line, Loader & Press. TLC.

Loader and Press. TLC.

The loader, which holds twenty mats, moves up and down incrementally to accept a mat for each of its twenty positions. According to design, it receives mats in even-numbered slots while moving down and odd-numbered slots when moving up. So in one cycle, down-and-up, it becomes fully loaded and ready to charge the press with twenty new mats as soon as the press ejects the preceding twenty-mat load into the unloader.

The press is five feet by eighteen feet in size and has a twenty-mat capacity. It can produce panels in increments of 1/16" varying from 3/8" to 1 1/2" finished-board thickness. Its electronic controls, like all others in the plant, are by Wonderware.

Press and Unloader.
TLC.

The remainder of the MDF factory operation can be summarized briefly. From the unloader, mats go to a wicket-type "board cooler" that can accommodate six press loads, 120 mats, at a time.

Board Cooler. TLC.

After cooling, mats are stacked to await sanding (next photo). A forklift transports mats to the eight-head, wide-belt sander, which finishes both sides at the same time. As panels leave the sander, human graders evaluate every panel on the basis of appearance and send each one to the appropriate grade bin. Finally, a Schelling book saw (second photo below) cuts some of the panels into boards. An automatic strapping machine (third photo below) bands units, which are stored in the warehouse until shipped.

Sander infeed & panels (L) being loaded on input ramp. TLC.

Schelling book saw cutting a stack of MDF panels. TLC.

Strapping machine & panels being readied for shipment. TLC.

At the warehouse, trucks load from two drive-in loading bays or from the sunken van-loading dock. Workers weigh the trucks in and out to assure maximum load without excess weight. Rail cars also load directly from the warehouse. Shipments go all over the country, with much of the plant's output being sent to furniture manufacturers.

Forklift loading a truck with MDF from the warehouse. TLC.

At the time of this writing, a new Langboard molding factory, located adjacent to the MDF facility, was scheduled to go on line in the summer of 2001. Once this plant became operational, it was to consume a significant portion of the MDF plant's production.

In summary, the Langdale MDF operation in Willacoochee is basically similar to that of their OSB facility in Quitman. Both employ elaborate processes to convert wood into sheets or panels of material suitable for use in some kind of construction. The two operations are different, however, in important ways. Whereas the OSB plant uses soft hardwoods as raw material, the MDF factory employs pine. In contrast to the OSB process, which basically involves glueing thin flakes of wood together in differently oriented layers to form panels, the MDF operation grinds the wood into tiny particles that are reconstituted with other materials to form panels. Another difference is that OSB, typically used as floor, roof, or wall sheeting in the building trade, is more resistant to water damage than MDF, which is always used indoors, often as furniture or interior molding. From the standpoint of the Langdales, both of these manufacturing enterprises serve the interest of the company by facilitating the marketing of products from their land, a key objective of Harley Langdale, Jr. since the 1930s.

11

Transition

The Langdale Company Today

While recognizing the essential contribution of Judge Harley Langdale in founding the company and sustaining it through the difficult period of the 1920s and 1930s, it is fair to say that the Langdale Company of today stands as a monument, above all, to the achievement of Harley Langdale, Jr. He has made the company in his image, or at least developed it in accord with his personality. It reflects his values, his ideas, and his decisions, even more than those of his father. This should come as no surprise to anyone, considering that Judge ran the enterprise for fifteen years and his son has run it more than sixty-three years. Of course it is true that they had much in common, and the work of the son has always to be considered as in part a legacy of the father, who remained company chairman until his death in 1972.

As of 2001, Harley, Jr. had been chairman of the company for about twenty-eight years, although he pretended to retire in 1993. At that time he gathered his correspondence and other papers into boxes and stored them, but he did not give up ultimate control of the company or turn over his office to anyone else. In fact, he continued after 1993 to rise early and reach his office by about 6 o'clock in the morning. To get there later would likely have caused him an acute attack of conscience. Early rising and early arrival at work were good examples that he believed a leader should set.

After handling his mail and reading the morning financial and manufacturing reports, he typically conferred with his nephew, Johnny Langdale, president of the company, and other managers as he and they deemed appropriate. When later in the morning he received outside visitors, they always found him well dressed, usually in a business suit, alert, soft-spoken, interested, and gracious. Like Judge Harley fifty years earlier, Harley, Jr. appeared as the epitome of the cultured

Southern gentleman, but of course the two Harleys were from different generations and wore different style clothing.

Although Harley, Jr. remained chairman and stayed active in the company after his "retirement" in 1993, he really did turn over day-to-day management to the president of the company, his nephew, Johnny Langdale. Harley, Jr. seemed to think of his role as mainly that of a steadying hand and a resource person. He consciously followed in the 1990s the pattern Judge Harley adopted in relations with him in the late 1930s. Harley, Jr. believed that a manager, including the president of the company, had to learn much of his managerial style and skill on the job. Any new manager is going to make mistakes, he commented in 1994; you just hope they won't be too damaging and experience will reduce their number and severity.

Harley, Jr.'s first priority during the 1990s clearly was to put into place a management team that could lead the Langdale Company effectively for many years to come. He sought to orchestrate an orderly transition. It appears that he succeeded, just as he succeeded in many other undertakings during his long tenure as leader of the company.

Johnny & granddaughter, Caroline. TLF.

Johnny Langdale (John W. Langdale, Jr.) assumed the position of president on 12 February 1992. Harley, Jr. chose Johnny for the company presidency to the considerable surprise of his father, who thought his son would not be interested in such a demanding executive job and might be temperamentally unsuited for it. Yet Johnny, in the typical Langdale pattern, had worked at various jobs within the company and had a good understanding of its operations. Johnny had also held several jobs with other employers. As a young man in college and supporting a family he accepted very little money from his father. John W. would have given his son more, but respected his desire for independence. John W.'s surprise at his son's promotion soon turned to pleasure as it became evident that Harley, Jr. had chosen well and Johnny had what it took to lead the company.[1]

In fact, the Langdale Company has prospered under Johnny's presidency as seldom before. An interviewer asked him in 1996 which event during his time as president gave him the most pride. He hesitated a moment, then reached into his desk drawer and pulled out a graph showing company performance over a long period of years. The line ascended steeply as it moved to the right on the page and showed no sign of leveling off. So what pleased Johnny most at that time was that the company made money at a record rate under his presidency.

With booming profits in the 1990s, Johnny led the company to acquire additional car dealerships and a bank. Similarly and more importantly, he took the company into the MDF (medium-density fiberboard) manufacturing business with the purchase of a massive plant located in Las Vegas, New Mexico, and the moving of it to Willacoochee, Georgia. Subsequently, at great expense, the Langdale Company replaced its existing sawmill with a new and much more sophisticated one. The company expanded further in February 2001 with purchase of an additional pole plant in Wadley, Georgia. A new factory to produce molding for the housing industry also went into operation in Willacoochee, Georgia, in 2001 as a satellite of the MDF plant. With Johnny Langdale as president, the Langdale Company moved vigorously to take advantage of opportunities afforded by the strong economy that existed for several years leading up to early 2001. In the sphere of employee relations, Johnny could take satisfaction in the fact that on his watch Langdale Forest Product Company employees voted their local labor union out of business. Some of these events will be discussed in more detail later.

This list of major achievements during Johnny's presidency, he would be the first to say, could not have happened without a strong economy and without the hard and effective work of many others. Certainly these things could only have been done with the acquiescence and support of the chairman of the board, Harley, Jr., whose leadership since 1937 brought the Langdale Company to a position of prominence within the forest products industry.

For the sake of perspective, it seems appropriate now to recapitulate briefly a few of Harley, Jr.'s achievements. Upon graduation from the forestry school of the University of Georgia in 1937 he joined his father's firm and soon took charge as general manager. While Judge Harley henceforth devoted his energies principally to the ATFA and to traditional agriculture, Harley, Jr. broadened the company's activities into the pulpwood business. He also moved toward greater efficiency in the naval stores enterprise by purchasing the assets of Judge's turpentine partners and shifting all distillation to a new centralized still erected in Valdosta in 1943. As one of the world's largest turpentine and rosin producers, of course, he received notice in trade publications, such as *Naval Stores Review*.

---

[1] Langdale, JWL Interview 14.

Harley Jr. and a group of leaders in naval stores. This photo appeared in *Naval Stores Review*. TLC.

In 1944 the company moved its headquarters from downtown Valdosta to the location adjoining the new still on the Madison Highway, where it remained in 2001. John W. Langdale and Billy Langdale returned to the family business at the end of World War II, the former part time and the latter full time.

Two years after the war, Harley, Jr. took the company into the preservative treating business. Another milestone occurred in 1948 with the complete reorganization of the family business into a new legal entity, the Langdale Company, which had about twenty subsidiaries in 2001.

By 1959, as John F. Kennedy and other politicians maneuvered for advantage in the upcoming presidential campaign, the *Valdosta Daily Times* considered the Langdale Company's size and diversity very impressive. According to the paper, "its vast operations include the production of naval stores, crossties for railroads, creosoted wood products, lumber and also farming."[2] This report, which today can be treated as the verbal equivalent of a photo snapshot, affords a convenient point of departure for describing the transition from the company of the 1950s to the Langdale Company of today.

In 1959, as the *Times* stated, the Langdale Company operated one of the most modern naval stores processing plants in the country. Its main components were built entirely of stainless steel. The distillation process employed in this facility had been developed by the United States Agricultural Research Station at Olustee, Florida. The plant had the capacity to process one barrel of crude gum every three minutes. The Langdales then had 130,000 drums of rosin worth $5.5 million stored on their yard. This was thought to be the largest concentration of stored rosin in the world.

Langdale's wood preserving division in 1959 still employed a creosote and creosote coal tar solution for treating crossties, utility poles, cross arms, construction poles, fence posts, barn poles and lumber. (Nobody at the company suspected at the time that those chemicals might some day become a problem.)

---

[2] "Langdale Is Vast Forest Industry."

The pressure-treating facility made use of two large cylinders 8 feet in diameter. One of these had a length of 78 feet and the other 120 feet.

John W. Langdale showing utility poles to a visitor. These poles, in the process of being "framed" on the Pole Yard, were treated with CCA, a chemical combination that Langdale executives considered superior to the older creosote-based wood preservative, which they discontinued decades ago. TLC.

As for the lumber division, the Langdales were proud that, thanks to a new method of mechanical unloading, log trucks could be sent back to the forest within minutes of their arrival. Once logs were unloaded, they went through the Swedish-invented debarker, then to a pair of German-made gang saws that cut the lumber to size. The saws had a sawing capacity of 50,000 board feet per eight-hour shift. Newly sawed lumber, after having both ends trimmed, traveled into an automatic stacker in preparation for loading into the dry kiln. Waste slabs, chipped into small pieces, went to paper mills.

Judge shows prize tobacco in the 1960s to James Blanchard of C & S National Bank. Tobacco then was more admired than it is today. TLC.

Harley, Jr. reasserted in 1959 a basic management concept from which he never seemed to waver since his return to Valdosta from forestry school in 1937. The Langdale Company strove to employ the most modern forestry practices, to produce the most wood per acre per year and to achieve the highest profit for the company and for neighboring landowners, many of whom were Langdale suppliers. The company aspired to use every part of every tree harvested and to produce a higher grade and more uniform product that would be more appealing to consumers and, therefore, more marketable and profitable.

As for their farming operations in the year preceding Kennedy's election, the Langdale Company specialized in corn, tobacco, peanuts, and cattle. Langdale farms operated in Brooks, Clinch, Echols, Berrien, Lanier, and Lowndes counties.

Harley, Jr., Tommy Stalvey, and Wayne Warren admire tall corn on a Langdale farm. Langdale agricultural methods, like their manufacturing processes, are among the most advanced. Wayne Warren manages the farming operation. TLC.

With passing years after 1959, the Langdale Company experienced a number of positive and a few negative developments. A positive event came in the early 1970s when the company installed new dry kiln equipment and started operating kilns twenty-four hours a day, using a high temperature (230 degrees) technique. Until that time air-drying required them to keep nearly two months' inventory of lumber stacked on the yard. By quickly running that existing inventory through the dry kilns they saved almost enough money to pay for the new equipment.[3]

In 1975 an event of the negative type occurred, sale of the Langdale turpentine still. Of course the Langdale naval stores operation had already ground to a halt, so selling the still was a financial plus. Yet it was a sad event, for it marked the symbolic end of the turpentine era in south Georgia. Julian Presa & Associates, Inc. of Guatemala City, Guatemala, bought the still, dismantled it, and shipped it to Guatemala. The Presa company expected to produce turpentine in Guatemela for less than the cost of importing it.[4]

The turpentine business had been declining for a number of years. When the Langdales stopped production, their still had only four workers. The main problem for their naval stores operation, according to John W., was the shortage of labor. This resulted in large measure, he thought, from the welfare program, which made

---

[3] Robert H. Langdale, interview by author, audio tape, 16 October 2000, The Langdale Company, Valdosta GA, Harley Langdale, Jr., Papers, Valdosta GA.

[4] "Langdale Company Sells Gum Process Machinery," *Valdosta Daily Times*, 27 August 1975.

it possible for men to stay home and draw welfare payments equal to their wages in the woods. As John W. phrased it, "they can draw welfare, stay at home, and still come out the same on a net basis."[5] Although turpentine production continued on a limited scale in south Georgia until the end of the century, the industry was essentially finished.

Notwithstanding the demise of their turpentine business, the Langdale Company continued to prosper in the 1970s. Annual sales, which had been about $7,000,000 in 1958, approached the $15,000,000 mark in 1976, the year Georgian Jimmy Carter won the US Presidency.[6] The annual payroll for the 485 persons directly employed by the company approximated $4 million, and the company transplanted an estimated 1,500,000 pine seedlings.[7]

In the 1970s issues related to the environment and conservation captured much of the nation's attention. The Arab oil embargo and resulting gas lines in the United States and other Western countries added immediacy to the question of oil supplies. Presidents Nixon, Ford, and Carter struggled with these issues. So did private companies, which critics often accused of contributing to the degradation of the environment.

On behalf of the Langdale Company in 1977, Gene Quick had responsibility for conservation activities. To reassure the public of the company's interest in ecology and conservation efforts, in June 1977 he detailed some of those measures.[8]

In the previous year, said Quick, the Langdale Company had transplanted about 1,500,000 trees on their land. This required a large amount of work by men and machinery to prepare the sites beforehand to assure a satisfactory survival rate. It also implied a commitment to look after the young trees, protect them from fire, and thin them usually three times during their growth to maturity. Obviously, this involved much expense. As for benefits, one acre of pine trees, he pointed out, produced enough oxygen daily for the needs of eighteen people. Based on calculations of scientists, he observed, all machines in the world then running on coal and petroleum could be run on the alcohol produced by 1/30 of the world's trees. So planting and growing trees clearly improved the environment and conserved coal and petroleum, at least potentially.[9]

According to Quick, the company at that time leased about 100,000 acres of its land to hunting clubs. Aside from the obvious recreational benefits to local sportsmen, the club members took an interest in the areas of their leases and actually helped supervise and conserve plant and animal resources.

---

[5] Ibid.

[6] Langdale, "Brief Facts."

[7] "Judge's Motto Lives on at the Langdale Company," *Valdosta Daily Times*, 26 June 1977.

[8] "Langdale Co. Didn't Wait," *Valdosta Daily Times*, 26 June 1977.

[9] Ibid.

The company cared deeply about environmental concerns, Quick asserted, and worked hard to protect the environment. For example, the company filtered water coming out of equipment to remove oil, etc. "All our wastes are contained right here on company property," he declared.

Five years ago (1972), Quick noted, the Langdale Company produced tons of sawdust and bark every day, which they burned as waste, creating streams of black smoke rising to the clouds. Now sawdust and bark were burned as fuel for boilers producing steam for the pressure treatment plants and dry kilns. The mixture of sawdust and bark produced very little smoke, he pointed out. Moreover, sawdust and bark were being used instead of natural gas and fuel oil that had previously been consumed for that purpose; this conserved petroleum. Although the incinerators formerly employed to burn waste sawdust and bark remained on site, said Quick, they were unused. Excess sawdust and bark not needed by the Langdale Company was sold to others for fuel.

Quick estimated the company burned 200 tons of bark and sawdust each day, the equivalent of 2,165,000 cubic feet of natural gas or 73.4 tons of bituminous coal, or 2,162 gallons of fuel oil.

Harley, Jr. accepts US award in 1990 for conservation. TLC.

Over the years the Langdale Company's sensitivity to environmental concerns has been recognized by several awards. In 1990, for example, the US Soil and Conservation Service gave a merit award to the company in recognition of its efforts to promote good land and water use. Harley Langdale, Jr. accepted the award on behalf of the company in Salt Lake City during the 45th Annual Meeting.[10]

Environmental matters, which rose to national prominence in the 1960s and 1970s, remained a matter of high priority for the Langdales at the turn of the century. Being in the forest products business and owning more than 200,000 acres

---

[10] Susan A. Smigielski, "Lowndes Firm Gets Merit Award," *Valdosta Daily Times*, 19 August 1990.

of land, they obviously had to deal with clean-water issues. Federal and state laws determined how close to streams logging could be carried on, for example. A portion of Langdale land was low and swampy, so care had to be taken to comply with regulations relating to wetlands. Wesley Langdale (John W. Langdale III), Johnny's eldest son, was responsible in 2000 for managing the Langdale land. It was strict company policy, he stated, to comply with the "Best Management Practices" manual put out by the Georgia Forestry Commission for such issues.

John W. "Wesley" Langdale, III. TLC.

Ideas on conservation have changed radically in the past fifty years. For example, in the mid-twentieth century a farmer with a boggy place could bring in a bulldozer and make himself a pond. He would receive praise from soil conservation experts and sometimes also be given money from the government to help pay for construction of the pond. By the late twentieth century, thanks to advancing ecological knowledge, conservation experts usually valued the boggy place much more than the pond that might be constructed there; and the farmer had to be careful, should he choose to build a pond, that he did not violate federal or state law.

Although Langdale executives unanimously asserted their acceptance of and compliance with environmental controls in 2000, they were still in the process of correcting a soil contamination problem created through error long ago. In the early period of their pressure treatment of poles, posts, etc., they used creosote and coal tar as wood preservatives. This was the standard product. Neither the Langdale Company nor other firms engaged in the same business at the time knew of the environmental hazards that eventually became well known. It turned out that the plant in Sweetwater, Tennessee, and the one in Valdosta had contaminated soil.[11]

Robert Harley "Bob" Langdale. TLC.

Bob Langdale, a mechanical engineering graduate of Georgia Tech (one of Billy's sons), was in charge of designing a system to rectify the situation. The method he developed in consultation with university researchers, enabled the company over a period of time to correct the problem at a lower-than-usual cost.

Though considerable, the expense of cleanup did not seriously impair company prosperity. By 1985 Langdale's annual sales rose to $75 million, an impressive increase from the $15 million of 1976. The number of employees had gone up relatively little in that time to something in excess of 500 in 1985. In contrast to the modest increase in the size of the work force, however, during the same nine-year period the payroll had more than doubled to approximately $9 million.[12]

The rise in sales occurred despite intense competition from Canadian lumber, which became a growing threat to United States lumber producers from the late 1970s. The Langdale Company sold lumber in 1979 for 25 percent higher prices on average than it received seven years later (1986). As Harley, Jr. noted in 1986, the weak Canadian dollar in comparison to the US currency drove Canadian exports to the south. Besides that, he complained later, the Canadian government sold timber to Canadian lumber producers at a price far lower than the price United States producers could pay for their timber, giving the Canadian producers an unfair competitive advantage.[13] Still, Harley, Jr. had little doubt their business would remain prosperous. To help assure that result, the company continued to

---

[11] Langdale, RHL Interview 01.
[12] "Langdale Company Brings Work Ethic to Forefront."
[13] "Langdale Timber Roots Deep in Lowndes," *Valdosta Daily Times*, 26 April 1987.

update machinery in the mid-1980s, installing computerized equipment to replace manually-controlled machines.[14] Harley, Jr. saw technological modernization as essential to being able to compete with the Canadians,[15] and the company pursued the process of modernization right on into the twenty-first century.

The problem with regard to Canadian lumber remained serious in 1987. Harley, Jr. noted reports that half of the lumber consumed in Western Georgia and perhaps 1/3 of all lumber used in the United States then came from Canada. Yet the situation had perhaps stabilized in that it seemed to be getting no worse. The Langdale Company was shipping 100,000,000 board feet of timber including poles pilings and lumber, each year to twelve eastern states. Having made $75 million in sales the previous year, Harley, Jr. was, as usual, optimistic about the future.[16]

His optimism may have dimmed temporarily as a result of labor problems later in the year. The United Food and Commercial Workers Union #442 represented about 250 Langdale workers. Their contract expired 4 October and, when negotiations failed, the union called a strike. Issues included job security, seniority, wages, and insurance benefits. During the strike, which was short, the plant continued operations, with administrative personnel filling in for striking workers. Twenty workers, two of them union members, reportedly crossed picket lines to work. The company and the union soon agreed on a new contract, which the workers approved by a 98 percent favorable vote on Friday, 6 November. All were back at work on the following Monday. The strike, unusual for south Georgia, was tame by comparison with typical events up North.[17]

James Harley "Jim" Langdale.
TLC.

---

[14] "Langdale Company Brings Work Ethic to Forefront."

[15] "Langdale Timber Roots Deep in Lowndes."

[16] Ibid.

[17] Terry Richards, "Striking Langdale Workers Return Monday," *Valdosta Daily Times*, 10 November 1987.

By the end of the century, Langdale workers no longer relied on a union to represent them in dealing with the company. By vote of the membership, a request for decertification of the local union was approved. Although the union contested this action in court, as of early 2001 the decertification remained in effect. For most companies this would be like a dream come true, and the Langdales obviously were pleased with the development. Officials at the plant gave much of the credit for the decertification to Jim Langdale whose excellent rapport with the workers and skillful management of the sawmill operations gave the employees confidence that their concerns and interests would be suitably respected.[18]

Jim (James Harley) Langdale, son of Johnny and grandson of John W., rose to his position through what he jokingly called the FTP, which stood for "Family Training Program." Both he and his elder brother, Wesley (John Wesley Langdale III), graduated from their dad's special version of the FTP. Johnny Langdale put his sons to work with non-family employers at twelve or thirteen years of age. He wanted them to have the experience of working for someone other than family. As young boys they had electrical, plumbing, and farming jobs. Later, during high school and college, they went to work part-time for the Langdale Company, each in an area suitable to his personality. Wesley liked working in the forest, so he apprenticed under the direction of registered forester, Jim Barrett, and others. Wesley worked as a locator and marker of lines, assistant surveyor, marker of trees to be cut, fire-fighter, tractor operator, and basically anything related to land management. According to Wesley and Jim, their father saw to it as best he could that they were treated like other employees, without favoritism.[19]

Jim Harley got his first job with the Langdale Company one summer during high school. He and two cousins, Joe and John Langdale, sons of John J., Jr., worked for Jim Fielding of the forestry department painting land lines and eradicating kudzu with chemicals. "The second time I worked for the company," Jim remembered, "was after my freshman year of college, I did a summer job again at Langboard in Quitman, I worked on the utility crew, clean up, sweeping, shoveling. I did that for about 2 months and then they put me on shift and I worked as shift utility which was kind of the bottom shift job, cleaning up, running a bobcat and picking up logs, just wherever they needed me.[20]

In Jim's freshman year, he attended Abraham Baldwin Agricultural College in Tifton and took some courses at south Georgia College in Douglas. After the summer job with Langboard, he moved to Alabama and worked on a ranch (owned

[18] Hickman, JDH Interview 01.
[19] Langdale, JWL Interview 14.
[20] Langdale, JHL Interview 01.

by the family of a friend he met at ABAC) for more than a year while taking night courses at Auburn University at Montgomery.

"Then," he said,

> I moved back here and went back to work with the company—that was January of '91 or '92. When I came back here, I started working the night shift at the sawmill. Basically, they wanted me to learn the whole process of the mill operations. They started me on a shovel. It wasn't long.... They were pretty sure I learned how to use a shovel over at Langboard, so they changed to having me run every piece of equipment in the mill—the debarker—basically do all the jobs in the mill. Then they tried to train me how to work people in the mill. I was going to VSU at the time in the daytime and working at night. I worked the night shift for 8-9 months. When I left the sawmill I went to the lumber sorter. Then I went to the dry kilns and learned how to dry lumber, then to the planer mill to plane lumber.[21]

Jim Harley enjoyed working with machines and showed aptitude for dealing with people. As he worked in each position involved in lumber manufacturing, he did so under the same circumstances as anyone else. This is reminiscent of the training that Judge Harley put his sons through in the turpentine woods seven decades earlier. It is the same pattern employed by John Wesley Langdale with his sons near Council, Georgia, at the end of the nineteenth century.

While going through the "Family Training Program," Jim became well acquainted with the workers and they with him. Other than his personal qualities and evident dedication to his responsibilities, this seems to be the source of his unusually good rapport with the workers. Although Jim was still a young man, longtime executives of the company commented that Langdale lumber manufacturing had never been managed better, and one declared the company's entire management team to be the best it had ever been.[22] Harley, Jr., still very much involved in the business in October 2000 at eighty-six years of age, expressed his delight at the performance of Jim and his brother, Wesley. Both, he said, had exceeded his expectations as managers.[23]

Jim Harley's sawmill went through a major upgrade in 1998, in keeping with the Langdale policy of continual modernization. Actually, this was more than an upgrade; they installed a completely new mill at a cost of about $27 million. Among other advanced features, the new mill had the capability of sawing lumber from crooked logs. Its saws could track a log's curve and consequently get more

---

[21] Ibid.

[22] Hickman, JDH Interview 01.

[23] Harley Langdale, Jr., interview by author, audio tape, 19 October 2000, The Langdale Company, Valdosta GA, Harley Langdale, Jr., Papers, Valdosta GA.

lumber and correspondingly less lower-valued byproduct from the crooked log. Considering that many logs do have some curvature, this innovation was one more way to enhance profit and stay competitive with other producers, especially the Canadians, who still posed the greatest challenge.

While Jim Harley supervised lumber manufacturing in October 2000, his brother, Wesley, managed the Langdale land. Wesley described his job modestly as a middle management position. Compared to his brother, Wesley had relatively few people reporting directly to him in the Woodlands Division, but he had very large responsibilities. Fortunately, said Wesley, he could depend on excellent people to help him do his job, including some who had assisted in his training.[24]

About twenty employees, most with associates degrees in forestry and one with a four-year degree, worked with Wesley in taking care of the Langdale land, which totaled about 228,000 acres in October 2000. In general, these employees had been with the company for several years and had gained much of their education on the job. They surveyed, painted land lines, marked boundaries, took care of forest roads, and maintained data in the Langdale GIS system, which referenced all their land-related activities. They supervised tree harvesting and site preparation, devised and kept up with management plans, decided which species of trees should be planted on which sites, negotiated the work of contractors, and oversaw hunting and fishing clubs leasing their land. Land trades and purchases also fell under Wesley's jurisdiction, as did relations with neighboring landowners. Wesley and his Woodlands Division managed prescribed burns and, when necessary, fought wildfires in cooperation with government fire fighters. Anything related to fire they coordinated with government agencies in Florida or Georgia, as appropriate.

Wesley regarded the Langdale fire-fighting capability as among the best. The men were well trained, he said, and well equipped. Each had a D-6 crawler tractor with a large V-blade on the front and a four-disk plow on the back for creating firebreaks. Each bulldozer and its equipment rode to a fire site on its own low-boy semi-trailer. Sometimes when there was high risk of fire an operator took the entire rig home with him at night to be able more quickly to respond to the outbreak of fire, should it occur.

Upon arrival at a fire site, before unloading his equipment the operator received directions from the appropriate area supervisor, five of whom existed with authority over the five geographical areas into which all Langdale land was divided for administration. While giving direction to the bulldozer operator/fire-fighter, the area supervisor coordinated with the state fire tower and fire station. The area supervisor also reported to the general supervisor, normally Hal Rowe, who was in charge of fire operations for the Langdale Company.

---

[24] Langdale, JWL Interview 14.

In summertime, especially, the men patrolled at night on the lookout for fire. During times of lightning activity in daylight, too, patrolling became important because the forestry commission's lookout towers then had to be evacuated for safety. Certain areas, such as the flatlands of Echols and Clinch Counties, required more patrolling than others. Often members of hunting and fishing clubs using Langdale land also patrolled for fires on their own initiative, said Wesley. Such help in spotting fires was one of the advantages to the company in leasing to these clubs.

Wesley Langdale's Woodlands Division had among its many responsibilities the supervision of timber harvesting on their land. In this activity as in others technology had changed dramatically since the 1950s. Chain saws now came into play only sometimes for trimming branches. Trees were typically cut down by mammoth machines called "feller bunchers," one type of which (called the shear type) could cut off a tree as large as twenty-six inches in diameter with a single hydraulic squeeze. A second version of the machine, which Langdale executives preferred over the shear type, used a circular saw as the cutting mechanism. Operators of these and other tree-harvesting equipments sat in air-conditioned cabs and seldom set foot on the ground. Machines loaded the machine-cut and machine-trimmed trees onto semi-trailer trucks for the trip to the Langdale mills. There Jim Harley and his crew, with their new crooked-log-sawing mill efficiently turned the produce of the forest into lumber for someone's new house. Of course if these logs were to be used as poles, not lumber, they went to the pole mill.

Installation of the new sawmill took place at the same time as the company's major investment in an MDF plant located in Willacoochee, Georgia. These large simultaneous expenditures, commented Johnny Langdale, probably caused him to lose a few hairs, but everything turned out well.[25]

MDF, medium-density fiberboard, is similar to OSB, (oriented stranded board) which the Langdales began manufacturing in Quitman, Georgia, in 1988. The OSB plant used soft hardwoods as its raw material and produced 4' by 8' sheets of material typically employed for roofing and floor underlayment. After some years of successful operation, the plant expanded its product line to include 3/4" tongue-and-groove sheets, which proved very popular with builders. John Robinson, general manager of the Langboard plants in Quitman and Willacoochee, commented that his own house had this tongue-and-groove material, which he, of course, strongly endorsed.[26]

John Robinson came to work for the Langdales in 1988 from Eufaula, Alabama. There he had started at the bottom, sanding floors, and worked his way to the top of management in an MDF plant. As a manager and as a person he

[25] Ibid.

[26] John E. Robinson, interview by author, audio tape, 17 October 2000, Langboard (OSB) Plant, Quitman GA, Harley Langdale, Jr., Papers, Valdosta GA.

received high praise from his fellow executives at the Langdale Company. They admired his technical expertise, his skill at managing people, and his business acumen. Under his direction the OSB and MDF plants had exceeded company expectations.

Asked to name his greatest source of pride about these incredibly advanced and automated plants that could be run with a crew of nine or ten workers, John replied unhesitatingly, "the people."[27] This was the standard response from all Langdale executives. Notwithstanding their great emphasis on constantly modernizing technology, they consistently credited the quality of employees with determining the success of the company. And to a man, they praised their employees as conscientious workers dedicated to doing the best job they could in their particular areas and constantly looking for ways to improve performance of their assigned tasks.[28]

The basic task of the Langdale MDF plant at Willacoochee was to transform southern yellow pine chips identical to those used in paper mills into a building material suitable for use in furniture, interior molding, plaque-making, and such. Although the raw material for MDF—pine instead of hardwood—and the final product differed from those of the Quitman OSB operation, the process was similar. Tiny pieces of wood (ground-up particles in the case of MDF) were glued together and shaped into useful products for which there was a market. The glue, also differed in the two plants, being of an exterior type in Quitman and an interior type in Willacoochee. Consequently, OSB products could be used outdoors (though not designed for permanent exposure to water), and MDF material had to be used indoors.[29]

The push to go into MDF manufacturing came principally from John Robinson and company president Johnny Langdale. They and other executives had been studying the pros and cons of doing this when they saw an opportunity to acquire an existing plant in New Mexico at a bargain price and move it to Georgia. This twenty-year-old plant, having reportedly run into problems securing raw materials and dependable labor, had been shut down by its owners. Generally aware of the situation from reports in trade publications, Langdale representatives inquired and eventually made an offer, which was accepted.

The Langdale Company arranged to have the manufacturing equipment and buildings disassembled piece-by-piece, with each item carefully marked, transported to Willacoochee, Georgia, and reassembled. The same company dismantled the plant in Las Vegas, New Mexico, and put it back together at Willacoochee. Some idea of the size of this undertaking may be gained from the fact that it took 400 semi-trailer trucks to carry all the pieces. The Langdale Company had some of the

---

[27] Ibid.

[28] Hickman, JDH Interview 01.

[29] Robinson, JER Interview 01.

equipment refurbished and some replaced with state-of-the-art machines. They also added some new capabilities. When production began in Willacoochee, the Langdale MDF facility met the standards of a new plant, but it had been acquired at half the usual cost of a new factory. Visitors to Willacoochee who had formerly toured the plant at Las Vegas could scarcely recognize it as the same facility, it was so much improved.

Within a year after start-up the plant reached full production, a rare achievement in the industry. Part of the explanation was that John Robinson hired several experienced MDF managers that he knew in Alabama to work and train additional people from the Willacoochee area. The Alabamians still working there in October 2000 made up about half the management group. The plant employed about 140 people, total.

One of the advantages of MDF is that it is more flexible than OSB in that it can be used in more ways. The market for MDF, therefore, is capable of greater expansion. As of October 2000, plans were under way to add a satellite plant at Willacoochee to manufacture interior molding for the housing market. Production started in 2001.[30] Plans for expansion in other areas were in progress, too, as the Langdale Company moved vigorously to develop the company's potential in the twenty-first century.

Although the Langdale story does not end, and much more could be written, this account must be brought to a close. From what has been related in this chapter it is quite clear that the transition process that Harley, Jr. initiated in the early 1990s succeeded. He installed a competent new generation of Langdales to lead the Langdale Company into the future. For this he could justifiably take comfort and pride.

The Langdale story as told in these pages began with Josiah Langdale a farmer of Yorkshire, England. Josiah became a Quaker, undertook missionary journeys, and married Margaret Burton. They had two children. Their daughter, Mary, became Mrs. Samuel Coates of Philadelphia, and their son, John, married Sarah Hudson of the same city. All of these and their children were Quakers. Samuel Coates was a merchant; John Langdale was a tanner, as was his father-in-law, William Hudson, Jr.

John and Sarah Hudson Langdale had eight children to live beyond childhood, four of each sex. Their eldest son, Josiah, married out of unity with the Society of Friends and was disowned by the Philadelphia Monthly Meeting in 1764. He was by trade a "house carpenter," according to Quaker records. Shortly before the start of the Revolutionary War a Josiah Langdale, described in a land deed as a "house carpenter" was living in Colleton District, South Carolina. This Josiah, almost

---

[30] Ibid.

certainly the son of John Langdale of Philadelphia, is known to be the ancestor of the Colleton County, South Carolina, and south Georgia Langdales.

A grandson of Josiah Langdale of Colleton, John Robert Langdale, born in 1815, migrated with other Colleton Countians to south Georgia in the 1830s. He and his wife, Harriet Griffin, had a number of children, the eldest of whom was Noah. John Robert and Noah both died in Confederate service, leaving widows and children. A child of Noah and Elizabeth Burnett Langdale, John Wesley Langdale, established his home close to the later town of Council very near the place where the Suwannee River flowed out of the Okefenokee swamp. John Wesley started out poor but, by the standards of the day, died rich in 1911. His sons later incorporated his estate as the J. W. Langdale Company, and eldest son John J. Langdale managed the estate until his death. Subsequently, John J. Langdale, Jr. managed it.

John Wesley's youngest son, who came eventually to be known as Judge Harley Langdale, established in 1922 a separate turpentine business that was incorporated after World War II as the Langdale Company. In the 1990s Judge's sons, who already held part of the stock in the J. W. Langdale Company (inherited from Judge Harley), purchased all of the remaining stock from the other heirs. Consequently, the owners of the Langdale Company now held all the property that once belonged to John Wesley Langdale of Council, plus much more.

If John Wesley Langdale, Okefenokee and Suwannee woodsman, alligator hunter, turpentiner, shingle-maker, crosstie maker, and hog-caller extraordinaire could see the Langdale Company of today, he would certainly be amazed. He would be pleased, too, no doubt, to see what great things his sons and grandsons accomplished in business and in their communities. Certainly he would be touched to view his portrait in the lobby of the Langdale Company's corporate office and to know that his descendants look to him as the founder of this extraordinary enterprise.

And what about old Josiah Langdale who grew up driving a horse-drawn plow in Yorkshire, became a Quaker minister, and opted for life in the New World in 1723? What might he think? Probably he would feel a tinge of sadness to see that these descendants had wandered from the Quaker path to join such groups as the Primitive Baptists, Southern Baptists, and Methodists. Yet he, too, would be proud to see that a work ethic quite acceptable to Quaker businessmen of his day still prevailed among those bearing his name, and he would derive comfort from that. So might his descendants, and so might we all.

Appendix A

Retirees And Employees Of The Langdale Company And Affiliated Companies
August 31, 2000

The Langdale Company & Affiliates

With Date of Entity Inception/Affiliation and Identity Code

Company, Date of Origin, & Manager	Identity Code
The Langdale Company, 1894 *Harley Langdale, Jr., Chairman* *John W "Johnny" Langdale, Jr., President*	TLC
The Langdale Company - Woodlands, 1894 *John W "Wesley" Langdale, III, Manager*	LCW
The Langdale Company – Farms, 1894 *Wayne Warren, Manager*	LCF
Langdale Forest Products Co – 1944 *James H. "Jim" Langdale, General Manager* *Hugh Kicklighter, Blackshear Plant Manager* *Jim Culpepper , Chauncey Plant Manager* *Steve Borris, Sweetwater Plant Manager*	LFP
Southern Builders Supply Company – 1945 *Thomas C. Anderson, Manager*	SBS

Langdale Fuel Company – 1962   LFU
Gerald Ryan, Manager

Comfort Inn – 1963   INN
Wayne Ross, Manager

Langdale Ford – 1965   LFD
Steve Everett, Manager:

Industrial Saw Works, Inc. – 1973   ISW
Charles Cowart, Manager

Southern Reman, Inc. – 1983   SRE
Ben Hightower, Manager

Greenleaf Wood Products, Inc. – 1985   GWP
David Christian, Manager

Langdale Industries, Inc. – 1986   LIN
John W "Johnny" Langdale, Jr., President

Southland Forest Products, Inc. – 1987   SFP
Gwinnette Aldridge, Manager

Langboard, Inc. (OSB) – 1988   LBD
John E. Robinson, General Manager
Chris Reid, Plant Manager

Langdale International Trading Corp. – 1988   LIT
Bryan Harvey, Manager

Commercial Banking Company – 1995   CBC
Stanley Fillion, President

Langdale Auto Mall – 1996   LAM
Robert "Bob" Larramore, Sr., Manager

Langboard, Inc. (MDF) – 1998   MDF
John E. Robinson, General Manager
Mike Adams, Plant Manager

Langdale Chevrolet/Pontiac/Oldsmobile – 1999   LCH
Jeff Thorne, Manager

TLC Benefit Solutions – 2000   LBS
Barbara Mulligan, Manager

****

Judge, Harley, Jr., John W., and Billy in the 1950s. A typical morning
meeting in Judge's office, with clockwise seating, according to seniority.
TLC.

Langdale Family Management Personnel

J. W. Langdale	Founder	1894-1911
Harley Langdale Sr	Founder	1912-1972
Harley Langdale, Jr	Chairman of Board	1926-present
John W. Langdale	Ex-President/Board Mbr.	1945-1998
Johnny Langdale	TLC/LI President	1974-present
Wesley Langdale	Manager-TLC Woodlands	1987-present
Jim Langdale	General Mgr. LFP	1990-present
W. P. (Billy) Langdale	Board Member	1945-present
Bob Langdale	Environmental Engineer	1971-present
Bill Langdale	Corporate Attorney	1972-present

Harley, Jr. congratulates John W. upon 50 years service. TLC.

Long Term Employees

The Langdale Company

Harold Bennett	First Sales Manager	47-78
Alec Skoropat	General Manager	48-83
L.V. (Lewis) Richardson, Sr.	Lumber Mills Manager	58-69
L.V. (Lewis) Richardson, Jr.	Lumber Mills Manager	58-83
Jim Hanahan	Gen. Mgr-WPD & Lumber Div.	45-73
T.E. (Buck) Connell	Forest Mgt/Surveying/Procur	44-82
J.S. Cross	Forest Mgt/Procurement	not known
Rex Nance	Forest Mgt/Procurement	not known
Alan Neese	Forest Mgt/Procurement	not known
Fred Blanton, Sr.	Garage Manager	47-85
Frank Eye	Asst Garage Manager	74-85
Raymond (Bill) Lee	WPD Assistant Manager	52-84
Clyde Wilson	Boiler Supervisor	52-85
Bill Herman	Lumber Sales Manager	58-89
Harris Mathis	Customer Service Manager	65-84
Jean Johnson	Administration	71-94
Evelyn Timmons	Administration	47-73
Nona Clayton	Administration	60-89
Leslie Robinson	Pole Mill Supervisor	59-96
Lawrence Zeigler	Forest Lease & Land Manager	56-92
Bob Bass	Pilot/Purchasing	68-91

Langdale Forest Products

Tom Stewart	VP-WPD Sales-GA	51-87
Henry Parrish	VP-WPD Sales-Fla	56-89
Auston Hancock	Wood Preserving Manager	55-95
Aubrey Saunders	Quality Control Manager	54-90
Paul Robbins	Sweetwater Production Mgr	61-98
Junior Ray	Maintenance Superintendent	56-94
Winston Donahue	Treating Supervisor	66-97
James Beauford	Sorter/Stacker Supervisor	63-97
Glen McGraw	Trucking Supervisor	55-94
Lawrence Haire	Lumber Grader	60-92
Gwen Stephens	Customer Service Rep	73-99
Buddy Hughes	Maintenance Supervisor	61-94
Paul Robbins	Sweetwater Prod. Mgr	61-98
Charles Wetherington	Pole Procurement Manager	49-98
Danny Castleberry	Sawmill Superintendent	73-96

Langdale Industries

Jim Respess	LI President	70-92
Wesley Street	LI General Manager	77-00

Langdale Farms

W.C. (Son) Hughes	farmer
Ellis Black	farmer
John C. Farmer	farmer
C.J. Junior Farmer	farmer
Jose Rodriquez	farmer
Willie Lightsey	farmer
Brogdon Family	farmer
Denver Roberts	farmer
Grays	farmer
Wallace Rhyms	farmer
Mike Royal	farmer
B.A. Warren & family	farmer

Naval Stores Division

J. G. Joiner	Turp. Still Manager
Walter Bennett	Turp. Operator & Partner
Jim & Jeff Bennett	Turp. Operator & Partner
Al Grant	Turp. Operator & Partner
K.C. Wilkerson	Turp. Operator & Partner
Joe Wetherington	Turp. Operator & Partner
Troy Dukes	Turp. Operator & Partner
Chester Cameron	Bookkeeper & Payroll
John Burnett	Turpentine Operator
Harry Burnett	Turpentine Operator
James Burnett	Turpentine Operator
W. W. Turner	Turp. Operator & Partner
D.M. Lassiter	Turp. Partner/Manager
Ike Langdale	Turpentine Operator
Frank Henderson	Turpentine Operator
Will Carter	Turpentine Operator
Fred Carter	Turpentine Operator
J.P. McDonald	Turpentine Operator
Will Morris	Turp. Still Employee

Back Row, L to R: J.G. Joiner, Fred Blanton, Alex Simmons, David Hart, Bishop Vinson, Luther Blue, John Lewis, Jim Jackson, Marion Brown, Tom Perry, Tom Henderson.
Second Row, L to R: Auston Hancock, Tom Stewart, J.F. Hanahan, Evelyn Timmons, C.M. Cameron.
Front Row, L to R: Horace Kier, M.C. Gordon, Julius Sharp, Rhodel Lewis.

Employees (Group 1) with 10+ years service in 1969. TLC.

Back Row, L to R: T.E. Connell, Troy Watson, Luther Neloms, James English, W.P. Langdale, Lewis Richardson, J.C. McDonald, J.H. Conner, Lawrence Ziegler, Junior Ray, Joe Henry, W.C. Taylor, Tommie Crews, Leon Tucker, R.L. Moore, T.J. Jones. Second Row, L to R: A.W. Skoropat, H.M. Bennett, Johnnie Loeb, W.D. Anderson, Harvey Shipman. Front Row, L to R: Gene Shuster, Johnny Wheeler, D.H. Jones, Edgar Rykard, W.H. Owens.

Employees (Group 2) with 10+ years service in 1969. TLC.

Back Row, L to R: Wallace Williams, Willie Lee McMillian, Lonnie Phillips, Artis Kirkland, William Moore, T.L. Atkinson, Lonnie Mitchell, Marvin Bennett, Charles Wetherington, Clyde Wilson, R.E. Lee, Harris Dees, Ike Langdale, Clarence Burgman. Second Row, L to R: J.W. Langdale, H. Langdale Sr., Delores Parish, Geraldine Clifton, Rhunelle Price. Front Row, L to R: Albert Lee Jones, Monroe Warren, Lee Russell Newsom, Willie Shelton, Verney Burgman.

Employees (Group 3) with 10+ years service in 1969. TLC.

Current Employees, August 31, 2000

Grouped by Time of Service
Showing Company Association for Each Employee

MORE THAN SEVENTY-FOUR YEARS
Harley Langdale, Jr TLC

MORE THAN FIFTY-FIVE YEARS
William P. Langdale TLC

MORE THAN FORTY-FIVE YEARS
David Hart LFP
Jack O. Howell LFD
Albert L. Jones LFP
Delores M. Parrish TLC

MORE THAN FORTY YEARS
Geraldine M. Clifton LFP
Samuel Savage LFP

MORE THAN THIRTY-FIVE YEARS
Harry Howell LFP
Russell B. McDonald LFP
J. Mack Peace LFP
B. L. Smith LFD
G. Franklin Staten LFP
Robert L. Strickland LFP
Curtis Wetherington LFD
Warren Wilkerson LFP

MORE THAN THIRTY YEARS
Clarence Burgman, Jr. LFP
Jim S. Fielding LCW
Mitchell Griffin, Jr. LFP
Nathaniel Jones LFP
Benjamin Matchett, Jr. LFP
Joe Mathis LFD
M. D. Meeks LFD
Luther Morrison LFP
Henderson Patrick LFP
Johnny B. Patrick LFP

Roosevelt L. Robertson LFP
Albert L. Rowan LFP
Thomas C. Smith LCW
Arnold E. Stewart LFP
Curtis L. Williams LFP
Mosel Williams LFP
J. H. Wright LFP

MORE THAN TWENTY-FIVE YEARS
Willie J. Alderman LFP
Sharon S. Arnold LFP
Gilbert R. Boxx LFP
William E. Browning LFP
James C. Culpepper LFP
Harvey Lee Daniels LFD
Franklin J. Eldridge LFD
John W. Langdale, Jr LIN
Robert H. Langdale LIN
Faye Long TLC
George E. Marsh LFP
Charles Millhorn LFP
Edward C. Minton LIN
James C. Moore LFP
Freemon Ponder LFP
Lewis M. Reed LFP
Hardy B. Stanley LFP
Steve C. Worthy LFP

MORE THAN TWENTY YEARS
Hayward Bennett LFU
Ervin J. Bighams LFP
Ralph Bryant LFP
Walter E. Butler LFP
David R Christian GWP
Ronald P. Craig LFP
Frank Croft LFP
Randy D. Folsom LFP

Janice Hall LFP
Thomas A. Hickey ISW
Johnny Holmes LFP
Van L. Hughes LCW
Ralph A. Lawrie LFP
Ronald V. Lightsey LFP
Dennis L. Lunsford LFP
Robert Mannings LFP
Charles McDougal LFD
Charles Miller LFP
Nathaniel. Miller LFP
Lucius W. Moore LIN
Roger V. Parrish SFP
William. Pittman LFP
Ali Rastegar LFP
Raymond O. Roberts LFP
Freddie N. Robinson LFP
Leroy Robinson LFP
Rose L. Rocheleau INN
Richard W. Sanders LFP
Herbert D. Smith LFP
Jerome Smith LFP
Thomas H. Strom LFD
Roosevelt Thomas, Jr. LFP
Charles L. Waldron LFP
Frank E. Watson LFP
Mizell L. Williams LFP
Walter Wilson LFP
Jerry B. Wood LFP
Maryann I. Zeigler SFP

MORE THAN FIFTEEN YEARS
Charles Allen LFP
Kenneth J. Allred SRE
Edward D. Arnold LFP
Craig A. Bennett LFP
Ronald A. Best LFP
Leland F. Bowden LFP
Randy Boyd LFP
James W. Boyle LFP
Julius V. Bridges LFP
Ricky J. Brown LFP
Carol Buescher LFD

G. Harris Ertzberger LFP
Teresa L. Etheridge LFP
David Eudy ISW
W. Greg Fielding LCW
Ronald Foster LFP
Larry K. Fudge LIN
William L. Gay LFP
Carroll J. Griffin LIN
Johnny E. Groover LFP
James D. Hickman LFP
Pete C. Joiner LFP
Robert L. Kier LFP
William F. Lee LFP
Gregory G. Martin LFP
Gareth G. Mathis LFP
Jerome C. Mope LFP
Stanley O. Nelson LFP
Robert L. Parrish LFP
Marc Perdue ISW
Sue A. Pike ISW
Karen M. Rawlins LFP
Torrie Renew LFP
Charles M. Rigoni LBD
Roger Riley LFP
Christopher P. Robbins LFP
Carl Russell LFP
Jimmie L. Stroud LFP
Fred Thomas LFP
D. Kevin Walker LFP
Wayne Warren LCF
Zollie Wolf, Jr. LFP
Cletus F. Woods LFP
Steve E. Zeigler INN

MORE THAN TEN YEARS
Joe C. Alderman LBD
Thomas C. Anderson SBS
Luther W. Armstrong, Jr. LBD
Leroy Arrington LFP
Gary T. Atkinson LBD
James T. Barrett LCW
J. Levi Beal LFP
Douglas L. Bearrentine LFP

Jerry Belcher LBD

Janet B. Belflower LIN

Ronald Bennett LFP

William L. Berry LFP

Donald F. Bonner, Jr. SBS

Dessie Brown LBD

E. Riley Brown, Jr. LFP

Horace Brown LBD

Kenneth D. Buchanan ISW

Joseph L. Burgman LFP

Donna C. Cain LIN

Robert J. Carroll LFP

Danny Carter SRE

Louis J. Cassotta LIN

Sidney Cherry LBD

Cary L. Combess LCW

Ronald E. Coppage, Sr. LFD

Bobby D. Courtney LBD

Henry Craven LBD

Margie Daniels CBC

Douglas J. Daugherty LFP

Len Davis LFP

Joseph Edmonson LFP

Solomon Edwards LBD

Julian Fifie LFP

Jerald W. Fisher MDF

Devan R. Fleming LFP

Richard Flint, Jr. LFP

Tobey A. Garrison LBD

Tommy Gibbs LBD

Joel Q. Godwin LFP

Randall D. Green LFP

Willie Griffin LBD

James M. Hall LBD

Thomas H. Hardeman LFP

Fomby Hardin, Jr. SBS

Nancy F. Hart SBS

Bryan L. Harvey LIT

Paul B. Hatcher, Jr. LFD

Brenda S. Highsmith LBD

Mark Holton LFP

Jack F. Howell LFD

Michael J. Hughes, Sr. LBD

James C. Hurley MDF

Anthony J. Jackson LBD

Joe L. Johns, Jr. LFD

Derrick L. Jones LFP

Ernest Jones LFP

Larry D. Jones LFP

Jack Kent LBD

Donald H. Kicklighter, Jr. LFP

Ernest J. King, Jr. LFP

Charles E. Lambert, Jr. LBD

George Lamons LBD

James H. Langdale ISW

John W. Langdale III LCW

Scott Lehman LBD

John S. Lindsey LFP

Farris R. Lowery LFP

Joshua Mabry, Jr. LBD

Sherman May LFP

Elijah H. McCall LBD

Steven G. McCormick LFD

Kimball R. McCrary LBD

Walter T. McCullough LFP

Herman L. McDonald SFP

Mike Y. McDonald LBD

Ira J. Mobley LBD

Rufus Morrison LBD

Marilyn E. Netter LIN

Clarence J. Newell LBD

Shawn A. O'connor LBD

James O'Quinn LBD

Jerry L. Paige LBD

John F. Peak LBD

Robert L. Pickle II LFP

Chris W. Reid LBD

Lonnie Reynolds LBD

Mark F. Richardson LFP

Frank Robertson LFP

John E. Robinson LBD

Jessie L. Rose LBD

Michael L. Royals LCW

Abigail Rozar LFP

Ralph Russell LFP

James H. Seay LFP

Glenda E. Short SBS
Ronald H. Sims LFP
Joseph K. Singley LFP
John B. Smith LFP
Tracy D. Southerland LBD
James A. Spates LFP
Tommy Stalvey CBC
Freddie Stone LBD
Gary Summerlin LBD
M. Joyce Swaney LFP
Wendell O. Tabor LFP
Kenneth J. Taw LFP
Larry M. Thomas, Jr. LFP
Pearlie H. Tucker INN
Eldon J. Turner LBD
Gregory M. Turner SFP
Roy Verdell, Jr. LFP
Earl W. Wade ISW
Jimmy B. Walker LBD
Arvinnie R. White LFP
Alford C. Williams SBS
Ellington R. Williams LFP
Lemuel A. Williams LFP
Ralph L. Williams SBS
Richard B. Williams LFP
Steve Williams LBD
Mark H. Wilson LIN
U-Vill Woods LFP
Edward A. Wooldridge LBD

MORE THAN FIVE YEARS
Curtis M. Aikens LFP
L. Gwinnette Aldridge, Jr. SFP
Larry A. Allen, Jr. LFP
Darren N. Anderson LFP
Ricky J. Austin LBD
Cecil W. Ayers LFP
Steven E. Bailey ISW
William H. Berryhill SFP
Tracy E. Bever LBD
Dan M. Blanton LFD
Donald F. Bonner, Sr. SBS
Steven J. Borris LFP

Marvin Brantley SRE
Jessie D. Brooker LFP
Carolyn S. Brown LBD
Harry L. Brown LFP
Jeffrey L. Brown SRE
Steven Browning LFP
Lossie M. Burkes LFP
Melanie R. Callaghan LFP
Eric J. Carlton LBD
Melinda K. Carlton LFD
Donald R. Carter ISW
Richard W. Carter LFP
Bobby G. Chambless LFP
Rodney K. Childree SBS
Jerry Clanton LBD
R. Charles Cowart, Jr. ISW
Roy Cowart LFP
Erik M. Cox SBS
Denise Dickey CBC
Denise E. Dickey LIN
James E. Dixon LFP
Howard J. Dunaway LFP
Chad Eason LFP
Jerome. Edwards LFP
Ted C. Elliott LFD
Anthony W. Evans LFP
Stephen A. Everett LFD
John H. Fead LFP
Roger Foster LFP
Irene R. Fuller LFP
Robert Gardner LFP
William T. Gay LFP
Otis L. Gibson LFP
Willie J. Gilbert LBD
Darleen Gist INN
Ellis Griffin LFP
Lawrence M. Griffith LFP
Charlie C. Gulledge LFD
Ernest Wayne Hall LFD
Gary L. Hall LFD
Tammy L. Harrelson SBS
Raymond D. Hendley LFP
Becky Herndon CBC

Benjamin S. Hightower SRE
Mark C. Howell LFD
Jeffrey E. Hutchinson LFP
Elizabeth S. Isgro LFD
Curtis A. Jackson LFP
Dennis Y. Jacobs, Jr. LFD
Gregory L. James LBD
Nathaniel Johns LFP
Jack Jones LFP
Stephen E. Kautzman LFD
Richard G. Keen, Sr. LFD
Yvonne Kimmel CBC
Derrian W. King, Sr. LBD
Lindy A. Kinsey LBD
Archie C. Lewis LFP
M. Dale Long LFP
Helicia Lopshire LFD
Elizabeth B. Macarages LIN
Johnnie B. Marshall LFP
Patrick. McCarthy LFP
Ronnie McClain LBD
James C. McCray LFP
Malgrum D. Meeks TLC
Roger D. Meeks, Jr. SBS
Frances S. Moody LFP
Tracey Moore LBS
Barbara A. Mulligan LIN
Barbara A. Mulligan LBS
Theresa G Neely LBD
Weldon Q. Nelums LFD
Patrick Newell LBD
Willie F. Newsome LBD
Charles D. Noecker LFP
James T. Page LBD
Jeffrey Palmer LAM
Perry M. Paul LFP
Timothy A. Peacock LFD
Lewis Peak, Jr. LBD
Willie Peak LBD
Deborah C. Price LBD
Jean Register CBC
Robert D. Roberts LFP
Tommy B. Roberts LFP

Johnny E. Robinson LFP
D. T. Rogers, Jr. LFP
Timothy B. Rose LFP
C. Wayne Ross INN
Allen H. Rowe LFP
William H. Rowe LCW
Robert G. Royals LFP
Gerald R. Ryan LFU
Steven Sanford LFP
T. Jeff Shave SRE
Reginald L. Sims LFP
Robert E. Slaughter LBD
Wayne R. Smith ISW
William Smith LAM
Tya C. Stalvey LFP
John I. Starling LBD
Jennifer A. Strickland LFP
Alan C. Tanner LFP
Robert D. Tapley LFP
Jeff Thorne LCH
J. Don Touchton LFP
Auston J. Vanosdol LFP
James A. Wainwright LFP
Marion T. Walizer LFP
Deborah K. Wardwell SBS
Donald K. Warren LIN
Steve D. Watts, Jr. LIN
Avery D. Wells LFP
Timothy C. Wilburn LFP
Bobby J. Williams SBS
Harold Williams SBS
Ronald Williams LFP
Valerie Williams CBC
Christine C. Yeh INN

LESS THAN FIVE YEARS
Nicole L. Adair INN
Guy W. Adams LFP
Larry Adams LAM
Michael D. Adams MDF
Robert W. Adams MDF
Paula J. Adkins LFP
Amanda Aldridge CBC

Scott F. Aldridge LFD

Charles H. Alexander LFP

Robert D. Alexander LFP

Terence L. Alexander LFP

Joseph C. Alexander. LFP

James W. Allen SRE

Donna T. Anderson LFP

John J Anderson LCW

Kelly D. Andrews LFD

Vashon C. Arnold LFP

David A. Ashburn LFP

William D. Austin LFP

Billie R. Baker MDF

David D. Ballance MDF

James T. Barrett, Jr. LCW

David J. Barwick SBS

Danny L. Beard LFP

Sandra Christine Beard LCH

Cindy L. Becton LIN

Michael B. Beggs LBD

Troy Q. Bell LBD

Jerry L. Bennett LFP

Mitch R. Bennett MDF

V. Eric Bennett, Jr. MDF

Perry L. Blake LFP

Mike Blalock LCH

William T. Boatwright MDF

Barbara Boler LCW

Anthony L. Booth LFP

Arthur Bowens MDF

Robert N. Boyd LFP

J. Houston Bozeman LFP

Darius V. Bradford LBD

Dennis R. Bradford LFP

Diane D. Bradley LFU

Joseph J. Bradley LBD

John Brand LCH

Matthew Brand LCH

Randy L. Brantley SRE

Robert Brantley LFP

Marcus S. Brinson LFP

Charles E. Brooks, Jr. LBD

Christopher A. Brown LFP

Charles R. Browning LFD

Cedric Bryant LFP

Gregory P. Bryant LFP

Thomas A. Bryant LBD

Michael J. Buchanan LCW

Bobby G. Bunch LFP

Gwen C. Burch MDF

James F. Burch MDF

Joseph L. Bush LFP

Jeremy Scott Buster LFD

Michael C. Butler SBS

Gretchen L. Cain LIN

Michael L. Calbert LFP

George Calloway LAM

Lee J. Campbell MDF

James H. Cannady LFP

Michael J. Carnegie LFP

Chad Carpenter CBC

Tony J. Carroll MDF

Darlene F. Carrube INN

Amber Carter LFD

Brenda L. Carter INN

Allan Casey LCH

Sandy J. Cason LFP

Luis Castillo SRE

Mitchell L. Cave LFP

Jennifer B. Chaney GW

Thomas Edward Chapman LFD

L. Shelly Chauncey MDF

Kevin H. Chitty LFP

Steve Chitty III CBC

Gavin K. Christian SBS

Marty Christian, Sr. LBD

Walter T. Christian LFP

John J Christie LFP

Annette Clark CBC

James N. Cleary ISW

Stan D. Clement MDF

Stanley D. Clement MDF

Bobby Clements LFP

Eddie. Clements LFD

Hugh T. Clements, Jr. SBS

Willie H. Clemson MDF

Maria I. Clingan MDF
John A. Cloyd, Jr. LFP
Alan S. Colwell LFD
Larry Conger LAM
Bennie W. Connell, Jr. LBD
Carlton Connell, Jr. LAM
David Connell LAM
Jennifer Connelly CBC
Phillip E. Coody LFP
April Corbett CBC
Susan E. Corbitt SBS
Timothy J. Corbitt SRE
Anthony D. Courson MDF
William D. Courson MDF
John W Courtney LBD
Benjamin B. Cowart LFP
Iris Cowart CBC
Margaret Joann Cowart LFD
James E. Cowen LFD
Joanne M. Cox SBS
Robert D. Craig LFP
Jeff M. Cravey LFP
Jesse L. Creed LFP
John T. Crosby MDF
Lamar Curry LFP
James Redding Daniels LFD
Willie Daniels LAM
John Darsey II LAM
J. Tommy Davis LFP
James L. Davis LFP
John F. Davis MDF
Maggie Davis CBC
Robert L. Davis LFP
Tawana L. Davis INN
Alvin H. Dawson LFP
Crystal Gail Dean LFD
Michael E. Dean MDF
Jose A. Deanda SRE
Gerald L. Demps, Sr. LBD
Leroy Demps, Sr. LFP
Burt Denson LBD
Linda F. Denson INN
Christopher Digiammarino LBD

Lowell B. Dillon LFP
Calvin Donaldson LFP
Jimmy E. Donaldson LFP
Jeffrey S. Doug LFP
Nathan Del Douglas LCH
Dennis R. Drott MDF
Daniel E. Dubberly MDF
Herman Durrance LAM
William J. Dyer LFP
Luc Ebner INN
Shawn Edith LFP
Tonya R. Edmondson LFP
Robert M. Elder MDF
Marvin A. Eleazer LFD
Eddie L. Emanuel LFP
Anthony J. Ennis LBD
Jeremy Daniel Eppley LFD
Mariano A. Espino LFU
Benny G. Evans LFP
Stacy L. Evans LFP
Wallace Evans SRE
Michael L. Everett LFP
Albert Farmer, Jr. LAM
Timothy Fiffie LFP
Stanley Fillion CBC
Kenneth F. Fletcher LFP
Stephen C. Fletcher LFP
Kenneth A. Fleury LBD
Jennie M. Flucas LFP
David R. Fortune MDF
Harold K. Foster LFP
Bernard Fowler MDF
Charles R. Fox LFD
John M. Fox LBD
Christopher S. Foy ISW
Terry T. Frasier MDF
Thomas S. Frazier LBD
Victor L. Fulton LFP
Edith Gaddis LFP
Monty L. Gaddis MDF
George A. Gardin LFD
Glen R. Garrett MDF
Lea Gibbs CBC

Dennis R. Giddens MDF
J. Charlton Gillis MDF
N. Marshall Gillis MDF
W. Dougal Gillis MDF
Darron D. Gilyard LFP
Vickie Godwin CBC
Jeffery L. Golden LBD
Michael J. Golson LFP
Brenna A. Gomez LFP
Jose L. Gonzalez LFP
Lori Jo Gouge LFD
Jerome Graham LFP
Kenny A. Graham SBS
Caleb Grant LCW
R. Cliff Grant, Jr. LCW
John C. Grantham MDF
Timothy L. Gray MDF
Annette Green CBC
Charles D. Green MDF
George B. Griffin MDF
Stacey L. Griffin LFP
Brandy Griffis CBC
Kristopher T. Griffis LFP
Chris Griner CBC
William J. Griner LFP
Mark A. Hadley LBD
Dennis W. Hall LBD
Gary W. Hall MDF
Jesse Hall LFP
Reggie N. Hall LFP
Kathleen E. Hamill INN
James Hancock LCH
Dewey W. Hand SFP
Jimmy R Hand MDF
William R. Hansel LFD
G. Anthony Harper MDF
Steve A. Harper MDF
Matthew T. Harrell MDF
Wesley R. Harrell LFP
Wiley Grant Harrell LFD
Sherman E. Harris MDF
Bradley D. Hartline LFP
Margaret Ann Hasty LFD

James C. Hawkins LFP
Yolanda H. Hayes MDF
William W. Haynes LFD
Sam Hayre LCH
David A. Heard LFP
Greg M. Henderson LFD
David A. Herrin MDF
Shane Hersey MDF
Lowell B. Hicks LFP
Lance M. Hiers LFD
Harold J. Hill LFP
Robert R. Hines LFD
Darren C. Hingson SFP
Christopher R. Hodnett MDF
Wayne T. Horten LFP
Richard D. Hunnicutt SBS
James A. Hunt LFP
Amanda Hunter LCH
Robert C Hunter MDF
Oliver A Hursey MDF
Patrick Hurst LAM
Thomas K. Hutchinson LFP
Larry G. Inman LFP
Glen D. Isgro LFD
Charlene Jackson LCH
Charles M. Jackson LFP
Pamela D. Jackson LBD
Vivian I. Jackson LFD
Derobert V. James SBS
Willie H. James LCH
Alan E. Jay LFP
James R. Jenkins LBD
Johnny Jenkins MDF
Roderick D. Jenkins LBD
Tracy R. Jenkins INN
Ann M. Johnson LFP
Bobbie D. Johnson LFP
Derring D. Johnson MDF
Ishuimul B. Johnson LBD
James R. Johnson LFP
Jared Daniel Johnson LFD
J. Russell Joiner MDF
Allen A. Jones MDF

Cecil L. Jones LBD
Derrick M. Jones LFD
Janice M. Jones INN
Meredith Jones LAM
Robert L. Jones LFP
Nancy L. Joyner LBS
William Brice Kautzman LFD
Woody Blake Kautzman LFD
Jerry Kersey LFP
Tony C. Keuma SRE
Glen T. Kier LFP
John L. King LFP
Tony Kirk LCH
Erin Elizabeth Kuiper LFD
Earl C. Lacey, Jr. LBD
Thurston Lamb SRE
Tracy Lane CBC
Casey P. Langdale LFP
Matthew Langdale LFP
Robert Larimore, Sr. LAM
Barton Latner LAM
Earnie E. Lawrence LFP
Julian R. Lawson LFU
David A. Lay MDF
Lorrie M. Leavell LFP
David T. Lee LBD
James Joshua Lehman LFD
Sharon G. Leslein LFU
John Letourneau, Sr. LAM
Herman L. Lewis MDF
Chet L. Linder LFD
Randall G. Loffmin LFP
Greg A. Long LFP
Debbie Lott MDF
Ralph Lott MDF
Robert H. Lott, Jr. LFP
W. Chad Lott MDF
Kerry D. Loveday LFP
Ronald H. Lowery LFP
Georgia A. Lynch INN
Katherina Lynch INN
Kathy Maartense CBC
Elton H. Mack SBS

Dafford Madison SBS
Danna Mallard LCH
James C. Manac LFP
Anthony W. Mancil MDF
Thomas J. March LFP
Dennis L. Marchessault SBS
Allen Marshall LFP
Tommy C. Martin, Jr. LFP
Jeffrey W. Massey MDF
E. Eugene Mathis, Jr. MDF
Ronald Matthews MDF
Kim McCarra CBC
Edward E. McCloud LFP
Michael C. McCorvey MDF
Darrell B. McCrae SRE
Karl E. McCranie MDF
K. Don McDonald MDF
Michael S. McDonald MDF
Andray L. McDougal LFP
Roderick E. McDougle LFD
Shawn R. McEady SBS
Dutch E. McElvey LFP
Clifton S. McFadden LFP
Ronnie H. McGovern MDF
Marvin B. McIver MDF
Annessonya Mcleod INN
Jessie W. McMillan MDF
Jennifer McMillian CBC
E. L. Meeks MDF
E. Landon Meeks MDF
W. Stacey Meeks MDF
Sabrina Y. Middleton INN
William H. Milam LFP
Franz K. Miles LFP
Tammie L. Miley LBD
James Miller LAM
Jeffery E. Miller LBD
Timotheos S. Miller LFP
Trascia L. Miller. INN
Greg A. Mincey LFP
Michael L. Mincey LFP
Marie R. Mitchell INN
Wilbert Mobley LBD

Willie A. Mohead LFP

Martha Moore CBC

Plenn Moore MDF

Robert H. Moore MDF

Allen Morgan LFP

Kathie S. Morrell INN

James D. Morris MDF

Thomas D. Morris LFP

Thomas J. Morris MDF

Anthony M. Moseley MDF

Billy J. Moxley MDF

Courtney S. Moye LFP

G. Francis Mullis, Jr. MDF

Zack Mullis LCW

Phil G. Murray MDF

Clayton A. Musgrove SRE

Cynthia D. Musgrove LFD

Heaven Nealey LAM

Sean C. Nelson LFP

Bartley T. Neugent MDF

Henry Neugent MDF

Kevin B. Neugent MDF

Kenneth D. Nixon MDF

Jason G. Norman LFP

Robert Eugene Norris LFD

Derrick V. Northern LBD

Timothy Norwood LFP

Danny A. Nose LFP

Jessica A. Nugent MDF

Roger T. Nugent MDF

Donald W. O'quinn LFP

Michael O'Steen CBC

Jerome C. Owens LFP

Keisha Owens CBC

Angela Palmer LAM

Ronnie E. Pate MDF

Dan R. Paulk MDF

Rick D. Peach LFP

David H. Peavy LFP

Mary C. Peek LCW

Frank B. Pelz MDF

Walter Pettiford LFP

Kevin G. Piland LBD

Anthony G. Pitts LFP

Raymond A. Poe LFD

Laura Polite INN

Ernest F. Polk LCW

Todd D. Pollard LFD

Danny E. Pollock LFP

Weyman Porter LAM

Aaron J. Powell LBD

Jared Powell LCH

Adam P. Pozos LFP

Edward Presley LFP

Guy S. Pryor LFP

D. Keith Purvis MDF

Josh Purvis LCH

Timothy M. Putala MDF

Johnny D. Pye LFP

Stephon J. Raiford LBD

Hugo Hernando Ramos LFD

Jamie L. Randall LFP

Jennifer Rasalam CBC

Jonathan Ray SRE

Michael E. Raybon LFP

David L. Register GW

Wyman C. Register LFP

Ricardo M. Regueiro SRE

Grover L. Reid MDF

J. Ricky Rewis TLC

Ester A. Reynolds LBD

Tameica L. Reynolds INN

Jada G. Richardson LIT

Leana Ridlon CBC

Laura Lynne Riemann LFD

Lewis R. Riley LFP

William E. Ritter, Jr. MDF

Edward D. Roberson INN

Andrew Charles Roberts LCH

Edwin B. Robinson LFP

James B. Robinson LFP

James Eugene Robinson LFD

Mark E. Robinson LBD

Samantha Robinson LBD

Wilson. Robinson, Jr. LFP

Juan Robles-Vazquez SRE

Enos Rodriguez SRE
Damon C. Rogers SRE
Joshua S. Rose ISW
Amy Ross CBC
Anthony M. Ross MDF
Judith M. Ross INN
Jason D. Rothrock LFP
Randy Rowan MDF
John D. Rowe MDF
Jason E. Rubenbauer LFP
Kenneth Ruehle LFD
Kimberly Runyon LAM
Weldon Rush, Jr. MDF
Anthony Sanders LFP
Craig Sanders LCH
Dustin P. Sanders SBS
Jerry L. Sanders LFP
Bobette S. Sapp LBD
Donald W. Sapp LFP
Lynn M. Sapp SBS
Joy Scarbrough CBC
Joseph A. Scott LFP
Rudolph Searcy MDF
James B. Sears, Jr. MDF
Angela M. Seither LFP
Brett D. Seither LFP
William B. Selby LFP
Christopher R. Sellars ISW
Angela V. Sharp SBS
Edward Shepherd LFD
Timothy Shirah MDF
Janet M. Simmons LFP
Ricky D. Simmons LFP
Tommy Simmons LBD
Keith L. Sims LBD
Ronald E. Sirmans, Jr. LBD
Donnie E. Sloan LFP
David R. Smith MDF
James A. Smith LFP
James K. Smith MDF
James W. Smith LFP
Jeffery Allen Smith LFD
Jeffery W. Smith MDF

Joey D. Smith MDF
Jonathan Smith MDF
Jonathan K. Smith MDF
Judy A. Smith LFD
Robert Smith MDF
Roger L. Smith MDF
Scott A. Smith MDF
Terri Smith CBC
Timothy W. Smith MDF
Hubert Souter LCH
Johnny L. Spencer, Jr. LBD
Vickie S. Spencer INN
David William Stacey LFD
Matt Stanaland CBC
Meredith Stanaland CBC
Felton L. Statum LFP
Kevin L. Stephens LFP
Thomas B. Stevens MDF
M.Kevin Steverson MDF
Paul Stewart LFP
Rickey D. Stewart MDF
Veronica L. Stewart INN
Jesse L. Stone MDF
Jonathan C. Stone MDF
Michael R. Stone MDF
Phyllis A. Storey LFP
Tina D. Stormant LFP
Jack Strayhorn LCH
Joshua D. Strickland LFP
Louie Stripling LCH
Richard Dewayne Stripling LFD
William L. Strom ISW
Wayne H. Sullivan SRE
Linda Summer CBC
Shannon M. Summers ISW
Jonathan Allen Suschinski LFD
George H. Sutton, Jr. MDF
Johnny J. Sweat MDF
Candice L. Tanner MDF
Alex Tass LFP
Annette M. Tatum MDF
Daniel C. Taylor MDF
Anthony G. Tedder LFP

Rodney G. Tenery, Jr. LCW
Michael S. Thacker LFP
Anthony C. Thomas LBD
Cythia G. Thomas INN
Deon L. Thomas LFP
Jacqueline P. Thomas LBD
Lori Thomas CBC
Mattie L. Thomas INN
Rhodesia K. Thomas LBD
Daryl B. Thompson LBD
Frederick P. Tillman LFP
Arthur L. Timmons, Jr. LFP
Aundra. Townsend LFP
Elijah Joe Tucker, Sr. MDF
Sandra B. Tucker INN
Francis K. Tuten, Jr. LBD
Matthew J. Varnadore LFP
Marvin T. Varnedore II LFP
Amos D. Vaughn LFP
Joshua M. Veal LFP
James G. Viar LFP
Henry D. Vickers MDF
Levonne Vining MDF
Wayne C. Vogenitz LFP
Christy L. Wade LBS
Howard L. Walk ISW
Dexter B. Walker MDF
Jennifer N. Walker LFD
Alicia Warren LBD
Amanda Warren CBC
Bradley W. Warren LFP
Ronald W. Warren LCW
Andrea Washington LFP
David L. Washington LFP
Tiesha F. Washington SBS
Kerry M. Waters SBS
Stacy L. Weaver MDF
Holly Webrand CBC
Calvin E. West LFP
Kathy Wetherington CBC
Jerry D. Wheeler INN
Jerry L. White MDF

Kendrick D. White LBD
Steve C. White MDF
Calvin V. Whited LFP
Felton C. Whitehead INN
Theresa G. Whitley LIN
Leisa K. Wickersham SRE
Freddie W. Wilkerson, Jr. MDF
Cary Williams CBC
Cedric L. Williams LFP
Dianne A. Williams LIN
Evelyn Williams CBC
James D. Williams LFP
Jennifer L. Williams LFP
Kareem J. Williams LBD
Lula A. Williams INN
Regina J. Williams MDF
Terence B. Williams LFP
Vince E. Williams LBD
Willie L. Williams LFP
Charles W. Williamson ISW
Stanley Willis LCH
Carey C. Wilson MDF
David Brian Wilson LFD
Felton Wilson MDF
John D. Wilson IV LFP
Robert F. Wilson LFP
Tara M. Wilson INN
Tony Wiseman LFP
Willie C. Wolfe LFP
Kay Wood LAM
Glen J. Worth MDF
Hertis L. Wright MDF
Fred L. Yarborough LFP
Billy R. Yawn MDF
Thomas B. Yawn LCW
Clifford. Yokley LFP
Craig A. Young MDF
Jason L. Young MDF
Peter I. Young INN
Todd Young LAM
John White Yow LFD

Appendix B
Family Connections

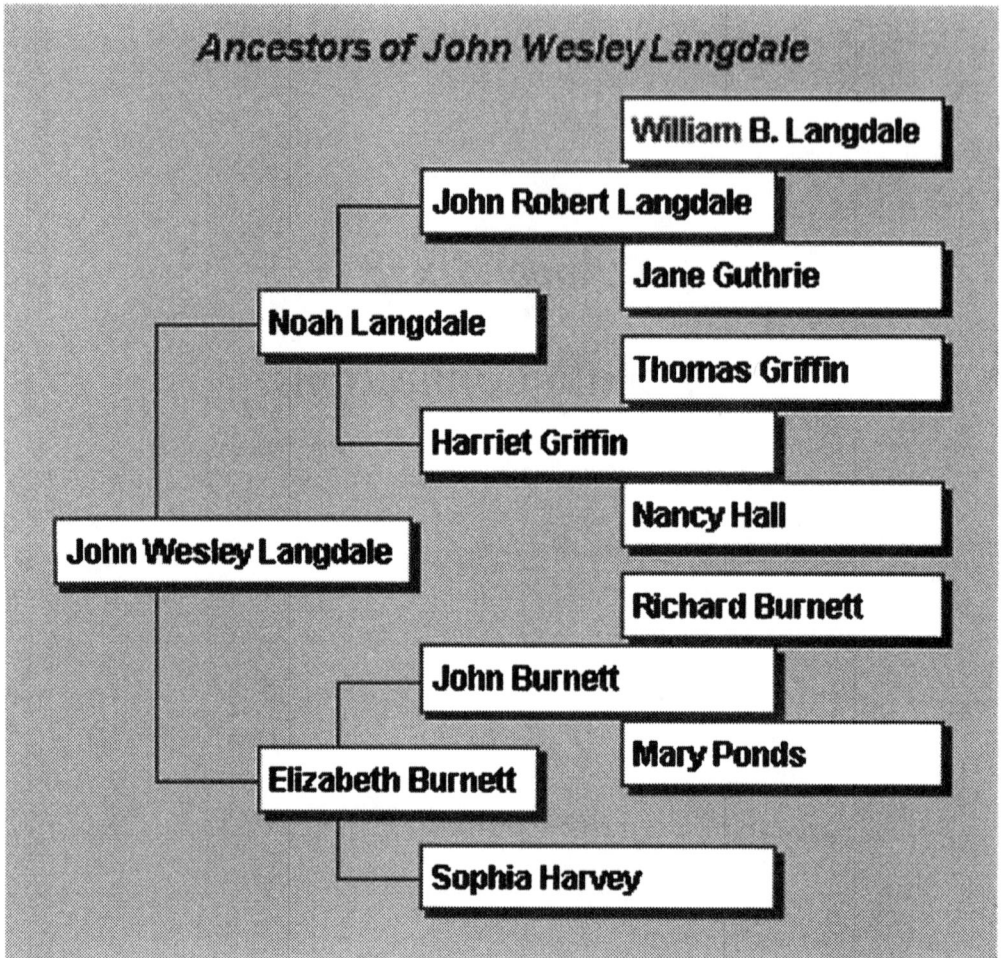

Ancestors of John Wesley Langdale

Ancestors of Harriet GRIFFIN

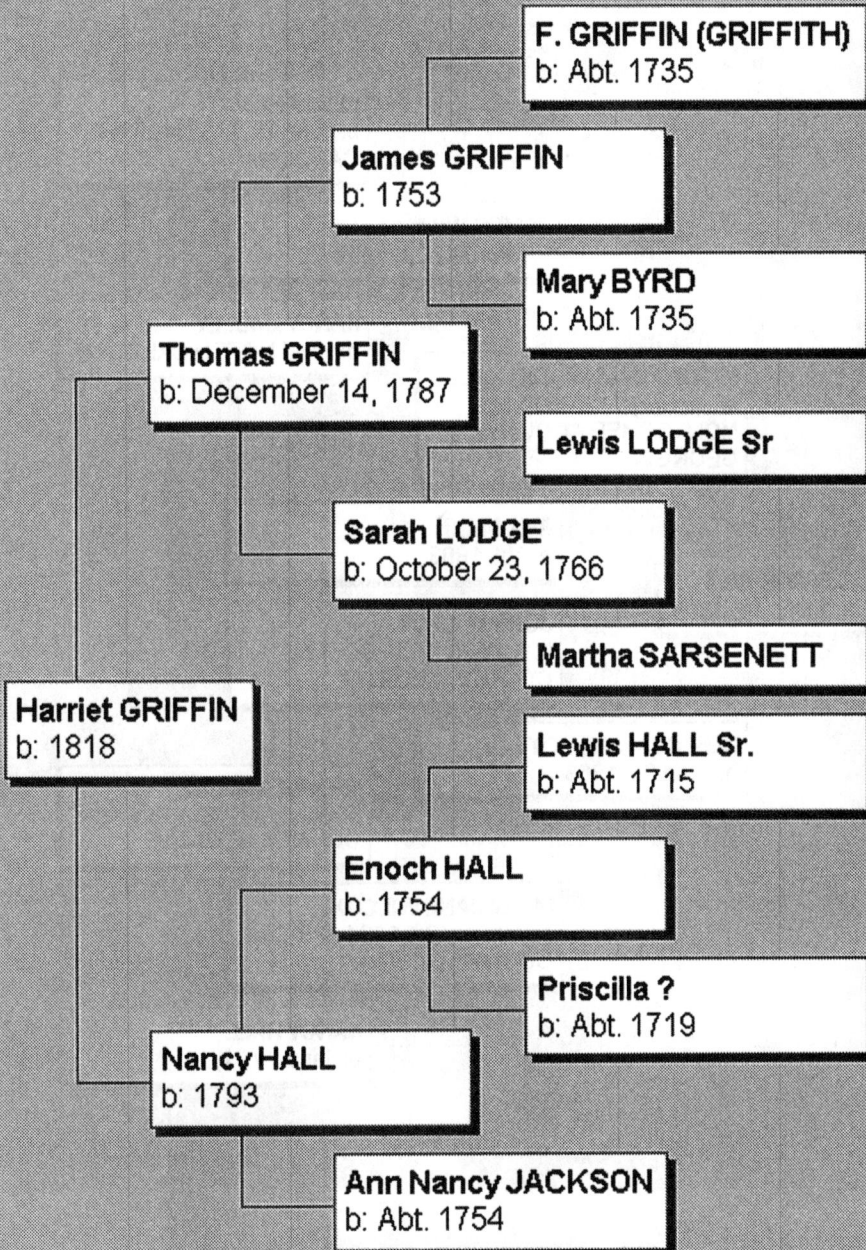

F. GRIFFIN (GRIFFITH)
b: Abt. 1735

James GRIFFIN
b: 1753

Mary BYRD
b: Abt. 1735

Thomas GRIFFIN
b: December 14, 1787

Lewis LODGE Sr

Sarah LODGE
b: October 23, 1766

Martha SARSENETT

Harriet GRIFFIN
b: 1818

Lewis HALL Sr.
b: Abt. 1715

Enoch HALL
b: 1754

Priscilla ?
b: Abt. 1719

Nancy HALL
b: 1793

Ann Nancy JACKSON
b: Abt. 1754

Ancestors of J. FRANK HALL

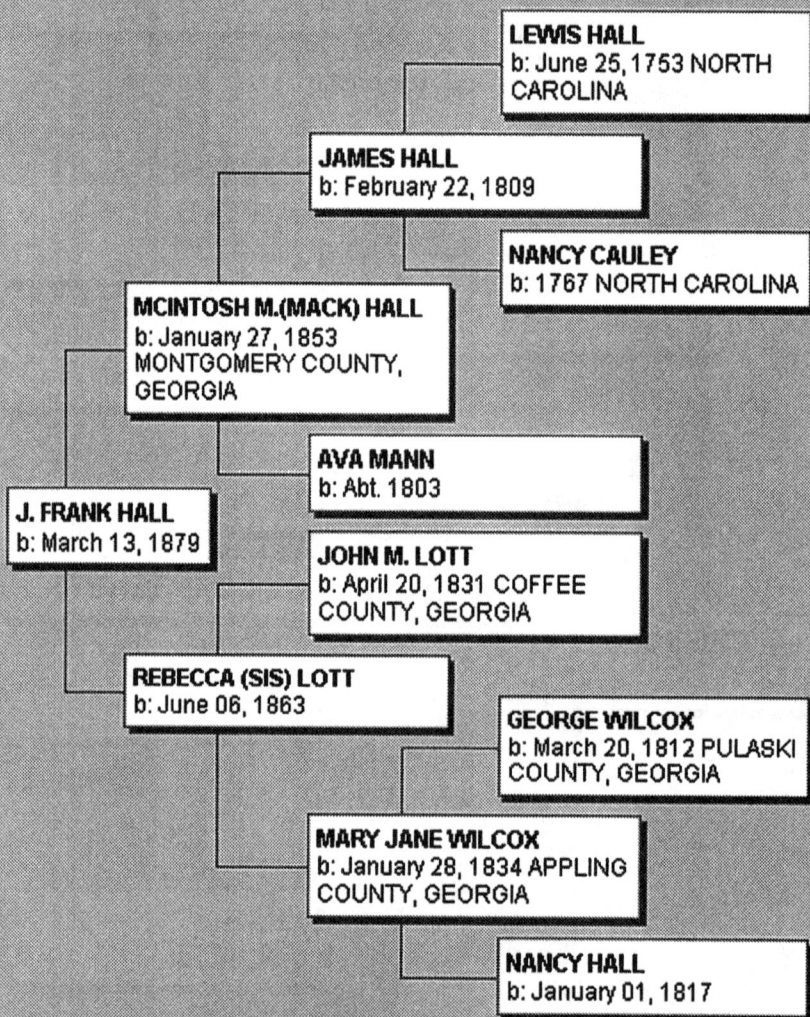

LEWIS HALL
b: June 25, 1753 NORTH CAROLINA

JAMES HALL
b: February 22, 1809

NANCY CAULEY
b: 1767 NORTH CAROLINA

MCINTOSH M.(MACK) HALL
b: January 27, 1853 MONTGOMERY COUNTY, GEORGIA

AVA MANN
b: Abt. 1803

J. FRANK HALL
b: March 13, 1879

JOHN M. LOTT
b: April 20, 1831 COFFEE COUNTY, GEORGIA

REBECCA (SIS) LOTT
b: June 06, 1863

GEORGE WILCOX
b: March 20, 1812 PULASKI COUNTY, GEORGIA

MARY JANE WILCOX
b: January 28, 1834 APPLING COUNTY, GEORGIA

NANCY HALL
b: January 01, 1817

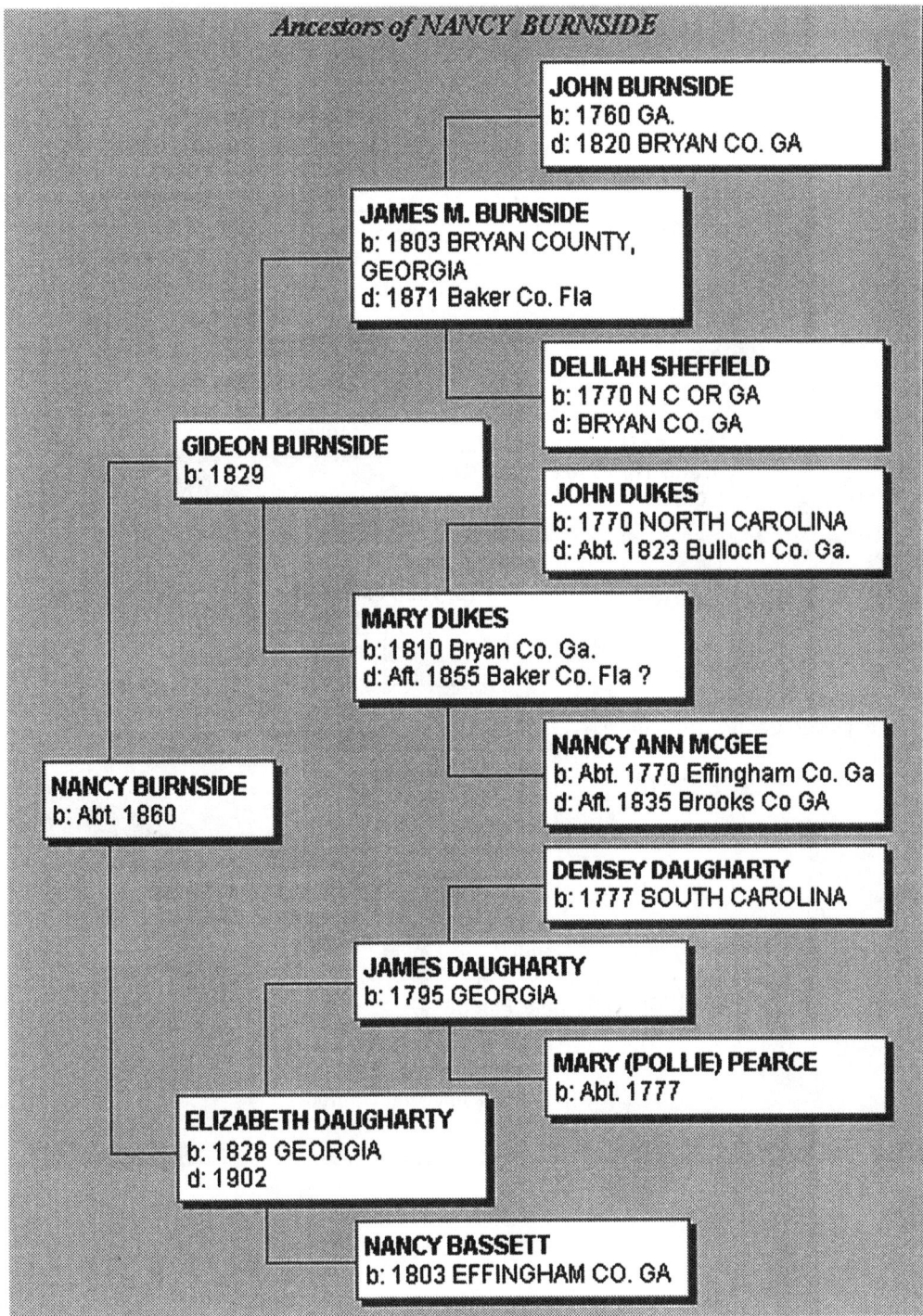

Ancestors of NANCY BURNSIDE

JOHN BURNSIDE
b: 1760 GA.
d: 1820 BRYAN CO. GA

JAMES M. BURNSIDE
b: 1803 BRYAN COUNTY,
GEORGIA
d: 1871 Baker Co. Fla

DELILAH SHEFFIELD
b: 1770 N C OR GA
d: BRYAN CO. GA

GIDEON BURNSIDE
b: 1829

JOHN DUKES
b: 1770 NORTH CAROLINA
d: Abt. 1823 Bulloch Co. Ga.

MARY DUKES
b: 1810 Bryan Co. Ga.
d: Aft. 1855 Baker Co. Fla ?

NANCY ANN MCGEE
b: Abt. 1770 Effingham Co. Ga
d: Aft. 1835 Brooks Co GA

NANCY BURNSIDE
b: Abt. 1860

DEMSEY DAUGHARTY
b: 1777 SOUTH CAROLINA

JAMES DAUGHARTY
b: 1795 GEORGIA

MARY (POLLIE) PEARCE
b: Abt. 1777

ELIZABETH DAUGHARTY
b: 1828 GEORGIA
d: 1902

NANCY BASSETT
b: 1803 EFFINGHAM CO. GA

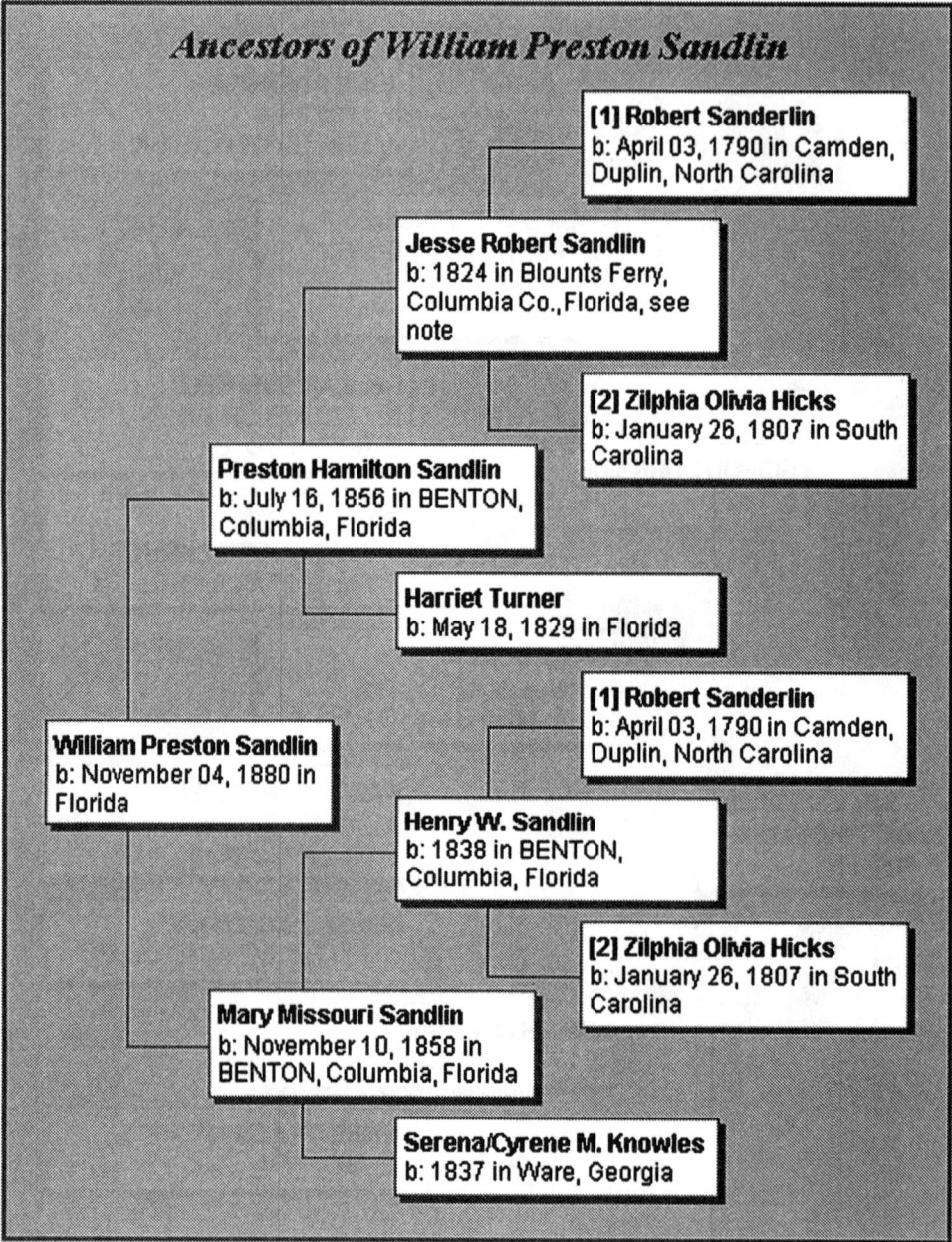

Ancestors of William Preston Sandlin

[1] Robert Sanderlin
b: April 03, 1790 in Camden, Duplin, North Carolina

Jesse Robert Sandlin
b: 1824 in Blounts Ferry, Columbia Co., Florida, see note

[2] Zilphia Olivia Hicks
b: January 26, 1807 in South Carolina

Preston Hamilton Sandlin
b: July 16, 1856 in BENTON, Columbia, Florida

Harriet Turner
b: May 18, 1829 in Florida

[1] Robert Sanderlin
b: April 03, 1790 in Camden, Duplin, North Carolina

William Preston Sandlin
b: November 04, 1880 in Florida

Henry W. Sandlin
b: 1838 in BENTON, Columbia, Florida

[2] Zilphia Olivia Hicks
b: January 26, 1807 in South Carolina

Mary Missouri Sandlin
b: November 10, 1858 in BENTON, Columbia, Florida

Serena/Cyrene M. Knowles
b: 1837 in Ware, Georgia

Appendix C

Yorkshire Origins Of Josiah Langdale,

(1673-1723)

Descendants of the Grandfather of
Josiah Langdale of Yorkshire

(Partial Listing of Four Generations)

This is a report produced with the genealogy program, *Family Tree Maker*, from a working file. It reflects research in progress, not a final product, and is placed here for the benefit of those interested in Langdale genealogy. Many genealogy questions remain unanswered, and some conclusions are, of course, tentative. Anyone desiring to correspond with the researcher regarding genealogy can do so through the Langdale bulletin board pages on the Internet, either by posting a message or by sending e-mail to the address listed there. URLs for two recommended bulletin boards are: http://genforum.genealogy.com and http://www.familyhistory.com.

The information here about Josiah Langdale and his parents differs from all published pedigrees the writer has seen.[1] Pedigrees contributed mainly by amateurs

---

[1] Published pedigrees stored on-line and on CD-ROM have been helpful in this study, although they vary widely in quality (most having been compiled by amateurs) and often have errors. Some of the better databases of pedigrees on CD-ROM include those by Everton Publishers included in this list: Automated Archives, *Automated Archives CD #100, Automated Family Pedigrees #1* (1994), CD, Automated Archives, *Automated Archives CD #161, Bulletin Board Messages--Volume 1* (1994), Broderbund, *Family Archives CD #012, Family Pedigrees: Everton's Computerized Family File, Volume 1, 1400s-Present* (Everton Publishers, 1998), Broderbund, *Family Archives CD #013, Family Pedigrees: Everton's Computerized Family file, Volumes 2 & 3, 1400s-Present* (Everton Publishers, 1998), Broderbund, *Family Archives CD #014, Family Pedigrees: Everton's Computerized Family*

(generally LDS church members) of widely varying skill are available as Pedigree Resource Files from the Family History Department of the Church of Jesus Christ of Latter Day Saints.[2] Similarly, Broderbund Software's World Family Tree volumes, include pedigrees contributed by individuals of differing abilities and published with little editorial control.[3] Pedigrees can also be found in databases on-line such as those of Ancestry.com, Genealogy.com, and FamilySearch.com

---

File, Volume 4, 1400s-Present (Everton Publishers, 1998), Broderbund, *Family Archives CD #018, Family Queries: Everton's "Roots" Cellar, 1640-1990* (Everton Publishers, 1998), Broderbund, *Family Archives CD #108, Family Pedigrees: Gentech95 & ARI, 1500-1989* (1995), Broderbund, *Family Archives CD #506, Family History: Lineages of Hereditary Society Members 1600s-1900s* (1999). The pedigrees and family group sheets by Everton are said to have come largely from professional genealogists.

[2] The Church of Jesus Christ of Latter Day Saints, having long offered to the public its Ancestral File and its International Genealogical Index (IGI), have recently begun selling data on CD-ROM. LDS titles used in this study include the following: Church of Jesus Christ of Latter Day Saints, *Family History Resource File: Master Index for Pedigree Resource File (for Discs 1-5)* (Intellectual Reserve, 1999), Church of Jesus Christ of Latter Day Saints, *Family History Resource File: Pedigree Resource File, Disc 6* (Intellectual Reserve, 2000), Church of Jesus Christ of Latter Day Saints, *Family History Resource File: Pedigree Resource File, Disc 7* (Intellectual Reserve, 2000), Church of Jesus Christ of Latter Day Saints, *Family History Resource File: Pedigree Resource File, Disc 8* (Intellectual Reserve, 2000), Church of Jesus Christ of Latter Day Saints, *Family History Resource File: Pedigree Resource File, Disc 9* (Intellectual Reserve, 2000), Church of Jesus Christ of Latter Day Saints, *Family History Resource File: Pedigree Resource File, Disc 10* (Intellectual Reserve, 2000), Church of Jesus Christ of Latter Day Saints, *Family History Resource File: Pedigree Resource File, Discs 1-5 (Master Index Included)* (Intellectual Reserve, 1999), Church of Jesus Christ of Latter Day Saints, *Family History Resource File: Pedigree Resource File, Discs 11-15 (Master Index Included)* (Intellectual Reserve, 2000), Church of Jesus Christ of Latter Day Saints, *Family History Resource File: Vital Records Index--British Isles* (Intellectual Reserve, 1998), Church of Jesus Christ of Latter Day Saints, *Family History Resource File: Vital Records Index--North America* (Intellectual Reserve, 1998), and Church of Jesus Christ of Latter Day Saints, *Family History Resource File: Vital Records Index--North America (Disc 1)* (Intellectual Reserve, 1998).

[3] A large source of pedigrees of varying quality is the World Family Tree collection produced and sold by Broderbund. These are now also available by on-line subscription from Genealogy.com. World Family Tree CD-ROM volumes consulted for this study include Broderbund, *World Family Tree Super Bundle 6 (Vols. 28, 29, 30, 31, 32)* (1999), Broderbund, *World Family Tree Super Bundle 7 (Vols. 33, 34, 35, 36, 37)* (1999), Broderbund, *World Family Tree Super Bundle 8 (Vols. 38, 39, 40, 41, 42)* (1999), Broderbund, *World Family Tree Super Bundle 9 (Vols. 43, 44, 45, 46, 47)* (2000), Broderbund, *World Family Tree Super Bundle 10 (Vols. 48, 49, 50, 51, 52)* (2000), Broderbund, *World Family Tree Super Bundle II (Vols. 53, 54, 55, 56, 57)* (2000), Broderbund, *World Family Tree Super Bundle I (Vols. 3, 4, 5, 6, 7)* (1996), Broderbund, *World Family Tree Super Bundle III (Vols. 13, 14, 15, 16, 17)* (1998), Broderbund, *World Family Tree Super Bundle IV (Vols. 18, 19, 20, 21, 22)* (1998),

Generation No. 1

1. JOSIAHSGRANDFATHER[1] LANGDALE He married
JOSIAHSGRANDFATHER LANGDALE WIFE.[4]

Children of JOSIAHSGRANDFATHER LANGDALE and
JOSIAHSGRANDFATHER WIFE are:
2. i. JOSEPH[2] LANGDALE, d. 1681, Nafferton, Yorkshire, England.
    ii. JOHN LANGDALE, m. JOHNLANGDALE WIFE.
3. iii. JUDITH LANGDALE, b. 1629; d. 1719.

Generation No. 2

2. JOSEPH[2] LANGDALE *(JOSIAHSGRANDFATHER[1])* died 1681 in Nafferton,
Yorkshire, England. He married MARGARET JOSIAHMOTHER. [5]

Child of JOSEPH LANGDALE and MARGARET JOSIAHMOTHER is:
4. i. JOSIAH[3] LANGDALE, b. 1673, Nafferton, Yorkshire, England; d.
        1723, aboard ship London Hope, anchored in the Downes near Deale
        in Great Britain.

3. JUDITH[2] LANGDALE *(JOSIAHSGRANDFATHER[1])* was born 1629, and died
1719. She married THOMAS LAYBOURNE, son of CHRISTOPHER
LAYBOURNE and ANN GOTT. He was born 1625, and died March 27, 1712.

Broderbund, *World Family Tree Super Bundle V (Vols. 23, 24, 25, 26, 27)* (1999), Broderbund,
World Family Tree, Volume 2, Pre-1600 to Present (1995), Broderbund, *World Family Tree,
Volume 8, Pre-1600 to Present* (1997), Broderbund, *World Family Tree, Volume 9, Pre-1600
to Present* (1997), Broderbund, *World Family Tree, Volume 10, Pre-1600 to Present* (1997),
Broderbund, *World Family Tree, Volume 11, Pre-1600 to Present* (1997), Broderbund, *World
Family Tree, Volume 12, Pre-1600 to Present* (1997), Broderbund, *World Family Tree,
Volume 13, Pre-1600 to Present* (1997), Broderbund, *World Family Tree, Volume 1, Pre-1600
to Present* (1995).

[4] Based on facts related in the partial autobiography of Josiah Langdale. This does not
support published genealogies identifying Josiah as a grandson of Marmaduke Lord Langdale.
Josiah mentioned no connection with the family of Baron Langdale. He stated that his
mother's name was Margaret, whereas the name of his mother if the Baron Langdale
connection were true would have been Elizabeth Savage.

[5] In his autobiography Josiah did not identify the parents of his father or those of his
mother.

Notes for JUDITH LANGDALE:

The identification of Judith Langdale as Josiah's aunt and of Thomas Laybourne as Josiah's Uncle Layborne is based on data from Linda Valdez, combined with information from Josiah's partial autobiography.[6]

According to his autobiography, before he became a Quaker Josiah Langdale was a member of the Church of England, as were his parents.

Josiah mentioned that two sons of his Aunt Fnu Layborne became priests, but Josiah did not state whether they were Catholic or Anglican. Since Josiah's family belonged to the Church of England, one can reasonably expect that his aunt and her family did also. That being so, Josiah's two cousins Layborne probably were Anglican priests.

Thomas Laybourne and Judith Langdale Laybourne had a son, Thomas Laybourne. The Linda Valdez notes for this man indicate he graduated from Cambridge University with bachelor's and master's degrees and became a priest 6 June 1680. This Thomas Laybourne (1657-1728) was born in Nafferton twenty years before Josiah, who was also born in the vicinity of Nafferton. Thomas Laybourne (the son) had children, so he was evidently married, which presumably rules out his having been a Catholic priest.

Henry Laybourne (1669-1755), youngest son of Thomas and Judith Langdale Laybourne, also graduated from Cambridge University. He apparently was also an Anglican priest. The information on this Laybourne family appears to fit the description from Josiah Langdale's autobiography.

From reviewing Linda Valdez's Laybourne data, it does not appear that Josiah Langdale's descendants had any contact with those of his Laybourne cousins in America. Coincidentally, however, some of the Laybournes and some of Josiah's descendants settled in Ohio in the early 19th century. One of Josiah's grandsons, Samuel Langdale (b. 1759 in Philadelphia), moved to Ross County, Ohio, after the Revolutionary War, perhaps around 1800. Like the Laybournes, some of the Langdales moved on to Illinois, Indiana, etc.[7]

---

[6] See Linda Valdez, Family History.com, Message #79, Sunday, 20 August 2000.

[7] For research on Quakers of this period an invaluable source is William Wade Hinshaw's six-volume *Encyclopedia of American Quaker Genealogy*. In addition to the printed version, it is also available on compact disc such as Broderbund, *Family Archives CD #192: Genealogical Records: The Encyclopedia of Quaker Genealogy, 1750-1930, 6 Vols.*, Ed. *William Wade Hinshaw* (Genealogical Publishing Company).

Other CDs very useful to this study, having voluminous documentary information for the Pennsylvania area, include Broderbund, *Family Archives CD #019, Genealogical Records: Egle's Notes and Queries of Pennsylvania, 1700s--1800s*, Broderbund, *Family Archives CD #113, Family History Collection: 217 Genealogy Books* (1996), CD, Broderbund, *Family Archives CD #114, Family History Collection: First Families of America* (1996), Broderbund, *Family Archives CD #130, Pennsylvania German Church Records, 1729-1870* (Genealogical

More About JUDITH LANGDALE:
_____

Burial: June 16, 1719, Nafferton, Yorkshire, England[8]

Children of JUDITH LANGDALE and THOMAS LAYBOURNE are:
     i.   ANN[3] LAYBOURNE, d. 1654.

More About ANN LAYBOURNE:
Burial: January 1653/54, Nafferton, Yorkshire, England

5.   ii.   CHRISTOPHER LAYBOURNE, b. 1656; d. 1736, Nafferton, Yorkshire, England.
6.   iii.   THOMAS LAYBOURNE, b. March 05, 1656/57, Nafferton, Yorkshire, England; d. 1728.
7.   iv.   ELIZABETH LAYBOURNE, b. May 06, 1660.
8.   v.   ROBERT LAYBOURNE, b. 1664; d. 1737, Pocklington, Yorkshire, England.
9.   vi.   WILLIAM LAYBOURNE, b. 1666.
10.   vii.   HENRY LAYBOURNE, b. April 25, 1669; d. March 1755, Cotterton, Yorkshire, England.

_____

Publishing Company), Broderbund, *Family Archives CD #163, Family History: Pennsylvania Genealogies #1, Pre-1600s to 1900s* (Genealogical Publishing Company), Broderbund, *Family Archives CD #166, Church Records: Selected Areas of Pennsylvania, 1600s--1800s,* Broderbund, *Family Archives CD #172, Pennsylvania Vital Records, 1700s-1800s* (Genealogical Publishing Company), Broderbund, *Family Archives CD #174, Virginia Vital Records #1, 1600s-1800s* (1997), Broderbund, *Family Archives CD #175, Ohio Vital Records #1, 1790s--1870s* (Genealogical Publishing Company), Broderbund, *Family Archives CD #182, Family History: New Jersey Genealogies #1, 1600s--1800s* (Genealogical Publishing Company), Broderbund, *Family Archives CD #193, County and Family Histories: Pennsylvania, 1740-1900,* Broderbund, *Family Archives CD #196, Birth Index: Southeastern Pa, 1680-1800* (John T. Humphrey), Broderbund, *Family Archives CD #209, Genealogical Records: Pennsylvania Wills, 1682-1834* (Family Line Publications), Broderbund, *Family Archives CD #210, National Genealogical Society Quarterly, Vols. 1-85, 1600s-1900s,* Broderbund, *Family Archives CD #213, Genealogical Records: The Pennsylvania Genealogical Magazine, Volumes 1-39.* (Genealogical Publishing Company), Broderbund, *Family Archives CD #305, Census Microfilm Records: Pennsylvania, 1850,* CD, Broderbund, *Family Archives CD #450, County and Family Histories: Ohio, 1780-1970,* CD, and Broderbund, *Family Archives CD #501, Immigration Records: Immigrants to Pennsylvania, 1600s--1800s* (Genealogical Publishing Company).

   [8] Ibid.; author's further e-mail correspondence with Linda Valdez, August 2000.

Generation No. 3

4. JOSIAH[3] LANGDALE *(JOSEPH[2], JOSIAHSGRANDFATHER[1])* was born 1673 in Nafferton, Yorkshire, England, and died in 1723 aboard the ship London Hope, anchored in the Downes near Deale in Great Britain. He married MARGARET BURTON 1710 in England, daughter of WILLIAM BURTON and ISABEL. She was born 1684 in England, and died 1742 in Philadelphia, PA.

Notes for JOSIAH LANGDALE:[9]

Josiah Langdale's autobiography[10] is a brief account of Josiah's boyhood and young manhood, emphasizing his spiritual struggle over several years that resulted in his leaving the Church of England to join the Quakers. It mentions but gives no details on his journeys to America. It includes a small amount of factual data on his family, which is discussed more fully in Gil Skidmore's excellent introduction and is summarized here. Some of the information included in this summary is from Ms. Skidmore's introduction, not Josiah's text.

Josiah names his parents as Joseph and Margaret Langdale of Nafferton, Yorkshire. Joseph had a brother, John Langdale, and an unnamed sister who was married to a man surnamed Layborne. The Laybornes had two sons, Josiah's cousins, who were priests. He says nothing about siblings, which implies he had none, but this is not definitely stated. At the age of twenty, he inherited land from his father, who had died in 1681 when Josiah was eight years of age.

At the death of his father in 1681, eight-year-old Josiah was sent to work on other peoples' farms to earn money. This essentially ended his formal education. After seven years (1688), Josiah's mother remarried (Josiah did not mention his stepfather's name), and Josiah, now fifteen, left home to earn his own way as a farm worker with an annual verbal contract. He plowed with a four-horse team, stacked hay, and tended livestock. After one year, he contracted to work for a Quaker named David Milner, with whose family he resided and labored for several years.

Josiah's account does not mention the Glorious Revolution and related events of 1688-89, says nothing about Newton's Law of Gravitation which the great scientist announced in 1687, and has no comment on John Locke's *Two Treatises on Government*, published shortly after the Glorious Revolution. From this one might reason that politics, philosophy, and natural science did not consume Josiah's

---

[9] Much of the information on the Quaker Langdale, Coates, and Hudson families is from *The Pennsylvania Genealogical Magazine*. Volumes 1-39. Reproduced on Broderbund Software's Family Archive CD #213 (Genealogical Records: *The Pennsylvania Genealogical Magazine*, Volumes 1-39). Hereinafter cited as FACD #213.

[10]"Josiah Langdale, 1673–1723, A Quaker Spiritual Autobiography," edited and with an introduction by Gil Skidmore (Sowle Press: Reading, England, 1999) iii-xix, and descendancy chart after page 27.

attention, or perhaps he regarded such matters as irrelevant to his readers. Josiah's autobiography reads as if he intended it as a testimony, such as one might deliver in a religious service, and from which politics and secular philosophy could reasonably be omitted. This is reminiscent of Primitive Baptist church records in south Georgia during the 1860s, which have almost no direct mention of the U. S. Civil War. [11]

In May of 1693 at the age of twenty, the same year he inherited his father's land, Josiah had a deep religious experience and was converted to the Quaker faith in a meeting at Bridlington. Within about a year, he felt called to the ministry and saw it as his mission eventually to travel to America to spread the faith. In the year 1700, at age 27, he began his first visit to America. He returned to England and reported on his work in 1705. This visit to America coincided with the early years of the War of Spanish Succession, known in America as Queen Anne's War, which continued until 1713.

In 1710, at age 37, he married Margaret Burton. Five years later, the War of Spanish Succession having ended, he made a second trip to America (1715-16), sailing first to Boston. [12] While he was away, Margaret did similar missionary work in Ireland, and, after his return, continued such activity on the continent. On these missionary trips Josiah and Margaret each traveled in the company of another minister of the same sex, which was the usual Quaker pattern.

By 1720 Josiah had resolved to move to America, so he sailed a third time across the Atlantic primarily, it seems, to make living arrangements for his family (1720-21). [13] By this time he and Margaret had a daughter, Mary, and a son, John. They all boarded a ship, the London Hope, in 1723 bound for Philadelphia.

---

[11] Crowley, *Primitive Baptists of the Wiregrass South,* 86–99.

[12] On 29 June 1716, Josiah Langdale and his traveling missionary partner, Thomas Thomson, requested certificates from the Philadelphia Monthly Meeting for their return to England via the West Indies. Langdale and Thomson had come to Philadelphia with certificates from their monthly meetings in Skypsea, eastern Yorkshire, and Hitching in Harford County, respectively. Those certificates "were read to the comfort and great satisfaction of this meeting." This information comes from "Early Minutes of the Philadelphia Monthly Meeting." *The Pennsylvania Genealogical Magazine* 7 (1918): 182. FACD #213

[13] A legal transaction, recorded in 1723 at about the time Margaret Burton arrived in Philadelphia with her two young children and news of her husband, Josiah Langdale's death, reveals that Josiah, probably during his last trip, had acquired property in Bristol. Specifically, on 8 June 1723, John Hall of Bristol, Bucks County PA, a cooper by trade, took out a mortgage on 6 1/4 acres located in Bristol. This land was described as "bounded by Mill street, Mill Creek, lands late Richard Burge's and those of John Abraham Denormandie, James Allen, Henry Tomlinson, Thomas Bill, Solomon Boom, Daniel Pegg, Josiah Langdale, Richard Mountain, and Neshamany Road." So Josiah evidently planned to live in Bristol. Although not important at this point in the story, the described transaction also shows that people of the surname Burge owned property in the neighborhood where Josiah Langdale of Yorkshire intended to live. Several decades later Josiah's grandson of the same name sold land in South Carolina to a Michael Burdge. There is no evidence here, however, that the Philadelphia

Unfortunately, Josiah died aboard ship, and Margaret arrived in Philadelphia a widow with two young children.[14] A little more than a year later, still carrying on an active ministry, she married Samuel Preston, a Quaker gentleman and merchant whose age exceeded hers by about two decades. She died in 1742 at the age of fifty-eight. Her husband, Samuel, died the next year.

Josiah Langdale's will, written on his deathbed before his ship actually left British waters, made his wife, Margaret, executrix and included mention of her parents' identity. She was the daughter of William Burton, a yeoman of Yorkshire, and his wife, Isabel. This information conflicts with other published data, but would appear to be definitive. Margaret was unquestionably there when her husband made his will, and she would certainly have known the names of her parents.[15]

When in June 1724 Samuel Preston and the widow Margaret Burton Langdale announced for the second time their intention to be married, the Quaker congregation, having followed their usual procedure and investigated the circumstances of bride and groom, saw to it that the widow's children would have their property rights protected. The examining committee reported to the meeting "that they find nothing to obstruct

---

Burges had any connection with the Michael Burdge to whom Josiah Langdale of Colleton SC, sold land in 1794. Appearance of the names Burge and Burdge in this instance, one supposes, was mere coincidence. The John Hall transaction with its mention of Josiah Langdale's land is from Mrs. William M. Mervine, contributor. "Abstracts of General Loan Office Mortgages, 13 April 1723 to 20 February 1723/4." *The Pennsylvania Genealogical Magazine* 6 (1915): 274. FACD #213.

[14] At the Philadelphia Monthly Meeting of 28 June 1723, certificates from the Bridlington Monthly Meeting at Skypsea in Yorkshire and from the York Quarterly Meeting "for our friend Josiah Langdale, Margaret his wife and two children, who were upon removing to America with intention to settle among us was read and well accepted, and tho' our dear friend Josiah did not live to reach us, yet his widow and children being here its ordered to be recorded." See "Early Minutes of the Philadelphia Monthly Meeting." *The Pennsylvania Genealogical Magazine* 7 (1918): 259. FACD #213.

[15] Abstracts of Philadelphia Co., Wills, 1682–1726, Will Abstracts Page 984; Reproduced FACD #209. The abstract reads as follows:

LANGDALE, JOSIAH. Late of Bridlington Key, Yorkshire.

February 14, 1723. June 28, 1723. D. 359.

Joseph Bond, Hannah Carpenter relict of Samuel Carpenter, deceased, mentioned.

Will signed on board the ship London Hope laying at anchor in the Downes near Deale in Great Britain, where he died.

Proved at Philadelphia.

Executrix: Wife Margaret (daughter of William and Isabel Burton, yeoman, late of Yorkshire, deceased).

Witnesses: John Annis, Senior, Commander of the Ship London Hope, Sarah Dinsdale, John Estaugh and Isaiah Cardel.

his proceedings, and that a settlement on her children is agreed to by the widow, & will be done before marriage." [16]

More About MARGARET BURTON:
LDS Ancestral File #: PHRX-HK

Children of JOSIAH LANGDALE and MARGARET BURTON are:
11.　i.　MARY[4] LANGDALE, b. May 26, 1713, of Bridlington, Yorkshire, England; d. December 23, 1770, Philadelphia, PA (age 57).
12.　ii.　JOHN LANGDALE, b. 1715, OF Bridlington, Yorkshire, England; d. September 18, 1769, Philadelphia, PA (Age 54).

Generation No. 4

11. MARY[4] LANGDALE *(JOSIAH[3], JOSEPH[2], JOSIAHSGRANDFATHER[1])* was born May 26, 1713 in of Bridlington, Yorkshire, England, and died December 23, 1770 in Philadelphia, PA (age 57). She married SAMUEL COATES June 13, 1734 in Philadelphia, PA, Monthly Meeting of Friends, son of THOMAS COATES and BEULAH JACQUES. He was born October 07, 1711 in Philadelphia, Philadelphia, PA, and died December 15, 1748 in Northern Liberties, PA.

Notes for MARY LANGDALE:

Frederick A. Virkus, *First Families of America,* describes Mary as "dau. of Josiah Langdale of the Yorkshire family." This statement, some would say, implies that Josiah and his daughter, Mary, descended from the famous Marmaduke Lord Langdale, Baron of Holme, or a near relative. The relationship, if any, between Josiah's father, Joseph Langdale, and the more famous Langdales is unknown by this researcher as of June 15, 2001.[17]

In March 1734 Samuel Coates and Mary Langdale declared to the Philadelphia Monthly Meeting their intention to marry. Their parents, present in the meeting, stated their approval.[18]

---

[16] "Early Minutes of the Philadelphia Monthly Meeting." *The Pennsylvania Genealogical Magazine* 7 (1918): 262. FACD #213.

[17] Frederick A. Virkus, ed., *First Families of America: The Abridged Compendium of American Genealogy (Volume 1)*, reproduced in Broderbund, *Family Archives CD #.114, Family History Collection: First Families of America,* 394/3246.

[18] "Early Minutes of the Philadelphia Monthly Meeting." *The Pennsylvania Genealogical Magazine* 7 (1918): 178. FACD #213.

Samuel Coates of the City of Philadelphia and Mary Langdale of Passyunk, Philadelphia County, PA, married on June 13, 1734, in a Philadelphia Quaker meeting. Among the more than fifty witnesses were the bride's mother, Margaret Burton Langdale Preston, her stepfather, Samuel Preston, her brother, John Langdale, and the groom's mother, Beulah Jacques Coates. Several other Coates relatives attended as well, but the groom's father, Samuel Coates, evidently missed his son's wedding.[19]

The Philadelphia Monthly Meeting of Friends recorded the death of a Mary Coates, age 57, on 10-23-1770. This fits perfectly with the date of birth for Mary Langdale Coates, daughter of Josiah Langdale and Margaret Burton, who was born in 1713. In the same place it is reported that there was also a younger Mary Coates, age 30, who died on January 28, 1769. Mary Langdale and Samuel Coates had a daughter, Mary, born in March 1738, who would have been a little less than 31 years of age if she still lived at that time and would fit the described chronological circumstances.[20]

Mary Langdale Coates made her will on April 4, 1769, and it was proved on November 16, 1770.[21]

Mary Langdale Coates and Samuel Coates had the following children, according to lists in Quaker minutes of monthly meetings.[22]

Samuel	May 17, 1735
Margaret	July 11, 1736
Mary	March 26, 1738
Beulah	January 28, 1739/40
Samuel	January 14, 1741/42
Sarah	September 1, 1743
Alice	September 11, 1744
Langdale	October 4, 1745
Thomas	October 27, 1746
Josiah	November 10, 1747
Samuel	October 24, 1748

---

[19] "Marriage Certificates Beginning with 1681 (Abstracts)." *The Pennsylvania Genealogical Magazine* 21900): 72. FACD #213.

[20] EAQG, II, 347.

[21] Abstracts of Philadelphia Co. Wills, 1763–1784, Will Abstracts [page 727]; reproduced on Family Archives CD #209

"COATES, MARY. City of Phila. Shopkeeper.

4 mo. 4, 1769. November 16, 1770.

Children: Margaret, Beulah, Alice Langdale, Thomas, Samuel, Josiah.

Execs.: Margaret and Beulah Coates, Alice Langdale, John Reynell.

Witnesses: Caleb Attmore, Wm. Wilson, Sarah Green.

Codicil. 9 mo. 7, 1770. Daughters: Margaret, Beulah, Alice Langdale.

Witnesses: Caleb Attmore, William Wilson, Hannah Jacobs. (P:13)"

[22] EAQG, II, 247.

Mary Langdale's husband, Samuel Coates, the fourth son of Thomas and Beulah Jacques Coates, was a merchant and an original shareholder of the Philadelphia Library. He alone of his siblings left surviving children surnamed Coates. Samuel inherited property near Frankford from his parents, but he and Mary lived in Philadelphia. When he died at age 38,[23] his youngest son was only nine weeks old. Two other sons, Josiah Langdale and Thomas, were fourteen and twenty-six months old respectively. The three young boys had four sisters, Margaret, Mary, Beulah, and Alice. The eldest daughter was just over twelve years of age.[24]

As executrix for Samuel Coates, Mary Langdale Coates placed advertisements in the Pennsylvania *Gazette* on December 27, 1748 (Item #10306), and July 27, 1749 (Item #10873). The first ad identified her as executrix for Samuel Coates, shopkeeper. To settle the estate quickly, she offered various items for sale on Second Street next door to Thomas Campbell. That was Mary's residence. The ad requested persons in debt to Samuel Coates to make payment right away. The second ad offered to "lett, for any term not to exceed eighteen years, a lot of ground, well fenced, in the Northern Liberties, within a mile of Franckford, and four miles from this city, containing 10 acres of good land." The property was described as having a creek, a dam, and a ditch for watering the meadow. Once again, she asked persons owing money to Samuel Coates to pay their debts speedily (C-1736, 1747, 1748).[25]

12. JOHN[4] LANGDALE *(JOSIAH[3], JOSEPH[2], JOSIAHSGRANDFATHER[1])* was born 1715 in OF Bridlington, Yorkshire, England, and died September 18, 1769 in Philadelphia, PA (Age 54). He married SARAH HUDSON Abt. 1735 in of Burlington Co., NJ, daughter of WILLIAM HUDSON and JANE EVANS. She was born July 30, 1718 in Of Burlington Co., New Jersey, and died August 05, 1780 in Philadelphia, PA.

---

[23] For Samuel Coates's will, made in September 1748 and proved on December 20 of that year, see *Abstracts of Philadelphia Co., Wills, 1748–1763, Will Abstracts* [page 11]; reproduced FACD #209

"COATS, SAMUEL. City of Philadelphia. Merchant.

September 1, 1748/9. December 20, 1748. J.14.

Wife: Mary. Children: Thomas, Josiah, Margaret, Mary, Beulah, Alice. Brother-in-Law: John Langdale.

Exec: Mary Coats.

Witnesses: Thomas Campbell, Jno. Reily."

[24] Linda Dudick Coates website, http://www.ancestrees.com, 12 June 2000;

James and Mary Watson gedcom file, citing *Family Memorials and Recollections: or Aunt Mary's Patchwork* by Mary Coates (1885).

[25] Linda Dudick Coates website, http://www.ancestrees.com, 12 June 2000.

Notes for JOHN LANGDALE:

On April 15, 1736, John Langdale attended the marriage of John Reynell and widow Mary Coates Nicholas. In addition to John, the forty witnesses included Beulah Jacques Coates (mother-in-law of Mary Langdale Coates), Rose ( ) Coates, Samuel and Mary Langdale Coates, Samuel and Margaret Burton Langdale Preston, and William Hudson (presumably the father-in-law of young John Langdale).[26]

Listed below are three deaths reported in William Wade Hinshaw's *Encyclopedia of American Quaker Genealogy* II, 387, that appear to fit the family of John Langdale, son of Josiah Langdale and Margaret Burton, in that John and his wife, Sarah Hudson, had children with the same or similar names.

1741 William (Langdall), son of John, died 9-21-1741.
1746 Jane (Landale), daughter of John, died 10-3-1746.
1747 Margrett (Langdall), daughter of John, died 5-18-1747.

Notes in the Bible of William Hudson, Jr., father of Sarah Hudson Langdale, indicate that:
William Langdale, born July 22, 1741, died on the 19th following.
Margaret Langdale, born September 9, 1744, died (date unspecified).
Jane Langdale, born July 17, 1746, died (date unspecified).[27]

The two sources differ somewhat, but this could be the result of the Bible records having been entered later, with imperfect recall of specific dates. The names are the same in the two sources, and the dates are basically consistent, so the three deaths recorded by the Philadelphia MM must be those of the children of John and Sarah Langdale.

John & Sarah had other children with names similar to those above. They were William Hudson (b November 22, 1747), Margaret (b May 1, 1752), and Jane (b May 1, 1755. The Philadelphia Monthly Meeting listed them among John Langdale's family members, including his wife, Sarah, being granted certificates to Haddonfield Monthly Meeting on June 24, 1763.[28]

At some time before December 10, 1745, Samuel Preston Moore lodged a complaint, undefined in the Quaker minutes, against John Langdale. A committee of

---

[26] "Marriage Certificates Beginning with 1681 (Abstracts)." *The Pennsylvania Genealogical Magazine* 2 (1900): 74. FACD #213.

[27] FACD #163, Pennsylvania Genealogies #1, Howard Williams Lloyd, "Hudson Family Records," 448.

[28] EAQG II, 576.

Friends mediated and reported to the December 1745 meeting that the matter appeared on the way to resolution.[29]

John Langdale's issue with Samuel Preston Moore and the Philadelphia MM may have had something to do with Samuel Preston's estate, with which both men would have been concerned. Samuel Preston, John Langdale's stepfather, died in 1743. Margaret Burton Langdale Preston, John's mother, had died in the previous year, 1742. Samuel Preston Moore was Samuel Preston's son-in-law and one of two executors of his will. The other executor was Preston Carpenter, a grandson of Samuel Preston. John Langdale's name appeared in his stepfather's will as a beneficiary, but without identification or description and without a specified bequest (as indicated by the abstract), so there could well have been some kind of dispute about the estate.[30]

At an unknown date after 1745 John Langdale and his family moved from Philadelphia to the vicinity of Norfolk, Virginia, and apparently lived there for some years, perhaps as much as one or two decades. It is conceivable, however, that John shuttled back and forth between Norfolk and Philadelphia during part of this time. A John Langdale witnessed a will for St. Lawrence Berford on March 13, 1750, in Norfolk, VA. This probably was the son of Josiah and Margaret Burton Langdale, considering that Norfolk was near the location of Western Branch Monthly Meeting of Friends in Isle of Wight County, VA, from which John and his family presented a certificate when they moved from Virginia to Philadelphia in 1761.[31]

---

[29] "Early Minutes of the Philadelphia Monthly Meeting." *The Pennsylvania Genealogical Magazine* 9 (1924): 172. FACD #213.

[30] *Abstracts of Philadelphia Co. Wills, 1726-1747, Will Abstracts* [page 774]; reproduced on FACD #209

PRESTON, SAMUEL. City of Philadelphia. September 5, 1743. September 22, 1743. G.68.

Brother: Thomas Berry.
Children: Carpenter, Margaret Moore.
Grandchildren: Mordecai Moore, Preston Carpenter.
Son-in-law: Samuel Preston Moore.
John Langdale.
Sisters-in-law: Mary and Margaret Coates, Ruth Webb, widow of Richard Rhoades.
Samuel Pemberton and William Orr.
Exec: Saml. Preston Moore and Preston Carpenter.
Trustees: Israel Pemberton, John Kinsey and Cadwalader Fooks.
Witnesses: George Plumly, Samuel Pennock and Richd. Hill, Jr.

[31] This probate record was extracted from microfilmed copies of the original Will Book. FACD #513.

John Langdale
Date: Mar 13, 1750
Location: Norfolk Co., VA
Record ID: 33721
Description: Witness

It is possible that John Langdale also resided for a time in Pittsburgh, In 1761 a census taken in Pittsburgh, Allegheny County, PA, recorded the presence of a John Langdale. Perhaps this was an interim stop for our John Langdale between Western Branch and Philadelphia Monthly Meetings. On the other hand, it might have been a different, unknown, John Langdale.[32]

On December 25, 1761, John Langdale presented himself, his wife, and their daughter, Rachel, for membership in the Philadelphia Monthly Meeting. For credentials, John had a certificate from the Western Branch Monthly Meeting, Isle of

---

Prove Date: Jun 21, 1750

Book-Page: I-166

Remarks: St. Lawrence Berford. Book I p. 166 --(torn)--(See Original Box 1711-1755). Dated 13 Mch. 1750. Proved 21 June 1750.... my real Estate in Ireland, but that the same shall descend according to the Rules of Law, all the sd personal Estate...I de[????].

[32] See FACD #310, Census Index: Colonial America, 1607–1789

Individual: Langdale, John

County/State: Allegheny Co., PA

Location: Pittsburgh

Page #: 344

Year: 1761

Other US Census indexes useful to this study include Automated Archives, *Automated Archives CD #291, Precision Indexing Databases, US Census Index Series: Georgia, 1870* (1994), Broderbund, Family Archives CD #020, Census Index: Ohio, 1880 (1995), Broderbund, Family Archives CD #285, Census Index: Western Pennsylvania, 1870 (1994), CD, Broderbund, Family Archives CD #286, Census Index: Eastern Pennsylvania, 1870 (1994), CD, Broderbund, Family Archives CD #287, Census Index: New York City, 1870 (1994), CD, Broderbund, Family Archives CD #288, Census Index: Baltimore, Chicago, St. Louis, 1870 (1994), CD, Broderbund, Family Archives CD #289, Census Index: North Carolina, South Carolina, 1870 (1994), CD, Broderbund, Family Archives CD #290, Census Index: Virginia, West Virginia, 1870 (1994), CD, Broderbund, Family Archives CD #291, Census Index: Georgia, 1870 (1994), CD, Broderbund, Family Archives CD #310, Census Index: Colonial America, 1607-1789 (1995), Broderbund, Family Archives CD #311, Census Index: United States Selected Counties, 1790 (1995), Broderbund, Family Archives CD #313, Census Index: United States Selected Counties, 1810 (1995), Broderbund, Family Archives CD #314, Census Index: United States Selected Counties, 1820 (1995), Broderbund, Family Archives CD #315, Census Index: United States Selected Counties, 1830 (1995), Broderbund, Family Archives CD #316, Census Index: United States Selected Counties, 1840 (1995), Broderbund, Family Archives CD #317, Census Index: United States Selected Counties, 1850 (1995), Broderbund, Family Archives CD #318, Census Index: United States Selected Counties, 1860 (1995), Broderbund, Family Archives CD #319, Census Index: United States Selected States/Counties, 1870 (1995), Broderbund, Family Archives CD #320, Census Index: United States Selected States/Counties, 1880 (1995), Broderbund, Family Archives CD # 312, Census Index: US Selected Counties, 1800 (1995).

Wight County, Virginia.[33] The Philadelphia MM received the Langdale family seventeen months later, on May 27, 1763.[34]

On this occasion the Langdales remained only briefly as members of the Philadelphia MM. According to the minutes, John Langdale & wife & six children, Rachel, William, Elizabeth, Jane, Margaret, & Samuel, were granted certificates June 24, 1763, from Philadelphia Monthly Meeting to Haddonfield Monthly Meeting. So, within a month after being accepted into the Philadelphia Monthly Meeting, John Langdale and his family moved on to Haddonfield Monthly Meeting. This did not include the two oldest sons, Josiah and John, Jr., who were 24 and 21 years of age, respectively, and apparently no longer lived with their parents.[35]

Further evidence that John Langdale and family resided for an extended period in or near Norfolk, VA, is the will of Christopher Perkins, an English merchant who lived in Norfolk for some length of time, moved back to London, and died in 1765. Christopher Perkins's will (dated July 27, 1765, and proved December 5, 1765), included bequests to several relatives and one to a friend, John Langdale. "To friend John Langdale late of Norfolk in Virginia, now of Haddon Field in West New Jersey L20 Virginia currency to buy a piece of plate, to be paid by friend Colonel Robert Tucker of Norfolk in Virginia." The specified location of John Langdale, according to Perkins's will, is consistent with the Quaker records reporting that John and his family transferred their membership from Western Branch MM in Isle of Wight County, VA, to Philadelphia MM and shortly afterward to Haddonfield MM. One observes that John Langdale was the only non-relative to receive a gift under Christopher Perkins's will and that Perkins had kept up with John Langdale's whereabouts in New Jersey. Since Langdale was a tanner and Perkins was a merchant, perhaps they were business associates, with John Langdale selling leather goods to Christopher Perkins. It would not appear that Perkins was a Quaker, for his will did not display the usual Quaker terminology for dates.[36]

The mid-1760s could not have been entirely happy years for the John Langdale family. Within six months after his parents moved their membership to Haddonfield, Josiah came into conflict with the Philadelphia MM, and in another six months was disowned. Within eighteen months of Josiah's disownment, his younger brother, John,

---

[33] "Early Minutes of the Philadelphia Monthly Meeting." *The Pennsylvania Genealogical Magazine* 12 (1933): 36. FACD #213.

[34] EAQG., II, 576, reports John Langdale and wife and daughter Rachel were received 27 May 1763, by Philadelphia Monthly Meeting on certificate from Western Branch, Isle of Wight County VA, Monthly Meeting, dated 10 June 1761. (Actually, Hinshaw has this event listed twice, with no date for the first listing.) But if, as this suggests, John and his family had to wait from December 1761 to May 1763 for acceptance of his certificate from Western Branch, one wonders why.

[35] EAQG., II, 576. See also, "Early Minutes of the Philadelphia Monthly Meeting." *The Pennsylvania Genealogical Magazine* 12 (1933): 262. FACD #213.

[36] Lothrop Withington, *Virginia Gleanings in England, 243–44.* in Broderbund, *Family Archives CD #186, Family History: Virginia Genealogies #2 1600s–1800s* (1997).

Jr., was disgraced and dead by drowning. These events are covered below in the notes for Josiah and John, Jr.

John Langdale resided and operated his tannery business in Haddonfield until his death in 1769. On May 6, 1769, shortly before his death he witnessed a will for a man named John Williams, a saddler and presumably a business associate.[37] By this time only one of his sons, Samuel, remained at home.

The Philadelphia Monthly Meeting of Friends recorded on September 18, 1769, the death of John Langdale, age 54, with no other identifying comment. The deceased John Langdale's birthdate would have been around 1715, which is consistent with what we know about the son of Josiah Langdale and Margaret Burton.[38]

Notes for SARAH HUDSON:

On November 28, 1777, shortly after the famous American victory in the Battle of Saratoga, New York, Sarah Hudson Langdale, her daughters Rachel, Margaret, and Jane, and her youngest son, Samuel, were received on certificate from Haddonfield Monthly Meeting.[39] Sarah had been for eight years a widow, her husband, John Langdale, having died on September 18, 1769, at fifty-four years of age.

The John Langdale family's return to Philadelphia came fourteen years after their departure in 1763 to live in Haddonfield. In the meantime, the Philadelphia Monthly Meeting had disowned Sarah's eldest son, Josiah, in 1764 for marriage contrary to discipline, and he had left Philadelphia. Also, Sarah's second son, John Langdale, Jr., had died by drowning in late 1765 under circumstances that would in all likelihood have led to his disownment had he lived. John Langdale, Jr.'s bride and first cousin (John Langdale's niece, Alice Coates Langdale) had been disowned for marriage to "a near kinsman," as the Quaker minutes described it. Moreover, only three months preceding Sarah Hudson Langdale's return to Philadelphia, the Philadelphia Monthly Meeting had disowned Sarah's daughter, Jane Langdale Parke, for marrying out of unity. Considering all of this, Sarah Hudson Langdale must have had mixed emotions as she rejoined the Philadelphia congregation. Her emotional state is unlikely to have improved with subsequent events, which included a conflict between her and the Philadelphia MM.

---

[37]*Abstracts of Philadelphia Co. Wills, 1763-1784, Will Abstracts* [page 584]; in FACD #209.

WILLIAMS, JNO. Neering. Phila. Sadler.

May 6, 1769. June 15, 1769.

Wife: Sarah. Execs.: Sarah Williams and John Howard (joiner).

Children: Joseph, John and Ann Catherine.

Witnesses: John Langdale, Samuel Simpson. Jos. Ogden and Paul Isaac Voto. (O:384)

[38] EAQG II, 387.

[39] EAQG II, 578.

Records show that on November 25, 1778, the Philadelphia Monthly Meeting of Friends disowned a Sarah Langdale for disunity and holding slaves.[40] It would seem that, if she had a husband, he, not she, would have been the one called to answer charges for such a transgression, so this implies she was a widow. Sarah Hudson Langdale, widow of John Langdale, who died in September 1769, seems to be the only Sarah Langdale referenced in the Philadelphia, Burlington, Falls, or Salem Monthly Meeting records of this period who was a widow of mature years. So, it appears that within a year after moving her membership from Haddonfield to Philadelphia, sixty-year-old Sarah Hudson Langdale was disowned by her monthly meeting. Evidently, Sarah did not agree with the Quaker teaching and policy with respect to slavery.

One can only speculate about Sarah's resistance to the pressure coming from the Philadelphia MM with respect to slavery. Her husband having been a tanner, he may have had one or more slaves trained in this work who remained after his death to work at the Langdale tannery, now the property of his widow, Sarah. It may have seemed to Sarah too great a hardship to divest herself of her slaves and, perhaps, her livelihood. It is known that John Langdale advertised his business for sale prior to his death and included a laborer with the assets offered. Whether he succeeded in selling the business is unknown, but if Sarah still owned the tannery, she may well have chosen to hold on to one or more bound or slave workers.

For some years Quaker leaders had been pressing an anti-slavery program.[41] A reflection of the anti-slavery campaign is this notation in the monthly meeting minutes for October of 1761: "Stephen Paschall was dealt with for trading in Negroes. A copy of the minute of the Yearly Meeting respecting those who buy and sell slaves had been delivered to him, and acquainted him with the result of this meeting thereon."[42]

Some members of the congregation rejected the anti-slavery policy and withdrew or were expelled, some accepted it with enthusiasm, and some yielded to official pressure for conformity. In what may have been an example of the last-mentioned scenario, a woman named Mary Robins, having evidently been reprimanded for selling slaves, "sent a paper in regard to her selling 2 slaves, which being read and considered, and the disposition of mind she has manifested giving grounds to hope it proceeds from sincerity, is accepted."[43] Evidently, Mary Robins was either persuaded by, or gave in to, the admonitions of the Philadelphia Monthly Meeting, and expressed her contrition for misconduct persuasively enough to retain her membership.

---

[40] EAQG II, 576.

[41] Jean R. Soderlund, *Quakers & Slavery: A Divided Spirit.* (Princeton NJ: Princeton University Press, 1985).

[42] "Early Minutes of the Philadelphia Monthly Meeting." *The Pennsylvania Genealogical Magazine* 12 (1933): 36. FACD #213.

[43] "Early Minutes of the Philadelphia Monthly Meeting." *The Pennsylvania Genealogical Magazine* 12 (1933): 262. FACD #213

About two years after Sarah Hudson Langdale's disownment for disunity and owning slaves, on August 5, 1780, the Philadelphia Monthly Meeting of Friends recorded the burial of a Sarah Langdale, age 62, without further identification.[44] This deceased lady's birthdate would have been 1718, which is about what one would expect for the wife of John Langdale, married about 1735, and starting to have children around 1736. With such consistency of fact, It is reasonable to identify the deceased Sarah Langdale as Sarah Hudson Langdale, who was born the daughter of William Hudson, Jr., July 18, 1718, and became the mother of eleven (eight surviving beyond childhood) children, including the Josiah Langdale who was by this time becoming identified with Colleton District, South Carolina. Records entered in the Bible of William Hudson, Jr. confirm that his daughter, Sarah Hudson Langdale, died August 5, 1780.[45]

In the two years between her disownment and her death, Sarah Hudson Langdale saw one more of her children come into conflict with the Philadelphia Quaker establishment. This was her youngest son, Samuel, who was disowned on February 26, 1779, for "engaging in a warlike expedition in the American Army."[46] Evidently, like many Quakers of the time, young Samuel Langdale, twenty years old at the time, chose American patriotism over Quaker pacifism.

Children of JOHN LANGDALE and SARAH HUDSON are:

    i.   RACHEL[5] LANGDALE, b. March 07, 1736/37; d. November 1773.

        Notes for RACHEL LANGDALE:

        LDS REFERENCES
        Film #: 177929, Page #: 500, Ordinance #: 19332

        Philadelphia Monthly Meeting records show Rachel Langdale buried January 23, 1773, age 36. Birthdate = about 1737. This would be the right age for John Langdale and Sarah Hudson's firstborn child, Josiah Langdale's elder sister [47]

    ii.   JOSIAH LANGDALE, b. December 18, 1739, of Burlington Co., NJ; d. November 30, 1817, Colleton County, near Walterboro, South Carolina; m. (1) MARY CURTIS OR CLEATON OR CLAYTON,

---

[44] EAQG II, 387.
[45] FACD #163.
[46] EAQG, II, 576.
[47] EAQG II, 387.

Abt. 1764, Philadelphia, PA; d. Aft. March 1794, South Carolina; m.
(2) MARY FLOWERS.

Notes for JOSIAH LANGDALE:

In November 1763, John Langdale's almost-25-year-old son, Josiah,
was in some kind of trouble with the Philadelphia Monthly Meeting
or some member of it. The minutes do not reveal the nature of the
problem but state that "the Friends appointed to treat with Josiah
Langdale, Report, they have assisted him so far that his affairs are in a
way to be settled."[48]

The next, and perhaps only other, mention of Josiah in the minutes of
the Philadelphia Monthly Meeting is a terse statement on June 29,
1764: "Josiah Langdale, late of this City, House Carpenter,
disowned,..."[49]

Hinshaw has the disownment occurring a month earlier. According to
EAQG, II, 576, Josiah was disowned on May 25, 1764, for marriage
contrary to discipline. He was 25.

The description of Josiah in the Quaker minutes as a "house
carpenter" is particularly important because it is evidence that Josiah
Langdale of Philadelphia and Josiah Langdale of Colleton are one and
the same. Notice that in the deed by which Josiah Langdale and his
wife, Mary, sold 200 acres of land to Michael Burdge in Colleton
District, South Carolina, in 1794, Josiah is there described as a "house
carpenter."

Also, the descriptive phrase, "late of this city," indicates that Josiah
had left Philadelphia. So where was he? By 1794 Josiah had been
living in Colleton District for about twenty years. As indicated by
surviving documents, he was there by 1774. His whereabouts during
the decade from his disownment in 1764 to the time of documentary
evidence of his presence in Colleton has not been determined for this
study. Neither is it known that he always resided in the Philadelphia
area before his departure in 1764. Considering that his parents, John

---

[48]"Early Minutes of the Philadelphia Monthly Meeting." *The Pennsylvania Genealogical Magazine* 12 (1933): 266. FACD #213.

[49]"Early Minutes of the Philadelphia Monthly Meeting." *The Pennsylvania Genealogical Magazine* 8 (1938): 27. FACD #213.

Langdale the tanner and wife Sarah Hudson, spent some time, perhaps as much as ten to fifteen years preceding 1761, in or around Isle of Wight County, Virginia, raises the possibility that Josiah may also have traveled, perhaps extensively.

Known events in the life of Josiah Langdale of Colleton (compiled by Dr. George W. Langdale)[50]

June 4, 1774
Josiah Witnessed Barbara Duke's will in Orangeburg District, St. Matthews Parish, South Carolina

September 26, 1780
Josiah Witnessed power of attorney, Berkeley Co., South Carolina

1781-1785
Josiah filed claims vs. South Carolina for provisions sold to Rev. War troops

1785
Tax collected by execution from Josiah in Colleton District, South Carolina

1790
Josiah possibly listed in US Census, Colleton District, St. Bartholomew Parish, South Carolina, as "Joseph Langle" (p. 35)

Dec. 24, 1791
Josiah sold sheep to John Youngblood

March 24, 1794
Josiah and wife, Mary, sold 200 acres to merchant Michael Burdge

1800
Josiah listed in US Census, Colleton District, South Carolina (nine in household)

June 1, 1802
Josiah listed as trustee of Island Creek Methodist Church

---

[50] Langdale, "Langdales of Colleton," 3–9.

August 26, 1803
Josiah filed suit vs. neighbors, members of the King family
Josiah's possessions then included several horses and a large yellow dog.

1810
Josiah listed in US Census, Colleton County, South Carolina (six in household)

1810-1812
Josiah negotiated land payment (Island Creek) with William Robinson

March 20, 1813
Josiah paid taxes in Colleton County, South Carolina

July 1815
Josiah sold 200 acres for $125 to Thomas Robertson

October 29, 1817
Josiah sold land to his 2nd son, John C. Langdale

November 30, 1817
Josiah died

Records of Josiah Langdale in US Census Records:

US Census of 1790 indicates the household of Josiah Langle (presumably an erroneous spelling of Langdale) included a wife, two female children, and two male children. Later evidence shows the males probably would have been William B. Langdale and John C. Langdale.[51]

US Census of 1800, lists Josiah Langdale as head of household including nine members.

US Census of 1810 lists Josiah Langdale as head of household including six members.[52]

---

[51] Langdale, "Langdales of Colleton," note, 6.
[52] Langdale, "Langdales of Colleton," 7.

Notes for MARY CURTIS OR CLEATON OR CLAYTON:

On March 24, 1794, Josiah Langdale and his wife, Mary, executed two documents, a lease (for one year at a price of one peppercorn) and a deed of release, by which they sold 200 acres of land to Michael Burdge for a price of 115 pounds of current South Carolina money. Mary, but not Josiah, signed with her x mark. Michael Burdge is described in both documents as a merchant. Josiah is described as a "house carpenter." Mary is identified in the lease as the daughter of the late John Curtes, deceased; in the release Mary is said to be the daughter of the late John Cleaton, deceased.

The land sold to Michael Burdge was originally granted to William Glover. It was bounded at the time of the original survey by the Edisto River on the northeast and on other sides by vacant land. According to these documents the land was depicted in a plat attached to the original grant and recorded in the secretary of state's office in Book ZZ, page 142.[53]

iii. WILLIAM (1) LANGDALE, b. July 22, 1741; d. August 19, 1741.
iv. JOHN LANGDALE, Jr., b. September 22, 1742, of Burlington Co., NJ; d. Bet. November 29 - December 21, 1765, by drowning at sea; m. ALICE COATES, October 26, 1765, Philadelphia, PA, Chirst Church; b. September 11, 1744, Philadelphia, Philadelphia, PA; d. May 18, 1787, Philadelphia, PA.

Notes for ALICE COATES:

Widowed by the death of her husband, John Langdale, Jr., in 1765, Alice Coates Langdale lived another twenty-two years.

Alice Langdale witnessed a will for Ann Tilbury, widow of Thomas Tilbury and sister of Thomas Evans, on January 3, 1778. Samuel

---

[53] Typewritten copy of lease and deed of release in possession of Dr. George W. Langdale of Athens GA.

Coates was one of the executors of this will.[54] Presumably this Samuel Coates was Alice's youngest brother, the one who had been a few weeks old at the death of their father, Samuel, in 1748.

On January 8, 1784, Alice Coates Langdale witnessed a will for Richard Humphreys of the City of Philadelphia.[55]

On May 17, 1787, Alice Langdale wrote her will, which was proved June 1, 1787. Executors were her brothers, Josiah Langdale Coates and Samuel Coates.[56] So the death of Alice Coates Langdale, widow of John Langdale, Jr., coincided with the completion of the Philadelphia Convention of 1787, which produced the United States Constitution that has been in force since 1789.

   v. MARGARET LANGDALE (1), b. September 09, 1744; d. 1744.

   vi. JANE LANGDALE (1), b. July 17, 1746; d. Abt. 1746.

---

[54] *Abstracts of Philadelphia Co. Wills, 1777–1790, Will Abstracts* [page 1005]; reproduced on Family Archives CD #209

TILBURY, ANN. City of Phila. Widow of Thomas Tilbury.

1 mo. 3, 1778. January 5, 1787. T.431.

Brother: Thomas Evans.

Niece: Mary Evans [Daughter of Brother Thomas Evans of Gwynedd].

Nephew: Hugh Evans.

Exec: Samuel Coates, Mary Evans, William Wilson.

Wit: John Evans, Joseph Crukshank, Alice Langdale.

[55] *Abstracts of Philadelphia Co. Wills, 1790–1802, Liber W* [page 331]; reproduced on Family Archives CD #209

HUMPHREYS, RICHARD. City of Phila.

January 8, 1784. November 17, 1793. W.552.

Wife: Mary. Children: Hannah, Richard. Friend: Sarah Robinson.

Cousin: Patience Jones.

Exec: Mary Humphreys, Son-in-Law John Litle, Nathan Sellers.

Wit: Thomas West, Alice Langdale.

[56] *Abstracts of Philadelphia Co. Wills, 1777-1790, Will Abstracts* [page 1044]; FACD #209.

LANGDALE, ALICE. City of Phila. Widow.

5 mo. 17, 1787. June 1, 1787. T.504.

Brothers and Exec: Josiah Langdale Coates, Samuel Coates.

Nephew: Samuel Coates, Junr.

Friends: Sarah Blake, Rachel Attmore, Mary [Wife of Richard Humphreys.

Wit: Charles Moore, Thomas Moore.

vii. WILLIAM HUDSON LANGDALE, b. November 22, 1747, of Burlington Co., New Jersey; d. December 1772.

Notes for WILLIAM HUDSON LANGDALE:

The Philadelphia Monthly Meeting of Friends recorded the burial on February 9, 1772, of a William Langdale, but without further identification.[57] It is reasonable to identify the son of John and Sarah as the person whose burial is noted, but there being no birthdate, age, or other information given for the deceased, the identification is less convincing than some others. With regard to Langdale deaths, see also the Notes for John Langdale, father of William Hudson Langdale.

viii. ELIZABETH LANGDALE, b. January 13, 1748/49, of Burlington Co., New Jersey; d. Aft. May 16, 1821, Bucks County, PA; m. JOHN BALDERSTON, Jr., February 09, 1797, Philadelphia, PA, Monthly Meeting of Friends; b. Of Solebury Township, near Philadelphia; d. Bet. November 09, 1820 - May 16, 1821, Bucks County, PA.

Notes for ELIZABETH LANGDALE:

On October 17, 1780, at age thirty-one, Elizabeth Langdale asked for permission to visit New York City, but the Pennsylvania authorities denied her request.[58] In the Revolutionary War situation, freedom to travel took second place to military security. Suspicions abounded. While some were denied permission to leave Philadelphia at times during the war, others were expelled as British sympathizers or worse.

On May 28, 1784, the Philadelphia Monthly Meeting received Elizabeth Langdale on certificate dated April 5, 1784, from Buckingham Monthly Meeting.[59]

---

[57] EAQG II, 387.

[58] "Petitions and Passes," annotated by Hannah Benner Roach, Volume 36, *The Pennsylvania Genealogical Magazine*, reproduced in *Genealogical Records: The Pennsylvania Genealogical Magazine*, Volumes 1-39, FACD #213

[59] EAQG, II, 576.

On December 8, 1794, Elizabeth Langdale witnessed a will for her friend Esther Fisher Lewis, widow of Samuel Lewis and daughter of Joshua Fisher, merchant, of Philadelphia.[60]

---

[60] *Abstracts of Philadelphia Co. Wills, 1790–1802, Liber X* [page 142]; FACD #209.

FISHER, ESTHER [LEWIS, LATE FISHER].

Widow of Samuel Lewis, Deceas'd. City of Phila.

January 27, 1791. February 27, 1795. X.202.

[A Daughter of Joshua Fisher, Late of said City, Merchant, Deceas'd].

To Exec. for Treasurer of the Monthly Meeting of Women Friends for Southern District [for poor of said Meeting] and to each of the two other Meetings of Women Friends [in this City].

To Overseers of School for Blacks under the care of the three Monthly Meetings.

Friends: Rebecca Jones, Hannah Cathrall.

To Exec. for Friends, as the Monthly Meeting May appoint for a Lot for the Quarterly Meeting of Friends and care of a Boarding School in the Country for any number not exceeding Fifty Boys or Girls.

To First Cousins: Phebe Vining, Benjamin Wynkoop, Esther Draper, Fenwick Fisher, Edward Fisher, Sarah Rowland [Widow], Isaiah Rowland, Sarah Mifflin [Widow], Susanna Emerson, James Blundell, Elizabeth Cogell, Mary Allston, Eunice Edmondson, Tabitha Jenkins.

Friend: Henry Shaw.

Sister: Lydia Gilpin.

To Brothers: Thomas Fisher, Samuel Rowland Fisher, Miers Fisher.

Nephews: Samuel Fisher Daws, Edward Daws [Children of Sister Sarah].

Exec: Brothers Thomas, Samuel and Miers Fisher.

Wit: Joseph Bringhurst, Ebenezer Cresson, William Waln.

Codicil: Signed December 8, 1794.

To Sister Lydia Gilpin, Cousin Phebe Vining. Revoking Legacy to Monthly Meeting [Southern District]. In Lieu thereof towards building a Commodious House for use of the Yearly Meeting held in this City.

To Exec. [In Trust] for Institution under the care of Yearly Meeting of Friends for Pennsylvania, New Jersey and for Instructing of Youth in one or more Schools.

To Exec. [In Trust] for Poor Widows and other objects of Charity who are not maintained by our Religious Society.

To Friends: Rebecca Jones, Hannah Cathrall, Abigail Duer, Rachel Offley, Hannah Pryor, Rachel Johns, Elizabeth Osborne, Margaret Porter, Sarah Bond, Jane Cord, Mary Houlton, Mary Longstroth, Elizabeth Langdale.

Niece: Sarah Rodman Fisher [Daughter of Brother Samuel].

Brothers: Thomas and Miers.

To Husband's Kinsmen: William Clifton, Ann and George Mifflin, Hannah Davis [Niece of Samuel Lewis], Joseph, John, Abel Lewis [Sons of Abel Lewis].

Wit: Cadwalader Evans, John Watson.

2nd Codicil: Signed December 8, 1794.

On March 31, 1797, Elizabeth Langdale Balderston was granted a certificate to the Buckingham Monthly Meeting. [61] This was a few weeks after her marriage to John Balderston, Jr. Elizabeth outlived her husband, who died in early 1821, for she is listed in his will written in January and proved May 16, 1821.[62]

ix. MARGARET LANGDALE, b. March 01, 1750/51, of Burlington Co., New Jersey; d. Abt. November 23, 1798, Philadelphia, PA.

Notes for MARGARET LANGDALE:

The Philadelphia Monthly Meeting of Friends recorded the burial of Margaret Langdale on November 26, 1798, at age 40. Subtracting to calculate the birthdate yields 1758, about six years after the recorded birth of Margaret, the daughter of John Langdale and Sarah Hudson. If the original manuscript had deteriorated or faded, however, it is conceivable that the "40" could be a misreading of "46." Anyway, this Margaret Langdale appears to be the only possible "fit" listed in the Philadelphia Quaker records of the period. The abstract of

---

To Workman: Prina Spruaner. Bound Girl: Elizabeth Wilston.

To Philip Rice [Husband's Relation].

Wit: Elizabeth Langdale, Thomas Gilpin.

Typed in margin: "Cod. 12 mo. 1794. I. Esther Lewis, late Fisher - mentions late husband Samuel Fisher".

[61]EAQG, II, 458.

[62] *Abstracts of Bucks Co., PA, Wills, 1785–1825, Will Book No. 10* [page 12] FACD #209 Page 15. John Balderston, Solebury Twp. May 16, 1818. Codicil November 9, 1820.

Do. dated January 17, 1821. Proved May 16, 1821.

Sons John and Mark exrs.

Wife Elizabeth.

Dau. Hannah, wife of John Michel of City of Baltimore.

Plantation in Falls Twp. whereon son John lives to daus. Merab and Ann Balderston.

Son Mark. Plantation whereon he lives in Falls Twp.

John 162 Acres whereon I live. Also 133 Acres in Loyalstock Twp., Lycoming Co., bought of William Watson.

Maryk 164 Acres 1 do. Patented September 1796 and 107 Acres in Muncy Twp., Lycoming Co., surveyed December 3, 1794.

Obligation on account of estate of Margaret Langdale, Deceased, executed to Thomas Savoy.

Wits: Joseph and William Rice, Robert Smith.

Margaret Langdale's will, listing her sisters Jane Parke and Elizabeth Balderson, confirm the identification.[63]

x. JANE LANGDALE, b. March 01, 1755, of Burlington Co., New Jersey; m. DR. THOMAS PARKE, August 15, 1777, Philadelphia, PA; b. Of Delaware and Philadelphia.

xi. SAMUEL LANGDALE, Sr., b. October 16, 1759, Philadelphia, PA; d. July 23, 1826, Clarksburgh, Ross, OH; m. (1) ELIZABETH BIDDLE; b. Ireland; m. (2) MARGARET LNU, Bet. 1779 - 1789; m. (3) ELIZABETH TRUITT, June 21, 1810, Ross, Ohio.

Notes for SAMUEL LANGDALE, Sr.:

A published history of Montgomery County, PA, edited by Theodore W. Bean and published in 1884, credits Samuel Langdale with heroic service under General Anthony Wayne at the Battle of Paoli in the Revolutionary War. A newspaper obituary in Ross County, OH, also referred to Samuel's military record.

Current research by descendants of Samuel Langdale indicates that he moved to Ohio shortly after the Revolutionary War and died in Clarksburgh. There is evidence that one of his sons, born in Chillicothe, Ohio, returned from Ohio to live near Philadelphia. Samuel's descendants are found in Ohio, Indiana, Illinois, and westward to California.

---

[63] EAQG II, 387; *Abstracts of Philadelphia Co. Wills, 1790-1802, Liber Y* [page 59]; FACD #209.

LANGDALE, MARGARET. City of Phila.

September 12, 1798. November 23, 1798. Y.68.

Sisters: Jane Parke, Elizabeth Balderson.

Nephews and Nieces: Ann, Thomas, Susanna, Joshua, Samuel Emblem, Robert Parke [Children of Sister Jane].

Exec: John James, Thomas Savory.

Testified as to wish of Testator: John James.

Appendix D

William B. Langdale

Descendants

(Two Generations)

This is a report produced with the genealogy program, *Family Tree Maker*, from a working file that includes data contributed by others and verified by them, not by the writer. It reflects research in progress, not a final product, and is placed here for the benefit of those interested in Langdale genealogy. Many Langdale genealogy questions remain unanswered and some conclusions are, of course, tentative. Persons desiring to correspond with the researcher can do so through the Langdale bulletin board pages on the Internet, either by posting a message or by sending e-mail to the address listed there. URLs for two bulletin boards are: http://genforum.genealogy.com and http://www.familyhistory.com.

Generation No. 1

1. WILLIAM B.[6] LANGDALE *(JOSIAH[5], JOHN[4], JOSIAH[3], JOSEPH[2], JOSIAHSGRANDFATHER[1])* was born Bef. 1787 in Colleton County, South Carolina, perhaps, and died Bef. November 28, 1821. He married JANE GUTHRIE Abt. 1814 in Colleton County, South Carolina. She was born January 15, 1802 in Ireland, according to a Walterboro newspaper article, and died December 24, 1880, in Colleton County, South Carolina.

Notes for WILLIAM B. LANGDALE:

Information is sparse. The earliest document so far found to mention William B. Langdale is a passport issued November 16, 1802, to enter the Cherokee Nation, work three months as a smith for James Vann, and return by way of Tellico.[64]

Military records list him and his brother, John C. Langdale, as privates in the War of 1812. They were both in Juhan's Battalion, South Carolina Militia. Also, there is reportedly a record of his having paid tax in 1824 on 195 acres at 20 cents per acre in Colleton District, South Carolina. The tax record is suspect, however, for it is thought that William died by 1821, leaving Jane a widow. Jane Guthrie Langdale married William's brother, John C. Langdale in November of that year.[65]

Sign pointing way to Island Creek Cemetery. This is north of Walterboro, South Carolina. It is also known as Ireland Creek. JEL.

---

[64] Dorothy Williams Potter, ed., *Passports of Southeastern Pioneers, 1770–1823* (Baltimore MD: Gateway Press, 1982), 97–98.

William Langdale has permission to go into the Cherokee Nation to the House of Mr. James Vann to work at the Smiths business for Mr. Vann for the term of three months & return back by the way of Tellico.

South West Point

16th Novr. 1802

R. J. Meigs, A. War[274]

[65] Langdale, "Langdales of Colleton," 11.

Notes for JANE GUTHRIE:

A "Jane Langdale" is listed in the LDS International Genealogical Index as born in South Carolina in 1802. Considering that Jane Guthrie Langdale was born in 1802, the IGI reference is presumably to Jane Guthrie Langdale.

Langdale Graves, Island Creek Cemetery. From L/R, these are grave markers of Margaret O'Bryan Langdale, Jane Guthrie Langdale, J. W. M. Langdale, and J. S. H. Langdale. The small wooden marker to the right of Jane Guthrie's monument has no identification. JEL.

More About JANE GUTHRIE:

Burial: December 1880, Island Creek Methodist Church Cemetery
Buried: Island Creek Cemetery, Colleton Co., South Carolina
Property: 1860, Estate valued @ $8663 ($7500 real & $1163 personal),
     US Census of 1860.
Pension: February 1879, War of 1812 pensioner
Occupation: 1860, A Nurse [says US Census of 1860]
Religion: Aft. 1878, Member Island Creek Methodist Church

Children of WILLIAM LANGDALE and JANE GUTHRIE are:
i.   CHILD[7] LANGDALE?.
ii.   MARY FRANCES LANGDALE.

2.   iii.   JOHN ROBERT LANGDALE, b. May 23, 1815, Colleton County, South Carolina; d. March 02, 1863, Fredericksburg, VA, hospital.

Grave marker of Jane Guthrie Langdale, Island Creek Methodist Cemetery, Colleton County SC. She was the mother of the children of William B. Langdale and John C. Langdale. Within about two years of Jane's burial here. owing to the deterioration of the meeting house, the Island Creek Methodist Church disbanded and its members transferred to other churches.

Generation No. 2

2. JOHN ROBERT[7] LANGDALE *(WILLIAM B.[6], JOSIAH[5], JOHN[4], JOSIAH[3], JOSEPH[2], JOSIAHSGRANDFATHER[1])* was born May 23, 1815 in Colleton County, South Carolina, and died March 02, 1863 in Fredericksburg, VA, hospital. He married HARRIET GRIFFIN August 08, 1835 in Lowndes (now Berrien) Co., GA (by Randall Folsom, JP), daughter of THOMAS GRIFFIN and NANCY HALL. She was born 1819 in Montgomery County, GA, and died August 1898 in Echols Co., GA.

Notes for JOHN ROBERT LANGDALE:

John Robert Langdale was born May 30, 1815, in Colleton District, South Carolina. He grew to a height of 5' 8" and had dark complexion. Moving from South Carolina, he lived for a time in Camden County, GA, and later in Berrien and Clinch counties. On August 8, 1835, he married Harriet Griffin. Randall Folsom, JP, performed the ceremony.

John Robert enlisted five times for military service, starting as a private under Captain John Pike from April to December 1836 in the Indian War. The following year he enlisted again, beginning December 23, 1837, under Captain W. C. Newbern/Northern. Twenty years later he went into military service again against the Indians, this time under Captain William H. Cone. For this duty he enlisted at Tampa Bay on July 1, 1857, and was discharged in the same city on January 22, 1858.

The final two enlistments were in the Confederate army. He went in as a private on August 1, 1861, and was discharged at Savannah on August 18, 1862. Less than two months later, on October 7, 1862, he enlisted again as a privete in Company I, 50th Regiment, Georgia Infantry as a substitute for J. L. Sutton. The certificate showing John Robert's enlistment as a substitute was recorded in Berrien Co. Deed Book 13, p. 183. John Robert Langdale died of pneumonia at a Fredericksburg, VA, hospital on March 2, 1863.[66]

On Dec. 7, 1859, John R. Langdale of Echols County, GA, purchased from Silas A. O'Quin of Columbia County, Florida, a parcel of land one acre in size, more or less, in the town of Magnolia. The price was $125.00. Acting for Silas O'Quin was his attorney in fact, David O'Quin, who also, as clerk of the Clinch County Superior Court, recorded the deed in Deed Book A, Page 383. [67]

Children of JOHN LANGDALE and HARRIET GRIFFIN are:

    i.   NOAH[8] LANGDALE, b. 1835, Berrien Co., GA; d. May 20, 1862, Confed Service; Place unknown—Augusta, GA, perhaps; m. ELIZABETH BURNETT, 1857; b. May 02, 1836, Colleton County, South Carolina; d. January 12, 1878, Echols County, Georgia.

       More About NOAH LANGDALE:
       Burial: May 1862, Magnolia Cemetery, Augusta, GA
       Military service: March 04, 1862, Enlisted at Blackshear in Co. A, 50th GA Vols (Pierce County - Satilla Rangers)

       More About ELIZABETH BURNETT:

---

[66] Huxford Genealogical Library, Langdale File; Gretta Holcom, Bradenton FL, E-mail to John Lancaster, 11 March 1999.

[67]Photocopy of deed, Papers of John W. Langdale, Valdosta GA.

Burial: January 1878, Bethel P.B. Church
Christening: September 14, 1856, Baptized Bethel P.B. Ch, Echols,
Co., GA

ii.   MARY POLLY LANGDALE, b. 1842, Berrien Co., GA; m.
      GEORGE WARD.

iii. REBECCA LANGDALE, b. 1846, Berrien Co., GA; m. WILLIAM
      T. MEADOWS, March 01, 1868, Brooks County, GA.

iv.   MITCHELL GRIFFIN LANGDALE, b. September 14, 1848,
      Homerville, Clinch, GA; d. 1923, Homerville, Clinch, GA; m. (1)
      AMIE ANN GRINER, October 03, 1869; b. October 08, 1842,
      Nashville, Berrien, GA; d. September 24, 1906, Milltown, Berrien,
      GA; m. (2) ELIZABETH WOODS, Aft. 1906.

      More About MITCHELL GRIFFIN LANGDALE:
      Burial: Lakeland, Lanier, GA
      LDS Ancestral File #: 5BGF-9M

      More About AMIE ANN GRINER:
      Burial: September 26, 1906, Milltown, Berrien, GA
      LDS Ancestral File #: 5BGF-BS

v.   NANCY LANGDALE, b. 1851, Clinch County, GA; m. SAMUEL
      N. GRINER, March 10, 1867.

vi.   JOHN CURTIS LANGDALE, b. November 05, 1853, Worth Co.,
      GA; d. August 01, 1934, Sumner, GA; m. (1) MARTHA VAN
      MAULDING, Bef. 1878; b. August 11, 1858; d. April 23, 1878,
      Sumner, GA; m. (2) JOAN BOZEMAN, Bef. 1883; b. WFT Est.
      1844-1866; d. WFT Est. 1888–1955; m. (3) MISSOURI BRYAN OR
      TOMPKINS, April 07, 1883; b. February 15, 1848; d. September 10,
      1889; m. (4) LAURA ANNIE MEADOWS, January 09, 1889; b.
      December 21, 1870; d. October 21, 1962, Tampa, Florida.

      Notes for JOHN CURTIS LANGDALE:
      ───

      Occupation: Farmer. Married several times. Some of his children
      were: Noah Langdale, Carrie (Langdale) Hancock of Plant City,
      Florida, James Langdale of Sumner, Worth County, Georgia. Birth
      order and by which wife unknown at this writing.

More About JOHN CURTIS LANGDALE:
Burial: Abt. August 03, 1934, Wright's Chapel Cem., Sumner, GA

More About MARTHA VAN MAULDING:
Burial: Abt. April 25, 1878, Wright's Chapel Cem., Sumner, GA

Notes for MISSOURI BRYAN OR TOMPKINS:

Died in childbirth. Buried Abt. September 12, 1889, at the Tompkins
Family Cemetery, Worth County, Georgia.

More About LAURA ANNIE MEADOWS:
Burial: Abt. October 23, 1962, Myrtle Hill Cem, Tampa, FL

vii. JAMES D. LANGDALE, b. 1856; m. MARY ???.
viii. MARTHA N. LANGDALE, b. 1859, Clinch Co., Georgia.
ix. FNU LANGDALE, b. 1860, Echols Co, GA; d. 1860, Echols Co, GA.
x. MALINDA LANGDALE, b. 1862, Echols County, GA; m. ???
DEAN.

Appendix E

John C. Langdale

Descendants

(Two Generations)

This is a report produced with the genealogy program, *Family Tree Maker*, from a working file that includes data contributed by others and verified by them, not by the writer. It reflects research in progress, not a final product, and is placed here for the benefit of those interested in Langdale genealogy. Many genealogy questions remain unanswered and some conclusions are, of course, tentative. Persons desiring to correspond with the researcher can do so through the Langdale bulletin board pages on the Internet, either by posting a message or by sending e-mail to the address listed there. URLs for two bulletin boards are: http://genforum.genealogy.com and http://www.familyhistory.com.

Generation No. 1

1. JOHN C.[6] LANGDALE *(JOSIAH[5], JOHN[4], JOSIAH[3], JOSEPH[2], JOSIAHSGRANDFATHER[1])* was born December 29, 1787 in Colleton County, South Carolina, perhaps, and died December 10, 1846, in Colleton County, South Carolina. He married JANE GUTHRIE November 28, 1821, in Colleton County, South Carolina. She was born January 15, 1802, in Ireland, according to a Walterboro newspaper article, and died December 24, 1880, in Colleton County, South Carolina.

Notes for JOHN C. LANGDALE:

_____

Dr. George W. Langdale found the following records for John C. Langdale.[68]

Sept. 30, 1821	Sunday School Certificate to John C. Langdale
May 7, 1828	Road grant
March 1, 1831	John C. paid general taxes to St. Bartholomew Parish
Nov. 12, 1832	Date of John C. Langdale's will preparation
Apr. 23, 1835	Date of summons for petit & common pleas jury duty
Jul 10, 1840	Business settlement with Christian G. Flete

In 1840 (the time of the 1840 US Census), John C. and Jane Guthrie Langdale had eight children, five girls and three boys, living at home. Evidence is as follows: The 1840 US Census for South Carolina, Colleton District, St. Bartholomew's Parish, lists heads of families and categorizes household members by sex and age. Names, except for the head of household, are not listed. Names and ages provided by family members, however, appear consistent with the census numbers and categories.

The census reports 1 male between 50 and 60 years of age. That would have been John C., age 53.

The census reports 1 male between 15 and 20. That would have been J. W.M., the eldest child, age 20.

The census reports 1 male between 5 and 10. Presumably that was John R. C., age 8.

The census reports 1 male under 5 years of age. This presumably was J.S.H. , said to have been 6 years of age. Perhaps he was actually a year younger.

The census reports 6 female members of the household, 1 of whom was between 30 and 40 years of age. That would have been Jane Guthrie Langdale, age 38.

According to the census, there were 3 girls between 10 and 15 years of age. That is consistent with the ages of Mary, 14; Eliza, 12; and Caroline, 11.

The census reports 1 female between 5 and 10. That is consistent with the age for Ann, who was 6.

The census reports 1 female under 5 years of age. The youngest child, Margaret, was born in 1840, the year of the census.[69]

---

[68] Langdale, "Langdales of Colleton," 10.

[69] Census numbers provided by John W. Langdale, from notes taken in the US National Archives. Ages of children based on G. W. Langdale, "Langdales of Colleton," which on

More About JOHN C. LANGDALE:

Event: Burial in Island Creek Cem., Colleton Co., South Carolina
Event: Abt. 1812, Pvt, Juhan's Battn, South Carolina Militia, War of 1812
Event: December 28, 1814, Witness to land sale
Event: October 29, 1817, Purch. Island Creek land frm. Josiah L.
Event: December 10, 1823, As Sgt., particip. in court martial/Colleton
Event: 1832, Planter [he called himself, in will]

Military: Bet. 1812 - 1830, South Carolina Militia service, approx. dates
Religion: 1828, Trustee, Island Creek Methodist Church
Property: 1824, Tax return, Colleton District., 947 acres

Grave marker of Margaret
O'Bryan Langdale, Island Creek
Cemetery, Colleton County SC.
JEL.

Children of JOHN LANGDALE and JANE GUTHRIE are:
2.
     i. JOSIAH WILLIAM MARMADUKE[7] LANGDALE, b. December 09, 1822,
Colleton County, South Carolina; d. March 17, 1862.

---

pages 12–13 includes text of John C. Langdale's 1832 will. In the will, John C. named five
children as his heirs: Marmaduke, Mary, Eliza, Caroline, and John.

ii. MARY R. C. LANGDALE, b. June 20, 1824; d. November 03, 1867.
iii. ELIZABETH CAROLINE "BETSY" LANGDALE, b. April 23, 1826; d. March 30, 1862.
iv. JANE CAROLINE LANGDALE, b. May 26, 1828; d. July 22, 1879.
v. JOHN R. C. LANGDALE, b. May 26, 1831; d. August 29, 1857.
vi. SARA ANN CAROLINE LANGDALE, b. May 26, 1834; d. January 12, 1861.

3.
vii. JEREMIAH SAMUEL HUDSON LANGDALE, b. April 24, 1837, Colleton County, South Carolina; d. June 12, 1903, Colleton County, South Carolina.
viii. MARGARET O'BRYAN LANGDALE, b. April 13, 1839, Colleton County, South Carolina; d. February 21, 1920.
ix. JOHN WILLIS LANGDALE, b. 1841, Colleton, Colleton, South Carolina.

Grave markers of Josiah William Marmaduke and Jeremiah Samuel Hudson Langdale, Island Creek Methodist Cemetery, Colleton SC. JEL.

Generation No. 2

2. JOSIAH WILLIAM MARMADUKE[7] LANGDALE *(JOHN C.[6], JOSIAH[5], JOHN[4], JOSIAH[3], JOSEPH[2], JOSIAHSGRANDFATHER[1])* was born December 09, 1822, in Colleton County, South Carolina, and died March 17, 1862. He married MARGARET E. CROSBY Abt. 1847, daughter of HUMPHREY CROSBY and SARAH SAVAGE. She was born Abt. 1827, and died 1897.

More About JOSIAH WILLIAM MARMADUKE LANGDALE:
Fact 2: Bet. 1861 - 1865, Civil War: Pvt., 11th South Carolina Vols.
Residence: 1850, Colleton Co., South Carolina

More About MARGARET E. CROSBY:
Burial: Walterboro, South Carolina
Fact 1: burried at Pleasant Grove Baptist Church, Colleton Co., South Carolina
Fact 2: 1860, Census lists 7 children, all under age 11
Fact 3: 1900, Lived with son Archy [1900 US Census]
Fact 4: 1900, 4 of 5 sons families totaled about 40

Children of JOSIAH LANGDALE and MARGARET CROSBY are:
     i.   JOSIAH WILLIAM MARMADUKE[8] LANGDALE, b. July 15, 1849; d. 1934; m. (1) S. HETEY OR HETTIE BELL CROSBY, Abt. 1870; b. 1852; d. 1889; m. (2) AGNES M. SLOMAN, Bef. 1896; b. 1860; d. 1944.
     ii.   JULEAN EMALINE LAURA LANGDALE, b. September 29, 1850; d. 1923; m. JAMES SAULS.
     iii.   JOHN C. LANGDALE, b. April 29, 1852.
     iv.   HUMPHRY BENJAMIN H. LANGDALE, b. March 06, 1854, Colleton Co., SC; d. March 12, 1919, Colleton Co., South Carolina; m. MARTHA MILDRED HICKMAN, March 27, 1876; b. March 24, 1859, Colleton Co., South Carolina; d. February 23, 1941, Colleton Co., SC.
     v.   ARCHEVILLE HENRY OWENS LANGDALE, b. April 11, 1856; m. SARAH HICKMAN, Abt. 1881; b. May 26, 1851; d. 1925.
     vi.   CHARLY LAWRENCE MAZON LANGDALE, b. May 30, 1858; d. March 31, 1935; m. (1) BELLE SMITH; m. (2) JANIE HIOTT; b. 1861; m. (3) MARY LACEY; m. (4) BELLE MARTIN.
     vii. SARA JANE REBECCA LANGDALE, b. August 31, 1862, Colleton, Colleton, South Carolina; d. October 29, 1926; m. JIMMY JORDAN.

3. JEREMIAH SAMUEL HUDSON[7] LANGDALE *(JOHN C.[6], JOSIAH[5], JOHN[4], JOSIAH[3], JOSEPH[2], JOSIAHSGRANDFATHER[1])* was born April 24, 1837 in Colleton County, SC, and died June 12, 1903 in Colleton County, SC. He married VICTORIA A. SMITH. She was born June 26, 1846, and died December 16, 1924.

More About JEREMIAH SAMUEL HUDSON LANGDALE:
Burial: 1903, Walterboro, SC
Fact 2: Bet. 1861 - 1865, Civil War: Sgt., 11th SC Volunteers

Fact 3: Civil War: Hospitalized at Richmond

Children of JEREMIAH LANGDALE and VICTORIA SMITH are:
    i.   JULIUS SAMUEL HUDSON[8] LANGDALE, b. July 22, 1863, Colleton County, SC; d. March 16, 1946, Gadsden, AL.

More About JULIUS SAMUEL HUDSON LANGDALE:
Burial: March 1946, Union Hill Cemetery, N. Gadsden, AL
Fact 2: Several sisters taught school, Colleton CO, SC
Occupation: Methodist minister/ businessman
Residence: 1900, Resided Attalla City, Etowah Co, AL (US Census of 1900)

    ii.   MATILDA E. LANGDALE, b. December 30, 1866; m. JOHN SAMUEL KENT; b. July 24, 1852; d. January 25, 1931.
    iii.   JANE MINERVA LANGDALE, b. March 22, 1871, Walterboro, Colleton County, South Carolina; d. December 15, 1909, Walterboro, Colleton County, South Carolina; m. WILLIAM STEPHEN THOMAS; b. April 02, 1875, Smoaks, Colleton County, South Carolina; d. May 24, 1923, Walterboro, Colleton County, South Carolina.
    iv.   LAURA LANGDALE, b. 1873.
    v.   MARGARET LANGDALE, b. 1874.
    vi.   LALLA LANGDALE, b. October 18, 1875; m. H. A. SMITH.
    vii.   VIOLA CARRY LANGDALE, b. May 24, 1880; m. PAUL K. WALTER; b. May 31, 1882.
    viii. CROMWELL LANGDALE, b. December 1885; m. MAGGIE BELLE WIMBERLY.

Appendix F
Noah Langdale
Descendants

(Two Generations)

This is a report produced with the genealogy program, *Family Tree Maker*, from a working file that includes data contributed by others and verified by them, not by the writer. It reflects research in progress, not a final product, and is placed here for the benefit of those interested in Langdale genealogy. Many genealogy questions remain unanswered and some conclusions are, of course, tentative. Persons desiring to correspond with the researcher can do so through the Langdale bulletin board pages on the Internet, either by posting a message or by sending e-mail to the address listed there. URLs for two bulletin boards are: http://genforum.genealogy.com and http://www.familyhistory.com.

Generation No. 1

1. NOAH[8] LANGDALE *(JOHN ROBERT[7], WILLIAM B.[6], JOSIAH[5], JOHN[4], JOSIAH[3], JOSEPH[2], JOSIAHSGRANDFATHER[1])* was born 1835 in Berrien Co., GA, and died May 20, 1862 in Confed Service; Place unknown—Augusta, GA, perhaps. He married ELIZABETH BURNETT 1857, daughter of JOHN BURNETT and SOPHIA HARVEY. She was born May 02, 1836, in Colleton County, South Carolina, and died January 12, 1878, in Echols County, Georgia.

More About NOAH LANGDALE:
Burial: May 1862, Magnolia Cemetery, Augusta, GA
Military service: March 04, 1862, Enlisted at Blackshear in Co. A, 50th GA Vols (Pierce County - Satilla Rangers)

Harley Langdale, Jr. and John J. Langdale Jr.
view the monument to John Wesley and Nancy
Burnsed Langdale, Bethel Primitive Baptist
Church Cemetery near Fargo, Georgia, in 1995.
JEL.

More About ELIZABETH BURNETT:
Burial: January 1878, Bethel P.B. Church
Christening: September 14, 1856, Baptized Bethel P.B. Ch, Echols, Co., GA
Children of NOAH LANGDALE and ELIZABETH BURNETT are:

2.	i.	MARY JANE[9] LANGDALE, b. December 19, 1858, Echols County, GA; d. June 28, 1908, Echols Co., GA.
3.	ii.	JOHN WESLEY LANGDALE, b. February 10, 1860, Echols County, GA; settled in Clinch, Co., GA, 1884; d. June 07, 1911, Jasper, Fla.
4.	iii.	JEFFERSON DAVIS LANGDALE, b. January 20, 1862; d. November 08, 1918, Valdosta, GA, probably.

Generation No. 2

2. MARY JANE[9] LANGDALE *(NOAH[8], JOHN ROBERT[7], WILLIAM B.[6], JOSIAH[5], JOHN[4], JOSIAH[3], JOSEPH[2], JOSIAHSGRANDFATHER[1])* was born December 19, 1858, in Echols County, GA, and died June 28, 1908, in Echols Co., GA.

Notes for MARY JANE LANGDALE:
Never married. Buried at Bethel Primitive Baptist (Boney Bluff) Cemetery.

Loaned money to nephew Harley for college (according to Rose Langdale Johnson and Virginia Langdale Miller).

Children of MARY JANE LANGDALE are:
  i.   LOU[10] LANGDALE.
  ii.   JIM LANGDALE.

3. JOHN WESLEY[9] LANGDALE *(NOAH[8], JOHN ROBERT[7], WILLIAM B.[6], JOSIAH[5], JOHN[4], JOSIAH[3], JOSEPH[2], JOSIAHSGRANDFATHER[1])* was born February 10, 1860, in Echols County, GA; settled in Clinch, Co., GA, 1884, and died June 07, 1911, in Jasper, Fla. He married NANCY BURNSED 1884 in Echols Co., GA, daughter of GIDEON BURNSED and ELIZABETH DAUGHARTY. She was born April 08, 1863, in Charlton County, GA, and died November 03, 1913.

Notes for JOHN WESLEY LANGDALE:

NEWSPAPER OBITUARY, 1911

Born in Clinch County, GA; main business interests at Council, Clinch Co., GA. Lived in Jasper, FL, at time of death from Typhoid fever on June 7, 1911. Died at home after illness of about six weeks.

"Mr. Langdale was a native of Clinch county and one of the most prominent men in that county. He had large interest in the Southern portion of Clinch county and leaves an estate valued at something like 150,000."

"It is said that he had 35,000 or 40,000 in cash in the bank. He was only 51 years of age and was in the prime of life. It was said that he was not only a good citizen but a splendid neighbor, and many people who was less fortunate than he was in accumulating money shared bountifully what he made."[70]

More About JOHN WESLEY LANGDALE:

Burial: 1911, Bethel P.B. Church, Echols Co., GA
Cause of Death: Typhoid Fever
Family/Heirs: Survived by wife & six children, 4 grown
Occupation: 1911, Naval stores & cattle business
Property: 1911, Estate estimated value of $150, 000, with $35, 000 to $40, 000 in bank.
Religion: Assoc. with (not a member) Bethel P.B. Ch., Echols Co., GA
Residence: 1911, Council, Clinch Co., GA, & Jasper, FL

Children of JOHN LANGDALE and NANCY BURNSED are:
    i.   JOHN J.[10] LANGDALE, b. March 16, 1885, Clinch County, GA; d. August 10, 1955; m. ROSALIE TALLEY CORNELIUS, December 02, 1923, Homerville, Clinch Co., GA; b. August 02, 1901, Clinch County, GA; d. January 03, 1967, Echols Co., GA.

           More About JOHN J. LANGDALE:
           Burial: Abt. August 12, 1955, Homerville, Clinch Co., GA

    ii.   NOAH LANGDALE, b. July 16, 1886; m. JESSIE C. CATLEDGE.

---

[70] *Clinch County News*, 16 June 1911, reprint of article from *Valdosta Times*.

Notes for NOAH LANGDALE:

Facts, History of Lowndes County, Georgia, 1825–1941[71]

1926   Bought interest of J.M. Youngblood Co. & formed GA Lumber & Supply Co.
Feb 12, 1934   Elected to Valdosta, GA, City Council.
March 6, 1940   Elected to Valdosta, GA, City Council

iii.   HARLEY LANGDALE, b. January 24, 1888, Clinch County, GA; d. April 10, 1972, Valdosta, GA; m. THALIA MAUDE LEE, August 14, 1913, Lynchburg, VA; b. February 14, 1885, Gretna, Virginia, near Lynchburg.

More About HARLEY LANGDALE:

Burial: April 12, 1972, Sunset Hill Cem., Valdosta, GA
Fact 8: Last residence: GA 31601
Fact 10: Social Security #: 257-10-8899
Fact 11: State of issue: GA
LDS Reference: Batch #: 1903520, Source Call #:

Notes for THALIA MAUDE LEE:

After the death of Silas Watkins Lee in 1900, his widow moved with her three children from Gretna to Lynchburg, VA. Mrs. Lee had two sons, Ernest and Richard Ivey, and a daughter, Thalia. "Mama got a job working at Allmans Store as a milliner making hats and was sent to New York and other places and later in about 1912 she was sent to Valdosta where she met our Father."[72]

iv.   SADIE LANGDALE, b. November 06, 1893; d. December 24, 1982, Wichita, Kansas; m. WILLIAM PRESTON

---

[71] D.A.R., General James Jackson Chapter, *History of Lowndes County, Georgia, 1825–1941*. Reprint. 1995, (Valdosta GA: General James Jackson Chapter, D.A.R., 1942), 200–201, 217.

[72] Harley Langdale, Jr., Report, 31 May 1983.

SANDLIN, April 28, 1915; b. November 04, 1880; d. October 09, 1941.

v. ISABEL LANGDALE, b. June 03, 1896; d. September 03, 1910, Valdosta, GA.

More About ISABEL LANGDALE:
Burial: 1910, Bethel (Boney Bluff) Primitive Bapt. Ch. Cem., near Fargo, GA

vi. NANCY "NAN" LANGDALE, b. May 26, 1898; m. ROY SIMMENS CAMPBELL, November 19, 1920.

vii. SUSIE MAE LANGDALE, b. May 02, 1900; d. October 26, 1978; m. HORACE ELBERT CAMPBELL, November 17, 1920; b. April 22, 1894, Cleveland, TN; d. April 07, 1983.

More About SUSIE MAE LANGDALE:
Burial: Abt. October 28, 1978, Sunset Hill Cem., Valdosta, GA

More About HORACE ELBERT CAMPBELL:
Burial: April 1983, Sunset Hill Cem., Valdosta, GA

4. JEFFERSON DAVIS[9] LANGDALE *(NOAH[8], JOHN ROBERT[7], WILLIAM B.[6], JOSIAH[5], JOHN[4], JOSIAH[3], JOSEPH[2], JOSIAHSGRANDFATHER[1])* was born January 20, 1862, and died November 08, 1918 in Valdosta, GA, probably. He married MARY MIMS. She was born Abt. 1862.

More About JEFFERSON DAVIS LANGDALE:
Burial: November 08, 1918, Valdosta, Ga

Children of JEFFERSON LANGDALE and MARY MIMS are:
i. BARNEY[10] LANGDALE, d. November 1972.

Notes for BARNEY LANGDALE:
_____

Individual: Langdale, Barney[73]
Birth date: Dec 4, 1891
Death date: Nov 1972
Social Security #: 250-14-3205

_____

[73] FACD #110.

Last residence: SC 29488
State of issue: SC

ii.   BERTHA LANGDALE, d. 1970, Jacksonville, FL; m. JAMES
       MCCABE.
iii.   DEWEY LANGDALE, d. 1958, Phoenix, Arizona; m. MIRIAM
       LNU.
iv.   DONELLA LANGDALE, d. 1944, Phoenix, Arizona; m. JOHN
       LNU.
v.   JAMES LANGDALE, d. 1965, Philadelphia, PA; m. MARIE LNU.
vi.   LEE LANGDALE, d. 1940, Brunswick, Glynn, GA; m. CHARLES
       NOAH CROFT.
vii.   MCELROY LANGDALE, d. 1945, Waycross, GA; m. ELLEN.
viii. NELLIE LANGDALE, d. 1983, Crawfordville, GA; m. FLOYD
       JENKINS.
ix.   ROSA LANGDALE, d. 1977, Atlanta, Fulton Co., GA; m.
       JEFFERSON STYLES.
x.   LILLIE BELLE LANGDALE, b. February 24, 1890, Milltown (now
       Lakeland), GA; d. December 06, 1969, Brunswick, Glynn, GA; m.
       ALONZO LEE GREENE.
xi.   EWELL LANGDALE, b. March 21, 1904, Georgia; d. August 1982,
       Jacksonville, FL; m. LEOTA LNU.

Notes for EWELL LANGDALE:

Individual: Langdale, Ewell[74]
Birth date: Mar 21, 1904
Death date: Aug 1982
Social Security #: 266-64-7786
Last residence: FL 32205
State of issue: FL

---

[74] Ibid.

Bibliography

Books

Bartley, Numan V. *The Creation of Modern Georgia*. Athens GA: University of Georgia Press, 1983.

Butler, Carroll B. *Treasures of the Longleaf Pines: Naval Stores*. Shalimar FL: Tarkel Publishing, 1998.

Chalker, Fussell M. *Pioneer Days Along the Ocmulgee*. Carrollton GA: Self-published, 1970.

Clifton, Geraldine McLeod, and others. *The Heritage of Lowndes County, Georgia—2000*. Volume 1 of *Lowndes County, Georgia, and Its People*. Valdosta GA: Genealogy Unlimited, Inc., 2000.

Coastal Plain Area Planning and Development Commission. *Remembered Places and Leftover Pieces*. Valdosta GA: Coastal Plain Area Planning and Development Commission, 1976.

Coldham, Peter Wilson. *English Convicts in Colonial America*. Volume 1. New Orleans: Polyanthos, 1974–1976.

Coleman, Kenneth, editor, and others. *A History of Georgia*. Athens GA: University of Georgia Press, 1977.

Cothran, Kay Lorraine. "Such Stuff as Dreams: A Folkloristic Sociology of Fantasy in the Okefenokee Rim, Georgia." Ph.D. dissertation, University of Pennsylvania, University Microfilms, 1972

Coulter, E. Merton. *Georgia: A Short History*. Rev. 3rd ed. Chapel Hill NC: The University of North Carolina Press, 1960.

Crenshaw, Russell S., Jr. Captain, USN (Ret). *The Battle of Tassafaronga*. Baltimore MD: Nautical and Aviation Publishing Company of America, 1995.

Crowley, John G. *Primitive Baptists of the Wiregrass South, 1815 to the Present*. Gainesville FL: University Press of Florida, 1998.

———. "Origins and Development of the Union Primitive Baptist Association of Georgia." M. A. thesis, Department of History, Valdosta State University, 1981.

D.A.R., General James Jackson Chapter. *History of Lowndes County, Georgia, 1825–1941.* 1942. Reprint, Valdosta GA: General James Jackson Chapter, D.A.R., 1995.

Echols County High School Composition Class. *Chinkypin.* Volume 2. Statenville GA: Echols County High School, 1976.

Hamilton County Bicentennial Committee. *A Brief History of Hamilton County, Florida.* Edited by Compiler Cora Hinton. Jasper FL: The Jasper News, 1976.

Herring, J. L. *Saturday Night Sketches: Stories of Old Wiregrass Georgia.* Boston: Gorham Press, 1918.

Holmes, William F., editor. *Struggling to Shake Off Old Shackles: 20th Century Georgia.* Savannah GA: Library of Georgia, 1995.

Huxford, Folks. *History of Clinch County, Georgia, Revised to Date.* Macon GA: J. W. Burke, 1916.

Janes, T. P. *Georgia, from the Immigrant Settler's Stand-Point.* Atlanta: N.P., 1879.

Lenz, Richard J. *Longstreet Highroad Guide to the Georgia Coast & Okefenokee.* Marietta GA: Longstreet Press, 1999.

Matschat, Cecile Hulse. *Suwannee River: Strange Green Land.* New York NY: Literary Guild of America, Inc., 1938.

McCall, Bevode C., editor. *Georgia Town and Cracker Culture: A Sociological Study.* Chicago: University of Chicago, 1954.

McDonald, Mary Lou L. and Samuel Jordan Lawson III. *The Passing of the Pines: A History of Wilcox County, Georgia.* Roswell GA: W. H. Wolfe Associates, 1984.

McQueen, Alexander Stephens and Hamp Mizell. *History of Okefenokee Swamp.* Clinton SC: Jacob Graphic Arts Co., 1939.

———. "History of Charlton County." Atlanta GA: Stein, 1934.

Mobley, T. R. *Old Days and Old Ways in South Georgia: A Short Story Collection.* Self-published, 1998.

The New World Book of Langdales. Bath OH: Halbert's Family Heritage, 1997.

Nugent, Nell Marion, Abstractor. *Cavaliers and Pioneers: Abstracts of Virginia Land....* Reprint, Baltimore: Genealogical Publishing Co., 1969.

———. *Cavaliers and Pioneers: Abstracts of Virginia Land...*Volume 3. Richmond: Virginia State Library, 1979.

Pikl, I. James, Jr. *A History of Georgia Forestry, Research Monograph Number 2.* Athens GA: Bureau of Business and Economic Research, University of Georgia, 1966.

Potter, Dorothy Williams, ed. *Passports of Southeastern Pioneers, 1770–1823.* Baltimore MD: Gateway Press, 1982.

Russell, Franklin. *The Okefenokee Swamp.* Edited by Charles Osborne. *The American Wilderness.* New York: Time-Life Books, 1973.

Shelton, Jane Twitty. *Pines and Pioneers: A History of Lowndes County, Georgia, 1825–1900.* Atlanta: Cherokee Publishing Company, 1976.

Soderlund, Jean R. *Quakers & Slavery: A Divided Spirit*. Princeton NJ: Princeton University Press, 1985.

Taylor, Roy G. *Sharecroppers: The Way We Really Were*. Wilson NC: J-Mark, 1984.

Thomas, Kenneth L., Jr. *McCranie's Turpentine Still*. Athens GA: University of Georgia, Institute of Community and Area Development, 1976.

Valdosta-Lowndes County Centennials, Inc., Pictorial History Committee, Tom D. Shelton, Chairman, ed. *A Pictorial History of Lowndes County, 1825–1975*. Valdosta GA: Valdosta-Lowndes County Centennials, Inc., 1976.

Williams, David. *The Georgia Gold Rush: Twenty-Niners, Cherokees, and Gold Fever*. Columbia SC: University of South Carolina Press, 1993.

Willoughby, James S. *The 'Possum Hunter and the Tar Heels: A Historical Novel of Post Civil War Days*. The Rock GA: Tall Timber Publishing Company, 1987.

Wright, Albert Hazen. *Our Georgia-Florida Frontier: The Okefinokee Swamp, Its History and Cartography*. Ithaca NY: Cornell University Press, 1945.

Articles and Papers

"Billy Langdale Elected D.O.T. Board." *Valdosta Daily Times*, 15 January 1988.

"Dollars Grow on Trees." *Atlanta Journal and Constitution Magazine*, 25 October 1953, 48–50.

"Funeral of Mrs. Langdale." *Valdosta Daily Times*, 25 November 1913, 5.

"Hiatus Over: Langdale Aims at Broome's D.O.T. Seat." *Albany* (GA) *Herald*, 16 October 1987.

"Judge Langdale to Be Honored Posthumously." *Valdosta Daily Times*, 7 October 1979.

"Judge's Motto Lives on at the Langdale Company." *Valdosta Daily Times*, 26 June 1977, 6C.

"Langdale Co. Didn't Wait." *Valdosta Daily Times*, 26 June 1977, 7C.

"Langdale Company Brings Work Ethic to Forefront." *Valdosta Daily Times*, 27 April 1986, 8A.

"Langdale Company Sells Gum Process Machinery." *Valdosta Daily Times*, 27 August 1975, 14.

"Langdale Is Vast Forest Industry." *Valdosta Daily Times*, 18 November 1959.

"Langdale Timber Roots Deep in Lowndes." *Valdosta Daily Times*, 26 April 1987, 17.

"Life of the Georgia Cracker." *Current Literature* 27 (1900): 30–31.

"Mrs. J. W. Langdale Dead: Well Known and Highly Esteemed Woman Died at Council." *Valdosta Daily Times*, 24 November 1913, 5.

"Southern Railroad Officials Dedicate Big Yards." *Valdosta Daily Times*, 5 February 1953.

"They've Promoted Pine Trees." *Valdosta Daily Times*, 26 June 1970.

"Timber Men Oppose Giving US Part of Okefenokee." *Atlanta Journal*, 22 April 1967.

Boyd, James. "Fifty Years in the Southern Pine Industry." *Southern Lumberman* 144/1817 (1931): 59–67.

Burnette, Harvey M. "Burnett History." Unpublished paper, typewritten, Burnsville NC: 1987.

Butts, Paul. "Other Forest Products: Uses and Trends." *Atlanta Economic Review* 20/12 (1970): 32–33.

Daughdrill, Brian. "Langdale Received Varied Education." *Valdosta Daily Times*, 24 October 1988.

Daughtry, Nina B. "Lydia Stone, the Lady with a Dream." *Savannah News-Press Magazine*, 21 March 1971.

Goff, John H. "Cow-Punching in Old Georgia." *Georgia Review* 1949, 341–48.

Lipscomb, Ed. "A New Kind of Agriculture Comes to the Piney Woods." *Nation's Business* 25/8 (1937): 34–36, 107–109.

Martin, Harold H. "He Converted a Wasteland." *The Saturday Evening Post*, 23 July 1955, 20, 91–93.

McKay, Archie. "Langdale Lived to See Dream Come True." *Valdosta Daily Times*, 1975, 1E, 10E.

McPhee, John. "Profile: The Pine Barrens." *The New Yorker*, 25 November and 2 December 1967.

Miller, Julian. "To Toast Langdale." *Valdosta Daily Times*, 13 November 1977.

Richards, Terry. "Striking Langdale Workers Return Monday." *Valdosta Daily Times*, 10 November 1987.

Smigielski, Susan A. "Lowndes Firm Gets Merit Award." *Valdosta Daily Times*, 19 August 1990.

Union Bag & Paper Corporation. "Advertisement." *Atlanta Journal and Constitution Magazine*, 25 October 1953, 4.

Valdosta Daily Times, 19 January 1909, 4.

Interviews, Correspondence, and Official Records

Burnsed, Elizabeth, and others. "Pension Applications of Elizabeth Burnsed, Widow of Gideon Burnsed, Drawer 272, Roll #8." In *Pension Applications of Confederate Soldiers and Widows who Applied from Georgia*. Georgia State Archives, Atlanta GA. Microfilm, Drawer 272, Roll #8.

Campbell, Nan Langdale. "Typewritten Copies of Handwritten Letters, 1986–1987, to Virginia L. Miller." John W. Langdale Papers. Valdosta GA.

Coleman, M. E. (Red). Letter to Byron Kirkland. Valdosta GA, 1 February 1977. The Langdale Company, Harley Langdale, Jr., Papers. Valdosta GA.

Contract for Timber Purchase. Lucy Crews to John Wesley Langdale, 20 June 1901. John W. Langdale Papers. Valdosta, GA.

Deed, C. B. Hitt of Richmond County, Georgia, to John Wesley Langdale, May 1888. John W. Langdale Papers. Valdosta GA.

Deed, H. M. Hitt of Richmond County, Georgia, to John Wesley Langdale, 10 November 1885. John W. Langdale Papers. Valdosta GA.

Deed, Henry C. Williams of Wilcox County, Georgia, to John Wesley Langdale, 1886. John W. Langdale Papers. Valdosta GA.

Deed, Henry Gay of Colquitt County, Georgia, to John Wesley Langdale, January 1888. John W. Langdale Papers. Valdosta GA.

Deed, Silas A. O'Quin of Columbia County, Florida, to John Robert Langdale. John W. Langdale Papers. Valdosta GA.

Hickman, James. Interview by author. Harley Langdale, Jr., Papers. Valdosta GA, 19 October 2000.

Huxford, Folks. "Langdale Folder." *Huxford Genealogical Society Library.* Homerville GA, n.d

Johnson, Rose Langdale. Interview by author. Audio tape. John J. Langdale, Jr., Papers. Valdosta GA, 13 June 1996.

Kennelly, Bradley. Interview by Lillian Stedman. Jacksonville FL, Federal Writers' Project. Library of Congress, Washington DC, 12 September 1939.

Langdale, George. Interview by author. Audio tape. The Langdale Company, Valdosta GA, 30 January 1996.

Langdale, Harley, Jr. "Brief Facts on the Langdale Company." Harley Langdale, Jr., Papers. Valdosta GA, October 1958.

Langdale, Harley, Jr. Interview by author. Audio Tape. Harley Langdale, Jr., Papers. The Langdale Company, Valdosta GA, 15 April 1995

———. Interview by author. Audio Tape. Harley Langdale, Jr., Papers. The Langdale Company, Valdosta GA, 21 March 1995.

———. Interview by author. Audio Tape. Harley Langdale, Jr., Papers. The Langdale Company, Valdosta GA, 22 March 1995.

———. Interview by author. Audio Tape. Harley Langdale, Jr., Papers. The Langdale Company, Valdosta GA, 24 March 1995.

———. Interview by author. Audio Tape. Harley Langdale, Jr., Papers. The Langdale Company, Valdosta GA, 27 March 1995.

———. Interview by author. Audio Tape. Harley Langdale, Jr., Papers. The Langdale Company, Valdosta GA, 28 March 1995.

———. Interview by author. Audio Tape. Harley Langdale, Jr., Papers. The Langdale Company, Valdosta GA, 29 March 1995.

———. Interview by author. Audio Tape. Harley Langdale, Jr., Papers. The Langdale Company, Valdosta GA, 8 April 1995.

———. Interview by Harold Steen, typewritten transcript. Harley Langdale, Jr., Papers. The Langdale Company, Valdosta GA, 1991.

———. "Lumber Prices 1951 to Present." Harley Langdale, Jr., Papers. Valdosta GA, 2 April 1997.

———. Personal Papers. The Langdale Company, Valdosta GA, 1950–1993.

Langdale, Harley, Sr. "Interview by Jane and Tom Shelton." *Jane Shelton Papers*. Valdosta GA, November 1969.

———. "Petition to Incorporate the J. W. Langdale Company, 1 April 1919." John W. Langdale Papers. Valdosta GA.

Langdale, Harriet Griffin, and others. "Pension Applications of Harriet Griffin Langdale, Widow of John Robert Langdale, Drawer 274, Roll #70." In *Pension Applications of Confederate Soldiers and Widows who Applied from Georgia*. Georgia State Archives, Atlanta GA.

Langdale, James Harley. Interview by author. Audio Tape. John W. Langdale Papers. The Langdale Company, Valdosta GA, 17 October 2000.

Langdale, John J., Jr. Interview by author. Audio Tape. John J. Langdale, Jr. Papers. Valdosta GA, 24 May 1996.

———. Interview by Harold Steen. Typewritten transcript. John W. Langdale Papers, The Langdale Company, Valdosta GA, 1991.

Langdale, John W. Address to Annual Meeting of Valdosta State University Chapter, Phi Alpha Theta History Honorary Society. Audio tape. John W. Langdale Papers. Valdosta GA, 30 May 1995.

———. "History of the Langdale Law Firms." John W. Langdale Papers. Valdosta GA, May 1996.

———. Interview by author. Audio Tape. John W. Langdale Papers. The Langdale Company, Valdosta GA, 17 February 1995.

———. Interview by author. Audio Tape. John W. Langdale Papers. The Langdale Company, Valdosta GA, 17 March 1995.

———. Interview by author. Audio Tape. John W. Langdale Papers. The Langdale Company, Valdosta GA, 23 March 1995.

———. Interview by author. Audio Tape. John W. Langdale Papers. The Langdale Company, Valdosta GA, 31 March 1995.

———. Interview by author. Audio Tape. John W. Langdale Papers. The Langdale Company, Valdosta GA, 3 April 1995.

———. Interview by author. Audio Tape. John W. Langdale Papers. The Langdale Company, Valdosta GA, 4 April 1995.

———. Interview by author. Audio Tape. John W. Langdale Papers. The Langdale Company, Valdosta GA, 7 April 1995.

———. Interview by author. Audio Tape. John W. Langdale Papers. The Langdale Company, Valdosta GA, 8 April 1995.

———. Interview by author. Audio Tape. John W. Langdale Papers. The Langdale Company, Valdosta GA, 11 April 1995.

———. Interview by author. Audio Tape. John W. Langdale Papers. The Langdale Company, Valdosta GA, 13 April 1995.

————. Interview by author. Audio Tape. John W. Langdale Papers. The Langdale Company, Valdosta GA, 14 April 1995.

————. Interview by author. Audio Tape. John W. Langdale Papers. The Langdale Company, Valdosta GA, 21 April 1995.

————. Interview by author. Audio Tape. John W. Langdale Papers. The Langdale Company, Valdosta GA, 24 April 1995.

————. Interview by author. Audio Tape. John W. Langdale Papers. The Langdale Company, Valdosta GA, 1 May 1995.

————. Interview by author. Audio Tape. John W. Langdale Papers. The Langdale Company, Valdosta GA, 2 May 1995.

————. Interview by author. Audio Tape. John W. Langdale Papers. The Langdale Company, Valdosta GA, 8 May 1995..

————. Interview by author. Audio Tape. John W. Langdale Papers. The Langdale Company, Valdosta GA, 15 May 1995.

————. Interview by author. Audio Tape. John W. Langdale Papers. The Langdale Company, Valdosta GA, 18 May 1995.

————. Interview by author. Audio Tape. John W. Langdale Papers. The Langdale Company, Valdosta GA, 22 May 1995.

————. Interview by author. Audio Tape. John W. Langdale Papers. The Langdale Company, Valdosta GA, 26 May 1995.

————. Interview by author. Audio Tape. John W. Langdale Papers. The Langdale Company, Valdosta GA, 15 June 1995.

————. Interview by author. Audio Tape. John W. Langdale Papers. The Langdale Company, Valdosta GA, 19 June 1995.

————. Interview by author. Audio Tape. John W. Langdale Papers. The Langdale Company, Valdosta GA, 25 January 1996.

————. Interview by author. Audio Tape. John W. Langdale Papers. The Langdale Company, Valdosta GA, 5 February 1995.

————. Interview by author. Audio Tape. John W. Langdale Papers. The Langdale Company, Valdosta GA, 13 February 1996.

————. Interview by author. Audio Tape. John W. Langdale Papers. The Langdale Company, Valdosta GA, 5 May 1997.

————. Interview by author. Audio Tape. John W. Langdale Papers. The Langdale Company, Valdosta GA, 6 May 1997.

————. Interview by Harold Steen. Typewritten transcript. Harley Langdale, Jr., Papers. The Langdale Company, Valdosta GA.

————. Letter to John Lancaster. Valdosta GA, 22 April 1997. Author's files.

————. "Memorandum, 12 November 1997, with Attachment, to John Lancaster." Valdosta GA, 1997. Author's files.

————. John W. Langdale Papers. The Langdale Company, Valdosta GA, 1941–1994.

Langdale, John W., Jr. Interview by author. Audio Tape. John W. Langdale Papers. The Langdale Company, Valdosta GA, 24 January 1996.

————. Interview by author. Audio Tape. John W. Langdale Papers. The Langdale Company, Valdosta GA, 13 February 1996.

————. Interview by author. Audio Tape. John W. Langdale Papers. The Langdale Company, Valdosta GA, 20 February 1996.

————. Interview by author. Audio Tape. John W. Langdale Papers. The Langdale Company, Valdosta GA, 1996.

Langdale, Robert. Interview by author. *Harley Langdale, Jr., Papers*. Valdosta GA, 16 October 2000.

Langdale, William P. Interview by author. Audio Tape. *William P. Langdale Papers*. The Langdale Company, Valdosta GA, 6 May 1997.

————. Interview by author. Audio Tape. *William P. Langdale Papers*. The Langdale Company, Valdosta GA, 24 April 1996.

————. Interview by author. Audio Tape. *William P. Langdale Papers*. The Langdale Company, Valdosta GA, 4 March 1997.

————. Interview by author. Audio Tape. *William P. Langdale Papers*. The Langdale Company, Valdosta GA, 5 March 1997.

————. Interview by Harold Steen. Typewritten transcript. Harley Langdale, Jr., Papers, The Langdale Company, Valdosta GA, 1991.

Miller, Virginia L. Interview by author. Audio tape. *Virginia L. Miller Papers*. Albany GA, .9 June 1995.

————. Interview by author. Audio tape. *Virginia L. Miller Papers*. Albany GA, 10 June 1995.

————. Interview by author. Audio tape. *Virginia L. Miller Papers*. Albany GA, .22 September 1995.

Option to Purchase Timber, John Wesley Langdale and others to Solomon Mobley, Jr., 28 November 1899. John W. Langdale Papers, Valdosta GA.

Order of Incorporation of the J. W. Langdale Company, Clinch County GA, 9 May 1919. John W. Langdale Papers, Valdosta GA.

Pitts, James E., Rev. Letter to Byron Kirkland. The Langdale Company, Valdosta GA, 3 February 1977. Harley Langdale, Jr., Papers. Valdosta GA.

Robinson, John. Interview by author. Audio Tape. Harley Langdale, Jr., Papers, Valdosta GA, 17 October 2000.

Talmadge, Herman E. Letter to Byron Kirkland, Washington, DC, 31 May 1977. Harley Langdale, Jr., Papers, Valdosta GA.

Trust Agreement, John Wesley Langdale and Others. John W. Langdale Papers, Valdosta GA, 1907.

Wansley, Lamar T. Letter to Byron Kirkland, Valdosta GA, 21 January 1977. Harley Langdale, Jr., Papers, Valdosta GA.

Wishart, R. W. Interview by Lindsay M. Bryan. Wishart residence, Tampa FL, 22 August 1939. Federal Writers' Project. Library of Congress, Washington DC.

CD-ROM and Internet Sources

Ancestry.com. *Alabama Vital Records: Marriages 1808–1920*. Provo: Ancestry.com, 2000. CD. More than 162,000 records from 54 of 67 Alabama counties.

———. *American Genealogical-Biographical Index*. Provo: Ancestry.com, 2000. CD. Nearly 4 million names; the equivalent of 200 printed volumes.20

———. *Ancestry Reference Library 2000: Deluxe Edition*. Provo: Ancestry.com, 2000. CD. 20 volumes.

———. *The Great Migration Begins: Immigrants to New England 1620–1633*. Provo: Ancestry.com, 2000. CD. More than 1000 sketches Originally published by Robert Charles Anderson in 3 volumes.

———. *Military Records: Civil War Muster Rolls*. Provo: Ancestry.com, 2000. CD. 5.3 million records on 3 discs.

———. *Military Records: Revolutionary War Muster Rolls*. Provo: Ancestry.com, 2000. CD. 426,000 records.

———. *Military Records: War of 1812 Muster Rolls*. Provo: Ancestry.com, 2000. CD. 580,000 records.

———. *Military Records: World War II & Korean Conflict Overseas Interments*. Provo: Ancestry.com, 2000. CD.

———. *South Carolina Records and Reference*. Provo: Ancestry.com, 2000. CD. Accesses thirteen databases including 20 volumes of South Carolina Magazine of Ancestral Research; also available in print from Brent H. Holcomb, Columbia SC.

Ancestry.com and Allen County Public Library. *Periodical Source Index*. Provo: Ancestry.com, 2000. CD-ROM.

———. *PERSI 2000 Periodical Source Index*. Provo: Ancestry.com, 2000. More than 1.3 million entries.

Automated Archives. *Automated Archives CD #100, Automated Family Pedigrees #1*. Banner Blue Software, 1994. CD. Lists 700,000 individuals, including European royalty; requires GRS.

———. *Automated Archives CD #161, Bulletin Board Messages—Volume 1*. Banner Blue Software, 1994. More than 400,000 messages between February 1992 and August 1994 compiled by Genealogical Information systems, Inc.

———. *Automated Archives CD #168, Salt Lake City Cemetery Records, 1847–1992*. Banner Blue Software, 1994. Burials from September 1848 through November 1992, including many Mormon pioneers and their families.

———. *Automated Archives CD #291, Precision Indexing Databases, US Census Index Series: Georgia, 1870*. Banner Blue Software, 1994. CD. AGLL Census Index; requires GRS.

———. *Marriage Records: Maryland, Virginia and North Carolina, CD #004*. Banner Blue Software, 1994. More than 600,000 records; Requires GRS.

Broderbund. *Family Archives CD #003, Marriage Index: AL, GA, SC, 1641–1944.* Novato CA: Broderbund Software, 1995. CD.

———. *Family Archives CD #004, Marriage Index: MD, NC, VA, 1624–1915.* Novato CA: Broderbund Software, 1996. CD.

———. *Family Archives CD #012, Family Pedigrees: Everton's Computerized Family File, Volume 1, 1400s–Present.* Novato CA: Broderbund Software, 1998. Images of family group sheets from Everton Publishers listing 389,000 persons, with index.

———. *Family Archives CD #013, Family Pedigrees: Everton's Computerized Family File, Volumes 2 & 3, 1400s–Present.* Novato CA: Broderbund Software, 1998. Images of family group sheets listing 478,000 individuals, with index.

———. *Family Archives CD #014, Family Pedigrees: Everton's Computerized Family File, Volume 4, 1400s-Present.* Novato CA: Broderbund Software, 1998. Images of family group sheets listing more than 374,000 persons, with index.

———. *Family Archives CD #017, Birth Records: United States/Europe, 900–1880.* Novato CA: Broderbund Software, 1995. CD.

———. *Family Archives CD #018, Family Queries: Everton's "Roots" Cellar, 1640–1990.* Novato CA: Broderbund Software, 1998. Alphabetical list of nearly 300,000 persons about whom queries were entered into Everton's "Roots" Cellar Ancestor Data Bank, plus the name of the contributor of each query.

———. *Family Archives CD #019, Genealogical Records: Egle's Notes and Queries of Pennsylvania, 1700s–1800s.* Novato CA: Broderbund Software, 1998. Page images of William Henry Egle's Notes and Queries published between1879 and 1900, first as newspaper columns (1879–1895) in the Harrisburg Daily Telegraph and later as annual volumes (1896–1900).

———. *Family Archives CD #020, Census Index: Ohio, 1880.* Novato CA: Broderbund Software, 1995. Contains records for all 87 Ohio counties existing in 1880, the total number of records being 800,000. Prepared by the Ohio Genealogical Society.

———. *Family Archives CD #108, Family Pedigrees: Gentech95 & ARI, 150–1989.* Novato CA: Broderbund Software, 1995. A linked-relationship database with 177,859 records, created by Automated Research, Inc.; requires GRS.

———. *Family Archives CD #110, Social Security Death Index: United States, 1937–1996.* Novato CA: Broderbund Software, 1997. Data on 55 million deceased persons listed in Social Security Death Benefits Collection of the Social Security Administration.

———. *Family Archives CD #113, Family History Collection: 217 Genealogy Books.* Novato CA: Broderbund Software, 1996. CD. Includes corrected versions of Frederick A. Virkus, *Abridged Compendium of American Genealogy* (Volume 1) and Savage, *Genealogical Dictionary of the First Settlers of New England* (Volumes 1-4); emphasizes New England & eastern US

———. *Family Archives CD #114, Family History Collection: First Families of America*. Novato CA: Broderbund Software, 1996. CD. Contains text of Frederick A. Virkus, editor, *The Abridged Compendium of American Genealogy, Volume 1* (1925); includes approximately 5,000 individual records & 7,000 lineages.

———. *Family Archives CD #115, the Genealogist's All-in-One Address Book*. Novato CA: Broderbund Software, Genealogical Publishing Company, 1996. Contains 3 books by Elizabeth Petty Bentley: *County Courthouse Book, Directory of Family Associations*, and *The Genealogist's Address Book*, totaling more than 21,000 addresses.

———. *Family Archives CD #119, Military Records: Confederate Soldiers, 1861–1865*. Novato CA: Broderbund Software, 1996. Names of 25,000 Confederate soldiers, sailors, & civilians who died in US prisons and hospitals, 1861–1865; complete contents of National Archives microfilm roll M918.

———. *Family Archives CD #130, Pennsylvania German Church Records, 1729–1870*. Novato CA: Broderbund Software, 1996. Contains all church records published in *Proceedings and Addresses of the Pennsylvania German Society*; previously printed by Genelogical Publishing Company in 3 volumes.

———. *Family Archives CD #144, Genealogical Records: Loyalists in the American Revolution*. Novato CA: Broderbund Software, 1999. Thirteen volumes of records with more than 87,000 names from Genealogica Publishing Company.

———. *Family Archives CD #146, Military Records: US Soldiers, 1784–1811*. Novato CA: Broderbund Software, 1995. Contains copies of microfilm records for 21,000 Revolutionary War volunteers from 22 states and territories.

———. *Family Archives CD #147, Revolutionary War Soldiers and Sailors, 1775–1782*. Novato CA: Broderbund Software, 1997. CD. Two discs containing all 17 volumes of *Massachusetts Soldiers and Sailors of the Revolutionary War*; records of about 688,000 persons, 20% of whom were enlisted & 80% were officers.

———. *Family Archives CD #156, Family History: Mid–Atlantic Genealogies, 1340–1940*. Novato CA: Broderbund Software, 1998. Eleven volumes of family histories from New York, New Jersey, Pennsylvania, Maryland, and Delaware.

———. *Family Archives CD #162, Family History: Virginia Genealogies #1, Pre 1600 to 1900s*. Novato CA: Broderbund Software, 1996. Page images of all five volumes of *Genealogies of Virginia Families* from *The Virginia Magazine of History and Biography*, originally published by Genealogical Publishing Company; references about 65,000 persons.

———. *Family Archives CD #163, Family History: Pennsylvania Genealogies #1, Pre–1600s to 1900s*. Novato CA: Broderbund Software, 1996. Contains 3 volumes of *Genealogies of Pennsylvania Families* from *The Pennsylvania Genealogical Magazine* and 1 volume of *Genealogies of Pennsylvania Families* from *The Pennsylvania Magazine of History and Biography*, amounting to several hundred family history articles and Bible records originally published by Benealogical Publishing Company.

———. *Family Archives CD #166, Church Records: Selected Areas of Pennsylvania, 1600s—1800s.* Contains text of 18 books.

———. *Family Archives CD #170, Immigrants to the New World, 1600s–1800s.* Novato CA: Broderbund Software, 1997. CD. Page images from 5 books: *New World Immigrants,* volumes 1 & 2; *Emigrants to Pennsylvania, 1641–1819; Immigrants to the Middle Colonies;* and *Passengers to America.* Contains nearly all articles that Harold Lancour identified in *Bibliography of Ship Passenger Lists, 1538–1825.*

———. *Family Archives CD #172, Pennsylvania Vital Records, 1700s–1800s.* Novato CA: Broderbund Software, 1997. Contains almost all articles on births, baptisms, marriages and deaths ever printed in *The Pennsylvania Magazine of History and Biography* and *The Pennsylvania Genealogical Magazine,* with events occurring mostly between 1740 and 1830. Originally published by Genealogical Publishing Company.

———. *Family Archives CD #174, Virginia Vital Records #1, 1600s–1800s.* Novato CA: Broderbund Software, 1997. Contains page images of six books originally published by Genealogical Publishing Company: *Virginia Vital Records, Virginia Marriage Records, Virginia Will Records, Virginia Land Records, Virginia Military Records,* and *Virginia Tax Records.* These articles first appeared in three periodicals: *Virginia Magazine of History and Biography, The Willliam and Mary College Quarterly,* and *Tyler's Quarterly.* References to 138,000 persons.

———. *Family Archives CD #175, Ohio Vital Records #1, 1790s—1870s.* Novato CA: Broderbund Software, 1997. Articles from *Gateway to the West,* Volumes 1 and 2, originally published by Genealogical Publishing Company.

———. *Family Archives CD #181, English Origins of New England Families, 1500s–1800s.* Novato CA: Broderbund Software, 1997. Contains page images of 6 books with articles from *The New England Historical and Genealogical Register* and references 143,000 persons. Originally published by Genealogical Publishing Company.

———. *Family Archives CD #182, Family History: New Jersey Genealogies #1, 1600s—1800s.* Novato CA: Broderbund Software, 1997. Volumes 1-65 of *Genealogical Magazine of New Jersey* (1925) published previously in two volumes as *Genealogies of New Jersey Families.* Originally published by Genealogical Publishing Company.

———. *Family Archives CD #186, Family History: Virginia Genealogies #2 1600s–1800s.* Novato CA: Broderbund Software, 1997. Contains all five volumes of *Genealogies of Virginia Families,* with articles first published between 1892 and 1942 in *The William and Mary College Quarterly Historical Magazine;* also page images of *Virginia Gleanings in England,* with articles first published in *The Virginia Magazine of History and Biography*, 1903–1926. Refers to more than 113,000 persons.

———. *Family Archives CD #187, Family History: Virginia Genealogies #3, 1600s–1800s*. Novato CA: Broderbund Software, 1997. Contains page images of *Virginia Colonial Abstracts* published in 34 paperback volumes, 1937–1949; also, all 4 volumes of *Genealogies of Virginia Families*, consisting of 350 articles that appeared originally in *Tyler's Quarterly Historical and Genealogical Magazine*. Refers to 130,000 persons. Previously published by Genealogical Publishing Company.

———. *Family Archives CD #192: Genealogical Records: The Encyclopedia of Quaker Genealogy, 1750–1930*, 6 Volumes. Editor William Wade Hinshaw/ Novato CA: Broderbund Software, 1998. Contains images of pages of Hinshaw's 6-volume *Encyclopedia of American Quaker Genealogy*. Originally published by Genealogical Publishing Company.

———. *Family Archives CD #193, County and Family Histories: Pennsylvania, 1740–1900*. Novato CA: Broderbund Software, 1998. Contains page images of 14 books including names of 275,000 individuals.

———. *Family Archives CD #196, Birth Index: Southeastern Pa, 1680–1800*: John T. Humphrey. Originally published as a 13-volume set entitled *Pennsylvania Births*.

———. *Family Archives CD #205, Family History: Virginia Genealogies, 1600s–1800s*. Novato CA: Broderbund Software, 1998. Contains page images of 17 volumes of family histories & Virginia genealogies referencing about 212,000 persons.

———. *Family Archives CD #209, Genealogical Records: Pennsylvania Wills, 1682–1834*. Novato CA: Broderbund Software, 1998. Pennsylvania probate records originally published in 27 volumes by Family Line Productions.

———. *Family Archives CD #210, National Genealogical Society Quarterly, Vols. 1–85, 1600s–1900s*. Novato CA: Broderbund Software, 1998. Contains articles originally published from 1908 to 1997, plus several supplements.

———. *Family Archives CD #213, Genealogical Records: The Pennsylvania Genealogical Magazine*, Volumes 1–39. Novato CA: Broderbund Software, 1998. Contains page images of the first 39 volumes of *The Pennsylvania Genealogical Magazine*, plus four supplements, published from 1895 to 1995. From Genealogical Publishing Company.

———. *Family Archives CD #226, Marriage Index: Georgia, 1754–1850*. Novato CA: Broderbund Software, 1995. CD. Lists about 84,624 marriages from 76 counties, starting with Effingham in 1754.

———. *Family Archives CD #229, Marriage Index: Selected Counties of KY, NC, TN, VA, WV, 1728–1850*. Novato CA: Broderbund Software, 1995. CD. Lists 582,185 marriages from 333 counties in 5 states.

———. *Family Archives CD #285, Census Index: Western Pennsylvania, 1870*. Novato CA: Broderbund Software, 1994. CD.

————. *Family Archives CD #286, Census Index: Eastern Pennsylvania, 1870.* Novato CA: Broderbund Software, 1994. CD.

————. *Family Archives CD #287, Census Index: New York City, 1870.* Novato CA: Broderbund Software, 1994. CD.

————. *Family Archives CD #288, Census Index: Baltimore, Chicago, St. Louis, 1870.* Novato CA: Broderbund Software, 1994 CD.

————. *Family Archives CD #289, Census Index: North Carolina, South Carolina, 1870.* Novato CA: Broderbund Software, 1994. CD.

————. *Family Archives CD #290, Census Index: Virginia, West Virginia, 1870.* Novato CA: Broderbund Software, 1994. CD.

————. *Family Archives CD #291, Census Index: Georgia, 1870.* Novato CA: Broderbund Software, 1994. CD.

————. *Family Archives CD #305, Census Microfilm Records: Pennsylvania, 1850.* Novato CA: Broderbund Software, 1998. CD. Eleven discs.

————. *Family Archives CD #310, Census Index: Colonial America, 1607–1789.* Novato CA: Broderbund Software, 1995. About 390,000 census records from 22 territories and states spanning a period of 182 years.

————. *Family Archives CD #311, Census Index: United States Selected Counties, 1790.* Novato CA: Broderbund Software, 1995. About 595,000 records for the year 1790 collected from US counties in the following 28 states: AL, CA, CT, DE, GA, IL, IN, KY, LA, MA, MD, ME, MI, MO, MS, NC, NE, NH, NJ, NM, NY, OH, PA, RI, SC, TN, VA, VT.

————. *Family Archives CD #313, Census Index: United States Selected Counties, 1810.* Novato CA: Broderbund Software, 1995. Contains 922,000 census records from the District of Columbia and various counties located in the following states: AL, AR, CT, DE, GA, IL, IN, KY, LA, MA, MD, ME, MI, MO, MS, NC, NH, NJ, NY, OH, PA, RI, SC, TN, VA, VT.

————. *Family Archives CD #314, Census Index: United States Selected Counties, 1820.* Novato CA: Broderbund Software, 1995. Contains 1,365,000 census records from the District of Columbia and counties located in the following 29 states: AL, AR, CT, DE, FL, GA, IL, IN, KY, LA, MA, MD, ME, MI, MS, NC, NH, NJ, NM, NY, OH, PA, RI, SC, TN, TX, VA, VT, WI.

————. *Family Archives CD #315, Census Index: United States Selected Counties, 1830.* Novato CA: Broderbund Software, 1995. Contains 2,160,000 census records from the District of Columbia and counties located in the following 33 states: AL, AR, AZ, CA, CT, DE, FL, GA, IA, IL, IN, KY, LA, MA, MD, ME, MI, MN, MO, MS, NC, NH, NJ, NY, OH, PA, RI, SC, TN, TX, VA, VT, WI.

————. *Family Archives CD #316, Census Index: United States Selected Counties, 1840.* Novato CA: Broderbund Software, 1995. About 2,612,000 census records from the District of Columbia and counties in the following 33 states: AL, AR, CT, DE, FL, GA, HI, IA, IL, IN, KY, LA, MA, MD, ME, MI, MN, MO, MS, NC, NH, NJ, NM, NY, OH, PA, RI, SC, TN, TX, VA, VT, WI.

————. *Family Archives CD #317, Census Index: United States Selected Counties, 1850.* Novato CA: Broderbund Software, 1995. Approximately 8, 380,000 census records from the District of Columbia and counties within the following 38 states: AL, AR, CA, CT, DE, FL, GA, IA, IL, IN, KS, KY, LA, MA, MD, ME, MI, MN, MO, MS, NC, NE, NH, NJ, NM, NY, OH, OR, PA, RI, SC, TN, TX, UT, VA, VT, WI, WV.

————. *Family Archives CD #318, Census Index: United States Selected Counties, 1860.* Novato CA: Broderbund Software, 1995. About 8,365,000 census records for 1860 gathered from the District of Columbia and from counties within the 39 states following: AL, AR, AZ, CA, CO, CT, DE, FL, GA, IA, ID, IL, IN, KS, KY, LA, MA, ME, MN, MS, MT, NC, NE, NH, NJ, NM, NV, NY, OK, PA, SC, TN, TX, UT, VA, VT, WA, WI, WV.

————. *Family Archives CD #319, Census Index: United States Selected States/Counties, 1870.* Novato CA: Broderbund Software, 1995. About 4,708,000 census records for 1870 from the District of Columbia and from counties located in the following 31 states: AK, AL, AR, AZ, CA, CO, DE, FL, GA, IA, ID, IL, IN, KS, KY, LA, ME, MN, MO, MT, NC, ND, NM, NV, SD, TX, VA, WA, WI,WV, WY.

————. *Family Archives CD #320, Census Index: United States Selected States/Counties, 1880.* Novato CA: Broderbund Software, 1995. Approximately 1,402,000 census records for 1880 collected from the following 14 states: AK, AL, AZ, CO, ID, IL, ND, NV, NY, OH, SD, TX, WA, WY.

————. *Family Archives CD #350, the Complete Book of Emigrants, 1607–1776 & Emigrants in Bondage, 1614–1775.* Novato CA: Broderbund Software, 1996. Data compiled by Peter Wilson Coldham & originally published by Genealogical Publishing Company in 6 volumes.

————. *Family Archives CD #399, Marriage Index: District of Columbia, Delaware, Maryland & Virginia, 1740–1920.* Novato CA: Broderbund Software, 1999. Lists marriages of 250,000 persons from 1740 to 1920.

————. *Family Archives CD #450, County and Family Histories: Ohio, 1780–1970.* Novato CA: Broderbund Software, 1998. CD. Thirty-five books with references to 700,000 persons.

————. *Family Archives CD #501, Immigration Records: Immigrants to Pennsylvania, 1600s–1800s.* Novato CA: Broderbund Software, 1999. Originally published in 10 volumes by Genealogical Publishing Company.

————. *Family Archives CD #506, Family History: Lineages of Hereditary Society Members 1600s–1900s.* Novato CA: Broderbund Software, 1999. Contains page images of 27 volumes originally published by Genealogical Publishing Company, with information on 440,000 persons.

————. *Family Archives CD #513, Genealogical Records: Viginia Land, Marriage and Probate Records 1639–1850.* Novato CA: Broderbund Software, 1999. CD.

Information on some 135,000 persons from counties of Spotsylvania, Augusta, Isle of Wight, and Norfolk.

———. *Family Archives CD #516, Genealogical Records: Early Georgia Settlers, 1700s—1800s.* Novato CA: Broderbund Software, 2000. Contains text of six books, including reconstructed censuses for 1790 & 1820, plus an index for the census of 1830. Also has some data on Georgia's relations with Creek and Cherokee Indians from Genealogical Publishing Company.

———. *Family Archives CD #517, Genealogical Records: Early South Carolina Settlers, 1600s—1800s.* Novato CA: Broderbund Software, 2000. Contains index to all recorded South Carolina wills preceding 1782 & extensive data on Scotch-Irish immigration from 1750 to 1775 from Genealogical Publishing Company.

———. *Family Archives CD # 312, Census Index: US Selected Counties, 1800.* Novato CA: Broderbund Software, 1995. Census records for 682,000 persons from District of Columbia and various counties located in the following states: AK, CT, DE, GA, IN, KY, LA, MA, MD, ME, MI, MO, MS, NC, NH, NJ, NY, OH, PA, RI, SC, TN, VA, VT.

———. *World Family Tree Super Bundle 6* (Vols. 28, 29, 30, 31, 32). Novato CA: Broderbund Software, 1999. About 8,000 family trees and about 6.3 million individuals are listed.

———. *World Family Tree Super Bundle 7* (Vols. 33, 34, 35, 36, 37). Novato CA: Broderbund Software, 1999. About 9,000 family trees with approximately 5.1 million individuals are listed.

———. *World Family Tree Super Bundle 8* (Vols. 38, 39, 40, 41, 42). Novato CA: Broderbund Software, 1999. Approximately 9,500 family trees with about 6.5 million persons are listed.

———. World Family Tree Super Bundle 9 (Vols. 43, 44, 45, 46, 47). Novato CA: Broderbund Software, 2000. Includes about 12,000 family trees including some 8.1 million persons.

———. *World Family Tree Super Bundle 10* (Vols. 48, 49, 50, 51, 52). Novato CA: Broderbund Software, 2000. These five CDs include12,000 pedigrees with about 8.1 million names.

———. *World Family Tree Super Bundle 11* (Vols. 53, 54, 55, 56, 57). Novato CA: Broderbund Software, 2000. Includes about 15,000 family trees and about 9 million names.

———. *World Family Tree Super Bundle I* (Vols. 3, 4, 5, 6, 7). Novato CA: Broderbund Software, 1996. About 24,000 family trees and 15 million individuals.

———. *World Family Tree Super Bundle III* (Vols. 13, 14, 15, 16, 17). Novato CA: Broderbund Software, 1998. About 15,500 family trees including 12.5 million persons.

————. *World Family Tree Super Bundle IV* (Vols. 18, 19, 20, 21, 22). Novato CA: Broderbund Software, 1998. About 13,000 family trees and about 10,000 persons.

————. *World Family Tree Super Bundle V* (Vols. 23, 24, 25, 26, 27). Novato CA: Broderbund Software, 1999. Approximately 14, 700 family trees and 9.4 million individual names.

————. *World Family Tree, Volume 2, Pre-1600 to Present*. Novato CA: Broderbund Software, 1995. About 6,000 family trees including nearly 3 million persons.

————. *World Family Tree, Volume 8, Pre-1600 to Present*. Novato CA: Broderbund Software, 1997. Almost 4,000 family trees including about 3 million individuals.

————. *World Family Tree, Volume 9, Pre-1600 to Present*. Novato CA: Broderbund Software, 1997. Almost 4,000 family trees including about 3,000,000 individuals.

————. *World Family Tree, Volume 10, Pre-1600 to Present*. Novato CA: Broderbund Software, 1997. More than 4,000 family trees and more than 3,000,000 persons.

————. *World Family Tree, Volume 11, Pre-1600 to Present*. Novato CA: Broderbund Software, 1997. More than 4,000 family trees with nearly 3 million individuals.

————. *World Family Tree, Volume 12, Pre-1600 to Present*. Novato CA: Broderbund Software, 1997. Over 4,000 family trees and nearly 3,000,000 individuals.

————. *World Family Tree, Volume 13, Pre-1600 to Present*. Novato CA: Broderbund Software, 1997. Approximately 3,700 family trees and nearly 3 million named individuals.

————. *World Family Tree, Volume I, Pre-1600 to Present*. Novato CA: Broderbund Software, 1995. About 6,000 family trees, including almost 3 million individuals.

Church of Jesus Christ of Latter Day Saints. *Family History Resource File: Master Index for Pedigree Resource File* (for Discs 1-5). Salt Lake City: Intellectual Reserve, 1999.

————. *Family History Resource File: Pedigree Resource File, Disc 6*. Salt Lake City: Intellectual Reserve, 2000. Lineage-linked pedigrees submitted to Family History Department of the LDS church.

————. *Family History Resource File: Pedigree Resource File, Disc 7*. Salt Lake City: Intellectual Reserve, 2000. Lineage-linked pedigrees submitted to the Family History Department of the LDS church.

————. *Family History Resource File: Pedigree Resource File, Disc 8*. Salt Lake City: Intellectual Reserve, 2000. Lineage-linked pedigrees submitted to the Family History Department of the LDS church.

————. *Family History Resource File: Pedigree Resource File, Disc 9*. Salt Lake City: Intellectual Reserve, 2000. Lineage-linked pedigrees submitted to the Family History Department of the LDS church.

————. *Family History Resource File: Pedigree Resource File, Disc 10.* Salt Lake City: Intellectual Reserve, 2000. Lineage-linked pedigrees submitted to the Family History Department of the LDS church.

————. *Family History Resource File: Pedigree Resource File, Discs 1-5.* Salt Lake City: Intellectual Reserve, 1999. Lineage-linked pedigrees submitted to Family History Department of the LDS church. Includes master index for discs 1-5.

————. *Family History Resource File: Pedigree Resource File, Discs 11-15.* Salt Lake City: Intellectual Reserve, 2000. Lineage-linked pedigrees submitted to the Family History Department of the LDS church; includes master index for discs 11-15.

————. *Family History Resource File: Vital Records Index—British Isles.* Salt Lake City: Intellectual Reserve, 1998. Five CDs listing 5 million births, christenings, and marriages from 1538 to 1888.

————. *Family History Resource File: Vital Records Index—North America.* Salt Lake City: Intellectual Reserve, 1998. Seven CDs listing births, christenings, and marriages in the US and Canada from 1631 to 1888, including about 4,000,000 names.

Glasscock, Pat. "File Patg.Ged." In *RootsWeb World Connect Project,* *http://www.rootsweb.com,* 20 January 2000.

Griffin, John Alfred. "File 17308.Ged." In *Ancestry World Tree,* *http://www.ancestry.com,* 14 May 2000.

United States Department of Agriculture, Economic Research Service. *A History of American Agriculture, 1776–1990: Farm Economy* USDA website,http://www.usda.gove/history2/back.htm, 15 September 1998.

————. *A History of American Agriculture, 1776–1990: Farm Organizations and Movements* USDA website, http://www.usda.gove/history2/back.htm, 15 September 1998.

————. *A History of American Agriculture, 1776–1990: Farmers and the Land* USDA website, http://www.usda.gove/history2/back.htm, 15 September 1998.

————. *A History of American Agriculture, 1776-–1990: Transportation* USDA website, http://www.usda.gove/history2/back.htm, 15 September 1998.

Index